The *Arabian Nights* in English Literary Theory (1704–1910)

This book is part of the Peter Lang Regional Studies list.
Every volume is peer reviewed and meets
the highest quality standards for content and production.

PETER LANG
New York • Bern • Berlin
Brussels • Vienna • Oxford • Warsaw

Muhsin J. al-Musawi

The *Arabian Nights* in English Literary Theory (1704–1910)

Scheherazade in England

An Expanded and Updated Version of the 1981 Edition

PETER LANG

New York • Bern • Berlin

Brussels • Vienna • Oxford • Warsaw

Library of Congress Control Number: 2021949981

Bibliographic information published by **Die Deutsche Nationalbibliothek.**
Die Deutsche Nationalbibliothek lists this publication in the "Deutsche
Nationalbibliografie"; detailed bibliographic data are available
on the Internet at http://dnb.d-nb.de/.

ISBN 978-1-4331-9757-4 (paperback)
ISBN 978-1-4331-8779-7 (ebook pdf)
ISBN 978-1-4331-8780-3 (epub)
DOI 10.3726/b18321

The first edition of this book was published in 1981 under the title
Scheherazade in England: A Study of Nineteenth-Century
English Criticism of the Arabian Nights © Muhsin Jassim al-Musawi

Peter Lang Publishing, Inc., New York
80 Broad Street, 5th floor, New York, NY 10004
www.peterlang.com

TO

Malcolm Ross
the man, the critic, the scholar

We travel not for trafficking alone;
  By hotter winds our fiery hearts are fanned.
For lust of knowing what should not be known,
  We take the Golden Road to Samarkand.
                                        —J.E. Flecker, *Hassan*

Contents

Figures

Preface

Very few books have cast such a spell on the reading public as Scheherazade's *One Thousand and One Nights,* better known as the *Arabian Nights' Entertainments,* a title which the first Grub Street English translator had chosen early in the eighteenth century when first coming upon Galland's *Contes Arabes.* The Arabian tales are still read with avidity, whereas such writers as John Barth and many others have drawn upon Scheherazade's mine of story-telling to introduce their views on the technique of writing or to ridicule modern attitudes and situations. But no matter how popular the tales are in the twentieth century, adaptations from or studies of the *Arabian Nights* have become so impersonal that one feels inclined to reintroduce the tales to the twentieth-century reader, a thought which had never bothered a Romantic or a Victorian essayist or critic. When Leigh Hunt, Dickens, or Morris, for instance, used to draw upon Scheherazade's mine of allusion and anecdote, they felt sure that their readers were so familiar with the tales that they had no need to check a "scholarly companion" to the *Arabian Nights.*

The framing tale in Scheherazade's collection is not hard to remember. The Vizier's charming daughter Scheherazade has requested her father to allow her to risk marrying the brooding melancholy and ruthless Sultan Schahriar. Betrayed by an adulterous wife, the Sultan avowed to marry each wife for a night, killing her upon the next morning in order not to be betrayed again. Unlike other unlucky females, Scheherazade draws upon her knowledge and wit. Bent upon entangling him in a new attachment to life, she disarms him by stories about the vicissitudes of fortune, and the cruelty of kings. She narrates other tales about the viles of women. More to her purpose, however, is to entangle him in the very web of story-telling. A story leads to another, and the sultan's mind lives in perpetual suspense for a thousand and one nights. By that time, Scheherazade is a mother, whereas the Sultan, divested now of his arrogance and distrust, is too enthralled by her art and affectionate care to think of sacrificing her. Such is the termination of the otherwise endless tales.

Although not given to allegorical explanations ourselves, it is only fair to agree with O.K. Chesterton that Scheherazade proves the autonomy of art. "Never in any other book," he says in the *Spice of Life* (pp. 56–60) "has such a splendid tribute been given to the pride and omnipotence of art." Such a despot like Schahriar may command multitudes, but he suffers to listen to a story-teller. It is Scheherazade's art, to be sure, which, so the tales suggest, saves her life.

Composite in nature, the volumes consist of romances, love stories, tales of roguery and adventure, accounts of some historical significance, and moralistic or philosophical pieces. Like literary productions of multifarious growth, the tales passed through many redactions since their early evolution in the ninth century, undergoing a number of changes, omissions, and interpolations in Baghdad, Syria, and in Cairo. Thus, a manuscript of a Baghdadi origin will definitely demonstrate some regional predilections. The same applies with equal force to the compilations of the Cairene origin. Twentieth-century scholarship has fared no better, so far, than the Victorian. Aside from Nabia Abbott's finding, a ninth-century fragment of the tales of a Baghdadi origin, there have been no further discoveries to illuminate the otherwise obscure genealogy of the *Arabian Nights*.

But as early as October 1838 and September 1839, the *Athenaeum* reviewer of the newly published English editions of the *Arabian Nights* came across some external evidence, corroborating the existence of a twelfth-century work in Arabic titled the *Thousand and One Nights*. The reviewer himself explained how the tales differ from pre-Islamic romances of chivalrous and warlike atmospheres. Scheherazade's tales, especially in their European redactions, draw quite heavily on urban manners and aspirations. Aside from a few pieces dealing with the supernatural, they are mostly concerned with domestic practices and intrigues. This very nature of the tales poses certain questions regarding their settings and authorship. The reviewer himself has also touched on this point, reaching some conclusions that must be included in any modern scholarly assessment of the history and people of the Arabian tales.

That the tales betray such urban predilections indicates that they began to evolve during the Abbasid reign. While possibly borrowing the framing tale from *Hezar Afsaneh* the story-tellers of Baghdad invented many others and adapted more to meet the increasing demand for entertaining tales under the starry skies of Eastern nights. In general, however, it is fair to say that the larger portion of the tales is genuinely Arabian. It continued to accumulate till the first half of the sixteenth century. There are tales that were Arabized to meet the taste of the Arab audiences. The expansion of the Arab Empire under the Abbasid rule drove many story-tellers to appropriate the light literature of other nations. But as the *Athenaeum* reviewer rightly noticed, even this portion is Islamic. Regulating and modelling manners and customs, Islam imposes a certain conformity ritual that defies clear-cut categorizations.

Many suggestions have been advanced regarding possible authors of the primary collections of tales that clustered around the framing tale. But while there should have been a certain author or a number of authors, storytellers or translators in Baghdad during the Abbasid reign, the fact that accumulation and sifting had continued until the first half of the sixteenth century impels scholars to search for manuscripts. These alone can demonstrate the additions, interpolations, and changes imposed upon the primary material by copyists and compilers. Such manuscripts will lead us to see through the regional predilections of such copyists and compilers, the redactors of the Arabian tales who have transmitted to Europe this mine of story-telling. Individual tales had found their way to medieval Europe through numerous channels, to be sure, but the *Arabian Nights* attained its tremendous vogue as a collection in the first decade of the eighteenth century when it was simultaneously translated into both French and English.

Since the appearance early in the eighteenth century of the anonymous Grub Street translation of Antoine Galland's *Mille et Une Nuits, Contes Arabes,* there has been no comprehensive assessment of the critical and popular reception accorded to the tales in England, at least not before 1978, the date of my doctoral dissertation. Despite their tremendous vogue and impact, the literary reputation of the Arabian tales has not been heretofore sufficiently recognized, as any cursory reading of standard historical and critical surveys will indicate. In this book, I have attempted to trace and evaluate the salient characteristics of the popularity of the *Nights*, especially with the nineteenth-century reading public. A survey of relevant eighteenth-century responses is unavoidable, however, not only because historical continuity and rupture invite response, but also because Galland's edition of the *Nights* was the one which enjoyed sustained popularity throughout the nineteenth century. Undeveloped and limited as the scope and criteria of literary scholarship and periodical reviewing were in the eighteenth century, basic patterns of reaction and response were nevertheless established at that time, leading to or evoking further critical insights and scholarly studies of the generic characteristics as well as of the origin and impact of the *Nights.*

But rather than dealing in the main with pseudo-Oriental modes or focusing on imitations and adaptations that fall at times outside the main currents of English literary taste, I have argued that a valid and substantial estimate of the literary reputation of the *Nights* must rest on a clear understanding of and adequate acquaintance with related contemporary criticism. Thus, my primary concern is with the nature and scope of critical responses as manifested in prefaces to translations and adaptations, in reviews and periodical articles, and in memoirs, recollections, and other miscellanies. But as these will largely testify to the preferences of the intellectual elite and the critical reader, I have made numerous references to adaptations, abridgements, selections, reprints, and "continuations" as a valuable index of popular taste.

This undertaking obviously indicates considerable dissatisfaction with the few existing studies of the vogue of the Oriental mode. Mainly preoccupied with the influence of the Arabian tales on English literature, many well-meaning critics have devoted their attention to servile imitations and adaptations without attempting to probe into the relevance of the *Nights* to the basic social and literary concerns of the period in question. Others have mentioned only in passing some nineteenth-century appraisals of Scheherazade's collection, concentrating instead on the allusions to it and borrowings from its mine of anecdote and detail. Useful as such researches certainly are, they nevertheless fall short of accounting for the enduring popularity of the *Nights,* a popularity which critical appreciations and estimates as well as statistical information on the popular market will surely explain and substantiate.

It is indisputable that the *Nights* exerted tremendous influence on English writing, particularly on drama and romantic fiction. In an essay for *Bookman* (1907, XXXI, 258), William E.A. Axon recognized this influence. While delighting the "literary palate" with their variety of sentiment and anecdote and with their impressive gallery of rogues, cobblers, fishermen, and scolding wives, the tales "may perhaps have had some share in encouraging the novelists when they did come to deal with homely scenes and common life." At a time when the modern novel was "as yet unborn" and when readers "were sick of sham classical romances of interminable and portentous unreality," Galland's volumes were very much in vogue. A year later, Martha Pike Conant published her monumental book, the *Oriental Tale in England in the Eighteenth Century* (N.Y.: Columbia

Univ. Press), bringing to the attention of many the nature of Scheherazade's contribution to the early evolution of the modern novel. She postulated that the tales could not have enjoyed such a sweeping success had they not met certain literary and popular needs. In their romantic machinery, their episodic plots and adventurous spirit, they supplied the very elements which the undeveloped English novel desperately needed to evolve beyond the dull practice of character sketching in periodicals (pp. 238–48).

Although a careful investigation of specific echoes and borrowings from the *Nights,* coupled with a survey of probable tributaries and channels of transmission and influence, will greatly substantiate and enrich any conclusions regarding literary vogue, I have found it impractical to concentrate on this area. Instead, I have cited only the most notable expressions of this influence that bear directly on the present discussion. A mere survey of recent standard bibliographies and indices will indicate the widening prospects of research for interested scholars. Aside from A. Nicoll's authoritative listing of dramatic adaptations from the *Nights,* both Robert D. Mayo's *English Novel in the Magazines, 1740–1815* and Walter E. Houghton's invaluable *Wellesley Index to Victorian Periodicals* (1966–) demonstrate how much is left to be done by those intending to assess the nature of the spell which Scheherazade had cast on the eighteenth- and nineteenth-century mind.

Further studies of literary influx may profit amply from the present estimate of the criticism of the *Nights* not only because of its direct relevance to contemporary critical issues and cultural taste but also because of the emphasis laid here on the nature of the major translations and editions that were accessible to the public in Augustan and Victorian England. Excepting Sheila Shaw's remarks on the value of Galland's version for early eighteenth-century fiction (*Muslim World*, XLIX [1959], 232–38; *PMLA*, XC [Jan. 1975], 62–68), there is virtually nothing written on the necessity of classifying and interpreting the impact of and responses to such various editions as those of Galland, Edward William Lane (1838–1841), John Payne (1882–1884), and Richard Burton (1885–1888). Central to my argument is the premise that these translations or redactions reveal much about contemporary predilections and must be seen as significant signs of the prevailing literary concerns of the times. Throughout the forthcoming chapters, these editions have been studied within their immediate socio-cultural context. In doing so, I have been led by two considerations. Aside from the historical and literary factors that would have unavoidably decided and shaped the attitude and method of each translator or editor, nineteenth-century writers, in particular, tended to entertain distinct impressions and maintain well-defined views of the available editions. Thus, the edition which appealed to Leigh Hunt, for instance, was not the same one that impressed Walter Bagehot. Significantly, the comments which each version evoked correspond to prevailing literary outlooks and aesthetic preferences and form therefore part of the temper of the given period. Being so widely popular and influential, the *Arabian Nights* in its various garbs elicited views and provoked arguments that should not be overlooked in any fair assessment of the evolution of literary theory in England. It is well to remember that in the early nineteenth-century dispute between the utilitarians and advocates of literary culture or in the late Victorian controversy between the new realists and the romanticists, the tales were often cited to substantiate diverse biases and attitudes.

A word must be said about the limitations of my topic. Although dealing with nineteenth-century (especially periodical) criticism of the *Nights,* writings on folklore sources and comparative mythology have been only sparingly referred to, simply because they fall outside the scope of purely literary trends. On the other hand, a few American, French, and German critics are included in this interpretive survey because their views were widely known in England at that time and were frequently cited in periodical reviews. The last point which needs some explanation is the ultimate purpose of this study. The reader may notice that I have not consistently striven to supply my own interpretations of the thematic and technical properties of the tales. Although a study of literary responses will inevitably shed some light on the contextual and generic characteristics of the work in question, this must not be seen as more than incidental to my primary intention to assess and interpret the vogue of the tales in view of and in relation to contemporary literary taste. In keeping with this purpose, extensive quotations from pertinent writings are deemed necessary, for it is only through such perspectives that we can fairly gauge the real meaning of the tales for the nineteenth-century reader.

Preface to the New Edition

The story of the first appearance of the *Arabian Nights* in France (*Les Mille Et Une Nuits: Contes Arabes*) in 1704–1712, and its continuation in 1717, is now a familiar one. Its immediate translation into English, 1705–1706 *as Arabian Nights' Entertainments*, is also as familiar. It was not so, however, in mid-1970s when I chose it as the topic for my doctoral dissertation. There were articles on its reception, or its Arab milieu, but there was no comprehensive reading of its popular and critical reception in England where it set the cultural scene on fire, invoking and inciting a variety of response from among different forums and groups. Martha Pike Conant was a pioneer in trying to study an "oriental" mode of writing that got accelerated by Antoine Galland's venture as the first translator in Europe of the *Arabian Nights*. The success of his translation of the "Seven Voyages of Sindbad the Sailor," 1701, encouraged him to embark on the translation of an incomplete manuscript, which he complemented at a later stage by some tales that were narrated to him by the Maronite from Aleppo, Hanna Diyab. The latter was as good as Galland in the art of story-telling, but the distinguished Arabist Galland had the knack for story-telling, a talent that enabled him to produce a readable version which, albeit its omissions and retentions, proved to be the most popular. Indeed, such avid readers, critics, and great writers like Jorge Luis Borges think of it as the most influential book, not only in partially generating a Romantic mode but also in setting the scene for a novelistic tradition. It was probably the most important literary event in eighteenth-century Europe in that soon after its appearance, it got serialized over years, and hence was able to appeal to a rising reading public that had to wait for the next issue. A popular mode of response was behind the rising culture industry that involved publishers, pseudo translators, imitators, editors, and writers. No one in that staid age remained oblivious to Scheherazade's web of enchantment. This is the domain that drew my attention to the enormous but diverse response to the *Arabian Nights*. The internet services which we take for granted nowadays were not available then, and one had to locate private and public collections and spend months perusing every article that was penned throughout the eighteenth and nineteenth centuries. Now as before, I argue that without that early engagement with that overwhelming cultural, political, and literary criticism, the story of the phenomenal rise of the *Arabian Nights* in world cultures remains incomplete. The outcome of that research and criticism is important first to students and scholars of English, French, and German. It is absolutely central to any pursuit of cultural or comparative studies. Although relatively popular upon its appearance in 1981, its Washington publisher (Three Continents Press, 1981) was more focused on Afro-Asian and Latin American literatures, a unique feat at that time. The publisher was the late Donald E. Herdeck, professor of modern poetry and poetics, whose publishing house was behind at least three Nobel Prize winners. *Scheherazade in England* could not reach the departments and readers who most need it: departments of languages and comparative literature. Although I published a few more books on the *Arabian Nights* in English and Arabic, *Scheherazade in England* remains central to my scholarly efforts as it laid the foundations for further explorations of translation, literary criticism, and cultural history. It was then inaccessible to many, and some scholars wrote to me later apologizing for being unaware of the book.

Its Peter Lang reprint is timely, for now there is a growing field of knowledge on and around the *Arabian Nights*, and there are courses offered at a number of universities that focus on Scheherazade's art. I kept the rest of the material as it appeared in that first print, but I added a chapter on "The Growth of Scholarly Interest in the Arabian Nights" that appeared in 1980 in *Muslim World*. I duly acknowledge the gracious support of the journal throughout my research in D. B. MacDonald's collection, Case Memorial Library, at Hartford Seminary Foundation. I also extend my thanks to Dr. Farideh Koohi-Kamali and Suma George and the production team from Peter Lang for making this reprint possible.

Acknowledgments

This study had its beginning in a doctoral dissertation submitted to Dalhousie University in 1978. With the advice of my supervisor, Professor Malcolm Ross, and my external examiner, Professor Richard Altick of Ohio State University, I have revised it and indeed rewritten it for publication as a book. I am indebted both to Professor Ross and Professor Altick for their encouragement and practical suggestions.

I should also like to acknowledge the friendly co-operation of the custodians of the Case Memorial Library, especially Dean Willem Bijlefeld, the librarian Duncan Brockway, and the archivist Nafi Donat. For many courtesies thanks are due to the staff of the Beinecke and Sterling Libraries at Yale, the Widener Library at Harvard, the Library of Congress, the British Library at the British Museum, the London University Library, and the London School of Oriental and African Studies. Nor can I forget the assistance of the interlibrary loan department at Dalhousie Killam Library for procuring a number of significant items and unpublished dissertations. And I should like to record my gratitude to a number of friends, especially to Edward Evans, and to Janet Lord for typing the manuscript. It would be churlish not to close with my love and gratitude to my wife Bahira and to my daughters (Rawa, Wafa, and Zeinab) who have been inconvenienced by my obsession with Scheherazade's admirers.

The Eighteenth-Century Reception of the *Arabian Nights*

But there were fictions wild that please the boy,
Which men, too, read, condemn, reject, enjoy—
Arabian Nights, and Persian Tales, were there,
One volume each, and both worse for the wear.
George Crabbe, "Silford Hall; or the Happy Day"[1]

Whate'er thy theme, whether the magic might
Of the stern Kings, that dwell mid ocean's roar,
Or Sindbad's perils, or the cruel wiles
Of Afric's curs'd enchanter charm us more
Or aught more wondrous still our ear beguiles,
Well pleas'd we listen to thy fabling lore,
And Truth itself with less attraction smiles.
Thomas Russell, "To the Author of the Arabian Nights Entertainments"[2]

To provide a comprehensive assessment of the *Arabian Nights* has been a laborious undertaking for Scheherazade's critics. One may not be at a loss to find a plausible explanation for her popularity either with the Romantics and their last descendants or with the Victorian reading public. But to account for the vogue of "imaginative" tales totally "at variance with all Western canons of construction" in the Age of Reason was frankly not such an easy task for the literary critic of the *Saturday Review* (Vol. LXXIV, November 12, 1892). He modestly acknowledged the serious implications involved in a venture of this kind and hurriedly supplied two solutions which, ironically, have never lost their validity. "It may be that what imagination there was, unsatisfied by the dignity of Racine and the splendid dullness of Richardson," wrote the cautious critic, "found relief in the unrestricted fancy of these stories." But feeling uneasy about the commonplaceness of this explanation, he unburdened himself to the reader: "Or it may be that they represent the first appearance of the spirit of history in fiction. If this is so, the eighteenth-century can boast the quintessence of Rationalism, imagination itself turned antiquarian." Other late nineteenth-century critics have supplied some elaborate interpretations of the immediate success of the Arabian tales. Writing for the *Atlantic Monthly* of 1889 (LXIII, 756–57), C.T. Toy, for instance, stressed the novelty of Oriental scenes, the charm of sentiment, the delicacy of humor, and the mystery of "the strange life" that took France by surprise. With an eye on the literary climate, Toy argued that "France has been nourished on the plays of Corneille and Racine, the discourses of Bossuet, and the skeptical philosophy of Bayle, with only Moliere to express the humor of life." Galland's translation brought something more exciting, different, and entertaining; ". . . here were opened the doors of unlimited and delicious romance. All Paris was full of the wonderful stories; it was a triumph resembling that achieved by the Waverley Novels." In the "Terminal Essay" to his *Thousand Nights and a Night* (Burton Club ed.; X, 92), Richard F. Burton provided a similar interpretation. What secured the *Nights* such an "exceptional success," he explained, were the "glamour of imagination," the "marvel of miracles and the gorgeousness and magnificence of the scenery." Being so unconventional and so "entirely without a purpose," the *Nights* startled, amused, and delighted the reading public. Useful as these suggestions and interpretations are for any evaluation of the critical and popular reception of the Arabian tales and other Oriental collections, they are not comprehensive enough either to explain the various literary estimates of the tales or to account fully for the developing popular interest in this new genre.

In her study of the Oriental tale (pp. 238–48), Miss Conant made no direct reference to the foregoing explanations; but her discerning intellect and scholarly insight enabled her to draw a few additional conclusions regarding the popularity of the *Nights*. She explained that the mere fact that the tales came through France ensured them popularity, for the French exerted a tremendous influence on English literature at that time. Furthermore, the truant desire to escape the strict rules of pseudo-classicism might have fulfilled itself in the perusal of these exotic tales of adventures and enchantments. In another place, Miss Conant mentioned the adaptability of the tales to the milieu which accorded them such a favorable reception, a fact which the endless array of philosophic and didactic imitations clearly substantiates. Unfortunately, Miss Conant's major argument centers upon the influence of the *Arabian Nights* and its immediate successors in the limited, though significant, sphere of Oriental fiction of the eighteenth century; as such, the few remarks she makes concerning the popularity of Scheherazade's tales might help to indicate the general features of literary influences without providing particular pieces of contemporary criticism either to substantiate such generalizations or to shed some light on the diversity of critical responses. As a matter of fact, hurried explanations of the vogue of certain genres tend rather to confuse than elucidate and clarify the issue, for, like late nineteenth-century critics, Miss Conant has overlooked the composite nature of the *Nights* and the socio-historical context of relevant literary tastes and responses since the first appearance of the tales in England.

Although the date of the first Grub Street translation of Galland's *Les Mille et une Nuits* (1704–1717) is unknown, the available evidence according to the Arabist Duncan Black Macdonald shows that the English version of the *Nights* was in print in 1706.[3] By 1713 it went through four editions and was soon followed by numerous reprints and "complete editions," countless "new translations," and "careful revisions" which "should make up a weighty chapter in the history of the great publishing humbug."[4] Marshall's list of chapbooks in 1708 contains the title *Arabian Nights Entertainments,* and the title was so appealing and popular that by 1709 there was the *Golden Spy... British Nights Entertainments.*[5] In 1783 James Beattie described the work as "a book which most young people in this country are acquainted with."[6] For soon after its appearance, it was received with delight and read with avidity by a large audience, making a "deep impression on cultivated circles," an impression that led to a series of imitations, abridgements, and adaptations throughout the century.[7] "Eastern tales, introduced to European literature early in the eighteenth century through Galland's translation of the inexhaustibly opulent *Arabian Nights,*" writes Howard Phillips Lovecraft, "had become a reigning fashion; being used both for allegory and for amusement." Blending with weirdness after the Eastern style, the story-teller's sly humor, according to the same writer, "had captivated a sophisticated generation, till Bagdad and Damascus names became as freely strewn through popular literature as dashing Italian and Spanish ones were soon to be."[8] Indeed, the increasing demand for these tales drove Grub Street hacks and booksellers to adapt and imitate so many of their anecdotes, episodes, and other properties that both Oliver Goldsmith and Horace Walpole followed the lead of Hamilton in satirizing those pseudo-Orientalists who derived their meagre information from a hasty and shallow acquaintance with the East.[9]

The numerous editions of the *Arabian Nights* at this time, and the numberless adaptations and abridgements from Scheherazade's repository provide but one testimony to its immediate success. No less indicative is Addison's response. As "a mirror of his readers' tastes and interests," Addison fell under the spell of the Orient, publishing a number of Oriental pieces in the *Spectator,* and thus making "one new significant addition to the repertory of eighteenth-century magazine fiction, the oriental tale."[10] The craving of the less critical reader for light literature encouraged some periodicals not only to publish fragments from the *Nights* but also to serialize these tales. Indeed, there is no better evidence to demonstrate their overwhelming appeal than the fact that the thrice weekly *London News* began on January 6, 1723, a serialization of these tales "which occupied three years and four hundred and forty-five instalments."[11] In 1720, the *Churchman's Last Shift* published "The Voyages of Sindbad the Sailor" in weekly parts, followed by another extract from the *Nights.* Their vogue continued unabated throughout the century, for in the last decades Thomas Bellamy, whom Robert D. Mayo described as "a shrewd judge of the popular market," serialized parts of the Arabian tales in his *General Magazine.* To revive the reader's interest, both the *Lady's Magazine* and *Monthly Extracts* published selections from the *Nights;* whereas the *Novelist's Magazine,* which "reflects the general contours of late eighteenth-century taste," published the *Nights* in full.[12]

Although indicating a deviation from neo-classical doctrines, this public approbation clearly manifests the requirements of the broad audience. The beginnings of the century witnessed the growth of a large reading class independent of the traditional critical standards staunchly held by ardent neo-classicists. Not necessarily bound by strict principles and rigid rules, the new audience favored the effortless, easy perusal of novel and romance which might prove no less useful for being entertaining. On the other hand, the failure of fiction to meet the established critical rules and its association with idleness provoked many eighteenth-century critics to maintain a hostile attitude towards the genre.

At variance with the established critical distaste for fiction, there was a growing popular tendency to appreciate light literature. Huet's treatise on the *Origin of Romances,* which prefaced Samuel Croxall's *Select Collections of Novels and Histories,* heralded the aesthetic preferences of a large audience among the middle class. In its emphasis on the entertaining element in writing and its applause of fictional literature that could be "comprehended without any great labour of mind," Huet's treatise voiced the predilections of the new reading public. It certainly assumes particular significance in the present context not only because Huet referred to a probable Arabian origin of romance but also because Galland corresponded with this learned friend of his regarding certain tales in the *Nuits*.[13]

That the *Nights* with its titillating accounts of adventure and romance and its blending of the real and the fantastic became popular with such a public is not surprising. Indeed, by calling Galland's *Nuits Arabian Nights' Entertainments,* the anonymous Grub Street translator showed a shrewd awareness of his semi-educated audience's taste for entertaining narratives. For no matter how disheartening the popular aesthetic preference for fictional literature was to men like Shaftesbury, the large feminine component of the reading public was clearly not afraid of being seduced by the "wondrous Tales" of the "miraculous Moor."[14] As a result, Grub Street hacks and booksellers found in the success of the *Nights* more than sufficient justification for flooding the market with reprints and imitations, until the pseudo-Oriental tale exhausted itself as a genre by the end of the century, leaving the *Nights* unrivalled.

Beyond all these considerations, it must be kept in mind that the quality of the book itself is of no less importance in accounting for its popularity. The English reader of the early eighteenth century was fortunate enough to have the Grub Street translator who, through scrupulous fidelity to Galland's version, retained that simplicity, urbanity, and vitality of style which made the work readable even for the semi-educated. Aware of the prejudices and inclinations of his early eighteenth-century audience, Galland avoided any outrageous deviation from acceptable literary tastes and conventions. Indeed, Galland was so responsive to his audience that he dispensed with the original introductory note to each tale, after some Parisians had made fun of it. "The Parisians, returning from their nocturnal revels," said Jos Von Hammer, relating an anecdote originally reported by Michaud, "would often stop before his door, and awake him from his soundest sleep, by calling loudly for him. Galland would open his window, to see what was the matter, and they would cry out: 'O vous, qui savez de si jolis contes, et qui les racontez si bien[,] racontez nous en un!' "[15]

Accordingly, Galland preferred the bare thread of narrative to the picturesque and highly exotic, omitting figurative and poetic passages, minimizing lavish detail, frenchifying dialogues and conversations, adding a few explanations and comments, and adapting the whole to the new literary and social milieu. Thus, when explaining the reasons for its immediate vogue, Sir Walter Scott stressed Galland's adequate adaptation of the tales to the French climate. In the "Dedicatory Epistle" to *Ivanhoe,* he argued that although the tales were less "purely Oriental in their first concoction," they were "eminently better fitted for the European market, and obtained an unrivalled degree of public favour which they certainly would never have gained had not the manners and style been in some degree familiarized to the feelings and habits of the Western reader."[16] Very pertinent in this respect, too, is James Beattie's remark on the French edition in his treatise "On Fable and Romance" *(Works,* II, 509–10). After doubting the authenticity of Galland's work, he drew the following revealing conclusion: "If they [the tales] be Oriental, they are translated with unwarrantable latitude; for the whole tenor of the style is in the French mode: and the caliph of Bagdat, and the Emperor of China, are addressed in the same terms of ceremony, which are usual at the court of France."

More concerned with the literary properties of the *Nuits* in his learned introduction to *Tales of the East* (Edinburgh, 1812; I, xxviii–xxix), Henry Weber noticed that Galland's main emphasis falls on episodic plots and elements of suspense and story-telling. Thus, the version which he submitted to the eighteenth-century reader's perusal abounds with stories of adventure, exquisite narratives of love and romance, and scenes of enchantment and transformation that have proved to be of enduring popularity. Indeed, such an acute critic as Robert Heron remarked in his preface to the 1792 Edinburgh edition of *Arabian Tales* (I, ix), ". . . it is probable that the *machinery* contributed, more than any other particular in their character, to obtain to the *Arabian Nights Entertainments,* the preference over most of the other works of imagination which were common in Europe at the time of their first appearance." Compared to the existing romances with their stock situations and plots, the tales were overwhelmingly appealing. "Magicians, Genies, Fairies, Lamps, Rings, and other Talismans, dance in such profusion through those volumes, as could not but make the reader wonder and stare, who was acquainted only with witches mounted on broom-sticks, and with little viewless elves, dancing occasionally by moonlight." But although the exotic appeal of the tales and their depiction of a world of wonder and wish-fulfillment might have been a major reason for their immediate success, the tales contain many thematic conventions that were not alien to early eighteenth-century readers. Many of these tales are rich with reflections upon the meaning of freedom, the sinfulness of pride and greed, the sacredness of duty and work, and the vanity of human wishes. Thus, although the eighteenth-century reader might have perused the tales for sheer enjoyment, he might have well agreed with Sindbad that there is no gain without pain, and that Providence rewards the honest, enterprising individual. He might have accepted Scheherazade's verdict that the magician in "Aladdin" deserves punishment and death for being so proud, calculating, and greedy. Moreover, the common reader might have found more than one reason to enjoy the elaborate descriptions of spacious palaces, scenes of domestic life, and other social and religious manners and customs. "I know not," wrote Robert Heron ("Translator's Preface," p. xii), "if even the gold, jewels, pearls, rubies, emeralds, the bales of rich stuffs, and superb pellices, the crowded kans, luxurious gardens, and apartments *beyond description sumptuous ...* have not insensibly a greater influence in dazzling and amusing the mind of the reader, than perhaps the pupil of taste will be willing to allow."

Even when discussing the romantic appeal of Scheherazade's tales, we should not limit ourselves to their scenes of transformation and supernatural machinery, for this mythological element is but one chamber in Alladin's spacious palace. In fact, the composite nature of the book makes it impossible to classify and categorize its popular appeal under one or two headings, a fact which Heron also recognized. After analyzing the threefold appeal of the *Nights* (its picture of social manners, its display of universal traits, and its machinery), Heron found his descriptive analysis incapable of covering the many-sided attraction of this "medley of comic, tragic, and heroic adventures." Indeed, when discussing the vogue of the *Nights,* one must agree with E.F. Bleiler that the appeal of this work consists in its being a repository of both realistic and fantastic themes told in a style wholly new to the eighteenth-century reader. "These stories," he rightly remarks, "appealed strongly to the Rococo mind, what with the wide range of opportunities they offered: delicacies of style, elaboracies of construction, adventure, eroticism, moralism, sensibility, fantasy, philosophy and irony."[17]

Another point which needs clarification before studying critical reactions is the reputed indecency of some of Scheherazade's tales. Under exaggerated conventional notions of Eastern polygamy, the impression that the Orient was a land of eroticism and licentiousness was widespread. But instead of maintaining the early clerical condemnatory attitude towards Islam and the East, early eighteenth-century writers dwelt on the topic "with gusto,"[18] especially at a time when the surplus of women posed a serious problem to early eighteenth-century England.[19] With its stories of veiled women and intriguing encounters, Galland's *Nights* established rather than effaced old impressions. Indeed, lady Mary Wortley Montague's letters, which were circulated privately in 1724, manifest a playful tendency to see the East from a perspective that was greatly influenced by the *Nights.* Along with a host of other travelers, Lady Mary wrote to prove that, "excepting the enchantments," the tales depict "a real representation of the manners" in Turkey.[20] Confusing difference and sites of splendour which her status allowed her with some orient, Lady Mary fed a stock of representations which the desiring nobility craves.

This taste for tantalizing visions should not be confused, however, with late nineteenth-century naturalistic tendencies; neither should Galland's version be confused with the unexpurgated editions of John Payne and Richard Burton. Although appealing to the growing love for exoticism and covert eroticism, Galland's version was meant to titillate rather than shock the eighteenth-century public. In the "Preface" to his own version of the *Nuits,* Galland explained that he attempted to be faithful to the original, except when "modesty" and "niceness of the French tongue and of the times" obliged him to do otherwise.[21] Accordingly, he deleted such licentious passages as the bath scene in the "Story of the Porter and the Three Ladies of Baghdad," and neglected others which he considered incompatible with good literary taste. According to the testimony of the eighteenth-century scholar Patrick Russell, who possessed a manuscript of the *Arabian Nights,* "a few scenes too licentiously described in the original, have with propriety been softened or supprest."[22]

Furthermore, as a product of his age with its dominating discursive emphasis on decorum, good manners and correctness, Galland attempted to assert the innate moralistic element in the *Nights.* In the preface to his translation (p. ix), he explained: "If those who read these stories, have but an inclination to profit by the example of virtue and vice, which they will here find exhibited, they may reap an advantage by it, that is not to be reaped in other stories, which are more proper to corrupt than to reform our manners." With the acute and perceptive awareness characteristic of writers very close to the literary market, Robert Heron appreciated this moral touch which, blending with the entertaining element, appealed to the layman and the learned alike. In the "Preface" to the 1792 edition of the *Arabian Tales* (I, vi), he severely criticized the "insipid obscenities of a Behn, a Manley, and a Heywood," whose books were "calculated, almost exclusively, for the debauchee and the women of pleasure," finding in the *Nights* something "for the entertainment of those, who chose to withdraw the mind occasionally from the realities of life, yet were unwilling to debase imagination, by turning it to dwell on the brutal grossness of sensual indulgence." In other words, Galland's version met the demand for a different species of writing, which, if not overtly moralistic, at least did not disturb the established standards of propriety and good manners. As far as this aspect of Galland's version is concerned, one must accept Weitzman's conclusion that "The *Nights* to which the eighteenth-century reader had access, as far as its tone and morality are concerned, did little to upset the traditional stoic moral code," for the tales "often addressed themselves to the moral and ethical issues which Europeans in the early eighteenth-century were attempting to solve."[23]

Weitzman's neat conclusion is tenable, however, only in so far as it applies to eighteenth-century popular taste, for it overlooks the hostile reaction to the *Nights* among such ardent neo-classicists as Atterbury, Lord Kames, and Henry James Pye. Then too, the conservative antipathy to fictional literature in general is not taken into account. These and other complications make it necessary to evaluate diverse critical and literary responses to the *Nights* and to examine them in relation to the dominant traditional standards of probability, propriety and balance. As the following sections will demonstrate, the neo-classic criticism of Scheherazade's aesthetics sets the tone for various other responses. These responses range from the general tendency on the part of her apologetic admirers to assimilate the tales into neo-classical backgrounds, to realistic and utilitarian views of the work as an accurate representation of Oriental life and manners.

When first introduced among the eighteenth-century literati, the tales were pronounced "ridiculous, improbable, unnatural," as B.E. Pote rightly concluded. Like many other early Victorian critics, Pote noticed how the neoclassicists vehemently opposed what, according to their doctrines, partook of the "absolute dreams of distempered fancy of the East." To them, such writings mock "all powers of analysis . . . leaving only their vague and confused impressions on the pulse of manhood and in the light of day."[24] Bishop Atterbury, Henry James Pye, and Lord Kames objected to the wildness of the *Nights,* to its style, and to what they considered its extravagant and disproportioned narrative details. In a word, they objected to what would have fascinated such pre-romantics as Hawkesworth, Beckford, Walpole and a host of other writers. Their objection to Scheherazade's *Nights* on aesthetic grounds, however, often entailed an objection to its moral standards, since Shaftesbury and others associated the exotic, the irregular, and the bizarre with uncharted freedom and laxity, looking upon structural wildness as a sign of irregular behavior. Hence, when Pope, for example, sent Galland's version of the *Arabian Nights* to Bishop Atterbury, recommending it for reading, the Bishop denounced it as wild, absurd, and infectious. "I have read as much of them as ever I shall read while I live," he assured Pope, explaining that he had no taste for their "romantic" machinery and stylistic extravagance. They "are writ," he continued, "with so romantic an air, and, allowing for the difference of eastern manners, are yet, upon any supposition that can be made, of so wild and absurd a contrivance, (at least to my northern understanding,) that I have not only no pleasure, but no patience, in perusing them." While admitting that they might supply entertainment and wonder, he insisted that they were too "monstrous" and "disproportioned" to be enjoyed: "They are to me like odd paintings on Indian Screens, which at first glance may surprise and please a little; when you fix your eye intently upon them, they appear so extravagant, disproportioned, and monstrous, that they give a judicious eye pain, and make him seek for relief from some other object." With an obvious dislike for this mode of writing, the Bishop rebuffed Pope, concluding that it was dangerous to fall under the Arabian story-teller's spell. "They may furnish the mind with some new images," he argued, "but I think the purchase is made at too great an expense: for to read those two volumes through, liking them as little as I do, would be a terrible penance; and to read them with pleasure would be dangerous on the other side, because of the infection." The Bishop's rebuff is pivotal, not only because of its *en bloc* geographical binary, but also because it encapsulates the rudiments of extreme neo-classicism in matters moral, stylistic, aesthetic, and compositional.[25]

This opinion, which William Lyon Phelps cited as "an unqualified condemnation" of Romanticism and which Horace Walpole ridiculed as showing lack of taste,[26] was shared by other neo-classicists who opposed the stylistic floridity, extravagant imagination, and lack of restraint and unity in some of the tales. Henry James Pye found deviation from probability in the *Nights* perplexing rather than entertaining, whereas Henry Home Kames considered this species of writing lacking certain properties, and wanting in simplicity and unity of construction.[27] In its artistic irregularity the *Nights* resembles the gardens of Versailles:

> I have often amused myself with a fanciful resemblance between these gardens and the Arabian tales: each of them is a performance intended for the amusement of a great king: in the sixteen gardens of Versailles there is no unity of design, more than in the *thousand and one Arabian tales:* and, lastly, they are equally unnatural; groves of *jets d'eau,* statues of animals conversing in the manners of Aesop, water issuing out of the mouths of wild beasts, give an impression of fairy-land and witchcraft, no less than diamondpalaces, invisible rings, spells and incantations.[28]

But rather than being limited to the Arabian tales, Kames' antipathy to this mode should be considered in the context of the eighteenth-century traditional reaction against the impending aesthetic challenge of the Orient.[29]

The neo-classical dislike for such tales was directed mainly against the unrestrained and lawless imagination which they were said to display. For Kames, this indulgence indicated immature taste, lack of morality, and backwardness.[30] In this attitude as well as in his distrust of wild imagination, Kames represents a general antipathy to romantic fiction. To Henry Fielding, for example, such a departure from the real and the probable in the *Nights* was simply incomprehensible: "I would by no means be thought to comprehend those persons

[Paul Scarron and the authors of the *Nights*] of surprising genius, the authors of immense romances, or the modern novel and Atalantis writers; who without any assistance from nature or history, record persons who never were, or will be, and facts which never did, nor possibly can, happen."[31] About forty years later, James Beattie echoed Fielding's objections to the romantic machinery of the *Nights;* Beattie, however, based his argument on more orthodox neo-classical standards which emphasized propriety and balance in language and subject matter. In his discussion of "Fable and Romance" (*Works*, II, 510), he noted that in the *Nights* there is "great luxury of description, without any elegance; and great variety of invention, but nothing that elevates the mind, or touches the heart." Influenced by the dominating conservative view of prose fiction, Beattie detects no obvious moral design in the tales. "All is wonderful and incredible; and the astonishment of the reader is more aimed at, than his improvement either in morality, or in the knowledge of nature." To conclude this survey of the conservative criticism of the *Arabian Nights,* it is fair to say that Kames, Atterbury, Pye, and Beattie were opposed to its extravagance, lack of instructiveness, and departure from reality. Considered within the context of the Augustan emphasis on regularity of form and conformity to classical models and established canons of construction, these reactions indicate that traditional literary critics detected in the *Nights* a new spirit capable of challenging the prevailing critical standards.

James Beattie's reaction, however, should not be regarded as strictly identical to that of Kames, for studied against the change in literary tastes in the last three decades of the century, Beattie's criticism reveals an ambivalent attitude. While adhering to the neo-classical standards of instructiveness and imitation of nature, Beattie showed no reluctance to pamper his contemporaries' susceptibility to the charms of Oriental literature. Thus, he based his criticism of Oriental fiction on the assumption common to critics throughout the century that romance and fiction originated in Arabia.[32] Whether meant as a criticism of incredible and supernatural accounts or as an endorsement of originality and imaginativeness, the assumption was held by many as a tenable premise at the dawn of comparative literature. Accordingly, Beattie contends (*Works*, II, 508–09) that the art of story-telling flourished in the Orient because of certain climatic and social circumstances which "have made them [Eastern kings and princes] seek for this sort of amusement, and set a high value upon it." He further argues that since Eastern princes are "idle, ignorant and credulous," they desire surprising, fabulous accounts rather than moral instruction. In the same place, Beattie also associates the florid Oriental style with the Eastern taste for "rich robes, gaudy, sumptuous entertainment; and palaces shining in gold, or sparkling with diamonds."

Anticipating Thomas Warton's and John Dunlop's emphasis on similar associations, he argues that instead of studying and conforming to the simplicity of nature and art, Eastern princes "pique themselves chiefly on the splendour of their equipage, and the vast quantities of gold, jewels, and various things, which they can heap together in their repositories." Thus, he concludes his argument with the contention that the Oriental mode is incompatible with the classical predilection for seemliness, propriety, and balance.

James Beattie's conclusions make a fascinating study, for while he appeals to the "circumstantial theory" with its emphasis on the necessity of studying each literature against its own social and cultural background, he never deviates from neo-classical standards and indefensible assumptions by which he evaluates and judges Oriental fiction.[33] An obvious lack of information concerning the circumstances attending the composition of such tales make Beattie and others incapable of understanding that the tales were never held in esteem among the learned and cultivated Arabs, and that they were compiled by story-tellers for the enjoyment of the common people, as late eighteenth-century travelers testified.[34] Consequently, instead of arriving at reasonable conclusions similar to those held by such Orientalists as Sir William Jones, James Beattie maintained a middle ground between the Orientalists and the neo-classicists. While evaluating the tales according to current neo-classical doctrines, he nevertheless appreciates two things in the *Nights* "which deserve commendation, and may entitle it to one perusal" (*Works*, II, 510). With an eye on contemporary taste for information, he wrote approvingly that the *Nights* "conveys a pretty just idea of the government, and of some customs, of those eastern nations." No less interesting is the comic and satiric strain that runs throughout the book. There is "somewhere in it," writes Beattie, "a story of a barber and his six brothers, that contains many good strokes of satire and comick description." Aside from this, Beattie admires the neatly constructed stories with their coherent action and apt characterization. To him, "the character of the Caliph Haroun Alraschid is well drawn; and . . . the story of forty thieves destroyed by a slave is interesting, and carefully conducted." Furthermore, the "Voyages of Sinbad claim attention: they were certainly attended to, by the author of Gulliver's Travels."

This admiration for the artistry and social content of the Arabian tales surely sets Beattie apart from the disparaging commentaries of Atterbury, Pye, and Kames, and associates him with a contemporary tendency to assimilate certain thematic and technical traits of the tales in a neo-classical frame. The conflict between the desire to enjoy the magic charm of this type of literature and the traditional standards which condemned its lawlessness was finally resolved in the tendency to rewrite some of these tales or to adapt them to suit the literary elite without denying the common reader the advantage of entertainment. Both Addison and Steele figure as representatives of and pioneers in the popularization of Oriental fiction. Although the acceptance of the Oriental tale still falls within the neo-classical premises of the age, it, nevertheless, reveals a restless search for new visions beyond the dull and limiting conventions. Addison, Steele, and, later, Johnson adapted the trappings and themes of the *Nights* and its successors for moralistic and philosophic purposes. By reducing the amount of Oriental machinery and colorful detail and by minimizing the fantastic and the supernatural in their adaptations, prominent writers and essayists of the period demonstrated their adherence to the accepted standards of probability and universal truths and to the whole dominant attitude towards fictional literature before 1760. In all cases a representational stand evolved in Augustan England that took some East as different but enticing and luring. A Manichean polarity began to show often in the writings of prominent thinkers in England and France. Samuel Johnson's *Rasselas*, 1756, goes as far as suggesting invasions.

In his capacity as a prolific essayist and popularizer, Addison considered popularity a sign of worthiness and, accordingly, he found himself committed to digest the new genre and to pamper his audience's susceptibility by reproducing as many of Scheherazade's pieces as possible. It is true that Addison retold "The Story of the Graecian King and the Physician Douban" and the story of al-Naschar's daydreams to lecture his readers upon the usefulness of bodily exercise and the vanity of extravagant hopes; yet, the real significance of these and numerous other contributions lies in the fact that he lent "the tremendous prestige of the *Spectator* to fiction in this mode," drawing the attention of critics and writers to some adaptable qualities in this goldmine of story-telling.[35]

Besides adaptations by well-known writers, anonymous contributors to eighteenth-century periodicals followed Addison's lead, although with less success. An anonymous contributor to the *Guardian* (No. 162, Sept. 16, 1713) retold the story of Shacabac and the rich Barmecide after stripping it of its rich Oriental attire and dramatic properties, to commend "complaisance" and good manners, as illustrated in this "little wild Arabian tale." Another contributor adapted the story of Parizade for the *Gentleman's Magazine* (XXIV, 1754, 222–23) to warn the fair sex against following "the fashionable world" or entertaining "vain and chimerical pursuits." Even Sir William Jones could not break from current classical doctrines. In his "Seven Fountains," for example, he adapted the "History of the third Calendar" to develop an allegory whose main purpose was to warn readers against insatiable craving for riches, and against vanity and sensual indulgence.[36] With this persistent tendency to deduce overt didactism from implicit and pale moralistic shades in highly dramatic and psychological pieces, the true implications of Scheherazade's story-telling were lost. It was only in the hands of nineteenth-century writers that allusions to the tale, rather than attempts at retailoring it, could retain and recapture the full impact and significance of the original.

The attempt to adapt tales from the *Nights* for different tastes continued throughout the century. Late eighteenth-century pantomime, for instance, drew heavily on the *Nights* to sustain the interest of the audience. As a result of the degeneration of the harlequinade into improper shows and because of the growing opposition to such performances, the English theater borrowed extensively from Scheherazade's fairy tales to furnish scenes for enchantment and transformation that would delight without shocking the middle-class *paterfamilias*. The *Nights* itself passed through a process of adaptation and emasculation. In the last decades and with the growth of an educated middle class reading public on the one hand and the increasing distrust of fictional literature on the other, adaptations in an Addisonian garb would no longer satisfy the adult reader. Instead, we witness a tendency either to adapt classics for children or to retell them in a manner acceptable to the growing middle classes. Arnaud Berquin's *Blossoms of Morality*, which appeared in 1789, contains, for example, two stories from the *Nights*: "The Beautiful Statue" and "Zeyn Al-Ansam." Following the common practice of minimizing detail and cutting off the elements of drama and suspense, Berquin supplied his helpless young readers with stories that were insipid and dull. In his "free" translation of the *Nights* in 1792, C.D. Piguenit avowedly attempted to render the tales compatible with the growing *bourgeois* demand for propriety and good manners. These efforts culminated in the Rev. J. Cooper's *Oriental Moralist; or the Beauties of the Arabian Nights Entertainment*, an adaptation which he accompanied with reflections and comments. In the preface to the second edition (1792), Cooper wrote,

> When I had finished reading the book [the *Arabian Nights*], it struck my imagination, that those tales might be compared to a once rich and luxuriant garden, neglected and run to waste, where scarce anything strikes the observer but the weeds and briars with which it is over-run, whilst the more penetrating eye of the experienced gardener discovers still remaining, though thinly scattered, some of the most fragrant and delightful flowers (p. 2).

Figure 1.1. Schabac offers his apologies to the Barmecide

His method was to expurgate, to retell, and to add certain reflections "to fortify the youthful heart against the impetus of vice." At times Cooper took a great deal of liberty with the original, making basic changes in the causal motivations and episodic sequences of the tales, as in the case of the incest theme in the "First Calendar's Tale." On other occasions, however, he attempted to assert the moral of some of the tales by appending lengthy reflections such as the following, by which he concludes Sindbad's adventures:

> During the whole course of these voyages made by Sindbad, my youthful readers will everywhere observe the interposition of the hand of Providence. Into whatever Calamities he was thrown, he always resigned himself to the will of God, who supported him in a miraculous manner. When at home in his own country, and secure from danger, his study was to relieve the distress of the poor and unfortunate; and, on the contrary, when reduced in foreign countries to the abject situation of a slave, he supported that character with a becoming decency and submission. Those, who can with fortitude bear up under the iron hand of adversity, will never be insolent in the sunshine of prosperity (p. 262).

Figure 1.2. Imperious woman with respectful nobleman

But when set against the conservative criticism of the tales and considered in relation to parallel attempts to rescue them from their opponents' imputations, Cooper's focus on "the beauties" of the tales is of primary significance. He sets the tone for other erudite discourses on the subject. The anonymous writer of the informed "Prefatory Discourse" for the 1807 Suttaby edition of the *Nights* has this to say about its moral purposefulness:

> The moral of his [the author's] tales is in general excellent, and he rarely fails to reward courage, fidelity, virtue, honour, religion, and the nobler qualities of the soul; and to punish cruelty, perfidy, ingratitude, fraud, irreligion, and those baser passions of human nature, which among men of every description of faith and complexion of features, are justly regarded as disgraceful and deserving of punishment (1, xvii).

On the pure literary level, the tendency to vindicate the Arabian tales against the charge of improbability and absurdity developed among critics who decided to meet hostile criticism on its own grounds. Intent upon demonstrating how foolish it was to alienate the *Arabian Nights* through misapplication of classical standards in literary criticism, many late eighteenth-century critics published erudite discourses and communications on the subject. Edward Gibbon, for instance, looked upon the *Nights* as equal in value to Pope's *Homer,* for both works "will always please by the moving picture of human manners and specious miracles."[37] Writing for the *Gentleman's Magazine* of September 1794 (LXIV, 783), "M.S." noticed that Scheherazade's tales create "the ardor of admiration" and "excite wonder." It is this early reading which "is often succeeded in riper years by superior energy of mind, and a thrift [sic] for more knowledge." This reading, the writer contends, is perhaps what Plato regarded as "the very source of philosophy itself," for it is similar to his sublime mythology which "was used merely with a view to excite wonder." Vicesimus Knox holds a similar contention regarding the salutary influence of the *Nights* on the youth. In a chapter entitled "On the Method of Exciting in Boys the Symptoms of Literary Genius" (*Essays Moral and Literary.* Enlarged ed., 1782, I, 314), he explains: "The Arabian Nights Entertainment, The Tales of the Genii, and the Death of Abel, though they may not be entirely approved by a mature understanding and taste, are well calculated to kindle a flame in the bosoms of boys."

The anonymous writer of "Prefatory Discourse" for the 1807 Suttaby edition of the *Nights* appeals to the neo-classical inclinations of some of his readers on two grounds. There is no other nation that "can boast of higher antiquity" than the Arabs. As such, the same methods of recognition and aesthetic enjoyment which we apply to Homer and Ovid should be applied to the supernatural elements in the Arabian tales. Furthermore, he contends that these elements seem strange to an English reader not because of their excessive and wild fancy, but simply because of our shallow acquaintance with Arab mythology and culture. To overcome this problem, he suggests as criteria the reader's "own passions and feelings" rather than conventional rules; such a premise will eventually lead, he thinks, to aesthetic understanding and adequate critical assessment:

> There is no other way of judging of compositions of this kind, but by trying them by the standard of our own passions and feelings; we do not admire or hate the genii of the Arabian Nights Entertainments, because we are told that some of them were virtuous and some of them malignant beings, endowed with a power to accomplish extraordinary things; but we lead ourselves to believe the miracles

that are related of them, in the same way that we are gratified with the wonderful relations of Homer's deities and heroes, or the metamorphoses of Ovid.

Elaborating on this point, he further explains that the same kind of "credibility is preserved in these tales, as the Greeks attached to the *speciosa miracula* of their poets." When perusing such writings, the reader willingly suspends "the operations of a severer reason" and "the fancy easily assents" because most of the romantic machinery and notions are "derived from hoary antiquity, and are sanctioned by popular belief" (I, xix).

Moreover, in the "regions of fiction" and improbability in the *Nights,* the author has the advantage of preserving human feelings and passions in extraordinary situations, depicting only the universal and the typical and maintaining the uniformity of human nature throughout the tales. Basing his further discussions of the question of probability on the preceding premise, the anonymous editor contends that the Arabian story-teller sustains interest "by the strain of natural feeling," and, simultaneously, leads the reader to believe that probability is maintained rather than violated in such narratives. Whenever the Arabian author "has recourse to supernatural agency," writes the same critic, "the personages whom he suffers to be under the species of influence, lose none of their human feelings, but, in the most extraordinary situations and circumstances, act under human motives and inducements." To substantiate his contention, the critic cites the story of Sidi No'man. The latter, he explains, "is transformed into a dog, and in that shape he does exactly as we should conceive any other human being would do, who should be placed in the same calamitous circumstances" (p. xxxii).

The anonymous writer's articulate argument was anticipated by a number of critics in the last decades of the century. In her *Progress of Romance* (Colchester, 1785), Clara Reeve devotes many pages to demonstrate that the story of Sindbad the sailor is comparable to the *Odyssey* and that the Arabian story-teller is preferable to Homer, since the latter "takes the liberty of sending his deities perpetually on the most trifling errands" (pp. 22–23, 58, 60–61). She contends that although "the Magicians of the Arabian perform very marvellous things, by the assistance of the good and evil Genii," they are "subordinate to the seal of Sultan Solomon the Son of David" (p. 23). Controlled as such, the supernatural agency in the *Nights* acts within the limitations of the Islamic mytho-religious system. In this region, however, eighteenth-century critics were kept in the dark because of their limited knowledge of Islamic culture, a point to which I shall return.

Whereas Clara Reeve was satisfied with drawing a comparison between the *Odyssey* and "Sindbad the Sailor," Taylor dwelt upon the point in his translation of *Pausanias]* concluding that the internal evidence which he traced in Sindbad's adventures is strong enough to indicate that many tales in Scheherazade's collection are not alien to classical literature:

> The readers of the most ingenious and entertaining work called the Arabian Nights Entertainment, will doubtless be agreeably surprised to find, if they have not discovered it before, that the interesting account of the preservation of Aristomenes in the deep chasm, has been taken from Pausanias, with some alterations, by the author of these tales, and forms one of the most curious parts of the history of *Sindbad the Sailor.*[38]

The probable classical origin of some of Sindbad's adventures became one of Richard Hole's primary tenets in his *Remarks on the Arabian Nights' Entertainments; in which the Origin of Sindbad's Voyages, and other Oriental Fictions, is particularly considered* (1797). Despite his avowed preference for classical harmony and simplicity as against Oriental magnificence and splendor, Hole's thesis is concerned with obviating the opposition to the supernatural element in these tales. Accordingly, his main appeal is to the classical preferences of the literati. He maintains that the same credibility is preserved in Scheherazade's tales as is to be found in the *speciosa miracula* of the Greek poets. Basing his argument on the available information concerning classical influences on medieval Arabic culture, Hole concludes that the Arabs borrowed Homeric episodes and inserted them in their tales of adventure. On the other hand, he allows the possibility of some Eastern influence on classical thought.[39]

Richard Hole's thesis, however, is not limited to such comparisons. Whereas the most extravagant incidents in the *Nights* are regarded as borrowings from classical sources, the others are verified by references to authentic accounts of historical personages and voyages. But Hole's attempt to verify geographical locations in his discussion of Sindbad's voyages provoked some critics to question the value of his labor. Thus, the *Monthly Review* of September 1797 (XXIV, 46) shrewdly remarked: "When we view him labouring to ascertain ... the scenes of the fabulous navigator's imaginary adventures, and attempting to 'give to airy nothing a local habitation and a name,' we feel inclined to ask whether it be probable that the Arabian fabulist has attended more to geography than to history?" Nevertheless, the questioning here indicates that Hole's work evoked some interest which cannot be seen apart from the vogue of the *Nights*. To gauge the real literary significance and impact of Hole's work, however, we must understand that it represents one of many zealous attempts to vindicate the supernatural element in the *Nights* on classical premises and, ultimately, to rescue the tales from belittling criticism. With good grounding in classical learning and considerable ignorance of Arabic literature, Scheherazade's apologetic admirers attempted to search for Greek elements in her tales to give some scholarly weight to their appreciative accounts of her art.

Seen in the context of late eighteenth-century scholarship, Hole's *Remarks* indicates the dearth of informative and authoritative studies in comparative literature, a fact to which Mahmoud Manzaloui rightly assigns a number of mistaken efforts either to trace all romantic accounts to Arabic origin as in Huet's and Warton's studies or to ignore Arabic classical literature because of shallow acquaintance with Islam and the Arabs, as in the case of Scheherazade' s opponents among the neo-classicists.[40] In both cases, the *Arabian Nights* was the basis on which zealous admirers and hostile critics alike built their theoretic discourses. The scholarly remarks, copious studies and investigations of Bolingbroke, Ockley, Sir William Jones, John Richardson, and a host of others, had not yet exerted any notable impact.[41] Travelers to the East were so enthralled by Scheherazade's descriptions of a glamorous Orient that they accepted Lady Mary's view that the *Nights* provides a faithful picture of Oriental life and manners. When considering travel accounts about the Arab East in the eighteenth century, one must agree with Wallace Cable Brown that early eighteenth-century travelers took "full advantage of the poetic license of a pre-scientific age, and of the privilege of the pioneer traveller to mingle inextricably fact and fiction."[42] We need to wait for Victorian scholars to dispel this thick cloud of illusion and to establish, albeit relatively, a well-informed background for comparative studies. Rather than figuring prominently as an impeachable source of information, the *Nights* itself was subjected to scholarly, although not necessarily merciless, dissection and annotation in Victorian England.

The apologetic admirers of the *Nights* in eighteenth-century England did, nevertheless, contribute to the development of two critical perspectives in the evaluation of the tales—the utilitarian and the purely aesthetic. Appreciated as a repository of information on Eastern manners, customs, and modes of life, Scheherazade's tales were read and appreciated by a large segment of the rising middle class. Galland himself has asserted this value of the *Nights*. Aside from the title page which communicates the same notion, he said in the "Preface" (p. viii) that the tales "must also be pleasing, because of the account they give of the customs and manners of the eastern nations, and of the ceremonies of their religion, as well Pagan as Mahometan, which are better described here, than in any author that has wrote of them, or in the relations of travellers." Others have also focused on this aspect. In discussing this side of the interest in the tales, the *Monthly Review* (XXIX, 1799, 475) observes, for instance,

> the curiosity and interest which they [the Arabian tales] so powerfully excite; the luxuriant descriptions with which they abound; and the accurate delineations of eastern manners, or (to speak more accurately) of the manners of the Moslems, which they exhibit, will always attract more attention than is usually allotted to the extravagant incidents of fabulous narrative.

Regarded as a subtle combination of the informative and the delightful, the tales were accorded considerable attention. Travelers, from James Capper and Vivant Denon to Lady Mary and James Dallaway, wrote at some length about this peculiar attraction of the tales, an attraction which impressed them so much that many of their accounts seem romanticized under Scheherazade's influence. Indeed, James Dallaway, chaplain and physician of the British Embassy to the Porte, saw the East from a perspective that was obviously colored by his readings of the *Nights*. Describing the romantic side of Eastern life, he explains that much of "the romantic air which pervades the domestic habits of the persons described in the Arabian Nights Entertainments, particularly in inferior life, will be observed in passing through the streets of Constantinople." Combining pleasure with information and historical detail, the tales deserve commendation. Hence, he concludes, "we refer with additional pleasure to a remembrance of the delight with which we first perused them, in finding them authentic portraits of every oriental nation."[43] This turn to representations of life practices and manners and no matter how general and platitudinous cannot be seen apart from an increasing colonial encroachment and the need for knowledge of native traditions.

In *Observations on the Passage to India* (1783), James Capper contends that the tales deserve more attention not only because of their accurate delineation of Eastern customs but also because of their impact on the Eastern auditor. Considered in relation to the growing emphasis on the need for a better under-standing of Eastern people, the *Nights* was deemed of great value at a time of colonial expansion:

> "The Arabian Nights" contain much curious and useful observation. They are universally read and admired throughout Asia by all ranks of men, both old and young. Considered, therefore, as an original work, descriptive as they are of the manners and customs of the East in general, and of the Arabians in particular, they surely must be thought to merit the attention of the curious . . .. But before

any person decides upon the merit of these books, he should be an eyewitness of the effect they produce on those who best understand them.[44]

With the increasing cultural interest in the East, especially in areas of Biblical studies and antiquarian investigations, and with the growth of British mercantile interests in India and Egypt, the emphasis on information became a recurrent theme in writings about the *Nights*. No longer looked upon as a mere collection of stories verging on the improbable and the absurd, Scheherazade's tales assumed considerable significance in the last decades of the century as a work worthy of the perusal of the learned. Being so entertaining, the tales were seen as more impressive, and, ultimately, more helpful than travel accounts. In Weber's discussion of the *Nights* (*Tales of the East*, I, ii–iii), for example, he maintained, "By the perusal of the *Arabian Nights, Entertainments,* and of other collections of similar nature, we obtain, in a manner the most impressive on the memory, and the most pleasing to the mind, a perfect insight into the private habits, the domestic comforts and deprivations of the orientals." Aware of the conservative opposition to fictional literature, Weber averred that the *Nights* provides social and historical information in the garb of amusing stories. "We are led," he continued,

> . . . to participate in their favourite amusements and acquire a knowledge of their religious sentiments and superstitions: and it thus happens that a boy, who has been indulged in the perusal of these ingenious fictions, is made as well acquainted with the peculiarities of Oriental manners, and the tenets of the Mahommedan faith, during the time of relaxation, as he is, during his school-hours, with the customs and mythology of the Greeks and Romans.

Beyond the emphasis on the *Nights* as a useful repository of information, there was a growing concern to verify this information by a study of the original manuscripts. Perhaps it was no longer entirely safe to trust the Galland version. Accordingly, by the end of the century, critics and scholars were insisting that fully accurate translations of the tales be undertaken. No sooner was the authenticity of Galland's version vindicated than Richard Hole and others called for an erudite, well-annotated and scholarly edition of the *Nights*.[45] In his *Remarks* (p. 221) Hole saw in the absence of such an edition a sign of contemporary negligence, which he held partly responsible for the controversy between neo-classicists and Orientalists. Had such a translation been available, it would have enabled both groups to trace common Grecian and Eastern themes to their origin. Robert Wood, James Beattie, and a number of correspondents with the *Gentleman's Magazine* raised many objections to Galland's version.[46] In the issue for September 1798 (LXVIII, 757), "W.W." contended that since Galland's edition "from which our English one is made, is generally supposed to be very defective," a new translation "would be gladly received by the publick, especially if it represented those fine poetical passages and moral reflections with which, we are told, the original abounds, but of which scarce a vestige remains in the present translation."

Nathan Drake felt that "had the translation been more faithful to the idiom of the original," and "better supported its peculiar spirit and strong features, and not mutilated a production of undoubted genius, these tales ... [would have] still further merited the attention of the philosopher and the historian."[47] After comparing their manuscripts of the *Nights* with Galland's version, both Patrick Russell and John Richardson expressed certain objections to Galland's method, especially his omission of poetical passages and abridgement of some tales. Speaking specifically of the story of the barber's fifth brother, Richardson remarked that "the deviation from the original is greater than even a free translation seemed to require." Although approving of Galland's expurgation of licentious passages, Patrick Russell, in a letter to the *Gentleman's Magazine,* noticed that "other descriptions ... expressive of Oriental *Costume,* have with less reason been omitted, particularly two Nights in Vol. II p. 155."[48] Conversely, however, both Edward Forster and Jonathan Scott seemed to disagree with such objections to Galland's version. In his omissions as well as emendations, Galland was regarded as worth emulating. Taking Warren Hastings' praise for Galland's French as authoritative, both embarked on providing the English reader with new translations from Galland's French after the Grub Street version had gone through numerous editions, unrivalled throughout the century.[49]

But had these diverse critical responses to Scheherazade's tales been the only ones in eighteenth-century England, a modern reader would have rightly pitied those learned critics who seem to have missed the pleasure, anxiety, and exquisite joy which usually accompany the perusal of these tales. History, however, has a different story to tell. Johnson, Rousseau, Voltaire, Pope, Addison, Steele, Swift, and Smollett—to mention only few—read those tales and borrowed extensively from them.[50] In fact, the medievalist Richard Gough strongly disapproved of Hole's contention that the tales "are held in contempt, more particularly by the grave and the learned," demonstrating in his preface to the 1798 new edition of the *Nights* (I, x) that "some of the *most grave* and the most learned retain with delight the impression made by the perusal of these volumes."[51] Besides the countless imitations for the magazines and adaptations for the theater, writers like Eliza Haywood, and, later, Maturin used the mechanism of the *Nights* in their works. Maturin's use is not limited to adapting the story-within-a-story structure but is also extended to the delineation of Melmoth, whose ancestors are not the villains of early Gothic romances, but Cazotte's "Maugrabi the Magician" in *Arabian Tales* (1792). Furthermore, Isidora's story clearly echoes the supernatural element in the *Nights*. In this romance, Maturin compares Isidora's anticipation of Melmoth's arrival to the Arabian damsels' attraction of some genie to interfere "at their nuptial hour."[52] But in spite of the significance of such readings and adaptations, there is perhaps no better testimony to the irresistible charm of Scheherazade's tales than the reported anecdote about Sir James Steward, Lord Advocate of Scotland. Having one Saturday evening found his daughters perusing Scheherazade's tales, he chastised them for spending the evening before the Sabbath in such frivolous and worldly amusements; "but the grave advocate became himself a prey to the fascination of these tales, being found upon the morning of the sabbath itself employed in their perusal, from which he had not risen the whole of the night."[53]

Along with the patterns of response already discussed, there was a parallel tendency to read the Arabian tales as a work of art, a blend of the fanciful and the realistic, rather than as an accurate representation of Oriental life and manners. This tendency corresponds to an obvious change in the whole critical attitude towards fiction after the 1750s. Instead of asserting imitation of nature as basic to literary evaluation, critics in the last decades of the century tended to recognize other elements that were incompatible with neo-classical standards.[54] No longer dependent upon the support of the literary elite, writers readily responded to popular demands for entertaining fiction. It is enough here to refer to a new wave of pseudo-Oriental tales, ranging from Johnson's "The Fountains" (1766) to Hawkesworth's *Almoran and Hamet*. In these, the emphasis is upon the marvelous rather than the probable, for romantic machinery and Oriental trappings were considered the right means for reaching and, consequently, instructing the reader. When reviewing Hawkesworth's *Almoran and Hamet*, Owen Ruffhead observed that "very few are disposed to relish the dry precepts of morality, or to connect a lengthened chain of reasoning; the majority must be entertained with novelty, humoured with fiction, and, as it were, cheated into instruction."[55]

In *Lectures or Rhetoric and Belles Lettres* (1762) Hugh Blair asserted the same tendency, intimating that "the wisest men in all ages have more or less employed fables and fictions, as the vehicles of knowledge." He argued that the Eastern nations developed the art of story-telling because it proved a suitable vehicle for their philosophical, religious, and political ideas. Citing the *Nights* to verify his thesis, Blair explained how these imaginative and amusing tales exhibit lively sentiments and accurate descriptions of people and manners: "The *Arabian Nights' Entertainments* are the production of a romantic invention, but of rich and amusing imagination; exhibiting a singular and serious display of manners and characters, and beautified with a very humane morality."[56]

From the 1760s onwards, great emphasis was laid on the equal importance of the marvelous and the moralistic in fiction. The rich imaginary world of the Orient was praised for its own sake and the florid Oriental style was imitated rather than ridiculed. Indeed, the fact that the focus of interest had shifted from copying nature to utilizing the improbable for instruction is too apparent to be overlooked, especially in relation to the critical attitude to Eastern tales. In 1759 the *Monthly Review,* for example, condemned deviation from probability and overt morality in some Oriental tales; in 1762 it recommended the adaptation of Oriental invention and description as a vehicle for moral and religious edification.[57] This same change can be detected in the *Critical Review.* When reviewing the *Tales of the Genii* for this periodical (XVIII, 1764, 40–41), Ruffhead praised these stories not only for their "eastern theology" but also for their figurative language, wonderful incidents, and glowing imagination.

No longer capable of capturing the attention of the prosperous middle classes, the early eighteenth-century moralistic and philosophic pseudo-Oriental tale gave way in the second half of the century to a series of fantastic imitations that were mainly written for the sole purpose of satisfying a popular craving for the amusing and the wonderful. Writing about the "numerous successors" of the *Nights,* the *Critical Review* remarked in 1786 (1st Ser. LXII, 38) that, "though of unequal merit, [they] still retain some credit, in consequence of this preternatural talisman." No critic, perhaps, expressed this increasing demand for the marvelous and the exotic better than Ruffhead, who, in the *Monthly Review* for 1762 (XXVI, 254), made this comment on Oriental imitations: "Such is the raging appetite for romance, that to engage the public ear, even academic gravity is forced to lay aside its didactic dignity, and sport in the flowery fields of fiction." He added that many "writers of distinguished talents have lately figured in the rank of novelists. The solemn Johnson had his Eastern Tale; Hawkesworth had his Genii; and Langhorne now leads us into the valley of Mesopotamia."

Theoretically, the break with neo-classical standards in criticism occurred in 1752, when Hawkesworth published his essay on "the most pleasing" narratives in the fourth number of the *Adventurer* (Sat., Nov. 18, 1752, p 24). Hawkesworth's argument is a justification of his own Oriental pieces which, "formed upon a single incident ... sufficiently uncommon to gratify curiosity, and sufficiently interesting to engage the passions, may afford an entertainment ... of the highest kind." On the basis of this concept, Hawkesworth concludes that histories, voyages, epics, old romances, and novels are deficient in one aspect or another. At the same time, he ridicules the neo-classical concept of imitating nature, asserting that "nature is now exhausted, all her wonders have been accumulated … yet fancy requires new gratifications, and curiosity is still unsatisfied." Thus, after rejecting the two classical tenets—generalized human nature and decorum—Hawkesworth appeals to the reader's spontaneous taste for the marvelous and the fantastic as basic to the pleasurable experience derived from reading a work of art. He argues that the overwhelming appeal of the *Nights* and its successful imitations indicates our readiness as readers to suspend our disbelief in order to be "rewarded by the new scenes to which we are admitted, and the unbounded prospect that is thrown open before us." In other words, Hawkesworth regards the genre established after the appearance of the *Nights* as the best among literary arts since it has no other purpose than to please the reader.

Hawkesworth's discussion of the reader's easy willingness to suspend his judgment in perusing such narratives was accepted by a number of his contemporaries. In his diary for December 17, 1797, Thomas Green explained how he used to react to the Arabian tales: "I have been for some time amusing myself with the Arabian Nights Entertainments, to whose fascinating influence I am quite ductile. Nothing can be happier than the leading plan of these tales." Rather than being shocked by their wildness, he perused them with rapture for "the stories themselves, though physically extravagant, are such, to which we yield, without scruple, what smoothes, without effort, all physical difficulties—a willing fancy; and their variety keeps expectation perpetually alive."[58]

This "willing fancy" seems to derive more enjoyment from reading the tales because of the existence of a mytho-religious structure which leads the reader to believe that he is reading about a world which is not completely alien to him. But this notion of the attraction of the *Nights,* to which Hawkesworth adhered, was rejected by Heron towards the close of the century. In his "Preface" to the *Arabian Tales* (p. x), the latter maintained that it is the strangeness of the machinery and the obscurity of motivations which arouse the reader's feelings of pity, sympathy, and fear: "It is surely the strangeness, the unknown nature, the anomalous character of the supernatural agents here employed, that enables them to operate so powerfully on our hopes, fears, curiosities, sympathies, and, in short, on all the feelings of our hearts." To him, it is this conflict between the human and the supernatural which stimulates the reader's interest and evokes his sympathy for people facing incomprehensible powers: "We see men and women," he argued, "who possess qualities to recommend them to our favour, subjected to the influence of beings whose good or ill will, power, or weakness, attention or neglect, are regulated by motives and circumstances which we cannot comprehend." Hence, he concluded, "We naturally tremble for their fate, with the same anxious concern, as we should for a friend wandering, in a dark night, amidst torrents and precipices." Whether accepting Hawkesworth's or Robert Heron's notions of the appealing nature of the supernatural in the *Nights,* the tendency among late eighteenth-century critics to appreciate the romantic machinery of the tales coincided with the interest in Gothic art. Indeed, the association between the Oriental and Gothic modes is too obvious to pass without brief comment. Late eighteenth-century critics were inclined to stress the interrelatedness of the two modes, remarking now and then that the Gothic romance was originally influenced by the Arabians.

Within relevant literary responses, Mrs. Barbauld's estimate of the supernatural element in the *Nights* is worth noting. In her essay "On the Pleasure Derived from Objects of Terror," Anna Laetitia Aikin i.e., Mrs. Barbauld, expounds on the appeal of "artificial" terror to the human mind. As a reaction against the conservatism and sobriety of the eighteenth-century, the essay deserves a place among pre-romantic writings. In so far as her views of the *Nights* are concerned, Mrs. Barbauld argues that Eastern tales, with their enchantments and magic, "will ever retain a most powerful influence on the mind, and interest the reader independently of all peculiarity of taste."[59] More than natural terror, the supernatural element in the *Nights* evokes religious awe and holy fear. As the pleasure derived from reading is in proportion to this feeling and to the wildness of the scenes described, Mrs. Barbauld concludes that the *Nights* provides the reader with the most pleasurable experience: "Hence, the more wild, fanciful, and extraordinary are the circumstances of a scene of horror," noted Mrs. Barbauld, "the more pleasure we receive from it; and where they are too near common nature, though violently borne by curiosity through the adventure, we cannot repeat it or reflect on it, without an over-balance of pain." Substantiating her argument with examples from the tales, she further explained: "In the *Arabian Nights* are many most striking examples of the terrible joined with the marvellous: the story of Alladin and the travels of Sindbad are particularly interesting."[60]

Horace Walpole's aesthetic appreciation of the wildness of Scheherazade's tales falls, perhaps, within the same current taste for this blending of the terrible and the marvelous. In a letter to Mary Berry he expressed a strong liking for the adventures of Sindbad and an appetite for the fantastic nature of many of the tales. Although the "Sultaness's narratives [are not] very natural or very probable," he observed, "there is wildness in them that captivates." The full significance

Figure 1.3. Elephant aloft in the talons of a monstrous eagle

Figure 1.4. Letchford Aladdin

of the letter, however, is not limited to its expression of Walpole's admiration of Scheherazade's artistry, for it also reveals the disparity between two different attitudes towards imaginative literature—the neo-classic and the romantic. With dashing satire, Walpole in this letter ridiculed Bishop Atterbury for refusing to continue reading the tales, indicating thereby the reaction against Augustan literary conservatism: "If you grow tired of the *Arabian Nights*," he amusingly noted, "you have no more taste than Bishop Atterbury, who huffed Pope for sending him them or the *Persian Tales,* and fancied he liked Virgil better, who had no more imagination than Dr. Akenside. Read Sindbad the sailor's voyages, and you will be sick of Aeneas's."[61] With Horace Walpole's sheer enjoyment of the wildness and imaginativeness which repelled early traditional critics, our survey of eighteenth-century critical responses seems to come full circle.

Studying the development of the critical attitude towards the *Nights* in the light of its popularity, one cannot avoid the conclusion that throughout the eighteenth century there was a developing interest in the marvels of these exquisite tales, and a persistent attempt to unravel their intricate designs and complicated artistry. No less significant than pseudo-Oriental imitations and adaptations are the critical comments which have been discussed. These comments, of course, reveal the changing standard and taste of the time. It is apparent that the critics, in some degree, were willing to modify their own earlier standards in accordance with the changing taste and interest of the reading public. It is therefore scarcely an exaggeration to say that the passion of the general reading public for these exotic stories did much to shape not only critical standards but also the literary tone of fiction writers alert to public demands.
Notes

Notes

1 George Crabbe, *Poems*, ed. Adolphus William Ward (Cambridge: Univ. Press, 1907), III, 197.

2 Thomas Russell, *Sonnets and Miscellaneous Poems* (Oxford, 1789), Sonnet No. V.

3 See "A Bibliographical and Literary Study of the First Appearance of the *Arabian Nights* in Europe," *Library Quarterly*, II (Oct. 1932), 405–06. For more information, see Burton's "Terminal Essay," and W.F. Kirby's "Contributions to the Bibliography of the Thousand and One Nights . . .," in Burton's *Book of the Thousand Nights*, X, 92–94 and 414–18 respectively. See also the British Museum Catalogue for editions; Victor Chauvin, *Bibliographie Arabe* (Liege, 1900), IV, 25–26; and "Notes on Sales: 'The Arabian Nights'," *TLS* (Mar. 16, 1922), 176. *The Cambridge Bibliography*

of English Literature assigns the period between September 1705 and March 1706 as the date of the first English translation. As early as December 16, 1706, Mrs. Manley's heroic drama *Almyna; or the Arabian Vow* was performed at the Theatre Royal. Mrs. Manley admitted in the preface that the theme was taken from Arabian sources, "with something of a Hint from the Arabian Nights Entertainments." After citing the preceding evidence, Adel M. Abdullah rightly concludes that this adaptation "corroborates the scanty evidence we have which points to the period between September, 1705, and March, 1706." See "The Arabian Nights in English Literature to 1900," Unpubl. Ph.D. Diss. (Cambridge, 1963), 225.

4 D.B. Macdonald, "On Translating the 'Arabian Nights,'" Pt. I, *The Nation*, LXXI (Aug. 30, 1900), 167.

5 For the comment on Marshall's list, see P.H. Muir's *English Children's Books, 1600 to 1900* (London: B.T. Batsford, 1954), 40, n. 4; and F.J.H. Darton's *Children's Books in England* (1932; rpt. Cambridge: Cambridge Univ. Press, 1958), 61.

6 "On Fable and Romance," in *Dissertations Moral and Critical, Philosophical and Critical Works*, II, 510. Hereafter cited as *Works* and incorporated with page number within the text.

7 Robert D. Mayo's phrase, in *The English Novel in the Magazines 1740–1815* (London: Oxford Univ. Press, 1962), 40–41.

8 Howard Phillips Lovecraft, *Supernatural Horror in Literature* (1927; rpt. New York: Abramson, 1945), 36–37.

9 For Goldsmith, see *The Citizen of the World* ... (London, 1762), I, 138; and for Walpole, *The Works of Horatio Walpole* (London, 1798), IV, 234–36.

10 Robert D. Mayo, 40.

11 Robert D. Mayo, 59. After the renewal of the stamp tax on newspapers, William Parker's *London News* came to an end in April 1725, and his *Penny Post* began to appear instead in four pages. It continued to serialize the rest of the *Nights* as "a front-page feature." See R.M. Wiles, *Serial Publication in England Before 1750* (Cambridge: Univ. Press, 1957), 35, 38, n. 2.

12 See Robert D. Mayo, 302, 303, 248, 366 respectively.

13 Reference to Huet is to the second (1729) edition, I, xiv. On the correspondence between the two, see Mia Gerhardt, *The Art of Story-Telling: A Literary Study of the Thousand and One Nights* (Leiden: E.J. Brill, 1962), p. 236 and n. 3; and Mahmoud Manzalaoui, "PseudoOrientalism in Transition: The Age of *Vathek*," in *William Beckford of Fonthill*, ed. Fatma M. Mahmoud (1960; rpt. Port Washington: Kennikat Press, 1972), 129 and n. 8.

14 Anthony Shaftesbury, *Characteristics*, ed. John M. Robertson (London, 1900), esp. 221–25.

15 Cited in the preface to *New Arabian Nights' Entertainments*, trans. George Lamb (London: Henry Colburn, 1826), I, v and n.

16 Everyman's, 1956, ed. W.M. Parker, 17–18.

17 "Introduction" to *Vathek* in *Three Gothic Novels* (New York: Dover, 1966), xxviii.

18 Norman Daniel's phrase, *Islam, Europe and Empire* (Edinburgh: Edinburgh Univ. Press, 1966), 20, 21–23.

19 For the eighteenth-century interest in this topic, see Ian Watt, *The Rise of the Novel: Studies in Defoe, Richardson and Fielding* (London: Chatto & Windus, 1957), 166; and J.B. Botsford, *English Society in the Eighteenth Century as Influenced from Oversea* (1924; rpt. New York: Octagon Books, 1965), 280.

20 See especially her letters of March 10, 1718 and April 18, 1717 to Lady Mar in *The Complete Letters* (Oxford: Clarendon Press, 1965), I, 385, 349–51.

21 *Arabian Nights' Entertainments* (London: Longman), I, ix. Quotations are from the 1783 four-volume edition.

22 "On the Authenticity of the Arabian Tales," *Gentleman's Magazine*, LXIX (Feb., 1799), 92.

23 "The Oriental Tale ... A Reconsideration," *Studies on Voltaire and the Eighteenth Century*, LVIII (1967), 1845. For similar conclusions, see also Richard F. Burton, "Terminal Essay," 101–02; and Sheila Shaw, "The Rape of Gulliver: A Case Study of a Source," *PMLA*, XC (Jan. 1975), 65.

24 "Arabian Nights," *Foreign Quarterly Review*, XXIV (Oct., 1839), 141. For authorship, see *Wellesley Index*, II, no. 552.

25 *The Works of Alexander Pope*, eds. Whitewell Elwin and William Courthope (London: Murray, 1871–89), IX, 22–23. See also the *Correspondence of Alexander Pope*, ed. George Sherburn (Oxford: Clarendon Press, 1956), II, 53.

26 William L. Phelps, *The Beginnings of the English Romantic Movement* (1893; rpt. New York: Gordian Press, 1968), 18–19. For Horace Walpole, see note. 61 below.

27 For Henry James Pye, see *A Commentary Illustrating the Poetic of Aristotle* (London: John Stockdale, 1792), 438–39.

28 Henry Home Kames, *Elements of Criticism*, ed. Abraham Mills (New York: Huntington & Savage, 1846), chap. 24, 447–48.

29 For more on this point, see Albert E. Richardson, *Georgian England* (1931; rpt. New York: Books for Libraries Press, 1967); A.S. Turberville, *English Men and Manners in the Eighteenth Century* (Oxford: Clarendon Press, 1926); Beverly Sprague Allen, *Tides in English Taste, 1619–1800* (Cambridge, MA: Harvard Univ. Press, 1937), 2 vols., esp. 1, 234; and Botsford, *English Society in the Eighteenth Century*.

30 Henry Home Kames, *Sketches of the History of Man* (London: Strahan and Cadell, 1778), I, 200.

31 *Joseph Andrews and Shamela* (Boston, MA: Houghton Mifflin, 1961), Bk. III, chap. 1, 158.

32 See, for instance, Huet's *A Treatise of Romances and Their Original*, London, 1672 (S. Lewis' tr. 1715); and Thomas Warton, "On the Origin of Romantic Fiction in Europe," prefixed to vol. I of his *History of English Poetry* (London, 1774–81).

33 Following Cicero and Quintilian, eighteenth-century Orientalists tended to relate stylistic and thematic peculiarities of literary productions to national and climatic circumstances and conditions. In line with the growth of Biblical studies and the attempt to justify the unclassical style of the Old Testament, this "circumstantial theory" gained in strength. For a discussion of this theory, though without my own references and applications to Beattie, see Husain F. Ali Haddawy, "English Arabesque: The Oriental Mode in Eighteenth-Century English Literature," Unpubl. Ph.D. Diss. (Cornell, 1962), v, 162–64, 226–41. I find the term "historical method" more convenient, especially in relation to the nineteenth-century interest in the thematic context of the *Nights*.

34 For a good survey of these references to story-telling and the *Nights*, see the Rev. Edward Forster's preface to his translation of the *Nights* (London: William Miller, 1802), I, xxiii–xliv, in which he covers the accounts of such travelers as M. Oliver, Lady Mary Wortley Montague, Dallaway, and James Capper.

35 Robert D. Mayo, 40.

36 *The Works* (London, 1807), X, 230–50.

37 See *Memoirs of My Life*, ed. Georges A. Bonnard (London: Nelson, 1966), 36. Whereas Gibbon and others discerned such similarities, pseudo-classicists were uncompromising in their rejection of the "wild" imagination displayed in the tales. "M.S." in the *Gentleman's Magazine* (LXIV; Sept. 1794, 783) considered the pseudo-classical approach to the *Nights* one sign of the many "eccentricities" of the eighteenth century. The imitation of models was, after all, a misconception of "Aristotle's remark that poetry is an imitation of an action." On this, see N.H. Clement, *Romanticism in France* (New York: MLA, 1939), 66, no. 47; and Henry A. Beers, *A History of English Romanticism in the Eighteenth Century* (New York: Henry Holt; 2nd ed., 1926). Beers expounds on the "incomplete, superficial concept of Hellenism" which neglected the "freer, more original spirit of Greek art," pointing out that, as an example of this intentional deviation, Addison, in *Spectator* (No. 160), apologized for Homer's failure to observe decorum. See p. 35, n.

38 *Pausanias*, I, 390. Cited in "The Prefatory Discourse," Suttaby's edition of the *Nights*, I, xii.

39 See, for example, his "Preface" to *Arthur; or the Northern Enchantment* (1789), v–vi.

40 "Pseudo-Orientalism in Transition," 135–36.

41 There were certainly a number of works dealing with Islam and the Arabs in the eighteenth century. Sale's authoritative introduction to the *Koran* (1734), Simon Ockley's *History of the Saracens* (1708–18), and Alexander Russell's *Natural History of Aleppo* (1756) were among many that paved the way for future scholarship. Bolingbroke's attempt to reveal and criticize highly prejudiced accounts of Islam is of special importance. See *On the Study and Use of History* (London, 1889), Letter IV, 93, 96–97. Adam Anderson, Thomas Astle, Adam Smith, Gibbon, and a number of Orientalists contributed much to the understanding of medieval Arab civilization

and its influence on Europe. For a survey of these, see Herbert Weisinger, "The Middle Ages and the Late Eighteenth-Century Historians," *Philological Quarterly*, XXVII (Jan. 1948), 63–79. See also Norman Daniel, *Islam, Europe and Empire*, 10, 25–30. In making my point about the prominence of the *Nights* in formulating the eighteenth-century image of the Orient, I should explain that, while the tales mainly enhanced old impressions of a gorgeous Orient, they also brought to the reader's attention the rich sources of Eastern wisdom and learning. Hence, I only partly agree with Professor Byron Porter Smith's opinion that "the popularity of the *Arabian Nights* did much to convince the reading public that something good could come out of the Moslem East. The use of the Oriental tale in England for didactic purposes would tend to strengthen the idea so vigorously set forth by Ockley, that Arabia was the fountain and source of wisdom." See *Islam in English Literature* (Beirut: American Univ. Press, 1939), 98.

42 "The Popularity of English Travel Books about the Near East, 1775–1825," *Philological Quarterly*, XV (Jan. 1936), 70. See also W.G. Rice, "The Early English Travellers to Greece and the Levant," *University of Michigan Publications*, X (1933), 205–60.

43 James Dallaway, *Constantinople Ancient and Modern* (London: Cadell & Davis, 1797), p. 72. See also Vivant Denon, *Travels in Upper and Lower Egypt* (London: J. Ridgway, 1802), I, ch. 13, 227–28.

44 James Capper, *Observations on the Passage to India* (1783; 3rd Ed., London, 1785), 40–3.

45 For a discussion of the authenticity of Galland's version, see *Gentleman's Magazine*, LXVIII (Sept. 1798), 757; LXIV (1794), 784; and *Monthly Review*, XXIX (1799), 475.

46 Robert Wood's reference to the "crude and hasty translation" from Arabic imaginative literature obviously applies to Galland's as the only available text of Arabian tales at that time. See *Essay on the Original Genius and Writings of Homer* (London, 1775), 173. Regarding Beattie's remark, see "On Fable and Romance," in *Works*, II, 509–10; and for Hole's see p. 9.

47 Nathan Drake, *Literary Hours; or Sketches Critical, Narrative, and Political*. 2 vols. (4th ed.; London: Longman, 1820), I, 229.

48 The quotation from John Richardson's monumental *Grammar* was cited by Patrick Russell in his communication "On the Authenticity of the Arabian Tales," 91–92.

49 Warren Hastings' opinion was cited by the Rev. Edward Forster in the introduction to his translation of *The Arabian Nights* (London: W. Miller, 1802), I, xxii. See also Jonathan Scott's "Preface" to *The Arabian Nights Entertainments* (London: Longman, 1811), I, xii.

50 For a survey of such readings, see Conant, Appendices A and B.

51 For the authorship of the "Preface," see John Nichols, *Literary Anecdotes*, VI, 318; Victor Chauvin, IV, 74; and William Lowndes' *Bibliographer's Manual of English Literature*, I, 59. Gough's work was cited by *Gentleman's* (VIII, 1810, 39) as one

used by Scott for his edition of the *Nights*. For additional remarks upon Gough's annotations, see Mahmoud Manzaloui's "Some English Translations of Arabic Imaginative Literature, 1704–1838," B. Litt. Unpubl. Thesis (Oxford, 1954), 82–83. Pope wrote to Judith Cowper on September 26, 1723 about his desire to tell a wild and exotic fairy tale, provided "there be an apparent moral to it." See Joseph Spence, *Observations, Anecdotes*, ed. James M. Osborn (Oxford: Clarendon, 1966), I, 151–52. As for Johnson, he wrote "The Fountains" in 1766 because he recognized that "babies do not want to hear about babies; they like to be told of giants and castles, and of somewhat which can stretch and stimulate their little minds." See Hester Lynch Thrale Piozzi, *Anecdotes of the Late Samuel Johnson* (New York: n.d.), 23. For more on Johnson's pseudo-Orientalism, see Carey Mcintosh, *The Choice of Life: Samuel Johnson and the World of Fiction* (New Haven, CT: Yale Univ. Press, 1973). Sir Joshua Reynolds seems to have read the tales, as the autographed copy of his (now available at the Beinecke Rare Book Library at Yale) indicates. See also Frederick Whiley Hilles, *The Literary Career of Sir Joshua Reynolds* (New York: Macmillan, 1936), 116. Voltaire himself admitted that he became a story-teller after he had read the *Nights* 14 times. See Ahmed Hassan Al-Zayyat, *Fi Usul Al-Adab* (1935), I, 42.

52 Eliza Haywood's utilization of the romantic properties of the *Nights* is discussed by George Whicher, *The Life and Romances of Mrs. Eliza Haywood* (New York: Columbia Univ. Press, 1915), 31–32. For references to Maturin, see *Melmoth the Wanderer* (Lincoln: Univ. of Nebraska Press, 1972), 393–94 and n. Other allusions are on pp. 10, 31, 51, 145, 182, 226, 255, 263, 290, 362, 372, 411.

53 Cited by Henry Weber, *Tales of the East*, xxi–xxii n.

54 For a discussion of this shift, see William Park's "The Change in the Criticism of the Novel after 1760," *Philological Quarterly*, XLVI (1967), 34–41; and Ioan Williams' "Introduction" to *Novel and Romance, 1700–1800: A Documentary Record* (New York: Barnes & Nobel, 1970).

55 Cited from the *Monthly Review*, XXIV (May 1761) in *Novel and Romance, 1700–1800: A Documentary Record*, 240.

56 *Ibid.*, 248. Cited from Blair's *Lectures on Rhetoric and Belles Lettres*.

57 See vols. XX (1759), 380, and XXVI (1762), 263–64. In making this point, I am indebted to William Park, 37–38, n. 12.

58 Thomas Green, *Extracts from the Diary of a Lover of Literature* (Ipswich: John Raw, 1810), 53–54.

59 Cited in Ioan Williams, *Novel and Romance*, 283–84. For assigning the article to Mrs. Barbauld, see Tompkins, *The Popular Novel*, 220 and n. I.

60 Williams, *Novel and Romance*, 285.

61 References are to the letter of June 30, 1789, *Correspondence of Horace Walpole*, ed. W.S. Lewis (New Haven,CT: Yale Univ. Press, 1954), XI, 20–21.

2

The Growing Vogue
of Scheherazade's Tales

When first your dimpled foot shall press
The enchanted carpet, who can guess
To what unhallowed crescent coast

It may transport you; to what host
Of turbaned aliens, clamoring,
Abandon you; or to what king?
　　　Grace Hazard Conkling, "To Elsa—with a volume of 'The Arabian Nights' "[1]

Is it an echo of something
　Read with a boy's delight
Viziers nodding together

In some Arabian Night?
　　　　　　　　　　　　　　From Tennyson's "Maud"

Consequent upon the English colonial expansion in India and the Arab East, the increasing social and cultural impact of industry, the growth of the newly enriched middle classes, and the progress of Oriental scholarship, eighteenth-century pseudo-Orientalism, gave way to an ardent search for accuracy and exactitude in information and details concerning Eastern settings, customs, and national peculiarities. There was a call for useful knowledge as befitting the

Utilitarian rising demand, which was in line with colonial expansion. Besides the appearance of a number of translations from Eastern languages, scholars and travelers published extensive researches and accounts about the area. Middleclass families began to tour the Near East, and travel books multiplied to the extent that the *Eclectic Review* alone published 46 reviews of such accounts between 1805 and 1825.[2] To meet the reader's demand for information on the Orient, Moore, Byron, and Southey supplemented their poetic visions of the East with copious illustrative notes. Although half met by the romantics, this demand for faithful representation of Oriental life and manners helped to stimulate the growth of literary and scholarly interest in the Arabian tales. Indeed, as early as 1838 the *Athenaeum* reviewer concluded that the imitations and reviews of the *Nights* were so impressive that a study of them "must form no uninteresting chapter in any comprehensive history of modern literature."[3]

In view of the tremendous social, political, and literary transformations and developments throughout the nineteenth century, drastic shifts in taste and patterns of response towards Arabian fiction were certainly inevitable. Numerous articles and reviews appeared dealing with various aspects of the *Nights*. The combined outcome of these popular and critical responses shows to what extent the tales had penetrated into the very core of English culture taking their place— as Robert Chambers remarked—"amongst the similar things of our own which constitute the national literary inheritance."[4]

Compared with early and mid-eighteenth-century responses, romantic and Victorian attitudes towards Scheherazade's tales are much more appreciative and informed. But despite the fact that such responses reveal drastic modifications of and reactions against already existing trends, this must not lead us to assume that no useful contributions were set forth in the eighteenth century. John Hawkesworth's and Robert Heron's literary estimates of the aesthetic charm of the tales must surely have paved the way for Leigh Hunt and others to enjoy and, simultaneously, evaluate the inherent attraction of Scheherazade's enchanting art. On the other hand, James Beattie's inconsistent appeal to the circumstantial theory and, later, Hole's call for appreciative understanding of Eastern literatures as requisite for the enjoyment of Scheherazade's artistry might have led to Edward William Lane's and Walter Bagehot's sociological approach to the *Nights,* as well as to James Mew's very penetrating remarks concerning the interrelationship between the supernatural element and the geography of the region.[5] It could have led as well to the *Eclectic* reviewer's call in 1840 to practice the "Catholic spirit of criticism," for the remote and the unfamiliar should be comprehended first in order to be appreciated, whereas the supernatural is a matter of belief rather than a mere flight of Eastern imagination.[6]

Late as this call might sound to a reader well-acquainted with the warm approbation accorded to the tales in the first quarter of the century, it was especially addressed to the readers of that periodical who, more than any, became the butt of Matthew Arnold's satire on middle-class smugness and lack of imaginativeness. The reviewer's appeal to the circumstantial theory is, however, indicative not only of the sweeping popularity of the tales but also of the persistent tendency to appreciate them for their own literary merits. Written in 1840, the review simultaneously indicates the changing taste of the period, from the romantic revel in the remote and the mysterious to the Victorian scientific, realistic, and significantly Utiliterian search for exactitude in information and details.

In the first quarter of the nineteenth century, however, these tales were read and enjoyed mainly for their exotic and fabulous enchantments, enchantments which continued to color and shape various literary and aesthetic attitudes and to inspire and evoke the intimate whisperings of many a poetic soul throughout the century. "There are few," wrote Henry Weber in his introduction to *Tales of the East* (1812),

> who do not recollect with pleasure the emotions they felt when the Thousand and One Nights were first put into their hands; the anxiety which accompanied the perusal; the interest with which their minds were impressed in the fate of the imaginary heroes and heroines; and the golden dreams of happiness and splendour which the fairy palaces and exhaustless treasures of the east presented to their imagination (I, i).

But more than evoking mere responses of delightful anxiety, the first encounter with the Sultana's tales were said to be an act of initiation into a dream-like world where steps lead "to a cavern stored with the precious rarities of an Eastern fancy" (*NR*, p. 46), and where every participant finds himself entangled in a web of enchantment and magic. "[There] was a time with us," wrote Walter Bagehot (*NR*, pp. 46–47), "when the *Arabian Nights* were not so much a story as a dream, when, with the same dim mingling of identities which we sometimes have in sleep, it is not Aladdin but ourself, and yet not ourself but Aladdin (Figure 1.4), who gazes on the jewel-bearing fruit-trees, marries the Vizier's daughter, and controls the resources of the lamp." Absorbed in such scenes and identifying himself with the main characters of the tales, he intimated, "we suffer and triumph with Sindbad, taste vicissitude with cameralzaman, enjoy the shrinking fondness of Zutulbe, travel upon the enchanted carpet, or mount the flying horse."

Considered in relation to the romantic scene in the first decades of the century, this thorough absorption in the tales, the subsequent subjective recreation of a seductive East, and the imaginary self-identification with Eastern characters constitute significant elements in the romantic movement in England. When adequately analyzed in connection with the new changes in popular and literary taste, this undercurrent will perhaps lead us to a fair evaluation of the romantic reception of the tales and to an estimate, through comparison and contrast, of other readings in the *Arabian Nights*.

A few premises are worth stressing at this point. Aside from the need for recognizing the social and literary implications of drastic changes in taste and their consequent bearings on the vogue of the work under consideration, due allowance must also be made for some patterns of response that are not exclusively romantic. Mere remembrance of "the blissful days of childhood, surrounded with a halo of Eastern splendour and magnificence," which the *Monthly Review* of 1826 (I, n. ser., 362) stressed as constituting the perpetual attraction of the tales for "the mature and well-informed," partakes of the romantic yearning after lost days and visions. Although such recollections are less romantic than Beckford's dream of "soaring on the Arabian bird roc, among genii and enchantments" or Thomas Wainewright's view of himself as a "concentration of all the Sultans in the Arabian Nights," and although these imaginings are different from Tennyson's and less impressive than William Henley's, they nevertheless indicate the general mood of a generation nourished on these tales and consequently unwilling to part with a land of bliss, which had become identified with childhood.[7] "To hear of more Arabian Nights," wrote Leigh Hunt in 1826, "was, to us like being told that we were to have a new piece of childhood,—three volumes of Rejuvenescence,—a springtime within the spring,—happy wonder,—a glut of willing credulity. It is the next thing to having wings on one's shoulders."[8]

Although this warm love for the tales might be considered symptomatic of a drastic change in taste during the first decades of the century, it should not lead us to assume that to maintain an attitude similar to Bishop Atterbury's was no longer possible. In fact, William Pattison, for example, was rather harsh in criticizing the tales despite Crabb Robinson's enthusiastic recommendation of them.[9] But being an exception, a case at variance with the prevailing literary and popular taste, Pattison's reaction poses no serious problem for a general evaluation of critical responses. More discrimination and tact are especially needed, however, when considering the responses of those who admire some tales or specific aspects of the work to the exclusion of others. Although Hazlitt, for instance, loved "the comic parts ... dearly," he nevertheless disliked the supernatural element. Being criticized by Coleridge for maintaining this attitude, Hazlitt found some solace in having such a formidable ally as Bishop Atterbury on his side in this matter. But the mere alliance with the Bishop provoked Leigh Hunt's criticism of Hazlitt's awkward blending of pseudo-classicism and romanticism: "Atterbury was a wit, and a swearing Bishop—a man of the world. His opinion is worth little on such a question. That of the author of 'Kubla Khan' and the 'Ancient Mariner' is worth a great deal; and we are glad to have him with us."[10] Leigh Hunt saw through Hazlitt's contradictions and regarded his very attitude towards the *Arabian Nights* as indicative of this confusion, for the man who criticized the utilitarian emphasis on facts himself devised limits and motives for fancy in his essay "On Reason and Imagination." Moreover, "Spenser and Chaucer, whom he [Hazlitt] admires so much, would, we may be sure, have been passionate admirers of the *Arabian Nights*. Milton would have called out for the conclusion of 'Sindbad the Sailor,' had it been left unfinished."[11]

It was Hazlitt's misfortune, perhaps, to be caught in the controversy with Coleridge and Leigh Hunt, for a few other critics maintained a similar attitude without inviting such biting remarks. Although strongly attached in youth to that "precious treasure he had long possessed, / A little yellow, canvas covered book, / A slender abstract of the Arabian Tales," Wordsworth later became a little apprehensive of its captivating spell, preferring the simple and the common to the glorious and the splendid.[12] No less curious was De Quincey's reaction. Although detecting a few examples of the sublime in "Aladdin" and while impressed by numerous descriptions of the / grotesque and the terrible in the Arabian tales, he found the authors of the tales, and Orientals in general, lacking in sentiment. If there were any sublimities in the *Arabian Nights,* they "first became such—a gas that first kindles—when entering into combination with new elements in a Christian atmosphere."[13] While accounting in part for translation as appropriation or even a requisition, De Quincey's is at the basis of an early nineteenth-century *new* philological binary that divides the universe in two language families: Semite and Aryan.[14]

No less bewildering is Ruskin's case. His vacillation between wholehearted acceptance and playful rejection of the "insidious" tales, for example, passed unnoticed by contemporary admirers of the *Nights*.[15] Besides including it in his amended list of Sir John Lubbock's "Best Hundred Books" and drawing heavily upon its wealth of allusions, he paid many a warm tribute to "those glorious Arabian Nights," which amply provided him with "luckily remembered" images to enrich his own compositions.[16] It was one of the favorite books for the family fireside reading. In fact, Lady Burne-Jones wrote that once her husband read aloud for the Ruskins the barber's tale from Lane's translation, "in which there is scarce a paragraph without some mention of God, the High, the Great, and at its conclusion Ruskin expressed great admiration for it."[17] Yet it was this same Ruskin who wrote to the *Pall Mall Gazette* on the fifteenth of February, 1886, that although he had read the *Nights* "many times over," he much wished then that he "had been better employed."[18]

In periodical criticism as well, one still finds traces of belittling remarks in the articles whose general tone is appreciative rather than hostile. Thus, one reads in the *Monthly Review* (I, n. ser., 1826, 362), for example, about such works as the *Nights* whose "brilliancy of imagination and wonderfulness of event, have, and always will have, attraction for the young and the ignorant mind." In 1859 Walter Bagehot mentioned the *Nights* as one of the "few books [that] have contributed more largely to uninstructive enjoyment and idleness *pur et simple*" (*NR*, p. 45). Such a remark is certainly pertinent and right, yet its tone and intention seem quite disparaging when set beside the typical romantic appreciation of the tales as shown in Coleridge's and Leigh Hunt's writings.

Nevertheless, when set against the sweeping romantic appeal of the tales, these uncertain responses and unimpassioned estimates seem mere eddies. Upon seeing a new edition of the tales many readers would perhaps have joined Leigh Hunt in his enthusiastic cry: "New Arabian Nights!—What! New Arabian Nights' Entertainments of the old stock! genuine! more Scheherazade and Dinarzade! more Zobeide and camaralzaman, and commanders of the Faithful, and ladies in veils, and enraptured linen-drapers, and genii, and magicians, and 'light of my soul,' and heads made no more of than turniptops."[19] Many, one might well imagine, did echo Coleridge's genuine yearnings for these tales of imagination and wonder: "Give me the Arabian Nights' Entertainments which I used to watch till the sun shining on the bookcase approached, and, glowing full upon it, gave me the courage to take it from the shelf."[20] Neither were Coleridge and Leigh Hunt the only passionate admirers of the tales. Emma Roberts never seemed to outgrow her childhood attachment to the *Nights*. "I had commenced reading the 'Arabian Nights Entertainments' at the age of five," she wrote; "since which period I had read them over and over again at every opportunity finishing with the last published number of the translation by Mr. Lane. This study has given me a strong taste for everything relating to the East, and Arabia especially."[21] Lady Burne-Jones mentioned how William Morris sent her sister Agnes "the priceless treasure of Lane's Arabian Nights," putting on the fly-leaf, "I write your name in pencil, in case you think it loathly." On the contrary, reported Lady Burne-Jones, "it entranced her and all of us, so that even the youngest sister would sit by the fire-side on her little stool, reading it as long as ever she was allowed, whilst the outer world passed away and her sisters were looked at with dim eyes and addressed as 'O daughters of my father'."[22] In fact, the appeal of the tales continued unabated throughout the first half of the century. The reviewer for the *Literary World* (III, No. 89, Oct. 14, 1848, 724) went so far as to assert that "we are prepared ... to say we would rather not consort with, in any relation or dealing, the man who is void of the sense to which they [the Arabian tales] appeal." Lending itself easily to every taste, Scheherazade's work was read and enjoyed by people as diverse in interest as the Methodist Benjamin Gregory, the Chartist poet Thomas Cooper, the Utilitarian Charles Knight, the Biblical scholar John Kitto, the Brownings, the Carlyles, the Ruskins, not to mention such devoted readers as the Brontës, Coleridge, Dickens, Hunt, Newman, Tennyson, and hundreds of others.[23] At the close of the century, many actually read in William Henley's charming tribute to Scheherazade their own admiration and love for the tales.[24]

As the popular market indicates, the appeal of Scheherazade's charming tales was so captivating that Leigh Hunt, upon reviewing six new editions for the *London and Westminster* in October 1839, could not refrain from concluding that the *Nights* "is the most popular book in the world."[25] Leigh Hunt was certainly right, for the "*Iliad* of romance," as George Henry Lewes called it,[26] enjoyed such an increasing popularity that the editor for the Select Library version asserted that "for the last fifty years few persons, making any pretensions to a taste for reading, have left unread these interesting volumes."[27] "Every rolling year," wrote James Mew in 1875, "seems to request a larger number of editions," and in view of the nature of the book, the critic did not find this fact surprising. "No decid-uous laurel is this book, from the leaves of which greedy Time steals gradually away the beauty and the verdure. As it once drew us, it still draws out children from the playground, and in the chimney corner its glittering conceits still carry consolation to old age."[28] Besides countless reprints from the Grub Street version, there were William Beloe's translation of a few additional tales in *Miscellanies* (1795), the antiquarian Richard Gough's "valuable" edition of 1798, the Rev. Edward Forster's translation from the French (1802), G.S. Beaumont's trans-lation from Galland (1811, 1814, 1817), Jonathan Scott's *Tales, Anecdotes and Letters* (1800) and *Arabian Nights' Entertainments* (1811), the Medievalist Henry Weber's composite edition of the *Tales of the East* (1812), the Rev. George Lamb's translation of Jos. Von Hammer's version (1826), and Henry Torrens' unexpur-gated first volume of the work. At the close of the century, the *Athenaeum* con-cludes: "It is a striking testimony to the lasting popularity of the 'Arabian Nights' that publisher after publisher brings out one edition after another (of uncopyright versions)."[29] In addition to standard and elegant translations, there were special volumes for railway reading, cheap ones printed for Limbird (1827, 1832), Dicks (1868), and William Tegg (1869). Besides pictorial penny and pocket series and reprints of individual tales, there were extracts, moral selections, and "continuations." The *Nights* was included in John Lubbock's "Best Hundred Books" as well as in Auguste Comte's Positivist Library.[30]

Editing and revising the tales engaged the attention of a large number of scholars and writers in England, France, and Germany.[31] The conservative 1st Earl of Beaconsfield Benjamin Disraeli, twice Prime Minister of the United Kingdom, thought of re-editing and supplementing them with a new volume of his own invention.[32] Schlegel and Coleridge found themselves entangled in the raging controversy over their origin and authorship,[33] a controversy which engaged the attention of such scholars as Hammer, De Sacy, and, later, Edward William Lane, provoking the *Athenaeum* (for the years 1838–1839) to publish some learned articles on the subject. On the popular level, the tales—more so than travel accounts and colonial expansion—largely contributed, it seems, to "Orientalizing" the reading public, a fact which did not escape Byron's attention. After the prodigious popularity of his subjective visions of the region in the "Turkish Tales," he advised Thomas Moore to "stick to the East," in evoking a semi-romantic Orient, sensuous and luxurious to the extreme.[34] Following Byron's advice in *Lalla Rookh,* Moore revealed to the public a picture which would evoke exotic longings and which, ultimately, would enjoy a tremendous popularity despite its being inferior to Coleridge's "Kubla Khan" and even to Southey's "Thalaba."[35]

This same impact of the *Nights* on the English mind and its evocation of a semi-romantic vision of the Orient manifested itself in a large number of travel accounts. Instead of reporting factual details and communicating objective truths, many romantic travelers gave vent to their highly subjective impressions and ecstasies, stimulated by the glamorous side of the Orient and enhanced by recollections of Scheherazade's tales. Thus, in Moyle Sherer's *Scenes and Impressions in Egypt and Italy* (1824) as well as in J. Carne's *Letters from the East* (1826), the *Nights* colors and shapes the travelers' descriptions of Eastern life and scenery.[36]

Aware of the appealing nature of Scheherazade's tales to the romantic imagination, adaptors and melodramatists borrowed extravagantly from this rich storehouse of episodes and scenes to satisfy the increasing popular demand for pantomimes, spectacles, and melodramas.[37] Indeed, the *Times* of April 5, 1825 (no. 12619) described the *Nights* as "a work to which our melodramatists are deeply indebted." As for prose and verse imitations and adaptations, the press teemed with numerous Oriental pieces, ranging from Julia Pardoe's tales and Sylvanus Hanley's *Caliphs and Sultans* to Richard Trench's *Poems from Eastern Sources* and Lord Houghton's *Palm Leaves*. Furthermore, a book studded with allusions to the *Nights* was taken as a necessary prerequisite for popularity. Dickens' advice for Miss Marguerite Power—to call her book *Arabian Days and Nights* and to cram it with allusions to Haroun al-Rashid and other "wonderful dramatis personae,"—tells much about the vogue of the Arabian tales in Victorian England.[38] The mere fact that major nineteenth-century writers have drawn heavily upon Scheherazade's endless treasure of allusions to verify their social and literary criticism, to add a dash of exquisite fancy to their prosaic descriptions, or to illustrate vividly certain ideas and tastes, indicates to what extent they could count on their readers' familiarity with the tales. Aladdin's lamp, the Barmecide's feast, al-Nashar's visions, Prince Hussain's carpet, and Ali Baba's "Open Sesame" had become familiar to all.

Nevertheless, when attempting to measure the changes in the literary reception of the *Nights* in nineteenth-century England, some caution is inevitable lest we confuse popular approbation with proper critical responses. One might, after all, regard the increasing popularity of Scheherazade's tales as a continuation of the eighteenth-century fascination with them, a popularity bound ultimately to increase in proportion to the growth of readership in urban areas. One could even detect in the numerous imitations and adaptations the same Augustan bias towards the moralistic or the satiric. George Crabb's "Confidant," George Croly's "Magic Lamp" (1830), and Ruskin's "King of the Golden River" (1841) are moralistic; whereas Marryat's *Pacha of Many Tales* (1835), Morier's *Mirza* (1841), Thackeray's *Sultan Stork* (1841), Dickens' *Thousand and One Humbugs* (1855), and G. Arthur A'Beckett's *Modern Arabian Nights* (1877) reveal an obvious satiric strain. In fairness to nineteenth-century imitations and adaptations, one must say, however, that they generally tend to be less diluted and emasculated, especially in matters of local color and detail, than the typical eighteenth-century pseudo-Oriental tale. Whereas this fact does not necessarily indicate a very drastic change in the literary reception of the *Nights* in nineteenth-century England, it nevertheless does tend to corroborate what the critics themselves asserted concerning this change which Leigh Hunt aptly summed up in the *London and Westminster Review* of October 1839. Referring to Richard Hole's treatise on the tales the critic remarked: "Forty years ago, a lover of the 'Arabian Nights' thought it necessary to pick his way into a public confession by the following polite style of concession to a 'severer taste'."[39] After citing Hole's apologetic admiration,

Hunt went on to quote what the former considered the main critical response of the age. "The sedate and the philosophical," wrote Hole in 1797,

> turn from them with contempt; the gay and volatile laugh at their seeming absurdities; those of an elegant and correct taste are disgusted with their grotesque figures and fantastic imagery; and however we may be occasionally amused by their wild and diversified incidents, they are seldom thoroughly relished but by children, or by men whose imagination is complimented at the expense of their judgement.[40]

In these Augustan attitudes Leigh Hunt discerned that "authoritative insipidity," "the ultra-material scepticism of the prevalent metaphysics," and that distrust of emotional intensity and imaginativeness which "had been gradually provoking a re-action" ("NT," p. 103). Writing especially about the vogue of the Arabian tales in 1839, Hunt detected in their popularity as well as in the preference for Galland's edition signs of this reaction which the scientism and utilitarianism of the new age seemed to consolidate and stimulate rather than smother and check. In Hunt's appreciation of Galland's version, one traces a nostalgic affection for and a feeling of loyalty to an old acquaintance. Annoyed by Lane's criticism of Galland in 1839, Hunt, for example, wrote: "Galland was nothing to him in the above requisites [erudition and exactness] and did pervert a thousand things in his translation most un-Arabically." Nevertheless, Hunt insisted on preferring him to Lane, simply because he first led the romantics to that world of romance, dreams, and happy childhood: "It was he that first opened to Europe this precious source of delight," went on Hunt; "he it was whose taste and enthusiasm led the way to the taste and enthusiasm of others, and without whom perhaps Lane himself would not have been ultimately led to favour us with his more accurate version" ("NT," pp. 110–11).

Whereas this melting sentimentalism might be partly due to the fact that Galland's version was the first to impress the romantic imagination and was as such closely associated with old recollections and boyish visions,[41] it does not necessarily preclude other reasons for Hunt's appreciation of Galland. The very nature of the translation, its simplicity of style and diction as well as its lack of "peculiarities," makes it appealing to both the romantic critic and the common reader: "Galland it was who first, at one happy impulse, made *every* body inclined to like the 'Arabian Nights,'" explained Hunt ("NT," p. 111), "greatly by reason of that very adaptation of his style to the prevailing taste and tone of conversation, in which, and in his inferior intimacy with Arabian manners, Mr Lane sees nothing but perversion."

With little emphasis on the peculiarities of the original, and with more stress on a skilful thread of narrative, Galland—as Stanley Lane-Poole and C.H. Toy rightly concluded—gave the reading public a picture of an intriguing and charming Orient which proved to be very attractive to eighteenth and nineteenth-century readers alike.[42] If some eighteenth-century readers took the picture for a real and authentic representation of Eastern life and manners, the romantics were obviously anxious to preserve this dear illusion. Finding in the tales descriptions of azure domes, seraglios with veiled women and eunuchs, magic mirrors, spells, vampires, and other "machinery" which evoke strong passions, they were titillated, tantalized, and enthralled. Their Orient was, nevertheless, a projection of their own desires, taking shape through an exquisite contact with the mysterious as well as the picturesque image of the East in Scheherazade's tales. It is a dream-like region, a languorous and enervating atmosphere, where there is passionate love and music, and where roads are sprinkled with rose water and palaces studded with gems and jewels. Appealing to man's perennial desire for power and love, the tales attained prodigious popularity. It is, evidently, this same picture, which Thomas Moore reproduced in *Lalla Rookh,* that led to his tremendous success. In Byron's Oriental tales, the East is a land of intriguing adventures, strong passions, and relentless cruelty. Woven into De Quincey's visions under the influence of opium, such Arabian tales picture a land peopled with calendars, cobblers, magicians, creatures, and birds of every kind, staring, hooting, chattering, and grinning at him.[43] Keats, on the other hand, with his admirable distillation of images and colors, fused with his classic material Scheherazade's spells and profuse details to create the domains and settings of some of his well-known poems. Through an intimate acquaintance with Wieland's *Oberon* and, thereby, with the most appealing Arabian tales, Keats blended his literary symbols and ideas with descriptions and stage properties from the *Nights*. In the matrix of "St. Agnes," "Endymion," and "The Cap and Bells," Oriental machinery and exotic detail coalesced with the myths of antiquity.[44]

Thus, whereas the universalist and classical tendency of the Enlightenment was for the typical and the general in human nature, the rebellious romantic imagination relished the very incidental qualities which eighteenth-century writers minimized or excluded from their pseudo-Oriental writings. Reveling in brilliant and colorful descriptions of domestic habits and scenes of love or ravenous lust, as well as in elaborate accounts of encounters between lovers in remote lands, the romantic mind reconstructed an imaginary Orient. Although only casually based on Scheherazade's tales of adventure, this romantic vision of the East is said to partake greatly of the very "murky sensualism, the unconscious masochism and sadism of the peaceful Western bourgeoisie."[45]

Despite the successive appearances of innumerable non-romantic travel accounts and the fact that a real picture of the East could be easily established, the romanticists fought hard throughout the first half of the century to preserve the happy illusion of a land of dreams which continued to lure them. Although not exactly related to this survey of English reactions, but indicative nonetheless of this same attitude, Washington Irving's disappointment at seeing the Turkish Minister at Barcelona plainly garbed demonstrates this tendency. In a letter of July 5, 1844, he intimated to his sister Mrs. Paris: "I confess I should rather have seen him in the magnificent costume of the East; and I regret that that costume, endeared to me by the Arabian Nights' Entertainments, that joy of my boyhood, is fast giving way to the levelling and monotonous prevalence of French and English fashions."[46]

In the editorial to his *London Journal* of October 1834, Leigh Hunt hailed this semi-romantic vision of the Orient, a vision which provided the imagination with new poetic heavens: "Hail gorgeous East! Hail, region of the coloured morning! Hail, Araby and Persia!—not the Araby and Persia of the geographer, dull to the dull, and governed by the foolish,—but the Araby and Persia of books, of the other and more real East . . . the Orient of Poets, the magic lands of the child, the ineffaceable recollection of the man."[47] Writing for the *London and Westminster Review* (Oct. 1839), Hunt explained what distinguished this imaginative vision of the East from the one depicted in prosaic travel accounts or in Lane's heavily annotated translation. Like other romantics, Hunt saw that Galland's version did establish and sustain the enthralling image of the East: "What is more valuable in the 'Arabian Nights' is not what concerns the Arabs as Arabs, but what concerns all the world as men, women, and children,—as lovers of surprising adventures, of visions, of luxuries, of beauty, of pomp and power, of endless variety and vicissitude" ("NT," p. 111). The main drift of Hunt's argument about Galland's preservation of "the Orient of Poets" becomes clearer when, at the conclusion to his article in the *London and Westminster Review,* he analyzes the sources of enchantment in the *Arabian Nights.* The mere repetition of exquisite names, the perpetual sense of adventure and vicissitude, the flattering of human desires for power and wealth, the very absence of overt moralism, the gallery of soft yet unyielding females, the neighborhood of the supernatural world, the towering ascendancy of immortal genius, and the very multitudinous and splendid life, all touched sensitive chords in the romantic imagination ("NT," pp. 135–36). In 1834 and under the unchallenged impact of Galland's version Leigh Hunt summed up the captivating attractions of this intoxicating, colorful, and restless world which defied neo-classical traditions and participated in setting the stage for the romantic reception:

> To us, the Arabian Nights are one of the most beautiful books in the world: not because there is nothing but pleasure in it, but because the pain has infinite chances of vicissitude, and because the pleasure is within the reach of all who have body and soul, and imagination. The poor man there sleeps in a door-way with his love, and is richer than a king. The Sultan is dethroned tomorrow, and has a finer throne the next day. The pauper touches a ring, and spirits wait upon him. You ride in the air; you are rich in solitude; you long for somebody to return your love, and an Eden encloses you in its arms. You have this world, and you have another. Fairies are in your moon-light. Hope and imagination have their fair play, as well as the rest of us. There is action heroical, and passion too: people can suffer, as well as enjoy, for love; you have bravery, luxury, fortitude, self-devotion, comedy as good as Moliere's, tragedy, Eastern manners, the wonderful that is in a commonplace, and the verisimilitude that is in the wonderful calendars, cadis, robbers, enchanted palaces, paintings full of colour and drapery, warmth for the senses, desert in arms and exercises to keep it manly, cautions to the rich, humanity for the more happy, and hope for the miserable.[48]

It is this vision of the Orient which both intoxicated and stimulated the romantic mind with ideal regions of freshness, spontaneity, freedom, intense emotions, opportunities and adventures, glory, and faith. Undoubtedly, responses to the moods and motifs which Hunt aptly summed up as constituting the attraction of the Arabian tales for the romantic imagination cannot be dissociated from each writer's personal inclinations and interests. Thus, Coleridge's great admiration for the organic universe of the Arabian tales and their fusion of the natural and the supernatural into one inseparable whole cannot be studied apart from his total transcendental vision.[49] Tennyson's aesthetic bent led him to recollect tales where realms of art represent the desired state for which he yearns. Thomson's melancholy led him to that petrified city of Zobeide, where a comely youth lives alone glorifying the name of God amid scenes of dying beauty and terrible desolation. It was not uncommon for even the sophisticated Victorian to look back to childhood with nostalgia and to renew his early enchantment with the *Nights* as a means of temporary escape from actuality. Although not especially concerned either with analyzing the formative influences of such readings or with tracing their echoes in the subtle workings of the creative faculty, this study cannot exclude such implications whenever readings or responses shade into each other. After all, it is only through a careful survey of the most representative cases of these recollections and readings that we can assess the real place of the *Nights,* not only in providing the romantic mind with motifs and colors to enrich and intensify yearnings after the infinite, the mysterious, the elusive, and the beautiful but also in supplying analogies and models that constitute the exotic strain in English literature.

In dealing with the more relevant readings of the tales and their consequent impact on creative writing, it might be helpful to follow a thematic rather than a chronological order, discussing first expressions of thorough infatuation with the tales, and of partial identification with their *dramatis personae,* before sketching the creative use of Scheherazade's machinery in reconstructing private mythologies and palaces of art.

The romantic reading of Scheherazade's tales involves a surrender to the art of story-telling which holds Sultan Shahriar spellbound, an art which lures and enchants and assumes ritualistic connotations when it dissuades ruthless kings, monsters, and genii from executing whatever evil designs they have in mind. As distinguished from critical perusal, the romantic reading is an act of thorough indulgence in a world of dreams and desires. The *Spectator* for November 25, 1882 (LV, 1513) partly explained the nature of this reading: "In the *Arabian Nights,* and in them alone of published books, can grown men enjoy the pleasure which children enjoy in story-telling, the pleasure of hearing exciting narratives without being called on for thought, or reflection, or criticism." Free from overt ethical instruction, these narratives supply pure pleasure. In reading them, we are "let loose, unreproved, in a world of wonders and brilliancies, of grand Kings and golden palaces and beautiful ladies and friendly or hostile genii; where all is unaccountable, but all happens as it should happen." Thus, the writer concludes that the "power of the *Nights* is the power of Romance in its elementary form; and the tales hold grown men—or, at least, those who can be so held—as fairy-stories hold children, or at least, those who can be so held, by ministering endlessly to their insatiable luxury in wonder."

But whereas this analysis of the romantic appeal of the tales might be applicable to the common reader's interest in romance, it fails to account for the romantics' infatuation with these tales. Rather than being a mere "insatiable luxury in wonder," their readings were no less than an aesthetic initiation into a charmed circle, spontaneously entailing a "willing suspension of disbelief" that Coleridge said (*Biographia Literaria,* chap. XIV) constituted "poetic faith." Thus, the young

John Nichol "revelled" in the tales "as in a new world of gorgeous dreams," whereas Leigh Hunt and others felt a lasting attachment to Scheherazade's "centre of miracles" which Henley enthusiastically celebrated at the close of the century.[50] Hunt's unqualified admiration for the tales may well represent, however, the attitude of the early romantics for whom the *Nights* opened new vistas of faith, superstition, beauty, adventure, art, and love. "Whenever we see the Arabian Nights," wrote Hunt in his *London Journal,* "they strike a light upon our thoughts, as though they were a talisman encrusted with gems; and we fancy we have only to open the book for the magic casket to expand, and enclose us with solitude and a garden."[51] It was this same world of wish-fulfilment and imagination which so impressed the young Newman that he "used to wish the Arabian Tales were true." In his close identification with the people of these tales, Newman's imagination "ran on unknown influences, on magical powers, and talismans." He said, "I thought life might be a dream, or I an Angel, and all this world a deception."[52]

This same habituation to the spiritual and the otherworldly could be traced in Coleridge as well, whose early loneliness and obsessive devotion to the Arabian tales intensified his inclination for dreaming: ". . . my mind had been habituated *to the Vast,* and I never regarded *my senses* in any way as the criteria of my belief. I regulated all my creeds by my conceptions, not by my *sight*—even at that age."[53] Whenever looking at his own volume of the *Arabian Nights,* he used to feel "a strange mixture of obscure dread and intense desire," a feeling which never left him throughout his life. On a number of occasions, he referred to this timorous passion for the Arabian tales, ". . . one tale of which (the tale of a man who was compelled to seek for a pure virgin) made so deep an impression on me (I had read it in the evening while my mother was mending the stockings), that I was haunted by spectres, whenever I was in the dark." He further intimated, "I distinctly remember the anxious and fearful eagerness with which I used to watch the window in which the books lay, and whenever the sun lay upon them, I would seize it, carry it by the wall, and bask and read."[54]

That the book stimulated Coleridge's imagination, stirred up his sense of credulity and wonder and imposed an aura of supernaturalism upon the common and the worldly was attested to by Coleridge himself.[55] It is evidently the dream-like quality of the work, its elimination of the boundaries between the natural and the supernatural, which engaged his attention and carried him to regions of limitless horizons: "I never knew but two men of taste and feeling," said Coleridge, "who could not understand why I was delighted with the Arabian Nights' Tales, and they were likewise the only persons in my knowledge who scarcely remembered having ever dreamed."[56] This thorough infatuation with the tales and the complete surrender to their tantalizing and dream-like qualities became even more evident in Coleridge's own dreams, for once he dreamt of being pursued by one of the female characters of the *Arabian Nights,* a fatal woman bestowing loathsome affection and deadly kisses instead of Haroun al-Rashid's gifts.[57]

Although different in nature from Coleridge's immersion in Scheherazade's world, William Beckford's reading of the Arabian tales shows similar entanglements in the intricate web of enchantment and magic. But whereas Coleridge's mind was steered towards the vast and the infinite, Beckford's readings intensified his exotic taste, his abnormal aptitude for sense experience, and his soarings into an Orient of voluptuousness, gorgeousness, intense passion, and intoxicating beauty. It was this picture, too, colored with Beckford's personal longings, which provoked Byron's praise and intoxicated the romantic mind in general.[58] In the course of this survey, however, we are concerned with the nature of Beckford's reading of the Arabian tales mainly because he stands as a major and influential figure in developing the exotic taste and intensifying the imaginative interpretation of the East.

At a time when young Beckford was obliged to lead a life of social isolation because of his mother's refusal to entrust his education to institutions, and when he was provided with everything which enormous wealth could buy, he came across a copy of the *Arabian Nights*. His biographers assert the tremendous influence which those tales exerted on the boy, who perused them with avidity and joy. In the words of Lewis Melville, "the impression they made on him was so strong that Lord Chatham [Beckford's godfather] instructed Lettice [his tutor] that the book must be kept from him." But, as Melville further explains, the "precaution came too late ... the oriental tales took possession of the impressionable reader to such an extent that he could never forget them. They had fired his youthful mind and held his imagination captive; their influence over him never waned all the days of his life."[59] Throughout his early life, young Beckford developed an inordinate taste for these tales, which provided him with a gorgeous, fantastic, and dream-like world that he took for granted as real and, ultimately, preferable to the external world. "I will seclude myself if possible from the world," he wrote, "and converse many hours with you, Moisasour and Nouronihar [referring to his 'Long Story,' 1777]. I am determined to enjoy my dreams and phantasies and all my singularity, however irksome and discordant to the worldlings around."[60] The more he was warned against over-indulgence in the world of the Arabian tales and the more his elders tried to wean him from them, the greater became his attachment to that exotic world of caliphs, cobblers, efreets, and genii.

Beckford's attraction to Scheherazade's world should be distinguished therefore from Victorian escapist attitudes. Unlike the young Dickens and Thackeray's Dobbin, for example, Beckford's infatuation with the tales was both a thorough identification with their *dramatic personae* and a deep emotional involvement in their thrilling adventures. It was not Haroun al-Rashid's glamorous court which attracted him, neither was it the valley of diamonds, but the Sultanic defiance of restrictions and his own wilful determination to delve into the mysterious, to enter forbidden subterranean recesses, and to defy or form pacts with powerful magicians and infernal powers. The full impact of Scheherazade's tales on the youthful, rich dilettante of Fonthill, can be fully estimated when we recall his early Sultanic leanings, for Beckford modelled his life upon the caliphs and sultans of the *Arabian Nights:* "He talked with evident satisfaction of the power of Eastern Satraps, the servility of their subjects, the pomp of their attendants," noticed Boyd Alexander. "He extracted similar obedience at Fonthill. His anger was unbridled when he was provoked or contradicted. He became imbued with the idea that he was descended from a race of Kings."[61]

Unlike his successors, and in particular Charlotte Bronte, who tended to domesticate the exotic, Beckford carried that streak of satrapism to the extreme. Despite his elders' efforts to encourage him to develop an interest in parliamentary affairs, Beckford bluntly rejected such participations, indulging instead in his own imaginary Orient. It was this imaginary kingdom of his, in which he figured as a sultan, that provided the setting for his imaginative writings. His own Fonthill as well should be seen as an expression of his craving for an "Aladdin-like retreat from the world," an oriental palace which Paul Elmer More considers a symbol of the romantic craze for isolation. "It was as if some one in that staid century had gained control over a group of genii out of the *Arabian Nights* and had set them to raising a magic structure for his delectation."[62]

Less infatuated with this Beckfordism, but entangled nonetheless in Scheherazade's web of story-telling, other nineteenth-century romanticists found echoes of their longings and desires in some of her stories. Christina Rossetti, James Thomson, and Meredith seized upon the story of the petrified city of Zobeide to evoke a sense of loss in an uncongenial world. The book which charmed and delighted Christina Rossetti throughout her life yielded not only that abundance of details which formed the exotic background of her "Goblin Market" and "A Birthday" but also that sense of the fleetingness of life with which she was obsessed.[63] In a romantic reverie, Christina imagines how she is carried into the petrified city of Zobeide, where death and decay reign in a kingdom which was once prosperous and happy. But while Christina Rossetti in the "Dead City" is concerned with recreating the vision of a wealthy kingdom punished for its inhabitants' pride and luxury, Meredith, in "The Sleeping City," focuses on the role of fate, a role which engages the romantic imagination because of its association with vicissitude, uncertainty, and perpetual fear.

Seizing upon the same theme, but endowing it with his own personal melancholy and disillusion in "The Doom of a City" (1857), James Thomson imagines a lonely voyager in a stormy night, finding his way to a petrified city whose inhabitants had been turned to stone amid fabulous luxury and wealth. But what makes Thomson's use of this Arabian theme worth associating with Christina's "Dead City" is the fact that Thomson had not yet rejected Providence. Although foreshadowing his well-known pessimistic "City of Dreadful Night," the 1857 poem reveals a faith in Providential benevolence which was replaced by utter despair in his later poetry.

Scheherazade provided the last romantics with another variation upon the theme of social dislocation and fear. The yearning for a lost paradise, emanating from this very social circumstance and restless search for ideal regions, finds no better expression than the story of Bharam, "The Man Who Never Laughed Again," after being exiled from the land of bliss and enchanting damsels. Throughout the century, this theme never lost its compelling appeal for the romantic sensibility. Tennyson's ". . . Exile of Bassorah" was but a variation upon this and kindred stories which were not overlooked by the first romantics.[64] Indeed, Keats read in Bharam's story not only the romantic endless longing to go beyond time into some intense, massive, and timeless experience but also the overwhelming fear of losing the desirable. In a letter of July 1819 to Fanny Brawne, Keats retold Bharam's story, stressing that strain of romantic agony succeeding moments of fulfillment: "I have been reading lately an oriental tale of a very beautiful color—It is of a city of melancholy men, all made so by this circumstance." Summarizing the plot, he explained how by turns these men "reach some gardens of paradise where they meet with a most enchanting Lady; and just as they are going to embrace her, she bids them shut their eyes . . . and on opening their eyes again find themselves descending to the earth in a magic basket." Like his La Belle Dame, the talismanic lady of the *Nights* left her victims dejected and forlorn, unable to retain the fulfilling intensity of that visionary experience. "The remembrance of this Lady and their delights lost beyond all recovery render them melancholy ever after." Although thematically identical with the common pleasure-pain paradox of his poetry, Keats' attraction to this tale is not limited to its main theme. Rather than driving him to disenchantment and withdrawal, it obviously stimulated his desire for potential participation in some concrete experience in the realm of human life. Thus, he wrote to Fanny Brawne, "How I applied this to you, my dear; how I palpitated at it; how the certainty that you were, in the same world with myself, and though as beautiful, not so talismanic as that Lady; how I could not bear you should be so you must believe because I swear it by yourself."[65]

Taking the tale "bodily from the Arabian Nights," and with an obvious stress on the "absorbing passion for the absent mistress," which Keats had already detected in the tale, William Morris recaptured the same mood of the original in his own "Man Who Never Laughed Again" in the *Earthly Paradise*. Such a reading and reproduction of the theme would not have concerned us, however, had it not been for the fact that Morris' own personality flowed into the tale, and tinged the original with intense pathos and romantic agony. In the original, the story-teller focuses on the dramatic action and the solution of the mystery of the forbidden door, whereas Morris' interest is centered upon the motivations and reasons which lie behind the hero's final action. Although reproducing the sense of predestination and loss, Morris "transposed it all into a higher key," as his daughter rightly concludes, making of Bharam's criminal curiosity an inevitable form of human behavior.[66] Moreover, in depicting the disparity between a lost paradise and a sordid reality, Morris obviously shares Bharam's longing for a lost world of enchantment and beauty. After all, Bharam's longing for an "isle of bliss" and a realm of beauty and art speaks for the yearnings of a whole generation forced to adapt itself to the drabness and sordidness of an industrial civilization.

Between Beckford's exoticism and William Ernest Henley's accommodation of art to life lies many Victorian attempts to maintain momentary escapes to a realm of spontaneity and freedom or to throw shades of fancy upon reality itself in order to make it more acceptable. Victorian readings of Scheherazade's tales demonstrate this vacillation between the tantalizing vision of the *Nights* and the immediate social and moral commitments. In Tennyson's "Recollections of the Arabian Nights," the realm of art appears triumphant, luring the poet into its domains of aesthetic pleasure. But although longing for Prince Hussain's magic carpet to escape from a dull and unhappy world, Tennyson simultaneously recognized that "the golden days of Faerie are over."[67] Instead of searching for a final retreat into Scheherazade's world, he finds some consolation in recalling his childhood revel in tales of splendor, love, and justice.

It is as a poetic recreation of his boyish dreams and his present willingness to submerge his fancy, temporarily, in an enchanting realm of exquisite beauty and pathos that Tennyson's "Recollections of the Arabian Nights" especially concerns us here. When reviewing the poem, Arthur Henry Hallam read it as an imaginative recreation of an early experience, an evocation of a vision subjectively conjured up to answer present desires and longings. While pitying those to whom the poem "calls up no reminiscence of early enjoyment," he quickly remonstrated against naive romantic trappings: "But let nobody expect a multifarious enumeration of Viziers, Barmecides, Fire worshippers, and Cadis; trees that sing, horses that fly, and Gouls that eat rice pudding!" Stressing "the idea which gives unity to this variety," Hallam maintained that Tennyson "has, with great judgement, selected our old acquaintance, 'the good Haroun Alrashid,' as the most prominent object of our childish interest." Along with this central idea, the poet "places us at once in the position of feeling," calling up "one of those luxurious garden scenes, the account of which, in plain prose, used to make our mouths water for sherbet, since luckily we were too young to think about Zobeide!"[68]

As a recollection of a scene so voluptuous and intriguing as to lure the religious Sheik Ibrahim into forbidden pleasure, the poem is especially concerned with evoking the delicate sensations aroused by reading the story of "Noureddin and the Fair Persian," a story in which the Caliph figures out prominently as the patron of the arts. With his usual method of suggestive description and word-painting, the poet recreates the enchanting atmosphere of the original scene in the Caliph's pavilion, to which the night journey leads. As John Sterling noticed, the poet does not seem "painfully striving after topics, images, variations, and originalities, but writing from lively conception of a theme which offered in abundance the material suited to his fancy and ear" (p. 115). The outcome, according to R.H. Hutton, "is a poem expressive of the luxurious sense of a gorgeous inward picture-gallery" (p. 353). But while contemporary reviewers have recognized this Keatsian matrix, no one seems to have searched for the poet's aesthetic preferences. In fact, Hunt, comparing it with the original tale, found it running too much "into mere luxury and exuberance," and lacking the "better part of stateliness and drapery of the East," as well as "the human variety of that wonderful set of stories" (p. 132).

Obviously, such contemporary reviews fall short of accounting for Tennyson's especial interest in the story of "Noureddin and the Fair Persian." As an imaginary self-identification with the characters of this specific tale, a subjective recreation of its action through a visionary night journey "adown the Tigris" towards the Caliph's pavilion, this poem invites some "symbolic interpretation" as J .H. Buckley suggests.[69] It is when reaching the level lake and the enchanted garden, "a realm of pleasance," that the narrator is initiated in the tantalizing and enervating scene. Leaving the boat, "as in sleep" he "sank / In cool soft turf upon the bank, / Entranced with that place and time." Led by some power, "With dazed vision unawares," he came upon the Caliph's pavilion. There, the narrator "trancedly" "Gazed on the Persian girl alone," for she is the "sweetest lady of the time." It is to be stressed at this point that the poet makes no allusion to Noureddin, for, as the original story indicates, it is the Fair Persian's beauty and her impressive singing to the lute which appease the Caliph's anger and lead him to overwhelm the lovers with his generosity. Seen within the thematic context of this poem, the narrator's specific attraction to the Fair Persian demonstrates a predilection for reenacting this aesthetic triumph in the realm of art. The night journey leads, after all, to the caliph himself, whom the narrator beholds, "his deep eye laughter—stirr'd / With merriment of kingly pride," enjoying the company of artists and bestowing his favors upon all. Accordingly, one must accept Buckley's apt conclusion that the progress of the night journey "through what seems to be a partial death into a rarefied and timeless life" indicates some "definite overtones of aesthetic meaning." "Haroun's Bagdad to the young Tennyson," he continues, "is essentially the city of eternal artifice, in a realm of self-subsistent reality beyond all movement and desire."

Although not identical with the typical escapist attitudes in the literature of the period, Tennyson's poem manifests a mood of dissatisfaction with ordinary life, a restless search for an ideal region. The mood itself becomes more obvious in a number of Victorian works that are professedly realistic. Conscious of the disparity between achievements and aspirations, between reality and dreams, many Victorians have seized upon al-Nashar's visions and the Barmecide's feast as symbols of their own frustrations, disappointments, and illusions. After Thackeray "lost his fortune," remarked Gordon N. Ray, "the story of Alnaschar and his tray of glass ... became for ... [him] a symbol of his own history."[70] In his *Vanity Fair,* Dobbin's reading of the *Arabian Nights* and his visions of the valleys of diamonds have become a symbol not only of his escape from a fashionable school where he is scorned for being a grocer's son but also of his idealism and impossible dreams in a highly materialistic and mechanistic world. Such readings transport him to an ideal region in which cobblers and fishermen may become wealthy merchants or influential wazirs, winning the hands of beautiful and charming princesses. Significantly, Carlyle reflected on the wisdom of shedding a romantic light on the drab reality. Although not exclusively drawn to Scheherazade's tales, he thought of them as imaginative creations, providing a release from the factual and the mundane. Writing to Mrs. Emerson on February 21, 1841, he said: "You are an enthusiast; make *Arabian Nights* out of dull foggy London Days; with your beautiful female imagination, shape burnished copper Castles out of London Fog! It is very beautiful of you;—nay, it is not foolish either, it is wise."[71] It is worth stressing that this land of happiness and dreams continues to lure the Victorians away from uncongenial reality. Rosamond and Lydgate in George Eliot's *Middlemarch* have never thought of marriage as more than a pleasurable experience. The author compares their romantic and idealistic visions to those which exist only in the remote world of the Arabian tales: "Ideal happiness (of the kind known in the Arabian Nights, in which you are invited to step from the labour and discord of the street into a paradise where everything is given to you and nothing claimed)," comments the writer, "seemed to be an affair of a few weeks' waiting more or less (Bk. IV, chap. 36)."

For many Victorians, Scheherazade's world was a symbol of ideal happiness, something desired but never attained, a correlative of lost childhood and frustrated aspirations. In this sense, Dickens' career might be regarded as representing the typical Victorian reading of the *Nights*. When young, Dickens used to act out scenes from the tales, always impersonating the character of the Caliph Haroun al-Rashid. In "The Ghost of Master B" *(The Haunted House)* we are told how he and other children used to act out the Caliph's adventures, until reality encroached upon this happy world of imagination in the shape of a sad event:

> *"Bless you, my precious!" said the officer turning to me; "your pa's took bitter bad!" I asked, with a fluttered heart, "Is he really ill?"*
>
> *"Lord temper the wind to you, my lamb!" said the good Mesrour, kneeling down, that I might have a comforting shoulder for my head to rest on, "your pa's dead!"*
>
> *Haroun Alraschid took to flight at the words; the Seraglio vanished; from that moment, I never again saw one of the eight of the fairest daughters of men.*
>
> *I was taken home, and there was debt at home as well as Death, and we had a sale there.*[72]

Alluding to his own father's imprisonment for debt, Dickens mentioned in the same story (p. 234) that should he compare his later misfortunes with his childhood dreams he would be "so worried, that I should have to drown myself in the muddy Pond near the playground." To escape such a suicidal end, Dickens—like such representative creations of his as Swiveller and Tom Pinch—entered into the spirit of his make-believe world; but, like Swiveller, he never let himself be completely swept away by fancy. Instead of being driven to disillusion and ennui, Dickens imposed an aura of fancy upon his realistic vision, creating thereby a fascinating combination of two worlds. In the words of George Gissing (1904, pp. 29–30),[73] Dickens "has put the spirit of the *Arabian Nights* into his pictures of life by the river Thames . . .. He sought for wonder amid the dreary life of common streets; and perhaps in this direction also his intellect was *encouraged* when he made acquaintance with the dazzling Eastern fables, and took them alternately with that more solid nutriment of the eighteenth-century novel."

It is this imaginativeness, stimulated and kindled by his readings of Scheherazade's tales, which becomes a talisman to preserve the integrity of his heroes and heroines or to protect them from danger in uncongenial circumstances. It is certainly this imaginativeness which helps David Copperfield gain Steerforth's sympathy and support after playing Scheherazade's story-telling role every night. It also enables Richard Swiveller in *Old Curiosity Shop* to cope with the grim realities of life and to transform these imaginatively into acceptable circumstances. Thus, upon recovering from a terrible fever, Swiveller adorns the real with the fanciful, drawing upon his readings of the *Nights* to add a romantic touch to the scene with the Marchioness (chap. lxiv). It is this same reading to which Sissy Jupe attributes her father's kindness (*Hard Times*, Bk. 1, chap. 9). Similarly, recollections of boyish visions of Ali Baba and Bedreddin Hassan restore to Scrooge an amiability and openness which he had lost in his pursuit of wealth. In *Martin Chuzzlewit*, Tom Pinch revels in this fusion of the fantastic and the real; whenever he feels the need for a temporary release from Pecksniff's pressure, he has only to "rub up and chafe that wonderful lamp within him" to summon the genie of story-telling, who will entertain him with scenes of enchantment and joy (chap. 5).

This same tendency to see the romantic side of life and to infuse it with recollections from early readings in Scheherazade's tales can apply to William Ernest Henley as well. With vigorous love of life, Henley imposed his vision of Scheherazade's world upon his personal life in an exquisite mosaic entitled *Arabian Nights' Entertainments*. Instead of mere nostalgic yearning for a remote place and time, the poet reveals a hearty delight in recollecting a boyish identification with the wonderful *dramatis personae* of the enchanting book:

> *I was—how many a time!—*
> *That Second Calendar, Son of a King,*
> *On whom 't was vehemently enjoined,*
> *Pausing at one mysterious door,*
> *To pry no closer, but content his soul*
> *With his kind Forty. Yet I could not rest*
> *For idleness and ungovernable Fate.*

> *And the Black Horse, which fed on sesame*
> *(That wonder-working word!),*
> *Vouchsafed his back to me, and spread his vans,*
> *And soaring, soaring on*
> *From air to air, came charging to the ground*
> *Sheer, like a lark from the midsummer clouds,*
> *And, shaking me out of the saddle, where I sprawled*
> *Flicked at me with his tail,*
> *And left me blinded, miserable, distraught.*

Instead of retreating into an ideal region of happiness, the poet shows a robust enjoyment of what the book offers: adventures, sweet sensations, and delightful scenes, all captured in a few deft impressions and word-strokes. Henley relates how, as he read the tales of the *Arabian Nights,* his own town of Gloucester was transformed in the imagination to Baghdad with all its cobblers, magicians, and rogues, and how scenes from the tales fused into pictures of real life:

> *Then, as the Book was glassed*
> *In Life as in some olden mirror's quaint,*
> *Bewildering angles, so would Life*
> *Flash light on light back on the Book; and both*
> *Were changed.*

Rather than recollections of lost visions, Henley's poem presents the narrator's exuberance, vitality, and sheer enjoyment of life. Throughout the poem, Henley figures as an active participant in the world around him. In his maturity, as in his childhood, the poet still derives nourishment and entertainment from the same old tales:

> *Thus the East laughed and whispered, and the tale*
> *Telling itself anew*
> *In terms of living, labouring life,*
> *Took on the colours, busked it in the wear*
> *Of life that lived and laboured; and Romance*
> *The Angel-Playmate, raining down*
> *His golden influences*
> *On all I saw, and all I dreamed and did,*
> *Walked with me arm in arm,*
> *Or left me, as one bediademed with straws*
> *And bits of glass, to gladden at my heart*

> *Who had the gift to seek and feel and find*
> *His fiery hearted presence everywhere.*

In this subtle interweaving of the romantic and the realistic, Henley was anticipated by George Meredith. The latter's ingenious understanding of Scheherazade's
thematic fabric and stylistic peculiarities makes him highly capable of penetrating to the core of her artistry, blending his own interest in human psychology
with her exquisite shades of fancy in his creative adaptations and imitations. As
Meredith's method precedes other adaptations of the tales to be made later in
the century, it is appropriate here to look at the two most striking examples of
his apprenticeship to the art of Scheherazade. "Shemselnihar" reveals Meredith's
preoccupation with psychology; the *Shaving of Shagpat* is an exercise in comic
method. Both draw on techniques and insights which Meredith found in the
Nights.

Basing his poem "Shemselnihar" (1862) on the story of the caliph's concu-
bine and her lover Ali Eben Beccar, Meredith dwells on the tensions and terrors
of a fateful love affair that terminates in romantic suffering and death. The poet's
main interest is centered upon a female torn between a strong passion for her
lover, and a binding sense of gratitude to the generous caliph. As a union with the
lover will not end her agony, she wishes instead to drive the caliph to hate her;
for it is this very hatred which will release Shemselnihar from her overwhelming
gratitude for his goodness:

> *Yes, I would that, less generous, he would oppress,*
>   *He would chain me, upbraid me, turn deep brands for hate,*
> *Than with this mask of freedom and gorgeousness*
>   *Bespangle my slavery, mock my strange fate.*
> *Would, would, would, O my lover, he knew—dared debar*
> *Thy coming, and earn curse of Shemselnihar!*[4]

In the *Shaving of Shagpat*, Meredith uses the Oriental setting and imagery of the
Nights to create an aesthetic distance from which to explore the evils of his own
time—materialism, exploitation, worldliness, dishonesty, and egotism. After
being tested and ultimately strengthened by a series of adventures and temp-
tations, the barber Shibli Bagarag understands the terrible consequences of his
own folly and pride. But enhanced by sprightly laughter and the love of a sensible woman, this understanding enables Shibli to shave Shagpat and to sever the
enchanted hair which is the symbol of backwardness, slavery, and bondage. Read

as an allegory, the history of Shibli Bagarag then represents the emerging spirit of reform which is bound to destroy an artificial social structure.

Meredith's successful imitation of the discursiveness, the fanciful abundance and light spirit of the *Nights* does certainly elude our search for overt moralism or philosophic premises. There is, to be sure, a deep meaning for those who are interested in allegorical interpretations, as George Eliot aptly remarked, but "to people more bent on enjoying what they read than on proving their acumen, the *Shaving of Shagpat* will be the thousand and *second* night which they perhaps longed for in childhood."[75] It was as such that the *Shaving of Shagpat* was read by Meredith's contemporaries, for "in exuberance of imagery, in picturesque wildness of incident, in significant humour, in aphoristic wisdom, the *Shaving of Shagpat* is a new *Arabian Night*. To two thirds of the reading world this is sufficient recommendation."[76] Indeed, Edmund Gosse went so far as to conclude that the genuine Oriental tales "pale before" Meredith's *Shaving*. Its "variety of scenes and images, the untiring evolution of plot, the kaleidoscopic shifting of harmonious colours" seem "of the very essence of Arabia, and to coil directly from a bottle of a genie."[77]

As far as mid-Victorian readings and patterns of utilization are concerned, Meredith's contribution stands as a landmark. Rather than providing a number of allusions to the *Nights* to evoke the atmosphere of a few tales or to intensify and enhance the dramatic effect of some situations in fiction, Meredith shows the possibility of recreating Scheherazade's tales by focusing on dimensions of internal characterization and ideas. Whereas the Eastern story-teller's interest is centered upon the bare thread of narrative, Meredith attempts to resurrect Scheherazade's other tools from oblivion and neglect. The full significance of Meredith's manipulation of such tools can be well appreciated when seen in relation to two obvious trends in creative and critical writings. Coinciding with the growing emphasis on illustrating and annotating the tales, Meredith's focus on Shemselnihar's character and his adroit evocation of Oriental scenes and ideas in the *Shaving* must be considered in line with the growing emphasis on realism. On the creative level, however, Meredith sets the tone for further manipulations of Scheherazade' s artistry to reconstruct private mythologies or comic settings. Thus, a large number of writers, ranging from Stevenson and Yeats to Sidney Grundy and F. Anstey, have found in the *Nights* cogent themes and details.

Meredith was partly anticipated by Charlotte Bronte in her semiautobiographical novel *Jane Eyre* (1847). Both modelled their heroines upon the characters of the *Arabian Nights,* especially upon Sultana Scheherazade herself. After reading the tales, Jane is introduced not only to the idea of magic, as Mrs. Leavis maintains, but also to Scheherazade's marvelous experience in taming the most embittered, disillusioned and sadistic Sultan literature has ever known.[78] Jane's method of counteracting Rochester's imperiousness and sarcasm is basically the same as Scheherazade's. Whenever Rochester summons Jane to his presence, she "prepares an occupation for him," telling him a story, showing him a picture or asking him to sing. Furthermore, Shahriar's appraisal of Scheherazade as "the deliverer of many damsels" seems to be in Jane's mind when she tells Rochester playfully that she will stir up a mutiny in his seraglio and liberate the "harem inmates" (chap. 24, 297). Throughout these scenes, however, she is bent upon "pampering that susceptible vanity of his," disarming him by her playful humor once and by her sarcastic submission next, until he is divested of his Sultanic imperiousness.

Such comparison might not be taken as indicating a conscious attempt on Charlotte Brontë's part to identify her heroine with Scheherazade and to project her subjective aspiration to attain the love of a man "invested with something . . .superb, impetuous," had it not been for the fact that Rochester himself seems to partake of the distinguishing traits of both Shahriar and Haroun al-Rashid. According to Winifred Gérin, Rochester "had no other antecedents but Zamorona," the ideal hero of her Angrian Saga, who "had been recognizably 'lifted' from the *Arabian Nights*."[79] Besides his virile exploits, his imperious manner and brooding mind, his desire to roam incognito like al-Rashid, and his possession of a horse called Mesrour, Rochester shares Shahriar's distrust of womankind. Moreover, both attract young girls who exercise their ingenuity to win their masters' love and admiration. Like Shahriar, Rochester appears in the concluding scenes of the narrative as one domesticated and subdued by an intelligent female. Shahriar concludes by saying to Scheherazade: "I receive you entirely into my great graces, and I will have you to be looked upon as the deliverer of the many damsels I have resolved to have sacrificed."[80] Similarly, Rochester admits that he has undergone a change due to Jane's influence: "I have never met your likeness, Jane, you please me, and you master me . . .. I am influenced—conquered; and the influence is sweeter than I can express; and the conquest I undergo has a witchery beyond any triumph I can win" (chap. 24, 289).

This use of thematic patterns from the *Nights* to project subjective aspirations and longings appears in a number of writings. Instead of drawing on geographical and anthropological information to recreate a semi-romantic vision of the East, such writers as Yeats and Stevenson retreat into aesthetic experiences of exciting adventures and tantalizing visions. In "The Gift of Haroun Al-Rashid," William Butler Yeats, for example, is not concerned with depicting a gorgeous picture of the Orient; neither is he merely interested in using a story from Scheherazade's collection as a vehicle for his own ideas. In this poem, Yeats delves into Scheherazade's rich lore to reconstruct a highly personal experience. Despite the speaker's suspicions of the caliph's melancholy mood and despotic bent of mind, the latter stands for him as a holy figure, whose precious gift (a female) should be accepted with gratitude, as she brings the recipient inspiration and comfort.

In this veiled autobiographical poem, Yeats withdraws to Scheherazade's world to maintain an aesthetic distance which enables him to express his own personal experience. Although of a different nature, Robert Louis Stevenson's *New Arabian Nights* (1882) represents a similar attempt on the writer's part to reconstruct an aesthetic realm of intriguing adventures in which he finds a release from overwhelming personal tensions and preoccupations. Indeed, Donald David Stone detects some significance in Stevenson's very use of the title: "In Stevenson's case—an invalid with romantic dreams of freedom—it is especially appropriate that he should have used such a title, since the original tales of Scheherazade are related by the narrator as a means of postponing the continuing threat of death."[81]

Since that happy night when reading the tales in the "fat, double-columned volume," Stevenson continued to derive pleasure and comfort from their stirring adventures which worked as an antidote for pain.[82] When perusing the tales, he used to submerge himself in their adventures, identifying himself thoroughly with their heroes and imaginatively accompanying "the caliph and the serviceable Giaffar."[83] Reflecting on the opiate power of such writings on his own mind, Stevenson regards Scheherazade's story-telling as the most attractive form in fictional writing. Imitating the bare narrative thread of her tales and adapting al-Rashid's adventures to a late nineteenth-century setting, Stevenson wrote his Arabian tales not only to capitalize on the popularity of the original but also to initiate a creative outlet for his own personal sentiments and feelings. It is significant in this connection that the *Westminster Review* of January 1883 (CXIX, 138), which had already criticized the use of Oriental thematic and technical patterns to project subjective visions (LXIX, n. ser. XIII, 1858, 291–93), chastised Stevenson for. taking the name of the original in vain: ". . . Mr. Stevenson's tales are Arabian only in name," remarked the editor, "the suicides, robberies, murders, which form their subject matter are perpetrated in our own day, not further off than London or Paris, and the treatment and colouring are essentially modern and realistic." The *Westminster* critic concluded that Stevenson's tales "much too nearly resemble glorified and mundane 'Penny dreadfuls' . . . to be regarded as legitimate successors of 'The Arabian Nights'."

This criticism of Stevenson's method, however, does not necessarily preclude the existence of circumstances favorable enough for the growth of such imitations. In fact, Stevenson's tales seem to have met the demands and interests of a large section of the reading public, a public looking for release from personal tensions or social pressures in compositions of an adventurous or comic nature. But within the limits of the present survey of readings and adaptations, it is worth noting that this same interest in romantic adventures and comic episodes corresponds to the revival of critical interest in romance at that time. Besides Stevenson's tales, however, there are two more adaptations that we need to evaluate in relation to this revival: Sidney Grundy's *Arabian Nights* (1887) and F. Anstey's *Brass Bottle* (1900).

Sidney Grundy's comedy is highly entertaining because of the author's acute awareness of the humorous implications involved in incongruous situations. Grundy's hero, with a hearty absorption of Scheherazade's tales, gets into the spirit of the caliph's nocturnal adventures, emulating al-Rashid's role in late nineteenth-century London. The subsequent events and complications give rise to the appealing comicality of this work. No less interesting is Anstey's manipulation of Scheherazade's spells to depict highly amusing situations in the *Brass Bottle*. As it is no longer possible to maintain the same amount of credulity required for the enjoyment of the supernatural element, Anstey turns the genie of the lamp into a comic agent, who compels others to perform the most entertaining and humorous adventures. In Anstey's hands, the element which used to inspire the first romantics with awe became a means of comic relief.

Despite the differences in manner of treatment, late nineteenth-century comic adaptations built upon an already existing tendency to utilize some of Scheherazade's tales for the stage. Besides being a main source for melodramatic adaptations in the first half of the century, the *Nights* provided pantomime and burlesque writers with machinery and settings, which they either turned into satirical shafts aimed at melodramatic conventions and stereotyped characters, or transformed into a blend of fantasy and down-to earth domesticity. A.J. Byron's villain in *Ali Baba, or the Thirty-Nine Thieves* (1863), for example, is advised to "update his style, dress elegantly, start fraudulent joint-stock companies, [and] swindle widows."[84] Written primarily for the pleasure of large middle-class audiences, these burlesques and pantomimes throve not only on satirizing the growing capitalist and managerial strata, but also on satisfying the craving for comic entertainment.

It is certainly one of the great ironies of the nineteenth century that, despite its enduring attraction for the romantic mind, the *Nights* could not escape the sweeping tendency to burlesque. Neither could its enchantment and talismanic powers dissuade J.R. Planche from ransacking its treasures to prove that some fun could be found "under a turban."[85] In his Dulac's painting, *Fisherman and the Genii,* for instance, Planche went so far as to present the Sultan in the kitchen with an ordinary nightcap. But like many other middle-class manifestations of pettiness and vulgar taste, this tendency to burlesque was not condoned by Scheherazade's romantic admirers. Upon watching with misgivings the playful use of Arabian legends for pantomimes and burlesques, the reviewer for the *Illustrated London News* made the following comment which may serve as a fitting conclusion to this survey:

> We are not sure whether our feelings of respect for the *Arabian Nights' Entertainments* are not somewhat upset, by finding its legends turned into pantomimes; for we ever believed in them to the fullest extent, and almost regarded the volume with awe, as we pondered o'er the doings of its Genii, and Ghouls, and African Magicians, in whom we placed such faith that we quite avoided Mr.

SO STRANGE OF FORM AND SO BRILLIANT AND DIVERSE IN HUE
(Page 114)
14

Figure 2.1. Dulac's painting of the fisherman showing his strange fish to the Sultan, MS 66

Lane's uncomfortable, although no doubt, correct nomenclature, which entirely altered all our friends the Caliphs and Viziers.[86]

Notes

1 *Century Illustrated Magazine*, LXXXVII (n. ser. LXV, 1913).

2 See Wallace Cable Brown, "The Popularity of English Travel Books …," p. 74 and n. 18.

3 Review of Edward William Lane's translation of the *Nights*, No. 572 (Oct. 13, 1838), 737.

4 Cited from his article "What English Literature Gives Us," in Alexander Ireland's edition of *Book Lover's Enchiridion: Thoughts on the Solace and Companionship of Books* (London: Simpkin Marshall, 1883), p. 287.

5 Walter Bagehot's "The People of the Arabian Nights" appeared in the *National Review*, IX (July 1859), 44–71. See the *Wellesley Index to Victorian Periodicals*, III, no. 154. Hereafter Cited as *NR* and incorporated with page number at the end of each quotation. For James Mew, see "Arabian Nights," *Cornhill Magazine*, XXXII (Dec. 1875), 713–14, 725. For authorship, see also the *Wellesley Index*, I, no. 1483.

6 "Lane's *Arabian Nights*," n. ser. VIII (1840), 644.

7 Cyrus Redding, "Recollections of the Author of 'Vathek,'" *New Monthly Magazine* (June 1844), p. 150. For the reference to Thomas Wainewright, see "Exhibition of the Royal Academy," reprinted from *London Magazine* (July 1821) in *Essays and Criticisms*, ed. W.C. Hazlitt (London: Reeves & Turner, 1880), p. 140.

8 "New Series of Arabian Nights' Entertainments," *New Monthly Magazine*, XVI (Ser. 2, 1826), 336–37. For authorship, see the *Wellesley Index*, III, no. 894.

9 See Edith J. Morley, *Life and Times of Henry Crabb Robinson* (London. J.M. Dent, 1935), p. 144.

10 *Leigh Hunt's Literary Criticism*, eds. Lawrence Huston Houtchens and Carolyn Washburn Houtchens (New York: Columbia Univ. Press, 1956), p. 246.

11 *Ibid.* Leigh Hunt expressed a similar notion when commenting upon Edward William Lane's beautifully worded description of the shopping scene in "The Porter and the Three Ladies of Baghdad." See "New Translations of the Arabian Nights," *London and Westminster Review*, XXXIII (Oct. 1839), 118. For authorship, see Burton's "Terminal,Essay," X, 92 n. 3, and Victor Chauvin, IV, 102 For Hazlitt's own remarks regarding Coleridge's criticism, see "On Dreams," in *Miscellaneous Works of William Hazlitt*, in 5 vols. (Philadelphia, PA: Carey and Hart, 1848), II, 155.

12 "The Prelude," V, 462–63. Wordsworth's early copy of the *Nights* to which he referred in "The Prelude" is still unidentified, and as such John Livingston Lowes' remarks have not lost their validity yet. See *Road to Xanadu* (Boston and New York: Houghton

Mifflin, 1927), p. 461 n. The Rydal Mount Sale List published in *Transactions of Wordsworth Society* (Vol. VI) indicates a late acquisition of Jonathan Scott's *Arabian Nights' Entertainments* (sale no. 456) and M. Galland's *Les Mille et Une Nuits, Contes Arabes* (12 tomes, 1729), sale no. 538.

13 See *Autobiography* in *Collected Writings of Thomas De Quincey*, ed. David Masson (London: A & C. Black, 1896), I, pp. 128–29 and n. 2.

14 See Edward Said, *Orientalism* (New York: Vintage Books Edition-Random House, 1979), 136–143.

15 See his letter of September 11, 1878 to Susan Beever in *Letters of John Ruskin, 1870–1889, Works of John Ruskin*, eds. E.T. Cook and Alexander Wedderburn (London: George Allen, 1903–1912), XXXVII, 258. Future references to Ruskin's writings will be to this edition unless otherwise indicated.

16 "Pre-Raphaelitism," *Works*, XII, 378–79; see also *Arrows of the Chace in Life of John Ruskin* (London: George Allen, 1912), II, 384, and *Works*, XXXIV, 583, for a facsimile of his emendations of Sir John's list.

17 *Life of John Ruskin*, II, 143; also Lady Burne-Jones, *Memorials of Edward Burne-Jones* (New York: Macmillan, 1904), I, 300.

18 *Works*, XXXIV, 585. See also "Mr. Ruskin on the Choice of Books," in *Best Hundred Books, Pall Mall Gazette*, "Extra"—No. 24, p. 8.

19 "New Series . . .," *New Monthly Magazine*, p. 336.

20 Cited from Tomalin's "Shorthand Report of Lecture V" in Ernest Hartley Coleridge's edition of the *Letters of Samuel Taylor Coleridge* (London: W. Heinemann, 1895), I, p. 11 and n. 1.

21 *Notes of an Overland Journey, through France and Egypt to Bombay* (London, 1841), p. 133.

22 Burne-Jones, *Memorials of Edward Burne-Jones*, I, 142.

23 For references to Cooper's, Gregory's, and Kitto's readings, see Richard D. Altick, *English Common Reader* (1957; rpt. Chicago, IL: Chicago Univ. Press, 1963), pp. 119, 218, 265; and for more information on other readers, see Amy Cruse, *Victorians and Their Books* (1935); (London: George Allen & Unwin, 3rd ed., 1962), pp. 286, 291, 292, 293. An excellent short survey of such readings is by Robert Calvin Whitford, " 'The Arabian Nights' and the English Novel," *Dial*, LX (Mar. 16, 1916), 270. Like Leigh Hunt, Dickens continued as an avid reader of the *Nights*. See Harry Stone's *Charles Dickens' Uncollected Writings from Household Words, 1850–1859*, 2 vols. (Bloomington: Indiana Univ. Press, 1968), I, 210 and n. 13, and his "Dark Corners of the Mind: Dickens' Childhood Reading," *Horn Book Magazine*, XXXIX (June 1963), 306–21. See also Jane W. Stedman, "Good Spirits: Dickens' Childhood Reading," *Dickensian*, LXI, No. 3 (Sept. 1965), 150–54. For information on Hunt, see his *Lord Byron and Some of His Contemporaries* (2nd ed., London, 1828), I, 438–39; and Mrs. James T. Fields, *A Shelf of Old Books* (London: Osgood, 1894), pp. 48–49. Thackeray's yearning for that paradise of childhood drove him always to read

Arabian and kindred tales. See, for example, his letter to Tennyson in *Letters and Private Papers of . . .*, ed. Gordon Ray (Cambridge, MA: Harvard Univ. Press, 1945–46), IV, 152. As for Burne Jones, we read that "Arabian and Persian stories fascinated him so that he gathered a treasure of them in his memory, and loved to talk of them . . . . That corner of Asia was to him like a far off country home, for in imagination he lived and travelled there from boyhood." *Memorials of Edward Burne-Jones*, II, 43, 55. In "Society and Solitude" Emerson wrote: "Scheherazade tells these stories to save her life, and the delight of young Europe and young America in them proves that she fairly earned it." Cited from James O'Donnell Bennett, *Much Loved Books: Best Sellers of the Ages* (New York: Boniard Liveright, 1927), p. 159. For information on Carlyle's reading of the *Nights*, see David Masson, *Edinburgh Sketches and Memoirs* (London & Edinburgh: Adam & Charles Black, 1892), pp. 229–31; and Frederick Roe, *Thomas Carlyle as a Critic of Literature* (New York: Columbia Univ. Press, 1915), p. 5. William Butler Yeats once remarked that he used to read the *Nights* daily. See Allen Wade, ed. *Letters of W.B. Yeats* (London: Rupert Hart-Davis, 1954), pp. 831–32. Finally we may look to George Bernard Shaw who saw in his own preference for the *Nights* a sign of a consistently good critical sense. "The two literary sensations of my childhood," he said, "were undoubtedly the *Pilgrim's Progress* and the *Arabian Nights*. This shows that I was as good a critic in my infancy as I am now, though I could not then give such clever reasons for my opinion." "Books of My Childhood," *Literary Digest*, I, no. 3 (Oct. 1946), 1.

24 Henley's essay was included in his *Views and Reviews, Works* (London: David Nutt, 1908), V, 249. This review has been considered a marvelous piece of writing, evoking, and recreating the real atmosphere of Scheherazade's world. J.B. Priestly wrote to Kennedy Williamson: "To me he [Henley] touches the top in such things as his appreciation of the Arabian Nights." Williamson's *W.E. Henley: A Memoir* (London: Harold Shaylor, 1930), p. 62. Kipling, too, was so charmed that he sincerely remarked that "if such things be merchandise in the next world [I] will cheerfully sell a large portion of what I have written for a single meditation—illumination-inspiration or what you please—that he wrote on the *Arabian Nights* in a tiny book of Essays and Reviews." *Something of Myself* (London: Macmillan, 1937), p. 82.

25 "New Translations," p. 106.

26 Cited from his review of Meredith's *Shaving of Shagpat* for the *Saturday Review* (Jan. 19, 1856) in Ioan William's edition of *Meredith: The Critical Heritage* (London: Routledge & Kegan Paul, 1971), p. 43.

27 "Preface" to *Arabian Nights' Entertainments* (London: James Burns, 1847), I, ii.

28 "The Arabian Nights," *Cornhill Magazine*, p. 712.

29 "The Thousand and One Nights," No. 3596 (Sept. 26, 1896), 412. (Review of Joseph Jacobs' edition).

30 Sir John Lubbock, "On the Pleasure of Reading," *Contemporary Review*, XLIX (Feb. 1886), 240–51. The article was originally a paper read at the Working Man's College,

containing Sir John Lubbock's selection. When published in the *Pall Mall*, it started a discussion in which many writers and scholars participated. Besides Lubbock and Ruskin, William Morris and E.J.E. Welldon (Headmaster of Harrow) and the traveler H.M. Stanley included the *Nights* in their selections of the best readable books. See *Pall Mall Gazette*, "Extra," No. 24, pp. 4, 7, II, 17, 22. Comte's selection has been included with an introductory note in Frederick Harrison's *Among My Books* (London: Macmillan, 1912), p. 402.

31 Chauvin, IV.

32 See Boris Segalowitsh's *Benjamin Disraeli's Orientalismus* (Berlin, 1930), pp. 34–35.

33 *Notebooks of Samuel Taylor Coleridge*, ed. Kathleen Coburn (London: Routledge, 1973), III, notes, entry: 2500/29. 190; also Schlegel's *History of Literature, Ancient and Modern* (Edinburgh, 1818), Lecture VIII.

34 For Byron's advice, see Rowland E. Prothero, ed. *Works of Lord Byron, Letters and Journals,* in 6 vols. (London: Murray, 1903), II, 255. (Letter of Aug. 28, 1813).

35 Moore's poem was criticized by a number of his contemporaries for its straining to create "a paradise of sweets." See, for instance, the *British Review*, X (1817), 31–32.

36 See, for example, p. 176 in Sherer's book and p. 90 in volume two of Carne's *Letters*. The same romantic absorption of the tales manifests itself in H. Light's *Travels in Egypt, Nubia, Holy Land* (London, 1818), p. 230; *B. Disraeli's Home Letters, Written by the Late Earl Beaconsfield in 1830 and 1831* (London, 1885), p. 105; and in Alexander Kinglake's *Eothen* (1884). For a good review of these, see Rashad Rushdi, "English Travellers in Egypt in the Reign of Mohamed Ali," *Bulletin of the Faculty of Arts* (Fuad Al-Awal Univ.), IV, Pt. II (Dec. 1952), 1–61; and Norman Daniel, *Islam, Europe and Empire*, pp. 48–49.

37 Besides standard histories of English drama and pantomime, the interested reader should consult the *Catalogue of Additions to the MSS. Plays Submitted to the Lord Chamberlain, 1824–1851* (London: B.M. Publications, 1964) and "Register of Lord Chamberlain's Plays," vols. I–VI, B.M. Add. MSS. 53, 702–07. See also A. Nicoll, *A History of English Drama, 1660–1900*. Rev. ed. 6 vols. (Cambridge, England: Univ. Press, 1952–59).

38 "A letter to Miss Power of Feb. 26, 1863," *Letters of Charles Dickens*, ed. by his Sister-in Law and His Eldest Daughter (New York: Charles Scribner's Sons, 1879), II, 226–27.

39 "New Translations of the Arabian Nights," XXXIII (Oct. 1839), 103. Hereafter cited as "NT" and incorporated with page number at the end of each quotation.

40 Hunt's own citation from *Remarks on the Arabian Nights' Entertainments*, p. 8.

41 It is worth keeping in mind that the romantics from Hunt to John Payne insisted on preferring Galland's orthography to Lane's accurate but startlingly new transliterations. Galland made a deep impression on the reader's mind, and his version became identical with youthful recollections. Thus, upon using the old spelling of

the caliph "Haroun Alraschid," Dickens sentimentally remonstrated, "Let me have the corrupted name again for once, it is so scented with sweet memories" (Cited from Sylvere Monod, *Dickens the Novelist* [Univ. of Oklahoma Press, 1968], p. 32). For Payne, see "The Thousand and One Nights," Pt. II, *New Q. Magazine* (Apr. 1879), 398–99.

42 "The Arabian Nights," *Edinburgh Review*, p. 167; and for C.H. Toy's article, see "The Thousand and One Nights," *Atlantic Monthly*, LXIII (June 1889), p. 757.

43 For De Quincey, see *Autobiography* and *Confessions of an Opium Eater* in *Works*, ed. D. Masson, vols, I, III, 128–29, 441–42 respectively.

44 See Sidney Colvin, *John Keats: His Life and Poetry, His Friends and Critics and AfterFame* (New York: Charles Scribner's Sons, 1917), pp. 173, 175, 184–85, 190–91, 195, 205; M.R. Ridley, *Keats' Craftsmanship: A Study in Poetic Development* (Oxford: Clarendon Press, 1933), 117–19, 124–25, 160–61, 164–65 and notes; Werner W. Beyer, *Keats and the Daemon King* (New York: Oxford Univ. Press, 1947), pp. 7, 17, 150, 175, 272; and Harry B. Forman, ed., *Poetical Works and Other Writings of John Keats* (4 vols., London: Reeves, 1889), I, 140–41.

45 Maxime Rodinson, "The Western Image and Western Studies of Islam," in *Legacy of Islam*, eds. Joseph Schacht and C.E. Bosworth, 2nd ed. (Oxford: Clarendon, 1974), p. 48.

46 *Life and Letters of Washington Irving*, by Pierre M. Irving (New York: Putnam, 1864), III, 348–49.

47 "Genii and Fairies of the East, The Arabian Nights, & C.," No. 30 (Oct. 22, 1834), 233.

48 *Leigh Hunt's London Journal*, No. 30 (Oct. 22, 1834), 233.

49 Neither is Coleridge's attitude separable from a whole movement which E.S. Shaffer recently subscribed to describing as "romantic Hellenism," of which "Orientalism" was only one aspect. Shaffer's view of Orientalism as closely bound "with new textual and historical scholarship exercised on the Bible since the Reformation" is only partly valid however. What he seems to overlook is that the movement had not assumed a distinct shape before the appearance of the *Arabian Nights*. See *'Kubla Khan' and the Fall of Jerusalem:* The Mythological School in Biblical Criticism and Secular Literature, 1770–1880 (Cambridge: Univ. Press, 1975), p. 14.

50 For Nichol's response, see *Memoir of . . .*, by Prof. William Knight (Glasgow: James MacLehose, 1896), p. 41; and for Henley, "The Arabian Nights' Entertainments" in *Works*, I, *Poems*, 61.

51 *Leigh Hunt's London Journal* (Oct. 22, 1834), No. 30, 233.

52 *Apologia Pro Vita Sua*, ed. David J. De Laura (New York: Norton, 1968), p. 14.

53 "To Thomas Poole, Oct. 16, 1797," *Letters of Samuel Taylor Coleridge*, ed. Ernest Hartley Coleridge (London: Heinemann, 1895), I, 16.

54 *Ibid.*, I, 12. "To Thomas Poole, Oct. 9, 1797." For other references see also p. 11 n. 9 and *Collected Works of Samuel Taylor Coleridge, The Friend*, vol. 4, pt. 1. Ed. Barbara E. Rooke (London: Routledge & Kegan, 1969), 148, n. 3. In the same place he mentioned how the exterior of an awe-inspiring mansion in the neighbourhood had been "long connected in . . . [his] childish imagination with the feelings and fancies stirred up in . . . [him] by the perusal of the Arabian Nights' Entertainments."

55 See John Livingston Lowes, *Road to Xanadu*, p. 459 n.

56 "Lecture VIII, Don Quixote," in Thomas Middleton Raysor, ed., *Coleridge's Miscellaneous Criticism* (Cambridge, MA: Harvard Univ. Press, 1936), p. 103. Besides Hazlitt, Coleridge perhaps had in mind Mrs. Barbauld whom he criticized for objecting to the absence of moralism and the excess of the improbable in the "Ancient Mariner." See the entry for May 31, 1830, *Table-Talk* in Raysor's, p. 405.

57 *Notebooks of Samuel Taylor Coleridge*, I, 848, 1250 n.

58 The influence of *Vathek* on Isa'ac Disraeli in *Mejnoun and Leila* (1799), Southey in *Thalaba* (1801), John Hamilton Reynold in *Safie* (1814), Thomas Moore in *Lalla Rookh* (1817), Disraeli in *Alroy* and, especially, Barry Cornwall (Bryan Waller Procter), has been noticed by many reviewers and critics. See Fatma Moussa Mahmoud, "Beckford, *Vathek* and the Oriental Tale" in her *William Beckford of Fonthill: Bicentenary Essays* (1960; rpt. Port Washington: Kennikat Press, 1972), pp. 81–83; and Marie Eide Meester, *Oriental Influences in English Literature of the Nineteenth Century* (Amsterdam, 1967; rpt. of 1915), pp. 19–22. In a note to *Giaour* (1813), Byron paid a warm tribute to Beckford's tale. Significantly, Paul Elmer More considers Beckford's *Vathek* "one of the main documents to anyone who wishes to study the sources of the romantic movement," and the image of the damned with flaming hearts which concludes the book, "the essential type and image of the romantic life and literature." *Drift of Romanticism*, Shelburne Essays, 8th ser. (New York: Houghton Mifflin, 1913), pp. 33, 36 respectively.

59 Lewis Melville, *Life and Letters of William Beckford of Fonthill* (London: Heinemann, 1910), p. 21.

60 Cited by J.W. Oliver, *Life of William Beckford* (London: Oxford, 1932), pp. 31–32.

61 Boyd Alexander, *England's Wealthiest Son* (London: Centaur Press, 1962), p. 41.

62 *Drift*, pp. 12, 14.

63 For Christina Rossetti's infatuation with the *Arabian Nights*, see her letter of July 18, 1876 to her brother Dante in *Family Letters of Christina Georgina Rossetti*, ed. William Michael Rossetti (London: Brown & Langham, 1908), p. 57. Christina Rossetti's "Dead City," which was based on the story of marble men in the *Nights*, gives a "foretaste" of the "Goblin Market," especially in its description of "glowing and incongruously assembled fruits," as Dorothy Margaret Stuart remarks in her *Christina Rossetti* (London: Macmillan, 1930), p. 16. Edmund Gosse detects in the same poem as well "the accents of the future author of *Goblin Market*." See "Christina Rossetti" in *Critical Kit-Kats* (New York: Dodd, 1897), p. 142. In "The Sources of

Christina Rossetti's 'Goblin Market'" (*Modern Language Review*, XXVIII, 1933, pp. 158–60), Ifor Evans explains how the "union of details derived from Keightley *[Fairy Mythology]* with an *Arabian Nights* motive has left a definite mark on *Goblin Market.*" For more information on these poems as well as on Christina Rossetti's use of exotic imagery from the *Nights* in "A Birthday," see also Evans, *English Poetry in the Later Nineteenth-Century* (1933; London: Methuen, 2nd ed. 1966), pp. 93, 95.

64 Tennyson's "Written by an Exile of Bassorah, while sailing down the Euphrates" (1827) might have been based on the story of Noureddin and the Fair Persian as Paden maintains. But the yearning for the paradisal city and the melancholy tone recall Bharam's experience in "The Man Who Never Laughed Again." See W.D. Paden, *Tennyson in Egypt: A Study of the Imagery in His Earlier Work* (Lawrence: Univ. of Kansas, 1942), p. 131.

65 Hyder Edward Rollins, ed., *Letters of John Keats* (Cambridge, MA: Harvard Univ. Press, 1958), II, 130.

66 This and the preceding references to Morris are from May Morris' "Introduction" to *Collected Works of William Morris* (New York: Russell & Russell, 1966), V, xxi, xxiv.

67 See *Alfred Lord Tennyson: A Memoir, by His Son* (New York: Macmillan, 1897), I, 34. Many Victorians expressed similar longings, alluding extensively to Scheherazade's spells of enchantment and magic. See, for example, Ruskin's allusions to Prince Hussain's carpet and al-Nashar's visions to express his frustrated desires in *Works*, XXXIV, 260, XXXVI, 443, and XXVIII, 352.

68 "On Some of the Characteristics of Modern Poetry," *Englishman's Magazine*, I (Aug. 1831), 621. Also reproduced in Isobel Armstrong, *Victorian Scrutinies: Review of Poetry 1830–1870* (London: Athlone Press, 1972); and in *Tennyson: The Critical Heritage*, ed. John D. Jump (London: Routledge & Kegan Paul, 1967). Allusions to other contemporary reviews of "Recollections . . ." will be to this last reference and will be incorporated hereafter within the text.

69 This and the following quotation are from his *Tennyson: The Growth of a Poet* (Cambridge, MA: Harvard Univ. Press, 1960), p. 39.

70 See his letters of September 1835 and April 1840 to William Ritchie and Mrs. Carmichael Smyth in *Letters and Private Papers of W.M. Thackeray*, I, 297 (n. 52), 439, respectively. Among many others, Mrs. Gaskell used the same story to describe her heroine's misfortune and disappointment. Mary Barton's dreams of prosperity came to the same end as al-Nashar's. (*Mary Barton*, chap. 7).

71 Thomas Carlyle, *Correspondence of Thomas Carlyle and Ralph Waldo Emerson: 1834–1872*, in 2 vols. (London: Chatto & Windus, 1883), I, 316.

72 Charles Dickens, *Christmas Stories*, ed. G.K. Chesterton (Everyman's Library, 1910; rpt. 1965), p. 233.

73 George Gissing, *Charles Dickens: A Critical Study* (London).

74 *Poems of George Meredith*, 2 vols. (Surrey Ed.; London: Times Book Club, 1912), I, 251.

75 Cited from her review of the book in the *Westminster* of April 1856 by loan Williams, *Meredith: The Critical Heritage*, p. 47.

76 *Ibid.*, p. 41. Cited from her review in the *Leader* (Jan. 1856).

77 *Gossip in a Library* (London: William Heinemann; 3rd ed., 1893), p. 326.

78 Q.D. Leavis, "Introduction," *Jane Eyre* (Penguin, 1972; rpt. of 1966), p. 13. Further references to this edition will be incorporated within the text.

79 Winifred Gerin, *Charlotte* Bronte: *The Evolution of Genius* (Oxford: Clarendon, 1967), pp. 333, 45–46, respectively.

80 *Arabian Nights' Entertainments* (London: Longman, 1783), IV, 312.

81 Donald David Stone, *Novelists in a Changing World* (Cambridge, MA: Harvard Univ. Press, 1972), p. 52.

82 See "A Penny Plain and Tuppence Coloured," in *Memories and Portraits* (New York: Scribner's, 1887), p. 218.

83 "An Autumn Effect," *Essays on Travel and in the Art of Writing* (New York: Scribner's, 1923), p. 132.

84 See Michael R. Booth's "Introduction" to *English Plays of the Nineteenth Century* (Oxford: Clarendon, 1976), V, 32.

85 As a widely accepted opinion in the early nineteenth century, "no fun under a turban" indicates how both writers and theater-goers took the Orient seriously. Planché challenged that tradition, imposing a comic element on his adaptations from the *Nights*. In juxtaposing the comic and the fearful, the fantastic and the common, Planché produced extravaganzas and revues which seem to have been greatly appealing to the public. See Booth, pp. 18–19.

86 From a review of Nelson Lee's pantomime, *Forty Thieves* . . . (Jan. 9, 1847), p. 26.

3

Patterns of Critical Response: The Romantic Appraisal of Scheherazade's Aesthetics

". . . I used to read to him to cheer his courage, and he was very fond of that. They were wrong books— I am never to speak of them here—but we didn't know there was any harm in them."

"And he liked them?" said Louisa, with her searching gaze on Sissy all this time.

"O very much! They kept him, many times, from what did him real harm. And often and often of a night, he used to forget all his troubles in wondering whether the Sultan would let the lady go on with the story, or would have her head cut off before it was finished."

Charles Dickens, *Hard Times,* chap. 9.

Rather than lagging behind the reading public, late eighteenth- and nineteenth-century critics and reviewers seem to have been avid readers of Scheherazade's entertaining tales. In their numerous articles, reviews, and introductory notes to various editions of the *Nights,* one detects a marked note of admiration which, on some occasions, amounts to a kind of thorough infatuation with its enchantments and tantalizing visions. "Dear, delightful Scheherazade!" exclaimed W.C. Taylor in 1834, "who is there that loves not to recall the hours of stolen pleasure, devoted to the stories with which, during a thousand and one nights, thou didst delay the stroke of fate, and change the stern resolve of the cruel Schahriar?"[1] At the same time, the *Athenaeum* for August 16, 1834 (No. 355, 605) remonstrated: "Who is there that remembers not with delight the time when he first read the Arabian Nights?—who that recurs not occasionally to their pages with renewed pleasure?" A few years later, the Select Library editor of the *Nights* made the following remark: "Not to be acquainted with the 'Arabian Nights,' argues a literary apathy, the imputation of which no one, we think, would be willing to bear."[2]

When studied against late eighteenth- and nineteenth-century conservative opposition to fiction, the increasing popularity of the *Nights* with critics and the tendency to defend its properties against the slightest condemnatory remark present an interesting paradox, which obviously demands an adequate explanation in the light of contemporary literary controversies. Aside from the few disparaging remarks levelled against its machinery in the eighteenth century, there were no serious objections to the tales on moral or social grounds, despite the fact that much of the criticism of fiction at that time partook of the evangelical and utilitarian antipathy to novel reading, not only as a frivolous, time-wasting occupation but also as an enervating and insidious practice. With this contemporary reaction to fiction in mind, the *Monthly Review* (I, n. ser., 1826, 363) expressed a deep attachment to the tales which such didactic and strictly orthodox writers as Mrs. Sherwood and Miss Edgeworth could never break: "We may respect the efforts of Mrs. Sherwood and her excellent and well-meaning fellow labourers, who endeavour to supplant the lying dreams of Oriental fancy by domestic and religious tales; but never, never will they interest and delight like the nameless authors of the 'Arabian Nights' Entertainment.'" Three years later, the *Asiatic Journal* (XXVIII, no. 167, July 1829, 560–61) carried an article by the celebrated Arabist, Baron De Sacy, in which he stressed the perennial charm of the *Nights*. Its success, he explained, "suffers no deterioration from the vicissitudes of fashion or the change of customs." While some works and literary genres were supplanted by others, the *Nights* "has always had editors and readers," and "the magical name of the work has served as a cover and passport to vast importations of contraband goods, without detracting one jot from its popularity." Writing for the *Foreign Quarterly* of December 1834 (XIV, 350) W.C. Taylor gave vent to his intimate feeling of love for these tales despite the growing Benthamite emphasis on practical truths; for "notwithstanding the hazard of incurring all the ridicule of this utilitarian age,—we still love to revel in these wild and wondrous scenes of oriental imagination."

It is not superfluous to mention here that critics often used the tales as touchstones in evaluating and appraising English fictional literature. Thus, when appreciating Scott's *Waverley* (1814) for its historical documentation, the Tory *British Critic* compared it to the *Nights,* explaining that *Waverley* "should be ranked in the same class with the Arabian Nights' entertainments, in which the story, however it may for a moment engage the attention, is but of little consequence, in proportion to the faithful picture which they present of the manners and customs of the east."[3] On the other hand, the *British Review* for November 1818 was rather attracted to Scheherazade's convoluted narrative art, citing this as its definitive criterion to estimate Scott's *Tales of My Landlord:* "The *Arabian Nights,* so long admired for never-ending incident and seducing narrative," said the *British Review,* "are not likely to be surpassed, at least in number, although they were in reality, what they are in name, a Thousand and One."[4]

More pertinent, however, is the fact that nineteenth-century critics approved of certain elements in the *Nights* which they would hardly have accepted from contemporary novelists, especially in matters of probability and moralism. Citing Stevenson's *New Arabian Nights* as a frame of reference, the *Saturday Review* (Nov. 4, 1882, 609–10) remarked, for instance, "We ... could not endure it if Mr. Stevenson ..., in his *New Arabian Nights,* were to change the President of the Suicide Club into a dog or a goat." After listing a number of objections to the same writer's "improbable" stories, "affected" style, and "morbid tone," the *Westminster Review* for January 1883 (CXIX, 138) chastised him for excluding explicit moral insights from his pseudo-Arabian tales: "The original 'Arabian Nights' no doubt left much to be desired on the score of moral edification," the *Westminster* critic contended, "but they possess in an extraordinary degree the merit of local colouring." Aside from this merit, their exquisite blend of the natural and the supernatural entails different criteria that are inapplicable to English fiction: "In that sunny land of mirage and unreality, peopled by Genii, and where everything is brought about by enchantments," continued the critic, "a stringent moral code could hardly be expected to obtain, but Stevenson's tales are Arabian only in name."

Although furnishing a subtle defense of what he considers an omission on Scheherazade's part and touching upon the two main aspects which make the book a source of amusement and information to nineteenth-century readers, and although his response falls within the common critical tendency to explain the irresistible charm of the tales, the *Westminster* reviewer does not provide us with enough insights into the diversity of reactions to their imaginative and moral value. Indeed, no description of the critical reception of the *Nights* would be complete without due awareness of the socio-aesthetic richness of Scheherazade's composite work, its capacity to satisfy every taste. It is this very nature of the *Nights,* after all, which provokes and simultaneously explains the diversity of responses to its stylistic and thematic characteristics. As most of these critical patterns of response were set forth in the first decades of the century, it is only proper to sketch briefly their early scope before following up their development and growth throughout the Victorian period.

In his informative preface to *Tales of the East* (1812, I, i), Henry Weber detected in this "storehouse of ingenious fiction and of splendid imagery" lessons in morality, which though not conveyed "in the austere form of imperative precept and dictatorial aphorism," appear "in the more pleasing shape of example." More than sixty years later, the *Cornhill* (XXXII, Dec. 1875, 732) carried James Mew's significant contribution on the *Nights,* in which he quoted with satisfaction some of these lessons, especially "the common-sense advice of that too-confiding Arabic tailor" who told the Second Calendar that such a practical job as wood-cutting is preferable to being a man of culture in a materialistic society. Mew even regarded Noureddin Ali's advice to his son to become a calculating man of the world as entitling the *Nights* to be called the " 'Evangel of the East,' worth of cedar, of covers adorned with jewels, and of letters of liquid gold on pages of purple parchment." On the other hand, the *Monthly Review* (I, n. ser. 1826, 365) anticipated the *Spectator* of November 25, 1882 (LV, 1513–14), in discerning a subtle stream of "pensive morality" running throughout the *Nights,* in general, and "The City of Brass," in particular, "to impress on the mind of the thoughtless and the gay a sense of the nothingness of life and earthly possessions."

It is worth noting parenthetically that the preceding concern with the innate moral purposefulness of the *Nights* falls within the broader context of the controversy over the value of fiction. Without being overtly moralistic, the tales center on a social and moral code which cannot be casually overlooked. Combined with their chief merit as imaginative productions, this characteristic helped establish their unique reputation in early nineteenth-century England. Unlike many other fictional writings, the *Nights* invited little or no carping comment on account of its content. It is perhaps this fact, among others, which explains why the *Nights* was often cited as an imaginative work which the enemies of fiction could not easily disparage.

No less significant for students of critical responses is the developing sociological interest in the *Nights,* which, although suffering from the dearth of information on the social context of the tales, figures quite prominently in John Dunlop's *History of Fiction* (1814) and Sismondi's popular *Historical View of the Literature of the South of Europe.* Both eminent writers emphasize the urban (*bourgeois*) origin of the most obvious cycles of tales in Scheherazade's collection, setting thereby the literary and critical scene for subsequent researches into the society of the *Nights* and stimulating such industrious scholars and writers as Edward William

Lane, Walter Bagehot, John Payne, Stanley Lane-Poole, and Richard Francis Burton to examine the sociocultural context of Arabic fiction. Approaching the tales with a lingering neoclassical bias, John Dunlop could not appreciate their deviation from "the simplicity of nature," but he, nevertheless, discerned in them a living picture of certain social orders.[5] Their "chief merit," he postulated, "consists in the admirable delineation of eastern manners, the knavery of slaves, the hypocrisy of dervishes, the corruption of judges, the baneful influence of . . . despotism . . ., and the boldness and artifice of the women, who risk so much the more in proportion to the vigour with which they are confined."[6] An heir to a neo-classical discourse, and much given to conservative perspectives on women and assistants [Dunlop's slaves], Dunlop presents a transitional case between two discursive positions, the Augustan and the romantic. Similarly, Sismondi dwelt on the urban setting of the Baghdadian tales, especially their pictures of mercantile adventures and commercial pursuits: "We recognise, in them," he explained, "the style of a mercantile people, as we do that of a warlike nation, in the romances of chivalry. Riches and artificial luxuries dispute the palm with the splendid gifts of the fairies." Elaborating on this side, he further remarked, "The heroes unceasingly traverse distant realms, and the interests of merchandise excite their active curiosity, as much as the love of renown awakened the spirit of the ancient knights."[7] The implications of such views will become evident in due course, for while Sismondi evaluates literary productions in the light of their own social milieu regardless of contemporary ethical or literary considerations, later critics like Walter Bagehot allow such strictures to interfere with their estimates of the aesthetics of the *Nights*.

Indicative of further critical interests as well are some early nineteenth-century efforts to expatiate on Scheherazade's sources of entertainment, and, ultimately, to rescue the tales from false imputations and conventional presumptions. The Suttaby editor of the *Nights* (1807), for instance, upholds in his "Prefatory Discourse" (p. xix) that the subtle blend of the realistic and the fantastic in Arabic fiction entertains the reader without luring him from reality into extra-rational realms. Haroun al-Rashid's adventures, for example, "though bordering at times on the improbable, are nevertheless within the sphere of human action, and might have been performed by human beings." But in stories involving supernatural agents, "where all bounds of reasonable probability are violated, and we confessedly enter the regions of fiction," the editor remarks that "our pleasure experiences no diminution from the moral certainty that the events which are read, could never have had existence, but is kept alive by the strain of natural feeling, which as wonder increases upon wonder, the personages operated upon never fail to display." This characteristic was also admired by Coleridge and Thomas Keightley. Both considered the tales well qualified for critical approbation, for by enhancing enjoyment without imposing demands and strains upon the reader's mind, and by preserving the distance that separates the reader from his own world, the *Nights* remains a source of irresistible and harmless attraction. In Keightley's words, such tales are preferable to the "modern novel" because "they go at once beyond the regions of probability, and cannot therefore injure by exciting romantic expectations of the fortune of the hero or heroine being realized in ourselves."[8] The significance of such responses lies not only in their relevance to contemporary attitudes towards the *Nights* but also in the fact that such estimates fall within the context of a general tendency to study and enjoy the tales on their aesthetic merits, a tendency which gained in momentum and strength as the nineteenth century wore on.

Inseparable from this pattern of response is another tendency which, while admitting possible climatic and social influences on Arabian fiction, sees through the confusion of the premature eighteenth-century use of the historical method. As has already been noticed, Thomas Warton wrote extensive dissertations on the assumed Arabian origin of romantic fiction, associating this art not only with climatic conditions but also with idleness, for Eastern monarchs are said to have encouraged story-telling to relieve their idle minds. This last conjecture was seized upon by John Dunlop. Basing his argument on some of Warton's views and echoing in one instance James Beattie's similar hypothesis, John Dunlop dwelt on this subject in his pioneering *History of Fiction* (1814), a work influential in the first half of the century, but regarded as wanting in scientific objectivity by some well-informed critics. Sir Francis Palgrave, for example, saw through John Dunlop's rambling thesis, remarking with pleasant sarcasm that "we have very little confidence in the influence supposed to be exercised by climate over the moral character of mankind: we doubt whether genius of any kind actually rises or falls with the mercury in the thermometer."[9] Concluding that John Dunlop "*Wartonizes* in his turn," and that both overlook historical and social facts when ascribing idleness to Eastern monarchs and, eventually, associating fiction with truancy, Francis Palgrave detects in their attitude "the conceited airs of superiority with which our writers usually regard the Asiatics" (p. 388).

Our immediate concern at the present moment, however, is not with the implications of the historical theory, but with the reviewer's insight into the nature of the Arabian tales, an insight which corresponds to and anticipates other literary efforts to disentangle the tales from conventional critical assumptions. Rather than depicting mere scenes of splendor and extravagance "where everything is carried on by prodigy," the tales reveal qualities that charm and entertain on a universal scope. "The Arabian fabulists," Francis Palgrave remarked (p. 389), "excel in ludicrous incident and genuine humour; and in showing how much can be effected by mere human contrivance. Has Mr. Dunlop forgotten the little Hunchback?" Disputing Dunlop's contention, he stressed that "whatever eastern 'magnificence and splendour,' and 'luxuriant ornaments' he may be able to find, they can scarcely be attributed to the 'scenery' and 'climate' of the Arabians." By emphasizing the ludicrous and the comic in the *Nights,* which Dunlop and others had overlooked, the *Quarterly* reviewer points out one of the main sources of entertainment for such exuberant writers as Thackeray and Henley, who enjoyed that sheer taste for sprightly humor which seemed to dominate every scene.[10]

Although this is not the right place to elaborate on the significance of the foregoing pioneering efforts to study the aesthetics of the Arabian tales and to dissociate them from traditional assumptions, it is still needful to stress the existence of such attitudes at the beginning of the century. No less important than this interest in the aesthetics of the *Nights* was the growing demand for editorial accuracy and textual exactitude. Voiced by Richard Hole in 1797 and by a number of contributors to the *Gentleman's Magazine* (1798, 1799), the call for an accurate translation that would satisfy the emerging scientific spirit led to the publication of new editions, which, although still based on the French of Galland, provided at least some illuminating introductory remarks concerning the sociological significance of the tales.[11] Confused and rambling as Jonathan Scott's lengthy introduction to his translation of the *Nights* is, it nevertheless stresses the dialectical interaction between the supernatural machinery of the tales and the socio-religious milieu they depict.[12] Considered together, these interests in the literary, historical, and philological context of the *Nights* represent its critical reception in the first decades of the century. Many of these responses have developed into well-defined patterns which roughly correspond to some major currents in nineteenth-century criticism.

It was as a story-book, to be sure, that the *Nights* enjoyed such a sweeping popularity, evoking some literary responses and comments that call for adequate assessment. Indeed, as early as 1786, the *Critical Review* (LXII, 38) noticed that the tales "attracted every reader by the splendor of their descriptions, and the magic of their enchantments, before we learnt that they exhibited a faithful copy of eastern manners, and oriental conversations." Irrespective of its genealogical or sociological value, the *Nights* is admired for its tantalizing visions and aesthetic luster. Writing for the *Atlantic Monthly* (LXIII, June 1889, 762), C.H. Toy wisely argued: "Fortunately our literary enjoyment of the Nights does not depend on our knowing their genealogy. Like all such literary organisms of slow growth," he further elucidated, "their beauties and treasures lie partly on the surface, partly deeper down. The adventure, magic, drollery, wit, and passion are easily recognizable; the profounder social and religious sentiments must sometimes be searched for."

But while aptly summing up the nature of the main nineteenth-century critical approaches to Scheherazade's tales—the intrinsic and the extrinsic— Toy throws no light on the implications involved in responding to these "recognizable" aspects. Rather than revealing a uniform and consistent appreciation of Scheherazade's aesthetics, a careful reading of nineteenth-century literary responses will indicate diverse and varying estimates and evaluations that form integral parts of the raging literary controversies of the day. Whereas the reading public as well as romantic critics saw in the very enjoyment of these recognizable beauties, the sole purpose of reading, others, especially mid-Victorian critics, devoted a great deal of their time and energy to the study and analysis of the tales from contemporary perspectives. Thus, while Coleridge, Henley, Hunt, James Mew, and Stevenson looked upon the tales as brilliant species of romantic fiction to be enjoyed and responded to imaginatively, Walter Bagehot and others sought to furnish a systematic study of their aesthetics, making use of a mixture of realistic and classical touchstones to interpret the literary text. Although overlapping whenever the discussion leads to childhood reminiscences and sentimental recollections, there still remains a borderline separating these attitudes.

As a conspicuous strain in the nineteenth-century critical reception of the *Nights,* romantic estimates invite some detailed analysis. In classifying these estimates, I shall concentrate on the interpretation of the text as an imaginative production of unlimited prospects, making due reference to the relevant implications of the fascination with the occult and the supernatural and associating this with the broader reaction against neo-classical rules and realistic prescriptions, as well as the geometric thinking and empirical spirit of the Enlightenment. I propose, too, to examine the fascination with the *Nights* in view of such marked romantic predispositions as the faith in the immanence of God and in an organic universe, and the search for the infinite and the mysterious beyond the limitations of logic and sensory experience. As there were a number of versions available for the nineteenth-century public, it is worth asserting that whether in the Grub Street form or in the English translations of Beaumont, Scott, and Forster, Galland's redaction continued throughout the period in question to appeal to the common reader as well as to the professional romantic critic. Despite the fact that it was superseded by a number of more accurate, literary, and scholarly editions,

Galland's version went through more than sixty editions (not to mention the countless reprints of single tales and juvenile editions), and supplied the theater with an abundance of stock themes and situations. Commenting upon Jonathan Scott's Aldine edition of the tales, the *Saturday Review* for December 13, 1890 (p. 688) rightly observes, "This is the form in which the youth of many generations have been set dreaming of the wonders of the gorgeous East, and it may safely be said to have had thousands of readers where the more learned edition of Lane has had hundreds, and the too-learned text of Burton only tens." On the other hand, the *Athenaeum* (no. 3752, September 23, 1899, 413) touches upon the aesthetic appeal of Galland's version when comparing it to other editions: "... it is his glory to have been the first to bring the 'Arabian Nights' to Europe, and ... his paraphrase, with all its defects, possesses the literary quality which has commended it to many millions of readers in many tongues for two hundred years." Whereas these estimates may well testify to the popularity of Galland's version with the reading public, the personal preferences for this edition of such writers as Walter Scott, Southey, Leigh Hunt, and, later, Ruskin and Henley, attest to its inherent literary charm.[13] In his own eloquent way of heightening literary impressions in a subjective fashion, Henley communicates to the reader the tantalizing visions which enraptured him when reading Galland's "work of art." Blending with his own intimate memories and youthful experiences due to Galland's own artistry, this version became for him the "sole, unparalleled Arabian Nights": "Nay, that animating and delectable feeling I cherish ever for such enchanted commodities as gold-dust and sandal-wood and sesame and cloth of gold and black slaves with scimitars—to whom do I owe it," he asks rather rhetorically in his impressive essay (*Views and Reviews, Works,* V, 255–56) "but this rare and delightful artist?"

Aside from the fact that Henley's compressed impressionistic recollections provide one of the best examples of that thorough submersion in the intriguing world of the *Nights,* they evidently indicate the existence of some material charm brilliantly brought into focus by the French translator. To understand this aspect of Galland's version, one must see it through nonromantic perspectives, stripped of that "golden cloud of vision" and halo of fancy, which Harriet Beecher Stowe beautifully described.[14] Writing for the *Edinburgh Review* of July 1886 (CLXIV, 167), Stanley Lane-Poole touches upon the appeal of Galland's version as "the most artistic version, the best literary paraphrase of the 'Nights' that exists." After citing his objections as a scholar to Galland's omissions, the critic concludes (p. 170) that "so long as a good story book is appreciated, Galland will hold his place, and many of us who have been brought up on him will probably continue to prefer the old favourite, with all his excrescences and shortcomings, to the most scholarly and complete translation that the heart of Orientalist can conceive." With his estimable sobriety, Walter Bagehot relates the romantic appeal of this version to Galland's capacity to project his own subjective mood into the translation: "... his version conveys just about as exact an idea of the *Thousand and One Nights* as they exist for Arabian readers, as Pope's translation of Homer does of the Greek *Iliad*. But as in the case of Pope so in that of Galland, there was a *vis* in the translator himself which gave a life to his work independent of the parent from whom it sprang" *(NR, p. 45)*. John Payne, the translator of the most complete literary version, expounds on "the intrinsic value" of Galland's work, on its communication of the true romantic spirit of the Orient in a style that unites in itself "simplicity and boldness, strength and grace." Writing for the *New Quarterly Magazine* of January 1879, he contends: "Indeed, it seems to me that this first effort, imperfect as it was, to transplant into European gardens the magic flowers of oriental imagination, can never entirely be supplanted, and that other workers in the field can only hope to supplement and not to efface it."[15]

With his acute literary sense, John Payne is too wise to underestimate the romantic appeal of Galland's version. Concentrating on bare incidents, romantic machinery and on the most exquisite shades of humor and pathos, Galland provides the public with stories to which, in Joseph Jacobs' words, "Edgar Allan Poe's epithets of 'wonder and imagination' apply in their full significance."[16] In his introduction to the 1896 edition of Edward William Lane's translation (pp. xxvii–xxviii), Jacobs explains that Galland has left an abiding impression because of his subtle awareness of the enduring appeal of the romantic and adventurous portions which make up the largest body of his translation. Fair as this statement might seem to a student of critical responses, it does nevertheless overlook the fact that incidents and adventures can never attain such a dazzling impression without an effective narrative. In other words, Galland's knack for story-telling impels him to strip the tales of a considerable portion of local color and "national peculiarities" in order to enhance the overflow of narrative, a procedure which Leigh Hunt greatly appreciated ("NT," p. 111) in opposition to Lane's censure of Galland on this account. Although minimizing local color, Galland does nevertheless preserve the catalogue-like quality of Scheherazade's style. Coalescent and interrelated as the style and machinery of the *Nights* are, they help make the natural and the supernatural, the possible and the impossible, the real and the ideal shade into each other, to the extent that the reader finds himself so bewildered and enthralled that he suspends his disbelief for a moment and responds with rapture and joy to Scheherazade's enchanting story-telling. In an eloquent contribution to the *American Review* of December 1847, G.W. Peck, for instance, dwelt on this aspect, stressing how Scheherazade's blend of the real with the ideal "causes the judgement to grow weary of attempting to distinguish them," letting thereby the "most extraordinary statements . . . acquire the force of truth" (p. 612). Scheherazade "makes no prefaces conciliatory to the fancy," he further explained in the same place; "she tells her tales, in fine, with such an unconsciousness of there being any doubt of her veracity, that she gives fictions absolutely impossible, more than the effect of truth." In the first half of the century, many romanticists were drawn, too, to this consummate fusion of fact and fiction. "Everywhere," notices James Mew in his essay for *Cornhill* (p. 175), "the narrator has craftily interwoven the woof of the vague and impossible with the warp of the actual and definite. The pendulum of her narration moves to and fro between the real and ideal, unconditioned conception and clearly limited fact." These are no ordinary interventions. The divide sustained in *Preface to the Lyrical Ballads* (1802) between Coleridge and Wordsworth, the uncanny and the strange versus the common is no longer an issue here. The faring and navigation between the natural and supernatural in subject matter and style takes place effortlessly.

In terms of reception, the storyteller subtly caters to the reader's instinctive desire for wonder and longing to delve into the mysterious, as well as to one's sense of helplessness in the face of an enigmatic universe. Scheherazade's literary tools in attaining such an effect are her distinctive merits as an enchanting storyteller. By blending the natural with the supernatural, she dupes the reader into thinking that the wonderful partakes of the real and the immediate of the remote. Furthermore, her artful violation of causal sequences usually passes unnoticed in a realm of faith and hope, where Providential intervention is taken for granted as inevitable and where different criteria apply to man's relation to the outside world. According to Joseph Jacobs ("Introduction," p. xxvi), as soon as the "chain of causation is broken," we find ourselves "in a mad world . . . where there is no measure between cause and effect. A drop of honey may cause the fall of a kingdom, a discarded peach-stone may harm and rouse the wrath of the invisible potencies by which we are surrounded." Significantly, this romantic element assumes its attraction from its orientation in Muslim mythology and faith. Over this world of the *Nights,* expounds Jacobs in the same place, "broods the grim figure of Moslem Nemesis known by the name of *Kismet,* who has his earthly representative in the person of the Commander of the Faithful."

Like Peck, Jacobs appreciates and understands the *Nights* as a work of fiction thoroughly imbued with the Muslim faith in the supernatural. This appreciation involves both susceptibility to the pervading trust in the Divine Presence and acquiescence to the absence of logical constructions in the tales. In other words, a complete submersion into and enjoyment of Scheherazade's world would not be possible without some romantic predilections. Such readings fit well in and carry on the romantic movement which had already evolved, in part at least, under the impact of German transcendentalism. It is hardly too much to say that Scheherazade's organic world, where the natural and the supernatural fuse into each other, must have represented one version of the religious reality for which the romantics searched. The transcendental truths that glitter in the collection are, after all, not that different from Novalis' transcendentalism. In this connection, it is worth mentioning that Carlyle, despite his distrust of fiction, discerned in the *Nights* images of reality and remains of eternal ideas, "things that *are* in thee, though only images of things." It is this nature of the *Nights* according to Carlyle, its projection of truths beyond the reach of reason, which "still leads captive every heart."[17] While coinciding with some romantic views on God and nature, the generic characteristics of the *Nights,* especially the narrator's suspension of causation in tales of some supernatural quality, answer to Coleridge's description of purely imaginative works of art.

Whether in the *Ancient Mariner* or in the *Arabian Nights,* the dreaming mind gives way to a flowing stream of associations, unrestrained by empirical reasoning or mechanical connections, and regardless of any moral causation. Speaking of the Arabian tales in Lecture XI, Coleridge remarks that in a dream or reverie, such a throng of associations gives rise to conceptions of a supernatural agency. In the *Nights* he detects "the same activity of mind as in dreaming, that is—an exertion of the fancy in the combination and recombination of familiar objects so as to produce novel and wonderful imagery."[18] On this very same point, G.W. Peck elaborates, describing the workings of fancy in individual episodes and details. Running on "at its sweet will, precisely as it does in dreams," fancy works in Scheherazade's tales with no obvious logical plan. Instead of attracting the reader's attention to a unity in action, it at times works on a quasi-musical level. The story of Prince Ahmed, for example, "resembles an overture, where the subject, instead of passing into a related key, should go boldly from the minor of one to the major of another, somewhere below, the modulation being through the iron door." A more striking dream-like passage is the one introducing Sindbad's sixth voyage: after being shipwrecked, with the consequent death of his shipmates, he abandons himself to the current, passing through a dark vault for days, mostly sleeping. When he awakes, he finds himself in an open sunny country in the midst of a large number of "blacks." According to Peck (pp. 613–14), this change "from the suffocating obscurity of the cave to the broad daylight of such a country as Serendib, is one of the most delightful surprises ever conceived." This story substantiates Peck's interpretation of fancy as a faculty "which works not in a sustained effort, but like the water at the top of a fountain, ever rising and falling, here burst upward with a sudden irrepressible buoyancy quite out of the reach of reason."

As for the general reader's own response to such imaginative writings, a number of nineteenth-century critics follow Coleridge's own verdict. According to him, these writings, while not outraging the reader's moral sense, excite no deep emotional involvement. He contends that "these tales cause no deep feeling of a moral kind—whether of religion or love; but an impulse of motion is communicated to the mind without excitement, and this is the reason of their being so generally read and admired."[19] In this respect they are comparable to his own visionary poems, particularly the *Ancient Mariner*, despite the open obtrusion of moral sentiment at the conclusion of the latter. Answering Mrs. Barbauld's objection to the lack of moral in this poem, he argues that the poem "ought to have had no more moral than the Arabian Nights' tale of the merchant's sitting down to eat dates by the side of a well, and throwing the shells aside, and lo! a genie starts up, and says he *must* kill the aforesaid merchant, *because* one of the date shells had, it seems, put out the eye of the genie's son."[20]

As productions of pure imagination, both the *Ancient Mariner* and the *Nights* emanate from passive minds, minds in a state of dreaminess or reverie, teeming with surging associations which, while flowing unburdened by conventional causation, naturally partake of the truth of pure sentiments and feelings as in a trance or a transcendental vision. Rather than precluding this latent moral dimension in such an organic universe (which is no mere "dead brute Steam-engine," according to Carlyle), Coleridge refers not only to the absence of the common conventional practice of obtruding moralism upon action in such narratives but also to the mysterious mytho-religious scope of the tales which eludes the common search for overt moralism. In a world where there is no line of demarcation between the natural and the supernatural, and where an apparently casual act entangles its doer in a controversy with the supernatural world, different criteria are needed to estimate and comprehend its own system. What applies to the merchant ought necessarily to apply to the mariner, for, whether killing an albatross or blinding the genie's son, both disturb the moral system of an organic universe. Instead of searching for didacticism, critics must look for the real imaginative value of these tales, a value which sets them apart from contemporary novels and makes them significant in nurturing the nineteenth-century mind and in providing stimulation and solace for a large number of readers.

A study of the romantic criticism of the *Nights* would not be complete, however, without taking into account contemporary discussions of the value of imaginative literature. Coleridge's foregoing defense of such literature was addressed, after all, to Mrs. Barbauld, who, collaborating with other moralists, tried her best to "transform juvenile literature from a treasure house of fancy into a repository of useful knowledge."[21] In approaching the controversy between the advocates and enemies of this literature, it is well to remember that if the Utilitarians and Evangelicals made no secret of their hostility to imaginative writing, the romantics proved no less vigorous in exposing and ridiculing their opponents' narrow-mindedness. What concerns us most at this stage is the relevance of this controversy to our topic. Because of its sweeping popularity, the *Nights* was often cited as attesting to the indispensable aesthetic value of imaginative fiction.

From Coleridge, Thomas Keightley, and Leigh Hunt to Dickens and James Mew, there was a growing tendency to emphasize Scheherazade's power to stimulate the imaginative faculty, to educate the sensibilities, and to fit the mind "for the better prosecution of its more arduous employment," as the Select Library editor of the *Nights* asserted in his preface (pp. vi, xv). It is true that both the Benthamites and the advocates of imaginative literature valued education; but while the former group—especially the early writers of the *Westminster Review*—limited the term to "useful knowledge," the romantics meant by it "a due mixture of direct and indirect nourishment and discipline," a notion which Wordsworth unreservedly defended.[22] The popularity of the *Nights* with both sides presents an interesting case; for while people like Charles Knight popularized the work as a social treatise which was no less useful for being a story-book, the romantics recommended the tales as nourishment to the mind. Wordsworth's preference for Arabian and other romances that "are eminently useful in calling forth intellectual power" is a case in point. Writing to "a friend" in 1806 concerning the education of the latter's daughter, he distinguished between reading fairy tales and romances and the mere acquisition of book-learning. He suggested "leaving her at liberty to luxuriate in such feelings and images as will feed her mind in silent pleasure," remarking further that this nourishment, "is contained in fairy tales, romances, the best biographies and histories." It was in this same letter that he criticized education which is mainly bookish or intellectual.[23] Thomas Keightley adopted a similar point of view in his evaluation of fictional literature, whereas Coleridge considered the tales the most desirable works of art that supply the mind with "a love of the Great and the Whole," as his letters of October 9 and 16, 1797 to Thomas Poole show.[24] Dickens' own personal experience would certainly corroborate the preceding views, for the *Nights* "kept alive" his fancy and his "hope for something beyond time and space."[25] In the second half of the century, James Mew expatiated on this attraction of the tales in his article for *Cornhill* (p. 714), concluding that "no book is better calculated to awake the faculties of the mind, and to summon up that ardent admiration of the ideal which is not seldom succeeded by superior energy and a thirst for what is popularly supposed to be higher knowledge."

More than any, Leigh Hunt strove to establish a sensible attitude towards this type of writing. His well-informed review of six new editions of the *Nights,* which appeared in the *London and Westminster* (Oct. 1839), deserves special attention not only because of the writer's brilliant evaluation of different translations but also because of his deliberate introduction of the *Nights* as a case study to correct the Benthamite antipathy to imaginative writing. Published at a time when the *Westminster* itself was undergoing some positive change in its treatment of literature, Hunt's article has to be seen as an appeal for a better understanding of fiction rather than a blunt denunciation of Utilitarianism. The unprecedented vogue of the *Nights* in a highly scientific age, he argues, testifies to the everlasting human need for imaginative writing: ". . . not only is this edition [Lane's *Nights*] one of many, that have been increasing in number for the last twenty years, but within that period, which has been the most practically and stupendously scientific in the history of the world," he argued, "the love of fictitious writing has absolutely grown with its growth and strengthened with its strength, as if on purpose to spite the prophecy." With the current suspicion of imaginative writing in mind, he continued, remonstrating: "Nay, let us rather say, as though nature herself, through the medium of art, had resolved to see fair play to all the faculties of man, and to let no merely mechanical utility arise that should not be accompanied with a like amount of feeling and fancy" ("NT," pp. 102–03).

In an age running wild with its steam engines, railways, and telegraphs, Hunt's primary concern is to demonstrate to dry materialists that the popularity of the *Nights* indicates that such scientific achievements neither eliminate the human love for imaginative literature nor discredit the latent faith in the supernatural. He contends that there are things invisible and mysterious with which mechanistic and scientific reasoning cannot cope. Indeed, man himself, no matter how scientifically trained, cannot escape an overpowering awe in the face of many an enigma in the universe ("NT," p. 108). He further argues that without the power of imagination and fancy, man is deprived of a faculty as central to his being as melody is to music. To exclude imagination and romance from one's life, to remain impervious to the attractions of the *Nights,* is to overlook basic human needs. In concluding this side of his argument, Hunt remarks that reason and imagination complement each other to form one harmonious and unified sensibility: "Very modest, in truth, was the expectation of the mechanical philosophers, that they were going to put an end to all poetry and romance. Let us just look at the little which they would have had to perform" ("NT," p. 106). The current disregard for the imaginative is indicative of narrow-mindedness, for, he upheld in the same place, to take "fancy and imagination" out of the mind is as impossible as attempting to take "the blue out of the sky," "melody and harmony out of music," or "fragrance out of the flowers."[26]

Speaking especially of the *Nights* in the light of its popularity in a scientific age, Hunt remarks that the tales themselves still challenge the reader's credulity with wonderful lamps, magic carpets, and "Open Sesame" that are more thrilling than modern inventions. Thus, when compared with Scheherazade's enchantments, modern mechanical achievements still lag behind, a fact which suggests to Hunt and other advocates of romance that the genre will continue to titillate human desire for the marvelous and the extraordinary. Significantly, in his article for *Cornhill* (p. 714) James Mew echoed Hunt's argument, contending with an obvious satisfaction that the popularity of the supernatural machinery of the *Nights* testified to the fact that "Romance has not yet been immolated on the altar of Science." It was Leigh Hunt's purpose, however, to work out a harmonious reconciliation between science and romance through an adequate understanding of their attributes. Because of its rich realistic as well as imaginative properties, the *Nights* fits well into the general pattern of his argument. As the romantic machinery of the *Nights* expresses a human desire to transcend the limits of reason or sensory experience, modern scientific achievements are but a materialization of similar aspirations to account for everything and to reach out into the unknown. Like Novalis, Hunt thought of the scientific pursuit as an exploration of the invisible, the infinite, and the mysterious. By emphasizing at once Scheherazade's unsurpassed imaginative attainments and the identical evolution of scientific or fictional invention, Hunt sought to round off his thesis with the conclusion that science and romance were compatible. If the vogue of the *Nights* in a scientific age proves this much, the fact that these tales are the creation of the same nation that introduced science and learning to medieval Europe should be claimed a conclusive testimony to the same effect: ". . . what is curious," he delightfully notices, "the people to whom we owe this book, are the very same that introduced to us the chemistry that was to undo our rainbow." After quoting Sismondi to verify this explanation, Hunt concluded that "this parallel accompaniment of fiction by science, of entertainment by knowledge, and *vice versa,* has taken place in small instances as well as great, and at all periods of history" ("NT," p. 106).

But had it not been for his emphasis on the intrinsic utility of such works as the Arabian tales, Hunt's endeavor to mitigate the Benthamite hostility to imaginative literature might have failed. Basing his argument on Sismondi's discussion of the *Nights* and anticipating Dickens' appreciation of the tales in the face of Gradgrind's factualism, Hunt remarks that the *Nights* extends the world beyond the visible, ushering the reader into realms of fancy, and enabling him to expand his vision and harmoniously to develop his faculties. While quoting Sismondi directly, Hunt incorporates a comment parenthetically to enliven the discussion with the Benthamites: " ' . . .they [Arab storytellers] are the creators of that brilliant mythology of fairies and genii, which extends the bounds of the world, *multiplies the riches and strength of human nature*' (hear this, ye statists and matter-of-fact men, who propose to live 'by bread alone!') 'and which, without striking us with terror, carries us into the realms of marvels and of prodigies' (p. 105)."[27] In another place, Hunt expounds on the real value of the tales, their immediate appeal to man's need for faith and sympathy with the unknown. Here, however, Hunt's immediate concern is with the romantic quest, with the restless interest in the remote and the mysterious as well as in the commonplace and the actual: "The *Arabian Nights*," he explains *(Leigh Hunt's Literary Criticism*, p. 246), "appeal to the sympathy of mankind with the supernatural world, with the unknown and the hazardous, with the possible and the remote. It fetches out the marvellous included in our common-places." Moreover, he considers the tales central to the literary culture, which elevates one's taste and recreates one's appetite for other pursuits. Although they "may produce mounting impatience and partial neglect of duties here and there," he argued in his *London Journal* for October 22, 1834 (p. 236), they ultimately help developing "a distaste to the sordid; elevate our anger above trifles, incline us to assist intellectual advancement of all sorts, and keep a region of solitude and sweetness for us in which the mind may retreat and recreate itself, so as to return with hope and gracefulness to its labours." On the other hand, he detects in the *Nights* lessons and ideas of practical value to the West, especially regarding such concepts as justice, hope and sympathy: "This wonderful work is still better for the West than for the East," he wrote in this leading essay to his *Journal* (p. 233). He further postulated that the "utility of a work of imagination . . . must outweigh the drawbacks upon it in any country," for aside from the fact that such a work as the *Nights* "makes people go out of themselves . . . and is thus opposed to the worst kind of selfishness," it also helps "to keep . . . [people] in order" by its stories of vicissitude and natural justice. The value of the *Nights* is not limited to these two aspects, however, for its cultivation of hope, according to Hunt, "comes in aid of the progress of society."

Intent upon demonstrating the value of this work, Hunt upheld that imaginative literature cultivates generosity and tolerance: "He may safely retreat into the luxuries and rewards of the perusal of an Eastern tale," he concluded, "whom its passion for the beautiful helps to keep in heart with his species, and by whom the behaviour of its arbitrary kings is seen in all its regal absurdity, as well as its human excuses."

But whether furnishing a retreat into a tantalizing land of romance or providing moral utility and information, the *Nights* maintains a special impact upon the literary scene as Leigh Hunt's remarks evidently indicate. What is more pertinent to our purpose, however, is to see this impact in relation to the growth of the romantic strain in fictional literature. James Beattie's and Robert Heron's comments on the influence of the *Nights* on the English novel, as well as Warton's speculations on the Arabian origin of the romantic fiction have already been discussed. Nineteenth-century critics have elaborated on the nature of this influence, whether manifested in borrowed techniques or in ingenious and servile imitations. Indeed, James Mew traced the very popular practice of serialization to Scheherazade's intriguing method of stimulating and sustaining Shahriar's curiosity for a thousand and one nights: "The custom, in periodicals, of sustaining interest by happily conceived divisions of the plot," he remarks (*Cornhill*, p. 717), "may perhaps be traced to this subtle artifice of Scheherazade." On the other hand, the same critic echoes George Eliot's contention that "almost all our good things ... [including] our nursery tales and romances, have travelled to us from the East."[28] With the countless eighteenth- and nineteenth-century imitations of the *Nights* in mind, Mew adroitly explains (p. 712) that "the fertile fancy of Scheherazade has given birth to children as strange as they are strong, as multiform as they are many. She is a very widow's cruse of fiction, a grain of musk bountiful of its sweetness, without any sensible loss of weight or substance."

Significant as the foregoing comments certainly are, they, nevertheless, fail to locate the *Nights* within an obvious critical frame in the romantic tradition. It is Leigh Hunt, again, who places his "illustrious friends" in the right context, associating them with other social, political, and literary forces that helped initiate the romantic reaction against eighteenth-century "ultra-material scepticism" ("NT," pp. 103–04). Seen within this context and in its French attire, Galland's version continued to appeal to the romantic mind throughout the nineteenth century. Its popularity and literary significance gained momentum especially after the revival of the romantic strain in taste in the last decades of the century. Whether in reaction against the crass materialism and scientific spirit of the age and the proportional growth of naturalism and realism in literary culture, or as an upsurge of individualism in the face of political democracy, romance was in vogue again and its advocates waged an unceasing struggle against the realists. What is relevant here, however, is the relation of the *Nights* to this vogue as it was seen and evaluated by late nineteenth-century critics and reviewers.

Held up as a literary model in the controversy with Henry James' and W.D. Howells' school of fiction, the *Nights* provided Robert Louis Stevenson with the best testimony to the efficacy of pure romance in meeting primary human desires and longings and in titillating the common man's latent aspirations. Contending in "A Gossip on Romance" that the vogue of a genre and, ultimately, its literary significance is in proportion to its material charm of romance, he writes in *Longman's Magazine* (I, 1882–83, 74) that the *Nights*, which is "more generally loved than Shakespeare, . . . captivates in childhood, and still delights in age." This work, however, is of no "moral or . . . intellectual interest." Dwelling on Scheherazade's episodes as the main source of amusement and delight, he continues: "No human face or voice greets us among that wooden crowd of kings and genies, sorcerers and beggarmen. Adventure, on the most naked terms furnishes forth the entertainment and is found enough." At a time when the Arabian tales were "in great request" according to the *Saturday Review* of November 4, 1882 (p. 609), Stevenson's reference to the *Nights* added a considerable weight to his own defense of the merits of romance. Siding with Stevenson in emphasizing "the immortal and indestructible value of incident pure and simple, of romantic event and composition," and taking issue with Howells on the same topic, the *Saturday Review* (p. 610) sees in the very popularity of Scheherazade's tales a definite testimony to the irresistible attraction of romance which modern fiction can never supply: "The world will soon be quite weary of 'analysis,' however scientific; but of good stories it will never be tired, and the treasure of good stories is *the Arabian Nights*." The *Saturday* reviewer seems to have maintained a fairly consistent attitude towards this subject throughout the period in question. Apart from the emphasis he laid upon the appealing attraction of entertaining episodic plots in the *Nights* (LXX, December 13, 1890, 688), he subtly satirized not only the editors of the *Nights* who have attempted to turn the story-book into a sociohistorical document but also the enemies of romance who, following Howells and James, have advocated a different fictional genre. Thus, when speaking of the defects of J.H. McCarthy's edition of the *Thousand and One Days* (LXXIV, November 12, 1892, 569), he said: "At any rate the slight inaccuracies of such graceful entertainment should not be carped at, lest Mr. McCarthy, put on his mettle as an Orientalist, should translate and annotate discourses of some earnest

Persian Prophet." Such an undertaking will conversely mean filling up "with instruction the few half holidays which our Fictional Moralists still allow us."

The preceding appreciations of Scheherazade's charming incidents and romantic events are representative of a common attitude in the eighties and nineties. Indeed, when writing "About Fiction" (*Contemporary Review*, LI, February 1887, 180), Rider Haggard cites the *Nights* and *Robinson Crusoe* as the best examples of the timelessness of romance and the promising "paths and retreats of pure imagination." Agreeing with the school of romance in his literary appreciation of novel writing, and emphasizing the theme of love and absolute "abandon" as dominant in the *Nights*, Stanley Lane-Poole followed a similar line in his article on the *Nights* (*Edinburgh Review*, July 1886, pp. 193–95), regarding the supernatural machinery and the "adventures of the restless Kalif Haroun" as mere ministers of love, an explanation which implies that all action in the tales partakes of the timelessness of the theme itself as woven into the enchanting web. Answering the increasing critical demand for realism and delineation of character, Lane-Poole contended (p. 196), as Henry Lewes had already done,[29] that each genre demanded its own critical standards. In the *Nights*, for example, "all serve to fill the picture of Moslem life, but none has much personal individuality." If we look for the romantic charm of the tales, it lies in the flowing narrative rather than in characterization: "The story and not the delineation of character is the essence of the 'Arabian Nights;' and we are not sure that this is much to be regretted." Provoked by the increasing emphasis on "portraiture" and "introspection," he sarcastically intimated, "We are afraid there still remain not a few barbarous folk who will like their 'Arabian Nights,' as they like their 'Montecristo' and their 'Ivanhoe,' not the less because there is not much introspection or philosophising in them." In such works as the *Nights*, he summed up (p. 196), the reader looks rather for entertainment than for well-delineated characters: "Delineation of character is very well in its right place; but we can conceive its being a foreign element in a story book pure and simple, and we confess we do not much miss it in the 'Thousand and One Nights'."[30]

Compared to early romantic estimates, one can detect an obvious note of defensiveness in these responses. Facing the increasing contemporary emphasis on internalization, delineation of character, realistic portraiture and causal sequence, late nineteenth-century romantics were eventually obliged to defend their own preferences. The implications of this defensiveness can be better understood when seen within the context of the romantic reaction against the sweeping scientific, materialistic, and, more significantly, democratic tendency of the age. Whether driving Blunt, Doughty, and Burton to explore the hearts of remote regions, stimulating others to probe into the mysterious implications of Oriental writings, or enhancing the personal desire of some to escape into aesthetic pursuits, the socio-economic and political transformations in late Victorian England provoked a new wave of romantic reaction. As far as the *Nights* is concerned, it is enough to remark that Galland's version provided Henley (*Views and Reviews*, p. 252) with "Hachisch-made-words for life," with an abundance of incidents and an inexhaustible mine of laughter and pathos. As for Stevenson, he found in its wealth of adventures and incidents a most needed refuge from his own pressing personal problems. Writing to Professor Meiklejohn, he said: "When I suffer in mind, stories are my refuge; I take them like opium; and I consider one who writes them as a sort of doctor of mind." Contending that "it is not Shakespeare we take to when we are in a hot corner; nor certainly George Eliot—no, nor even Balzac," he stated rather emphatically, it "is Charles Reade, or Dumas, or the Arabian Nights, or the best of Walter Scott; it is stories we want, not the high poetic function which represents the world." With this inordinate passion for tales, Stevenson concluded, "We want incident, interest, action; to the devil with your philosophy."[31]

It is with similar feeling that Richard Francis Burton used to respond to the tales before undertaking the more arduous task of providing an anthropological annotation to them. Apparently, it was as an escape from gloom that he indulged in studying and translating the *Nights*. In "The Translator's Foreword" (I, vii), he explains how the undertaking "proved itself a charm, a talisman against ennui and despondency: impossible even to open the pages without a vision starting into view; without drawing a picture from the pinacothek of the brain; without reviving a host of memories and reminiscences."

Whether enjoyed as an imaginative retreat or as an escape from despondency and ennui into an imaginary Orient, the *Nights* continued to touch the daemonic strain in the romantic imagination, evoking diverse feelings of ecstasy, delight, and relaxation. But whereas the early romantics derived from Galland's version an illusion of a gorgeous but insubstantial and remote Orient to which they could imaginatively retreat and which they could recreate to suit their own predilections, projections, and visions, the late romantics no longer maintained the same attitude. In his picturesque way, Burton aptly describes in his "Terminal Essay" (p. 102) the relation between the reader and the Orient as depicted in Galland's version. Galland's tales, he upholds, "arouse strange longings and indescribable desires; their marvellous imaginativeness produces an insensible brightening of mind and an increase of fancy-power, making one dream that behind them lies the new and unseen, the strange and unexpected." After Edward William Lane's publication of his well-annotated and profusely illustrated translation in 1838–41 and the appearance of numerous researches on the sociological and ethnological aspects of the *Nights*, the latter is seen as a record of life as well as an imaginative work. The emerging image of the East, especially as it appears in Lane's notes and Harvey's illustrations, is that of a complex socio-economic reality. Hence, instead of recreating a vision of a mysterious Orient which can suit his own questing soul, the late romantic could only relate to the *Nights* as an aesthetic or literary refuge from external or personal problems, finding in its mine of story-telling comfort and solace.

But to focus only on Stevenson's and Burton's imaginative retreat to Scheherazade's realm of art involves an obvious misrepresentation of the continuous romantic strain in the English literary reception of the *Nights*. If Stevenson derived comfort from perusing the caliph's nocturnal adventures, others like Yeats treated the world of the *Nights* as a literary symbol of the erotic, the sensuous, and the mystical. Then too, others, like Duncan Black Macdonald, responded with

Figure 3.1. William Harvey: Kamar ez-Zeman disguised as an astrologer from E.W. Lane, 1839–1839 edition

Figure 3.2. William Harvey: The father of Budoor urging her to marry

affection to this land as a domain of certitude and faith, stressing the Muslim trust in the Immanence of God. Comparing the tales with Apuleius' *Golden Ass*, Macdonald postulates that "the world of the *Arabian Nights* is God's world." Despite "all his belief in magic and his sense of the power of enchanters, the Muslim is a man," explains Macdonald, for the Muslim "stands on God's earth, beneath his sky, and at any time can enter that presence and carry his wrong to the highest court. Between him and Allah," concludes the writer, "there stands nothing, and he is absolutely sure of Allah."[32]

Such perspectives might have been impertinent, however, had they not been consistent with a late nineteenth-century tendency to regard the *Nights* as a work of art, purely imaginative and immensely enjoyable as such. Its very attraction to the romantic mind lay in its evocation of the illusion of reality without challenging the reader's inherited preferences and beliefs. In reaction against Lane's realistic and heavily Orientalized approach to the *Nights*, a keen interest in Galland's work developed in the last decades of the century. John Payne, himself a pioneering translator of the works of a number of French aesthetes, took the trouble to translate the whole work in 1882–84 as a production "of purely literary or fictional character," whereas Henley went back to Galland's version because it alone

SUPPOSING ME ASLEEP, THEY BEGAN TO TALK
(Page 155)

Figure 3.3. Dulac: The ensorcelled king feigned sleep, MS 67

could supply him with "a vast extravaganza of passion in action and picarooning farce and material splendour run mad."[33] At the close of the century, Duncan Black Macdonald wrote about the *Nights* as a story-book rather than as a social document. Disapproving of Lane's annotated translation which turned the *Nights* into a treatise on sociology, Macdonald remarks, "To the non-Arabist their [the tales] world is out of space, out of time; a land of enchantment whose like has never existed, never can exist."[34] After comparing and contrasting Galland's and Lane's versions, Macdonald concludes that Galland preserves the illusion of a gorgeous Orient, transporting his readers into a dream-like land, an experience which "an apparatus of commentary" will surely destroy. A person who "reads, and dreams, and wanders in lands of mystery beyond the mountain of Kaf," argues Macdonald in the same place, "has no need of learned crutches." Thus, whether referring to the *Nights* as a gateway to a desirable religious reality or as an imaginative recreation of agreeable illusions, Macdonald viewed Galland's version as the most appealing. Published at the turn of the century, his estimates may well represent the zenith of nineteenth-century romantic criticism of Scheherazade's tales.

Notes

1 "New Arabian Tales," *Foreign Quarterly Review*, XIV (Dec. 1834), 350. For author-ship see the *Wellesley Index*, II, no. 336.

2 *Arabian Nights' Entertainments* (London: James Burns, 1847), I, ii.

3 Cited by John O. Hayden, ed., *Scott: The Critical Heritage* (London: Routledge & Kegan Paul, 1970), p. 69.

4 *Ibid.*, p. 171.

5 *History of Prose Fiction*. Revised by Henry Wilson (London: George Bell, 1888), II, 507.

6 *Ibid.*, p. 508.

7 *Historical View of the Literature of the South of Europe*, trans. Thomas Roscoe, with Notes and a Life of the Author (3rd ed.; Henry G. Bohn, 1850), I, 62–63.

8 Thomas Keightley, *Tales and Popular Fictions, Their Resemblance and Transmission from Country to Country* (London: Whittaker, 1834), p. 33. For Coleridge's expla-nation of Scheherazade's appeal, see Lecture XI, pp. 193–94 in Raysor's *Coleridge's Miscellaneous Criticism*; and for his view of contemporary fiction as "injurious to the growth of the imagination, the judgement, and the morals." p. 195.

9 A review of "Dunlop's History of Fiction," *Quarterly Review*, XIII (July 1815), 385. Further references to this article will be cited with page number in the text. In identifying the authorship, I am indebted to Walter Graham, *Tory Criticism in The Quarterly Review, 1809–1853* (New York: Columbia Univ. Press, 1921), p. 46; and Hill and Helen Chadwick Shine, *Quarterly Review Under Gifford: Identifications of Contributors, 1809–1824* (Chapel Hill: Univ. of North Carolina Press, 1949), p. 48.

10 See, for example, Thackeray's *Journal from Cornhill to Cairo* in *Works* (Kensington ed.,New York: Scribner's Sons, 1904), XXI, 327; and Henley's "Arabian Nights . . ..," in *Views and Reviews, Works*, I, 254.

11 Richard Hole's view of Galland's translation is in *Remarks* . . ., pp. 9–10, 220–21. As for the notes in the *Gentleman's Magazine*, see LXVIII (Apr. & Sept. 1798), 304–05, 757–58; LXIX (Jan. 1799), 55; and LXIX (Feb. 1799), 91–92.

12 See "Introduction," I, xvii.

13 For Scott, Southey, and Ruskin, see "Dedicatory Epistle" to *Ivanhoe* (ed. W.M. Parker, Everyman's, 1965, pp. 17–18); *Complete Poetical Works* (New York: Appleton, 1856), Bk. I, p. 232 (notes to *Thalaba*); and "The Golden Water" in *Works*, XXXV, 639, respectively.

14 "Introduction," to *A Library of Famous Fiction Embracing the Nine Standard Master-pieces of Imaginative Literature* (New York: Ford & Co., 1873), p. viii.

15 "The Thousand and One Nights," Pt. i, II (Jan. 1879), 154. Attributed to Payne by W.A. Clouston, *Arabian Poetry for English Readers* (Glasgow: Privately printed, 1881), p. 364. This two-part article was reprinted in the ninth volume of Payne's edition of the *Nights* (1882–1884).

16 "Introduction" to the *Thousand and One Nights; or Arabian Nights' Entertainments*. Translated by Edward William Lane (London: Gibbings, 1896), I, xxvii.

17 See "Corn Law Rhymes," *Critical and Miscellaneous Essays, Works* (New York: Collier, 1897), XV1, 304; "Varnhagen Von Ense's Memoirs," XVI, 173; and "Count Cagliostro," XV, 487.

18 *Coleridge's Miscellaneous Criticism*, p. 193.

19 *Ibid.*, pp. 193–94.

20 *Ibid.*, p. 405 ("Table-Talk" of May 31, 1830).

21 Altick, p. 138, n. 22.

22 *Memoirs. . .*, by Christopher Wordsworth, ed. Henry Reed. 2 vols. (Boston, MA: Ticknor, 1851), II, 178.

23 Letter of Dec. 16, 1845 to S. Tremenheere in *Letters, the Later Years*, Vol. III, ed. E. De Selincourt (Oxford: Clarendon, 1939), 1269; the *Middle Years*, I (1937), 104, respectively.

24 For Keightley, see *Tales and Popular Fictions*, p. 33; as for Coleridge, references are to *Letters*, I, 12, 16.

25 *Life of Charles Dickens*, by John Forster. 2 vols. (London: Chapman & Hall, 1904), I, 9–10.

26 American critics, too, used the same argument in their protests against the utilitarian disregard for fiction. See, for example, E.G. Langdon, "The Origin of the Arabian Nights' Entertainments," Pt. V., the *Literary World*, III (May 13, 1848), 286. In identifying the authorship, I am indebted to Dorothee Metlitsky Finkelstein, *Melville's Orienda* (1961; rpt. New York: Octagon, 1971), p. 36, n. 20.

27 Quotations are from Thomas Roscoe's translation of *Historical View . . .*, I, 63. Italics are Hunt's.

28 A review of the *Shaving of Shagpat, Leader*, VII (Jan. 5, 1856). Cited in Ioan Williams, *Meredith: The Critical Heritage*, p. 40.

29 See, for example, his essay on "Shirley," *Edinburgh Review*, XII (Jan. 1850), 166. This same sober-mindedness can be traced in his own estimate of the *Nights* in a review of Meredith's *Shagpat* in the *Saturday Review*, I (Jan. 19, 1856), cited in Ioan Williams' *Meredith: The Critical Heritage*, 43–45.

30 Against this interpretation Richard Burton protests: "He [Poole] thus ignores all the lofty morale of the work, its marvellous pathos and humour, its tender sentiment and fine touches of portraiture, the personal individuality and the nice discrimination between the manifold heroes and heroines which combine to make it a book for all time" ("The Biography of the Book and Its Reviewers Reviewed," *Supplemental Nights*, VI, 350).

31 "Letter of Feb. 1, 1880," *Letters*, ed. Sidney Colvin, 4 vols. (New York: Scribner's Sons, 1911), I, 322.

32 *Religious Attitude and Life in Islam*. Being the Haskell Lectures on Comparative Religion, delivered before the University of Chicago in 1906 (Chicago, IL: Univ. of Chicago Press, 1909), pp. 138–39.

33 References to Payne and Henley are to "The Thousand and One Nights," Pt. II, p. 400; and "The Arabian Nights Entertainments," *Views and Reviews*, p. 249, respectively.

34 "On Translating the 'Arabian Nights'," Pt. II, 71 (Sept. 6, 1900), 185.

4

Lane and the Victorian Literary Scene

There was another; not quite so bad at first; but still a trying shop; where children's books were sold ... and there the mighty talisman, the rare Arabian Nights; with Cassim Baba, divided by four, like the ghost of a dreadful sum, hanging up, all gory, in the robbers' cave. Which matchless wonders, coming fast on Mr. Pinch's mind, did so rub up and chafe that wonderful lamp within him, that when he turned his face towards the busy street, a crowd of phantoms waited on his pleasure, and he lived again, with new delight, the happy days before the Pecksniff era.

Dickens, *Martin Chuzzlewit*, Chap. V

While the preceding discussion of romantic responses centers on Galland's version of the *Nights,* the more impersonal and scholarly approach to the study of the tales is closely associated with the publication of Edward William Lane's translation. In evaluating the differences between these translations and the nature of their vogue, Stanley Lane-Poole stipulates in his article on the *Nights* (*Edinburgh Review*, p. 192) that it was Lane "who first brought out the importance of the 'Arabian Nights' as constituting a picture of Moslem life and manners." Previously, the tales were treated as "romantic fictions." He further adds that "in the present day those who have been educated upon the English version after Galland would probably say that the tales consisted mainly of impossible adventures with genies and afrits, and such like supernatural elements." Although valid as far as popular responses are concerned, Stanley Lane-Poole's sweeping conclusion reveals the pitfalls of generalizations of this kind. He obviously takes into consideration some late eighteenth- and early nineteenth-century demands for a more accurate and annotated translation; but, nevertheless, he overlooks the fact that in the light of the dearth of information on the Orient, Galland's *Nights* was regarded by many as providing revealing insights into the life and manners of Eastern people. Indeed, such an industrious scholar as Henry Weber went so far as to assert in 1812 (*Tales of the East*, "Introduction," p. ii) that, as records of Eastern life and manners, "the value of these tales has been less disputed, particularly since the authenticity and *vraisemblance* of the portraits they convey has been established by the authority of some of the most faithful and best informed travellers in the East." Twelve years later, James Morier wrote in his "Introductory Epistle" to *Adventures of Hajji Baba* (Bentley's 1851 edition, p. vi), "of all the books which have ever been published on the subject, the Arabian Nights' Entertainments give the truest picture of the Orientals."

Insubstantial as those travelers' and writers' accounts and impressions might seem to such a learned scholar as Stanley Lane-Poole, they still represent one reading of Galland's tales which a scholar of his fame is not expected to ignore. Aside from this exception, we can agree with the general drift of Poole's argument; but it is proper to recognize at the same time that Galland's minimization of national peculiarities and his considerable concentration on romantic machinery and enchantments stamp on his version, in Walter Bagehot's words, "an ineffaceable character of uselessness," an omission which mid-Victorian critics are hardly expected to forgive despite their appreciation of Galland's knack for story-telling. Bagehot himself sums up this attitude in his discourse on Galland's version; for while it "sacrificed nothing of the liveliness and spirit of its original," its purpose was "neither to throw light on history, morals, nor manners; but to be read and to be found good reading" (p. 45).

Not all Victorian critics, however, maintained Walter Bagehot's robust and discriminating critical sense; neither did they all attempt to analyze the *Nights* from a detached perspective. The *Eclectic* reviewer (n. ser. VIII, 1840, 645), for example, looks upon Galland's version as worthless and undeservedly popular. Comparing this version with Lane's, the reviewer remarks that although "the old version ... has long been the delight of Europe, ... it must now inevitably yield to this vigorous successor." Denouncing it as unreadable and useless, he haughtily remonstrates: "Indeed, we may be allowed to express our surprise that it could ever have become so popular. We are free to confess that until Mr. Lane's translation was put into our hands, we never could get through more than a few of the 'Thousand and One Nights'." As "an injudicious exhibition of the substance of oriental fictions in a European dress," Galland's version, according to the reviewer, lacks "the peculiarities of the oriental style . . . [which] give the work an appearance of *naturalness*." The *Eclectic* reviewer's attitude may well manifest the non-romantic response to the *Nights*. While Leigh Hunt's preference for Galland in no way blinds him to the merits of Lane's edition, the *Eclectic* reviewer denies Galland's version even the liveliness which Bagehot has readily acknowledged. The purpose of this comparison, however, is not to scorn this lack of enthusiasm for the romantic properties of the tales, but to focus on a response that is at variance with the romantic reception of the *Nights*.

Appreciating the tales for the very qualities which Galland minimized in his version, the reviewer certainly agrees with Lane's criticism of Southey and others for assuming that Galland improved upon the original. The same reviewer also joins Lane in setting the tone not only for John Payne's and Stanley Lane-Poole's description of that version as "a fraud" but also for James Mew's sarcastic remarks upon Galland's *delicatesse et bienseance*.[1] To the former, too, the "period of 'make-believe' is gone by, and Jinne and Efreets have no power to cheat him [the adult reader] into a pleasing terror" (p. 657). Hence, rather than looking for mere romantic properties which the scientific age seems to discredit, the reviewer is interested in stylistic "peculiarities" and "naturalness," aspects which surely correspond to the increasing emphasis on exactitude, probability, and verisimilitude in novel criticism and writing. In preserving these qualities, Lane's edition must unavoidably be seen within the developing realistic tradition in English literature, a tradition which Richard Stang surveys in view of the writings of the period under discussion, and which lead him to see realism as the most fruitful mid- nineteenth century artistic movement. [2]

Although the call for an accurate and annotated translation was voiced by a number of critics at the close of the eighteenth and beginning of the nineteenth century, no effort other than Torrens' incomplete translation (1838) was made to reproduce the original after Lane's fashion. Corresponding to the growing realistic strain in writing under the impact of science and political democracy and the emphasis on reticence in literature, Lane's version gained wide recognition in mid-Victorian England not only as a drawing-room book but also as the best entertaining documentary record of what was perceived then as the medieval Arab society. Leaving out every objectionable passage and framing each story within a coherent socio-religious system by the use of heavy annotations, Lane catered to the prevalent taste as the following sections will indicate. Indeed, the immediate relevance of Lane's edition to the Victorian literary scene will become quite obvious when closely considered in relation to contemporary critical preoccupations with propriety, moral utility, and verisimilitude.

To understand Lane's reasons for expurgating his edition of the *Nights,* we should take into account the nature of his undertaking as well as the developing prudery of the middle-class reading public. Lane approached the *Nights* as tales originally recited for the entertainment of the vulgar, maintaining thereby an attitude which was identical with that of the nineteenth-century educated Arab who still looked down upon such stories as fitting only for the ignorant mind.[3] Meant for the entertainment of the populace, some stories revel in picturesque descriptions of the domestic, especially the sexual, life of the upper classes. Without going into psychological and sociological explanations for this notorious tendency among story-tellers, it is quite relevant to mention that Arab historians usually look down upon such narratives as insipid and unworthy of their attention. Appreciating the *Nights* mainly for its value as a repository of information, and considering details of "objectionable nature" incompatible with the purity of the Arab, Lane deleted such licentious scenes as the one in the story of the porter and three ladies of Baghdad, which he described as giving "a very erroneous idea of the manners of Arab *ladies*."[4]

Furthermore, Lane's omission of objectionable details must be seen in relation to the increasing squeamishness of the middle classes. As periodical responses indicate, Lane's family edition met a growing demand for a version that would comply with contemporary delicacy. In 1839 B.E. Pote wrote for the *Foreign Quarterly Review* (pp. 157–58) on this point, stating that the tales "now contain nothing that can deter the purest or the most fastidious from perusal." For him, as for many others, Lane's edition "is a public service, not national only because universal, from the universality of the tales." He further affirms that "when it is considered how influential they have been . . ., the effect of this purity upon every class of readers will be easily imagined." It is worth noting, too, that although Bagehot felt that Lane had been "a good deal hampered in his object by the exigency of making a drawing-room book, and adapting the Arab to the English tests of propriety" (p. 45), he nevertheless acknowledged the necessity of weeding the book "of all that can offend the fastidiousness of modern taste in respectable writings" (p. 64). Even Leigh Hunt, despite all his criticism of Lane's exaggerated propriety, agreed that the porter and his "fair trio" are "startling personages for the meridian of London" ("NT," p. 128). Of some relevance, too, is Stanley Lane-Poole's comment. Answering late Victorian criticism of his uncle's prudery, Lane-Poole states in his article for the *Edinburgh Review* (p. 171) that the translator's objective was to provide the "general public of both sexes" with a version which, while comprising the "best in the original," contains nothing that is "absolutely inadmissable among such an audience." We can probably fully understand Lane's circumstances when we become acquainted with writings calling for more excision. Indeed the *Eclectic Review* (p. 650) contends that "we should not have objected to a still further use in some cases of the liberty he has so rationally asserted."

No less pertinent is the fact that before the publication in the eighties of the "unexpurgated" translations of both Burton and John Payne, editors had followed Lane in conforming to the Victorian sense of propriety. Fyler Townsend, for instance, went so far as to bowdlerize Scott's retention of Galland's tales so that "the most innocently-minded maiden may read them aloud to her brothers and sisters without scruples or compunction."[5] Commenting upon this, the *Athenaeum* for October 28, 1865 (no. 1983, 573) shrewdly remarks that this version "has been 'expurgated' for better or worse." Paradoxically, in 1840 Hattersley defended Galland not for his artistry as other critics had been doing, but for his conformity to polite manners and delicate taste. In his article on the *Nights* (*Dublin Review*, February 1840, p. 113), Hattersley explained that prurient scenes would not fail to harm the impressionable reader, a problem from which they were saved in England because reticence was preserved in due respect for the delicate sex. In the face of the mounting demand for a complete version, Hattersley found Galland's selection justifiable on moral grounds; for the "eastern *raconteur* does not tell his tales either for boys or virgins; at least, if he did, neither class of his auditors would be benefited by his narrations." As such, much "picking of steps is necessary in making way through these otherwise delightful fictions; and many a story have we met with in manuscript collections, which no alteration or suppression could render fit to appear in print at all." After citing his own objections to "the character and circumstances of the people of the East" where men are "of violent passions" and where "*women* are not generally able to read," he complacently rounded off his thesis with a reference to the English woman: "We are, perhaps, but little aware of the salutary influence which the silent and passive censorship of the more delicate sex exercises over our literature." While capitalizing on traditional misrepresentations in order to justify conformity to Victorian moral idealism, Hattersley regarded bowdlerization as an inevitable procedure which no writer was expected to overlook.

Beyond this preoccupation with entertaining moralism and reticence in literature, Victorian critics were quite concerned with useful knowledge. As we have already seen, even such a romantic as Leigh Hunt tried to establish the utility of Galland's *Arabian Nights* in an age that appreciated books for their practical value.

In the late forties, the editor for the Select Library ("Preface," p. v) explained how the tales would present two sources of utility for the interested reader. Their very machinery, dramatic narrative, and social portraits convey a great deal of implicit instruction, whereas such tales as "Blind Man, Baba Abdalla" and the "Envious Sisters" overtly inform, teach, and edify. This classification is worth considering in the light of the growing taste for utility and didacticism, for while the early romantics were admittedly less interested in the last type,[6] Lane's generation developed a marked interest in the manners and customs of the East. It is of some historical and literary significance, to be sure, that such a popularizer of "useful knowledge" as Charles Knight was quite satisfied with Lane's edition, remarking with obvious contentment in *Passages of My Working Life* (London: Bradbury, 1864; II, 258) that "no other 'Arabian Nights' would meet the wants of those who really desired to understand Oriental customs and forms of speech," and that it "was worthy of the admiration of educated persons."

Since the appearance of Galland's emasculated edition there had been published numerous comments to substantiate its social context. But no matter how many essays and prefaces were written to corroborate or consolidate the image of the Orient depicted in that version, there was no edition other than Lane's that claimed to bring about a representation of the East in its complexity and perceived reality before the English public. This is at least what the *Athenaeum* for October 1838 (no. 572, 739), and the *Dublin Review* for February 1840 (VIII, 127), and the *Eclectic Review* for 1840 (n. ser. VIII, 650) unanimously agreed on. What may concern us at this point is the fact that Lane's very semi-scriptural style, which startled Hunt in the humorous passages ("NT," p. 112), appealed to a society accustomed to reading the Bible. By imitating the stylistic peculiarities of the Arabic language, Lane produced a readily accepted version on account of its stylistic resemblance to the Old Testament in the Authorised version. Indeed, the *Athenaeum* for October 13, 1838 (no. 572, 739) was the first to notice this appeal, remarking with obvious delight that Lane "adopted a phraseology which might appear antiquated or uncouth to any but Englishmen, trained as we are from childhood to read the Scriptures, themselves a close translation." It should not be surprising, therefore, that the *Eclectic Review* (p. 650) recommended the *Nights* to Biblical students as a book from which they would derive "a much clearer notion of oriental manners, customs, and scenery than from the most judicious books of travels ever written." E.G. Langdon, on the other hand, concluded his lengthy essay in the *Literary World* for May 13, 1848 (III, 286) with a remark which probably occurred to him because of this very stylistic quality of Lane's *Nights:* ". . . we may well be proud of a work which gave the first impetus to the mind of Dr. Adam Clarke, and to whose early attachment to which, we are primarily indebted for the most valuable Biblical commentary in existence."

While meeting contemporary critical demands for propriety and informativeness, Lane's edition catered, too, to the increasing taste for realism. By providing historical and sociological annotations to every tale, fixing the whole into a well-defined frame, and by relating incidents and anecdotes to their historical and social context, Lane supplies a substantial picture of what he lived or got associated with during his sojourn in Cairo. Thus, he relegates   the romantic machinery to a secondary place in the whole pattern of the tales. Understanding and evaluating the *Nights* accordingly, Lane maintains a realistic perspective which sharply contrasts with the romantic picture of the Orient. In correcting Leigh Hunt's view of the real value of the *Nights,* he remarks in the "Review" appended to the third volume of his translation (p. 686), ". . . its value consists in the fulness and fidelity with which it describes the character, manners, and customs of the Arabs, though its *enchantment* is doubtless mainly owing to other qualities." Rather than looking upon Scheherazade's machinery as an expression of man's desire to delve into the mysterious, Lane related this to a socio-religious context into which such supernatural agents as fairies and genii mean and assume definite propensities and roles: ". . . the most extravagant relations in this work are not in general regarded, even by the educated classes of the Arab people, as of an incredible nature," he wrote in the preface to his edition (I, xiv). To acquaint his reader with the circumstances attending the composition of the tales, he added, "I have resided in a land where genii are still firmly believed to obey the summons of the magician or the owner of a talisman, and to act in occurrences of every day." He expounds further that he had listened "to stories of their deeds related as facts by persons of the highest respectability, and by some who would not condescend to read the tales of *The Thousand and One Nights,* merely because they are fictions, and not written in the usual polished style of literary compositions."

Lane's attempt to give every detail an illusion of reality and a touch of plausibility cannot be seen apart from the contemporary taste for probability and verisimilitude. It is significant that the *Athenaeum* for September 25, 1841, concluded that the vogue of romance was almost over because it was "at variance with the spirit of the age. The nineteenth century is distinguished by a craving for the positive and the real—it is essentially an age of analysis and criticism."[7] Sometime earlier (October 13, 1838; no. 572, 739), this same journal praised Lane for "giving, in a series of illustrative notes appended to the several chapters, a faithful, and, as it were, living picture of the East," and for letting us "so fully into the privacy of domestic life among the Arabs." But the *Athenaeum* critic was not alone in commending Lane's realism. Hattersley, in the *Dublin Review* of February 1840 (p. 127), dwelt on Harvey's illustrations to this edition of the *Nights*. In his view, such illustrations "all but place the reality bodily before us, with a vividness and distinctness which all description in the world could never reach."

That Edward William Lane's edition does actually provide a picture of a substantial and complex reality is well indicated in three distinct patterns of response which will become obvious in due course. After the publication of his edition (1838–41), the romantic metaphor of a dream-like and mysterious East became no longer tenable, giving place instead to a "living picture" of a well-defined society, as Hattersley quite legitimately concluded (p. 127). As it is no longer possible either to confuse the world of the *Nights* with the real East or to maintain the same old romantic image in the face of this living reality, English fiction writers and critics had begun to distinguish between a 'real' East and the aesthetic retreats of the *Arabian Nights*. Thus, in an address to "Workmen and Labourers of Great Britain" (*Fors, Works*, XXVIII, 736), Ruskin draws upon the romantic machinery of the *Nights* to substantiate his distinction between the realistic and the factual on the one hand, and the imaginative and the fanciful on the other. Treating the tales as fictional, he argues that as long as they are comprehended as such they will entertain without overpowering the reader's mind. Dickens' own attitude furnishes a better example; for rather than confusing the *Nights* with a 'real' East, Dickens viewed Scheherazade's tales as fictional pictures of an exuberant and, for that matter, desirable life. Hence, upon waking from a fever to find the Marchioness sitting quietly in a neatly arranged room, Richard Swiveller's unsettled mind cannot distinguish between reality and fiction. His thorough acquaintance with the *Nights* leads him to believe that he has been caught up in Scheherazade's world of inexplicable and intriguing adventures:

> *"I'm dreaming," thought Richard, "that's clear . . . ."*

> *"It's an Arabian Night; that's what it* is," *said Richard.*

> *"I'm in Damascus or Grand Cairo. The Marchioness* is *a Genie and having had a wager with another Genie about who is the handsomest young man alive, and the worthiest to be the husband of the Princess of China, has brought me away, room and all, to compare us together." (Old Curiosity Shop, chap. 64)*

In *Vittoria* Meredith refers to Scheherazade's stories as mere "fancies" which his heroine must not confuse with reality. She has to check, therefore, such illusions "drawn from the *Arabian Tales* concerning the help of genies and enchanted birds, impressions so vivid that she feared her brain was losing its hold on things."[8]

In the *Shaving of Shagpat,* too, Meredith was more interested in imitating Eastern story-telling than in evoking a romantic picture of the Orient, a fact which did not escape the attention of such an acute critic as George Eliot. Reviewing Meredith's *Shaving of Shagpat* for the *Leader* of January 1856, George Eliot explains that the author proves capable of mastering Scheherazade's techniques, producing thereby a work that betrays no "incongruity between the thought and the form."[9] Such was George Henry Lewes' opinion as well. After indicating that *Shagpat* is more Eastern than Goethe's *Divan* and "less directly imitative than Ruckert's Oriental poems," he points out that Meredith "has thoroughly caught the spirit of Arabian romance, and pleasantly tinges his style with the colour and imagery of Arabian eloquence."[10] No less representative of relevant critical responses is the *Athenaeum* review of the same work for its issue of January 5, 1856 (no. 1471, pp. 6–7). Commending the author for his power of imagination and skill in construction, the reviewer stresses Meredith's pioneering handling of Oriental matter and technique. Rather than following other pseudo-Orientalists, Meredith filled "near four hundred pages with incidents, scenery, personages, customs, and language, all Arabian, without tripping."

No less significant in indicating the literary response to pseudo- Orientalism in mid-Victorian England is George Meredith's own criticism of Oehlenschläger's *Aladdin* in the *Westminster* of 1858 (LXIX, n. ser. XIII, 292).[11] In this article, one can detect the increasing awareness of the complex reality of the East, an awareness which provoked Meredith to warn poets "against the adoption of an Oriental model, or an Eastern theme, when they are peculiarly labouring under personal emotion." Unlike the early nineteenth-century superficial concern with local color and detail to recreate a romantic image of the Orient that allows them enough freedom to project their own preoccupations and aspirations, Meredith's emphasis on thorough absorption of Arab modes of feeling and thought obviously partakes of the mid-Victorian preoccupation with verisimilitude. According to him, a subjective rendering of the East distorts rather than recreates the Orient, not only because it outrages the sense of association but also because in such renderings writers "bring an alien element to bear upon the golden East with which it will never assimilate. They may amass heaps of imagery and paint the desert in vivid colors, but they will never themselves be taken for Arabs. The East teems with passion, sentiment, poetry, and humour, but these qualities are all entirely of a different texture from ours." Indeed, Meredith adds that to evoke the image of the Orient as it is made available after the publication of Lane's edition implies that a writer "must not only look on, his imagination must live in, the desert and the Arabian mind." Not many writers "can do it," he upholds, "because few have sufficient strength of sympathy and imagination combined to cast themselves loose from the West, and start freely; and moreover it requires a subtle dramatic and a mimetic power not common." Corroborating his argument with examples, Meredith cites besides Oehlenschläger a few other well-known writers. While "Göthe succeeded," Rückert was less fortunate. Both Freiligrath and Tom Moore failed, for they only "conjured up pretty pictures, one with fire, and one with tinsel." Taking issue with Moore in his *Lalla Rookh,* Meredith contends that while "industry enabled him [Moore] to get together vast hoards of costume," this poet "lacked the genius to give his stories more than artificial life." Hence, *Lalla Rookh* is rich only with a colorful detail which is "rendered sickly at times by clap-trap side-appeals to purely Western sentiments," for "Moore had not full faith in the East."

Apart from this literary awareness of the diversity and depth of Arab life and character, one can trace another response which is closely related to the critical reader's view of the purpose of reading. A romanticist reads the *Nights* to be absorbed in its realms of enchantment and to revel in its details, deriving his final enjoyment from the demands made upon his fancy to fuse incidents and scenes into one rich and vivid impression. Peck's elaborate discussion of this mode of reading contains some interesting insights. "Where the narrative is tediously minute," he elucidates in the *American Review* for December 1847 (p. 612), "the memory is bewildered and will not retain the impression of such a multiplicity." In pursuing Scheherazade's detailed description, the fancy is then "compelled to supply its place," by "instantly collecting, like a kaleidoscope, a heap of scattered particles into one symmetrical whole." He substantiates his argument by references to such paragraphs as the ones describing the presents of the King of Serendib to the Caliph. In reading these "at the usual rate and with the mind intent upon the progress of the story . . . the particulars of them are not so clearly before the mind, a moment after, as the richness of the whole." Referring to the preceding example, Peck maintains that such particulars and details "are at once fused in the alembic of the fancy into a single impression of a gift worthy of that powerful and magnificent monarch."

While this description of the process of responding to the tales beautifully sums up the nature of the romantic interest in Scheherazade's enchanting chambers, typical Victorian comments indicate a different attitude, an attitude of readers who had neither the time to linger long in the lands of fancy nor the poetic frame of mind to enjoy such moments of exquisite delight. In catering to the spirit of the age, Lane supplies the reader not only with a store of useful information but also with a large collection of illustrations which is meant to release the reader's fancy from the very demands which Peck describes. In a typical discussion of Harvey's illustrations, the *Eclectic* reviewer divides readers into children who derive pleasure from wonderful events in proportion to their truancy and limited experience, and adults who, while no longer enjoying preternatural machinery, derive pleasure from the scenes and pictures raised up in their minds when reading the tales: "His [the adult reader's] delight is to be found in other ways, and very principally in the pictures suggested by the narratives," the reviewer remarks (p. 658). Referring to some of Scheherazade's detailed descriptions as examples, he further explains that this reader "must be able to see mountains piled above the clouds, and the awful gloom of the valleys among which the Evil Jinns may be expected to become visible to mortal eyes." As the reader's pleasure is proportional to his ability to store these scenes in mind and to combine them into pictures, the critic concludes in the same place that such a process involves too much pressure upon the reader's mind. By supplying illustrations that reveal a thorough understanding of the text and consummate fidelity to natural scenery and manners, Harvey has not only spared the adult reader this tremendous demand on his fancy but also "superseded the efforts of the reader to portray for himself, even when he might have imagined something nearer to the description of the author."

This reasoning seems to have been taken for granted by other contemporaries. Writing for the *Foreign Quarterly Review* (XXIV, 1839, 157) about the same point, B.E. Pote described Harvey's illustrations as "appearing absolutely as the very dreams of the reader's own imagination spontaneously wrought into shape, and phantastically weaving them adown the margin as he reads the tale, that it is difficult to imagine a more pleasing or more perfect delusion than the graceful forms into which the pencil is running, constantly giving to unformed and embryo conception, the force and finish of reality." By supplanting the evocative power of the *Nights* through a determined effort to document and illustrate every detail, Lane and Harvey produced a book that was bound to fit into the dominating realistic trend. Indeed, soon after this domestication of the *Nights,* the Dalziel brothers as well as Arthur Boyd Houghton and other artists even embarked on providing Galland's version with illustrations that were meant to give a realistic touch to the whole. Writing about Houghton, Lawrence Housman remarks that "Houghton's illustrations [for the *Nights*] will supply humor or pathos or character-drawing, which the story itself has quite failed to convey. In his hands Aladdin's mother becomes a character of delicious comedy."[12] To conclude this discussion of the remarkable interest in illustrating the *Nights,* one must say that it indicates a tendency to enhance the vogue of the tales by re-establishing them within the dominant current of realism.

The preceding response is closely linked with the emerging realistic and neo-classical strain in mid-Victorian criticism of the tales. But although largely in keeping with the growing taste for verisimilitude and the reaction against subjectivism in writing, this new strain developed mainly in response to Lane's own version. In its scholarly and dignified garb, this edition was different enough to provoke some critics to break away from an age-old sentimental attachment to the *Nights* as a dear story-book associated with childhood and recalled with affection and melting emotion. Nevertheless, Scheherazade's passionate admirers never felt the desire to terminate this attachment. Thus, such romanticists as Dickens, Hunt, Henley, and Stevenson, to mention only a few, continued throughout their lives to read and recollect scenes from the *Nights*. In the face of the widespread obsession with factualism, writers like Keightley and W.C. Taylor expressed more than once a longing for such reminiscences to dispel "the dark and cloudy hours of life," despite their recognition that the "days are gone when . . . [they] gave full credence to the marvels of Alladin's lamp and ring."[13] Others who, like Bagehot, had been ardent readers of the *Nights* in youth and to whom the tales were then not "so much a story as a dream" found the return to them in maturity "a melancholy task" (*NR*, 46). In attempting to go back to Galland, Bagehot realized that the tales were no longer capable of delighting the mature reader's mind, not only because the scientific spirit of the age tended to discredit that world of aspirations and enchantments but also because "the years of discretion" put an end to egotism and ambition (*NR*, 47). With a note of resignation, Bagehot sums up his attitude as follows: "If we look at them with pleasure, it is mostly through a vista of old remembrances: we enjoy the revival of faded sensations rather than the excitement of new ones. The thing itself has lost the charm which once held us enchained" (*NR*, 46). The scenes which "used to strike us with awe" and the "startling" incidents, continues Bagehot, have lost their "power of producing an effect." But to "see things as they were to us," he suggests that "we must turn back in imagination to the gates of life, and recall the freshness of our youth."

To recognize the gap which separates the mature reader from his youthful impressions does not necessarily entail a use of the analytic faculty to criticize the *Nights* objectively. Indeed, to maintain critical detachment in order to see beneath Scheherazade's tantalizing narrative was not an easy task for Victorian critics. Retaining a considerable amount of emotional attachment to Galland's version which they had perused in youth, they found it extremely difficult to escape the impact of that "intellectual 'hasheesh'" which Walter Bagehot considered "an

Figure 4.1. Thomas Dalziel: Bedreddin Hassan and the pastry cook

Figure 4.2. Thomas Dalziel: The genie brings the hatchet and cord

Figure 4.3. Houghton: The old gardener and Gamaraalzaman

Figure 4.4. The African magician offers new lamps for old (Houghton's illustration, L. Houseman's *Arthur Boyd Houghton,* 1896, no. 36)

Figure 4.5. Houghton: The fisherman drawing his net

Figure 4.6. Houghton: Three blind men watched by a thief

intoxicating stimulant to that early imagination" (*NR*, 47). It was to their relief that Edward William Lane issued a new and annotated translation of the original which they could study and analyze. "As it is impossible," writes Walter Bagehot, "to revive the old feelings in their old force, it is pleasant, if we wish to re-peruse the Eastern stories, to have them in a form like that given to them by Mr. Lane; sufficiently different to leave our minds tolerably free from old distractions, and faithful enough to give play to a new set of interests" (*NR*, 47).

Instead of mere reveling in Scheherazade's enchanted chambers, Walter Bagehot and his contemporaries now attempted to focus on the aesthetic and sociological significance of the tales. "We ask ourselves," he remarks, "what intrinsic value they have as literary productions, and what sort of information they afford as to the people among whom and for whom they were written" (*NR*, 47). As we have already seen, the call for studying the tales as a social document was not new at the time of Bagehot's writing, neither was the interest in their aesthetic merits. What was new, however, was the attempt on the part of Victorian essayists and critics either to exercise a catholic spirit in studying foreign literature or to outgrow their early attachment to the tales in order to apply specific criteria to the work, as in Bagehot's case. Both attitudes are identical in purpose, and both have yielded some interesting results. But as I intend to reserve for the next chapter the discussion of the Victorian response to Islamic culture, I shall devote the remaining pages to mid-Victorian criticism of the tales, focusing on Bagehot's insights into their socio-literary context.

What makes Bagehot's study of the *Nights* especially significant is not only its author's fair acquaintance with the generic characteristics of some tales but also his method of treatment and analysis. As will become clear in due course, Bagehot applies a combination of classical, Elizabethan, and realistic criteria to evaluate a composite work which not only resists clear-cut categorizations but also requires different evaluative standards. Although not primarily elucidating Scheherazade's aesthetics, Bagehot's "People of the Arabian Nights" reveals a great deal about mid-Victorian critical preoccupations and represents, therefore, a literary attitude that notably varies from the romantic reception. Throughout this essay, Bagehot is highly prescriptive. He judges the *Nights* by such aesthetic touchstones that were held dearly by Victorian Neoclassicists, like the tragic contemplation of death, the response to reversals of fortune, the conflict between will and circumstance, the latent discontent of the Western mind, the active sense of free will in Western literature, and the minimization of chance and coincidence in writings emanating from a society believing in self-originating action and suffering. The whole argument is fixed into a contemporary frame of thought, which very strongly partakes of the realistic as well as the skeptical spirit of mid-Victorian England.

The writer develops two lines of argument regarding the narrator's style and the fanciful web of the tales. Like Peck, he recognizes the catalogue-like quality of the narrative, but what seems to him particularly characteristic is that "the whole style of the narrator is rather in keeping with his quietness and indolence" (*NR,* 70), revealing a disposition at variance with the narrative art in the West. Instead of skipping from one incident to another or omitting details of no particular bearing upon the event, the Eastern story-teller leads the reader to "travel over all the intermediate ground, and sometimes at a very slow pace," so that by the end the reader will be overwhelmed by an enormous variety of incident. Seen in the light of English literary conventions, the *Nights,* he believes, shows different narrative habits and techniques. While an "English novelist tells you that his hero called on a lady, and goes on to what passed at the interview," the Arabian story-teller "would tell you how he knocked at the door and rang; how it was opened to him by a servant clad in black apparel; how he entered, and having taken off his hat, ascended the stairs and was ushered in" (*NR,* 70). This differentiating schema is not a passing whim, or a personal perspective. It shows Bagehot's suave method of applying the *new* philologist dichotomous discourse that downplays a so-called East in relation to an empowered and empowering West.

When appraising the machinery of the *Nights,* Bagehot is of two minds about the implications involved in a writing that displays quickness, versatility, and superficiality rather than depth and strong firmness of grasp, which he assigns categorically to a West. He would obviously agree with Peck's discussion of the interrelated functions of style and fancy in such compositions as the *Nights,* but instead of wholeheartedly appreciating this characteristic, Bagehot disapproves of Scheherazade's elaborate descriptions and imaginative flights. He admires, for example, the story-teller's handling of the supernatural element, a handling in which he detects an unshaken faith combined with "an extraordinary reach of fancy" (*NR,* 69). Like Hunt ("NT," pp. 114–22), Bagehot finds Lane's rendering of such scenes as the Efreet's snoring, Sidi Numan's experience with the Ghoul and the emergence of the "Jinn" from the unsealed bottle, very impressive and unrivalled in "picturesqueness of effect" (*NR,* 69). What he criticizes, however, is "the tendency to run into extravagance," for "mere accumulation defeats its end, and crushes the centre point of faith around which fancy builds" (*NR,* 69). Citing scenes from the "Story of the City of Brass" to document his thesis, Bagehot analyzes these from a perspective entirely different from that of the romanticists in general and of Peck in particular. Unlike the latter, he is interested in writings that accord with his classical concept of proper composition. Hence, rather than merely responding to Scheherazade's descriptions, Bagehot's analytical mind looks for unified structural patterns that will excite without confusing the sober mind, concluding that "accounts of the fights of millions of Jinns, of armies of wild-beasts and crowds of devils, only weary us, and we are overwhelmed rather than excited by some of the descriptions of impossible wealth and magnificence" (*NR*, 70).

Bagehot's preceding objection to "this too common defect" (*NR*, 69) should be seen, however, in relation to his total view of the texture of the tales. It was his contention that the story-teller's handling of machinery and detail was informed by some basic socio-religious practices and beliefs. As such, he studied Arabian fictional modes as manifestations of "the Eastern disposition" (p.70), for "imaginative growths are the expression of fundamental social distinctions" (p. 49). Thus, in order to acquaint ourselves with the implications of his literary estimate, we need to consider at some length his analysis of the impact of the medieval Muslim milieu on human behavior as reflected in the *Nights,* for it is this primary consideration which tells quite plainly on Bagehot's critique of the aesthetic aspects of the tales. In response to Lane's restorative annotation, his monopoly over the tales, Bagehot treats the tales as documents. The confusion between the storytellers' practice and a medieval Islamic milieu is problematic. However, this is not the case for the mid-Victorians. Furthermore, we should recognize the limitations of his approach. His realistic predilection drove him, for instance, to focus on some tales of *urban* origin, excluding as a result a number of stories that had fascinated the romantics. On the other hand, his classical bent of mind led him to overlook the existence of a brilliant gallery of rogues and knaves who had been especially admired by such critics as Dunlop and James Mew.

Along with these considerations, Bagehot's study of the *Nights* will make more sense when set in its immediate literary context. It is well to remember, after all, that three years earlier W.C. Roscoe's significant contribution to the study of fiction appeared in Bagehot's *National Review*. In that essay on Defoe, Roscoe associates the growth of the novel as a genre with the development of political democracy, for the expansion of personal liberties involves a simultaneous recognition of the importance and value of the individual, a fact which is displayed at its best in the corresponding emphasis on internal characterization in fiction. With this same idea in mind, Bagehot evaluates the *Nights* in the light of medieval Muslim social conditions, concluding that the story-teller's lack of interest in character-drawing only manifests the corresponding absence of strong individualism in medieval Islam. In that milieu the state and religion impose a certain uniformity and sameness on the whole society. Bred up in strict social and religious observances from infancy and trained to conform to a number of obligations and ordinances, the individual melts into the community without feeling the slightest desire for dissent. These laws and obligations, explains Bagehot, "become as spontaneous as his digestion, and no more encumber him than do his flowing robes compared to the Transatlantic swallow-tail and trousers." Qualifying this statement, he mentions that a Muslim may have "far more play for personal peculiarities, or even eccentricities than perhaps most Europeans." But below this, he forcibly postulates, "lies a mass of entirely unstirred common life—beliefs never questioned and responsibilities never lifted" (*NR*, 56). This line of thought cannot be seen apart from Ernest Renan's discriminatory perspective, which was popular among Victorians. Although Bagehot does not resort to the latter's racist classifications, his categorization of an East in view of storytelling ends up with similar conclusions. Thus, he lays the blame for sameness in a collection of tales taken as document on Islam. He suggests there are other reasons for social fusion and general uniformity: "The possession of a theology and religion whose main dogmas and principles admit of no question, standing immovable upon a book which is not the record of a revelation, but itself the revelation." Aside from this socio-religious side, Bagehot stresses the despotic nature of medieval political systems. According to his reading of the *Nights,* this "political system . . . opens a minimum of play for the faculties, [and] in which genius and industry are no stepping stones to advancement, and incapacity and negligence no bar to favour" (*NR*, 55). Being mainly concerned with establishing the differences between Eastern and Western modes of writing, Bagehot conceivably associates such differences with corresponding social and political diversities. In case a reader of a controversial mind will attempt to challenge this thesis by adopting Mill's line of argument against public opinion to conclude that political democracy is no less stifling than Eastern social fusion, the writer furnishes a definite answer to this adverse criticism. Referring to Mill's distrust of a public opinion that limits man's tendency to expand by imposing tyrannical restraints upon private action, Bagehot contends that "Americanization," while an evil, is preferable to the Eastern tendency to absorb the private will: "In America public opinion crushes and constrains, in Egypt it absorbs. Both are bad, but the latter far more deep-reaching an evil. The one is but a chain, the other an opiate. The one chafes men most in small things, and leaves essentials free; the other gives ease in externals, and preys upon the vital forces" (*NR*, 56).

According to Bagehot's own reasoning, the preceding socio-religious conditions exert a destructive impact on literature. Taken and treated as social records, the Arabian tales show no interest in dissent or heroic action, a propensity to which he also relates the absence of well-delineated characters. To explain the social implications of this literary practice, Bagehot draws on the story-teller's stock devices to substantiate his thesis regarding the interrelatedness between literature and society. He contends that the *dramatis personae* exercise no trial of self-restraint because of the absolute faith in Providence and the conformity to social and religious teachings. Moreover, they demonstrate no penchant for working out their own fortunes in a society where the modes of gaining wealth rest upon uncertain mercantile adventures, unpredictable royal gifts, precarious acquisition, and sudden discoveries of hidden supernatural treasures. As these are the most prominent aspects of the adventurous pursuits related in the *Nights,* Bagehot considers their romantic uncertainty—which by the way, titillates Hunt's imagination ("NT," p. 135)—another reason for the individual's passivity and indifference. Taken together, all the foregoing factors are responsible for the narrator's lack of interest in character-drawing. In line with this reasoning, Bagehot finds that Eastern and Western perspectives are incompatible. He argues, for instance, that in Western fiction the person involved usually exerts a substantial effort to shape incidents and to attain a goal, whereas the hero in an Eastern tale has no "motive power," for he is a shadowy figure whose accomplishments help him little in this world: "All that is required of a hero is to accept with expressions of reliance on Providence whatever may be done for him. No trial of self-restraint is required greater than that of not pronouncing the name of Allah when borne near heaven by an evil spirit, or of not opening an interdicted door" (*NR*, 53–54). It is certainly to the credit of storytellers whom Bagehot treats as historians and sociologists that their celebrated tales of more than nine centuries ago invited such a powerful writer like Walter Bagehot to compare them to the flourishing European fiction in the age of empires.

Unacquainted with other Arabic writings and limited in scope by his self-imposed prescriptive and regulative criteria, Bagehot was bound to reach incongruous conclusions. His view of social fusion and reliance on God led him to contend that the medieval socio-religious system stifled the creative faculty and drained the imagination. Compared with some classical and English writings, Scheherazade's tales appeared to him as a product of fancy rather than imagination. While the latter is usually stirred by the deeper realities of life and a vigorous search for truths, fancy flirts with the surface of things: "Imagination will always be found exhausting the matter in hand; fancy roving and selecting over a wide range. The one plucks the heart out of a mystery, the other makes captive every flying grace" (*NR*, 48). Distinguishing further between the two, he explains, "In little space the one lays bare the secrets of all hearts, and claims not only the deepest but the most universal sympathies; the other dilates upon trifles, and makes playthings of the feelings and ideas of men." To substantiate this contrast, he draws the reader's attention to classical writings. "Read Homer. How deeply the story lies founded in the characteristics of a few individuals!" Bagehot exclaims. "It is not the tale of Troy, it is the wrath of Achilles, that is sung. It is not what befell men, but what certain men did and were, that forms the matter upon which imagination works." The last distinction is central to Bagehot's whole argument, for what he considers especially cogent in imaginative writing is human action rather than narrated incidents and adventures that satisfy the romantic mind. In English history and literature, he detects this consistent awareness of heroic action and its consequences in an "inter-tangled play of will and circumstance" (*NR*, 49). Overlooking the very city origin of the tales, he applies criteria that have been in vogue since Matthew Arnold's advocacy of classical critical standards in the 1853 "Preface." The implications involved in Bagehot's previous distinction lead him to develop a system of differences between the typical Eastern tale and the highest form of Western imaginative fiction, relating to such topics as human life and death, tragedy and pathos, and reversals of fortune. He contends that as a profound concern with human action indicates a proportional sense of life and death and an active awareness of the individual's commitment, the absence of such concern in the Arabian tale suggests a genre inferior to the best forms of imaginative fiction. For rather than showing an attachment to the profound realities of life, the Arabian story-teller glosses over death as no more than "an element or a break in adventure" (*NR*, 49). Although well-placed in mid-Victorian literary analysis, Bagehot's essay makes the wrong choice in selecting medieval Arabic-Islamic tales that were popular with readers in the East and in Europe, and applied to them neo-classicist critical standards with a tinge of realism that was a dominating trend among his contemporary literati. On the other hand, his analysis runs counter to the other contending trend of romantic fiction that was espoused by a substantial segment of his early and late contemporaries, including G.L. Stevenson.

Inseparable from the emphasis on human action and the sense of responsible commitment in classical and Elizabethan writings (which are Bagehot's main points of reference) is the focus on man's personal mode of reaction to the vicissitudes of external fortune. "But in the Eastern stories," he remarks, "you are never asked to sympathise with the man, but always with what happens to him" (*NR*,

50). On the other hand, these vicissitudes of fortune assume different aspects and consequences in Western imaginative literature. In the latter, such reversals may emanate, among other things, from the hero's personal discontent and introspectiveness, or from any tragic flaw which he cannot ultimately control. But in these Eastern stories of urban life, riches and a beautiful wife "are assumed as the certain and unfailing constituents of human felicity" (*NR*, 50). Conversely, the loss of such possessions entails misery and suffering. Dwelling on the reasons behind this attitude, Bagehot, nevertheless, quite rightly explains that in medieval Arab society, riches assume this importance not only because of their practical value but also because of the possibility of their being taken from their owner whenever whimsical rulers decide to do so. As such, there is a romantic uncertainty about riches which makes property a recurrent theme in tales of *urban* life.

What Bagehot considers a serious omission, however, is the narrator's "coldness and *insouciance*" when reciting incidents of anguish or suffering; for rather than focusing on the sufferer's reaction, the story-teller dwells upon the event itself, mentioning as a set-off a neighbor's readiness to help the protagonist out of some miserable situation. Bagehot's criticism is not limited to this omission on the part of the narrator, for he feels that the tales as a whole demonstrate no sensitive awareness of delicate emotions. Provoked by Lane's—and by implication Hunt's ("NT," pp. 122–23) and Peck's (p. 611)—assertion that pathos forms the special excellence of Scheherazade's art of story-telling, Bagehot contends that elements of tenderness or suffering in this art must not be confused with pathos. Even the story of Shems-en-Nahar seems to him "a tale of passion rather than of pathos, and the whole handling inspires a European mind, at least, with the impression that it is an extravagant picture of the weakness of indulged passion" (*NR*, 51). While informative with respect to mid-Victorian criticism, this line of analysis collapses a traditional storytelling that happened to take Europe by surprise and challenge its literary canons, with a strong novelistic growth that distinguished the literary scene in France and England.

No wonder Bagehot lays emphasis on characters. What he takes as omissions indicate that the display of character in prosperity or adversity is never the direct object of these tales.Bagehot regards this lack of interest in human action as the cardinal point of difference between English fiction and the *Nights,* a difference around which all other social and imaginative distinctions gather to form independent and, as such, incompatible genres: "English fiction is like paintings of persons, the *Arabian Nights* like landscapes with figures introduced," he states rather emphatically, affirming that in these Eastern tales there "is no such thing . . . as a sustained interest developed out of individual character or influence," for "men and women are woven like embroidery into the tissue of the story, they are a sort of puppets whereby strange occurrences can be represented" (*NR*, 49).

Notwithstanding his attempt at comprehensiveness, Bagehot overlooked some significant issues of direct bearing upon his subject. Foremost among these is the thematic and technical diversity of Scheherazade's tales which cannot be easily gauged by some regulative criteria. Thus, although indicating the growing mid-Victorian bias in favor of realistic and classical modes, Bagehot's method threw little light on the socio-literary context of the tales. The discrepancy between his method and the nature of the *Nights* led to a number of false conclusions regarding the meaning of the tales and the relevance of their social context. Begehot knew that these Arabian fictions "are simply part of the light literature of a people of active, bright, and, in some respects, highly cultivated intellect" (*NR*, 48), but he nevertheless tended to overlook the nature of this "light literature," confusing thereby the popular with the more introspective and critical mind. Being prescriptive, he overlooked, too, the generic characteristics which distinguish the Egyptian tale from the Baghdadian, and the conventional love story from the one of urban life. Furthermore, he could not fully account for such stories of ingenuity and perseverance as those of Sindbad and Ali Baba's slave, nor could he justify the considerable intellectual ferment to which many tales eloquently testify. In fact, Bagehot's misunderstanding of the Muslim reliance on God's munificence led him to cite only the examples that would square with his thesis. Eventually, he glossed over many topics that needed elucidation. Although he ardently believed in the impact of social modes on imaginative writing, he, for instance, provided no explanation for the absence of empirical causation in the *Nights,* neither did he solve the implications of the seeming passivity and unconcern with life and death in Arabian fiction. The inadequacy of Bagehot's evaluative standards will become obvious when set beside other nineteenth-century perspectives. Peck, for instance, used an analogic method similar to that of Bagehot, comparing Scheherazade's *dramatis personae* to those of Shakespeare. But rather than overlooking the social background of each type, he found the former consistent with urban life.

After admiring the story-teller's characterization of Haroun, he observed that Shakespeare's Kings "are a different style of men, and some of them, Lear and Hamlet for example, were placed in more trying circumstances than he [Haroun] had to encounter," for the latter's reign, he continued, "appears to have passed so placidly that he had little to do after business hours but to enjoy himself going about Baghdad incog., and picking up adventures" (p. 605).

To understand the reasons behind Bagehot's dissatisfaction with Scheherazade's aesthetics, we must examine the applicability of his criteria to the Arabian tale as an independent genre. Basing his critical discussion on the prominence of figural representation and human action in Western imaginative literature, Bagehot was bound to overlook the very core of medieval Muslim thought, the belief in God's absolute sovereignty. To dwell upon death or to paint human figures implies a blasphemous interference with God's omnipotence, an interference the mere imputation of which no pious Muslim would like to bear. From the same perspective as well, life is looked upon as enigma, designed by and known only to the Creator. Thus, to simplify life in fiction within some prescriptive conventions and to impose human values on God's creation mean a breach of faith. Although at times impatient with his own beliefs, the story-teller was always on his guard, commencing and concluding each tale with fervent invocations of God's compassion and guidance lest the devil should lure him away from such religious commitments. A careful consideration of medieval Muslim art and writing will tell a great deal about their suggestive and symbolic dimensions. Within the scope of the present discussion, it is worth mentioning that the medieval Arab artist developed an outlet for his creative impulse in the shape of the most intricate and symmetrical Arabesques that human ingenuity ever attained. What applies to figural representation in painting applies with equal force to delineation of characters in fiction. As a result, the story-teller developed after the same fashion a labyrinthine narrative of fascinating events and wonderful incidents, a pattern which was not entirely lost upon English critics. Although not well-acquainted with these religious implications, early nineteenth-century critics, for instance, were aware of the aesthetic dimensions of Arab story-telling. Thus, in an essay on "Eastern Story-Tellers" one reads in the *London Magazine* of May 1828 (XX, 186) that the "Arab begins every tale as far back as ever it is possible." Instead of "hurrying the auditor into the middle of the scene," the narrator attempts to "lead him about through two or three halls of entrance, so that he remains for a long time uncertain of where the true approach to the scene of the tale will be."[14] Moreover, to dwell upon daily human occurrences as man's reaction to vicissitudes of fortune is inconceivable, not only because of the frequency of such happenings which makes them too common a theme to captivate the auditor's interest but also because resignation to God's will implies the acceptance of Providential justice. No less interesting to students of literary criticism is the disparity between the Arabian story-teller's own unshaken trust in Providence and the general mid-Victorian attitude towards coincidence in fiction. With the growing prestige of realism and scientific determinism, and with the corresponding spread of skepticism, critics began to assert the importance of sequential causation and logical mechanism that leave no place for coincidence as signalizing divine intervention. Conversely, in the basically religious background of the *Nights,* the ardent belief in Providential intervention entails that chance and coincidence are no less motivational and effective than the most logical connections in a well-constructed novel.

Although betraying an obvious classical bias and arbitrary application of dramatic critical tenets to fiction in general and the Arabian tale in particular, Bagehot's essay does contain favorable estimates of some literary aspects of the tales. Like many eighteenth- and nineteenth-century critics, Bagehot states some exceptions to his generalization concerning the lack of well-drawn characters in the *Nights.* For him, such comic characters as the loquacious barber are among the best-sustained in these tales, revealing "a sprightly and genial way of handling subjects of jest which could only have arisen among a people with a taste for wit and fun, and glad to take occasion for mirth and laughter" (*NR,* 60). More to Bagehot's taste, however, are the characters of the caliph Haroun al-Rashid and his gracious minister Ja'far. In a very intelligent survey of the caliph's deeds and actions (*NR,* 61–62), Bagehot discerns those conflicting desires and unpredictable moods which make Haroun al-Rashid such a great romantic figure. Based upon his thorough reading of Haroun's cycle as well as upon Lane's copious notes, Bagehot's penetrating account of the caliph's character stands among the most significant contributions to the study of characterization in the *Nights.* It has obviously influenced all subsequent analyses of al-Rashid's character including John Payne's brilliant, but not necessarily right, psychological study of the reasons behind the caliph's nocturnal adventures.[15] Aside from this interest in the caliph's personality as revealed in the *Nights,* Bagehot holds this well-drawn character in high esteem for reasons closely related to his own classical taste for unity of construction. Endowed with tremendous powers and heroic attributes, and combining "the immunities of royalty with the freedom of private intercourse" (*NR,* 62), Haroun al-Rashid gives unity to action and imposes a meaningful design on the whole: "The presence of this defined and imposing character, wielding irresponsible power and commanding unlimited resources … this stately, magnificent centrepiece," he affirms, "gives a certain unity and substance to this collection of tales, which even with its aid they too much want: for this book is, in many respects, a jumbled gathering" (*NR,* 63).

Regardless of its exclusive concern with some tales of city origin, Bagehot's study still occupies an important place in the critical reception of the *Nights.* By focusing on what seems incompatible with the classical standards of composition,

Bagehot carries further Richard Hole's brilliant contrast between the Grecian temple and the Oriental mosque, an architectural analogy which he draws to sum up the patterns of similarity and variance between the classical and Oriental modes of composition.[16] But the merit of Bagehot's study is not limited to his sober development of such a late eighteenth-century approach, for his main contribution lies in his attempt to dissociate the tales from romantic sentimentalism, provoking thereby further considerations of Scheherazade's artistry and social portraits.

Seen in relation to Edward William Lane's pioneering contribution to the study of the *Nights,* Bagehot's article is the most thoughtful literary estimate of the tales, taken by mid-Victorians as a record of social and cultural customs and manners. In asserting the interrelatedness between imaginative forms of writing and socio-cultural contexts, he surely helps consolidate a prominent eighteenth- and nineteenth-century tendency to appreciate the tales as a rich storehouse of information on Eastern life at a time when the societies for useful knowledge proliferated. On the other hand, in minimizing the significance of events and in depreciating the interest in vicissitudes of external fortune, he overlooks the appeal of the tales to the romantic mind. As a matter of fact, Bagehot associates the romantic mind with boyhood, for both the romanticist and the schoolboy derive enjoyment from "their facile power of self-identification with the subject of the adventures" (*NR*, 50). In concentrating upon reversals of fortune without exploring the sufferer's deep responses, the tales, he thinks, "excite the fancy and the intellect rather than the emotions" (*NR*, 51). Bagehot's essay was written in 1859, in the same year Leigh Hunt died. Had he been asked to comment on Bagehot's association of this appeal of the *Nights* with the schoolboy's mind, he would probably have referred to his essay in the *London and Westminster Review* of October 1839. In that essay (p. 104), he ridiculed eighteenth-century neo-classicists who made similar associations, unaware of the "superior instinct of wisdom in the childish nature." Bagehot's personal wish to outgrow his early sentimental attachment to the tales clearly drove him to underestimate the very romantic attributes which fascinated him in youth, as they still fascinate many a romantic soul.

But in evaluating such diverse responses, it is well to remember that most of these display varying patterns of relation and reaction to individual translations. By its romantic nature Galland's version evoked responses that were different from the ones stimulated by Lane's annotated edition. On the other hand, although the *Nights* again became a story-book in Payne's hands (1882–84), his own medieval predilections turned the tales into chivalric romances written in a style which, in Macdonald's words, partakes of the "richness and strangeness of Wardour Street furniture and of medieval tapestries."[17] Following the same pattern of relation and reaction to translations and apparently attracted by this medieval atmosphere, the Reverend Cameron Mann wrote a comparative study of "Morte D'Arthure" and the *Thousand and One Nights* to the disadvantage of the latter.[18] The same pattern may apply as well to literary appraisals of Burton's edition. Impressed by Burton's emphasis on character-drawing in the *Nights,* J.F. Hewitt finds the tales shining with unfading luster in their dramatic presentation of characters. When comparing the Arabian story-teller with modern dramatic novelists, he considers the former no less successful in "making the characters draw their own likenesses and those of their surroundings in their conversation, actions, and their consequences," a statement which clearly contradicts Bagehot's as well as Stevenson's and Stanley Lane-Poole's contentions.[19]

Apart from those patterns of response, there has been developing a consistent attempt to search for the general truths and universal themes that have made and still make the tales so appealing to man's imagination. Besides the topics which Leigh Hunt has already considered, John Eagles sheds some light on the permanent attraction of the tales.[20] In "A few words about Novels—a Dialogue" (p. 472), the writer contends that those who cannot appreciate these tales "must be very scantily gifted with a conciliating imagination, though they may very possibly be the most reasonable of human beings." Anticipating some late nineteenth-century discussions of the perennial charm of the tales, the writer argues that the "charm that renders the *Arabian Nights* acceptable in all countries" arises from the vivid touches "which speak of our common nature." Apart from the "great use made of the obscure," there "is here and there, too, a sprinkling of simpletonianism in a foreign shape, showing that all nations have something akin." This universalization of the *Nights,* its cosmopolitan power that makes it popular everywhere, sets another track that would gain momentum in the next few decades.

But no matter what literary approaches were developed throughout the century, and whether emphasizing the sociological, the romantic, or the universal merits of the tales, the mere endeavor to study the *Nights* at length and to apply to this study all the available contemporary critical tools should be seen as another testimony to its tremendous popularity with readers and critics. Considered in relation to nineteenth-century critical currents, the *Nights* has evoked from a large number of critics and writers responses that deal with significant issues in literary criticism and constitute thereby a significant chapter in the history of nineteenth-century critical thought. In concluding this study of literary estimates, one feels inclined to go back to Bagehot, who, despite all his classical preferences, ends his own article with remarking "that no small attribute of admiration is due to the genius of the unknown enchanter, whose magic influence has exercised its charm upon so countless a multitude of readers" (*NR*, 71).

Notes

1 For the comments of Lane-Poole, Mew, and John Payne on Galland's omissions, see "Arabian Nights," *Edinburgh Review*, p. 168; "Arabian Nights," *Cornhill*, pp. 718–19; and "The Thousand and One Nights," Pt. 1, *New Q. Magazine* (Jan. 1879), pp. 152–53, respectively.

2 Richard Stang, *Theory of the Novel in England 1850–1870* (London: Routledge & Kegan Paul, 1959), p. 139.

3 It is needless to stress that the stylistic vulgarity and coarseness of the tales account for a great deal of this disregard. In his remarks "On the Origin of the 'Arabian Nights'," *Asiatic Journal* (July 1829), p. 560, Baron De Sacy explains that the *Nights* enjoyed no "distinguished station in the literature of the East," and that it was "unfit ... owing to its style, to be classed amongst the models of eloquence and of correct taste." Numerous references to the fact that the *Nights* never occupied a distinguished place in Arabic literature appeared in nineteenth-century writings. See, for example, the *Athenaeum* (no. 572, Oct. 13, 1838, 739); Burton's reference to Al-Nadim's comment in "The Terminal Essay," p. 71, and to nineteenth-century Egyptian attempts to remodel the tales, p. 147. See also, Payne, "The Thousand ...," Pt. II, p. 381; Stanley Lane-Poole, "The Arabian Nights," p. 185; and Anna Leach, "The Real 'Arabian Nights'," *Cosmopolitan*, XXVI (Mar. 1899), 483. Significantly, Lane reported with approval Shaykh Abd-E-Rahman El-Jabartee's attempt to rewrite the *Nights*. According to Lane, that native Egyptian was "so delighted in their [the tales] perusal that he took the trouble of refining the language of a copy of them which he possessed, expunging or altering whatever grossly offensive to morality without the somewhat redeeming quality of wit, and adding many facetiae of his own, and of other literati" (*Thousand and One Nights*, ed. Edward Stanley Poole [London: Bickers, 1877], I, chap. 1, n. 18, 66). Inseparable from this Arab objection to coarseness is the emphasis on instructiveness and utility. For many among the erudite, the *Nights* is a wasting-time book. Nothing is more relevant to our purpose, perhaps, than the comment which appeared in *Al-Muqtataf* (Cairo), 10 (July 1, 1888), 648, in which an Egyptian asked the Jesuits to publish something useful in medicine or other fields instead of editing such a work as the *Nights*.

4 *Thousand and One Nights*, ed. Edward Stanley Poole (n. 22 to chap. 3, vol. I, 193).

5 *Arabian Nights' Entertainments*. A New Edition, Revised with Notes by the Rev. Fyler Townsend (London: Frederick Warne & Co., 1866), "Preface," p. v. This

same edition was reissued in 1869 (Chando's Classics), 1874, 1887 (Warne), 1891 (New York: Frederick A. Stokes), and in 1892 (Routledge).

6 See, for instance, Hunt's comment on the moralistic stories in his "New Series . . .," *New Monthly Magazine*, pp. 338–39.

7 Cited by Richard Stang, p. 146.

8 *Works* (Memorial Ed.; New York: Scribner's Sons, 1909–12), VII, 281.

9 Cited by Ioan Williams in *Meredith: The Critical Heritage*, p. 47.

10 *Ibid.*, p. 43.

11 For authorship, see Gordon S. Haight, "George Meredith and the 'Westminster Review'," *Modern Language Review*, LIII (Jan. 1958), 13.

12 "Introductory Essay," *Arthur Boyd Houghton: A Selection of His Work* (London: Kegan Paul, 1896), p. 24. It is of some significance, to be sure, that Harvey's illustrations were appended to Routledge's 1854 reprint of Galland; see Chauvin, IV, 75. The following illustrated editions of Galland's version are worth citing: *Dalziels' Illustrated Arabian Nights' Entertainments*, with upwards of two hundred illustrations by eminent artists (Ward & Lock, 1863–65); *Arabian Nights' Entertainments*, with one hundred and fifty original illustrations drawn by Thomas B. Dalziel (Routledge, 1877); another edition with upwards of one hundred illustrations on wood drawn by S.J. Groves (1865, 2 vols. Edinburgh: Nimmo; reprinted in 1866 and 1868); Dick's edition with numerous illustrations by Frederick Gilbert (1868); Tegg's illustrated *Arabian Nights* (1869); and the People's Edition of the *Arabian Nights' Entertainments*, illustrated by J.E. Millais, J. Tenniel, J.D. Watson (London: Ward & Lock, 1882).

13 For Keightley and Taylor, see *Tales and Popular Fictions*, p. 33; and "New Arabian Tales," p. 350, respectively.

14 Notwithstanding the casual reference to Von Hammer which was meant to give a shade of originality to this material, the *London Magazine* article was bodily taken from the German critic's "Arabian Poetry, especially the Romance of Antar" which had already appeared in the *New Monthly Magazine* (Jan. and Apr. 1820), Pt. I, esp. pp. 16–18.

15 For Payne's essay, see "The Thousand and One Nights," *New Quarterly Magazine* (Jan. 1879), p. 162.

16 For Hole, see *Remarks*, pp. 17–18.

17 See "On Translating the Arabian Nights,"—I, the *Nation*, 71 (Aug. 30, 1900), 168.

18 "'The Thousand and One Nights' and the 'Morte D'Arthur'," *North American Review*, 184 (Jan. 18, 1907) pp. 150–56.

19 For Burton's view, see his "Terminal Essay," X, 130, 131, 138, 139, 167. Hewitt's "History as Told in the Arabian Nights," appeared in *Westminster Review*, CXLIII, No. 3 (1895), 254.

20 *Blackwood's Edinburgh Magazine*, LXIV (Oct. 1848), 472–73. For authorship, see the *Wellesley Index*, I, no. 2796.

5

A Panorama of Eastern Life

Viewed as a tout ensemble in full and complete form, they [the tales] are a drama of
Eastern life, and a Dance of Death made sublime by faith and the highest emotions, by
the certainty of expiation and the fulness of atoning equity, where virtue is victorious,
vice is vanquished and the ways of Allah are justified to man. They are a panorama
which remains kenspeckle upon the mental retina.

Burton's "Terminal Essay," p. 139.

In order to evaluate the critical efforts to penetrate the contextual implications
of the Arabian tales and to reconstruct their socio-cultural and moral environ-
ment, we have to be familiar not only with the basic patterns of the sociological
criticism of the *Nights* and the relation of this criticism to the English milieu
but also with the nineteenth-century translators' perspectives and methods of
redaction and annotation. Because of its very composite nature, the *Nights* passed
through different processes of domestication and adaptation, displaying in its
English garments each redactor's view of things and the cultural outlook of his
period. On the other hand, considered as an epitome of Muslim life since its first
appearance in Galland's garbled translation, the *Nights* has evoked numerous
reactions which largely, although not exclusively, fall within the dominant cultural trends of the time and correspond to some prevailing impressions of Islam

and the Arabs throughout the eighteenth and early nineteenth centuries. But no matter how numerous these discourses on the socio-religious content of the tales are, they either fall short of providing a comprehensive assessment of the shifting panorama of Eastern life or partake of some traditional misrepresentations of the Muslim faith. Indeed, mid-Victorian critics were neither sanguine about the impact of these writings on the English mind nor sure that the existing travelers' accounts had ever "penetrated beyond the mere outward shell and husk of the Oriental character."[1] Torn between conventional distortion of Islam and the dearth of profound studies on Arabic culture, critics found themselves unable to go beyond the surface of Scheherazade's narrative and to deal with the more involved aspects of the narrator's ideas. "If we endeavour to overcome the dazing influence of the tales themselves, to look with a critical eye upon the sequence of the ideas," argued Bernard Cracraft in 1868, "if we try to reascend by analysis and imagination to the springs of authorship, and to reconstruct the society out of which the stories grew, we pass abruptly into another world of thought, and tumble at the entrance into a sea of speculation" (*Essays*, p. 72).

Bewildered as Cracraft seems to be, he nevertheless gives evidence of the very sobriety and critical detachment which distinguish a large body of mid-Victorian criticism.[2] Rather than succumbing to conventional presumptions, he raised questions about the relativity of impressions and searched for a firmer grasp of the meaning of the tales for the medieval Arab. It is only when placed in their medieval context, he states, that the tales can furnish clues to the real ideas and feelings of medieval Arab audiences. Detecting considerable ingenuity behind the "apparently elemental simplicity" of the *Nights,* Cracraft is especially concerned with the "inner idea" of the medieval Arab and its "external evolutions . . . in literary monuments" (*Essays*, pp. 76, 73). Even without historical evidence to corroborate the cultural richness of the immediate conditioning milieu of the tales, their popularity is sufficient testimony to their thematic depth. "No book," he argues, "ever took possession of the world without . . . an antecedent national pedigree of overwhelming literary power and force" (p. 75).

Although providing no substantial contribution to the reconstruction of the cultural and social conditions which the tales partly display, Cracraft is at least aware of the richness as well as of the problems involved in discussions of this kind. The questions he raised still demand some accurate answers, whereas the difficulties to which he alluded indicate how much meticulousness and tact are needed to tackle the implications of such an enquiry. In fact, it is almost impossible to supply a fair survey of nineteenth-century attempts to study the socio-cultural content of the tales without taking into account such intricate topics as the adaptability of the *Nights* to the English milieu, the thematic nature of various translations, and the lingering hostility to Islam as alien theology and culture. It is necessary, therefore, to begin by discussing these issues, taking antipathy to Islam as a starting point and focusing on some of its variants as manifested in nineteenth-century discourses on the *Nights*.

A reader can easily trace the traditional hostility to Islam in such writings as P.Q. Keegan's "Gleanings from Anglo-Oriental Literature," where the author furnishes a racial interpretation of religion that squares with the plans and aspirations of the advocates of colonial exploitation. Rather than basing his conclusions concerning Oriental customs and beliefs on primary sources, Keegan limits himself, in this article for the *New Monthly Magazine* of June 1877 (n. ser. IX, 674–87), to such pseudo-Oriental and picaresque imitations as Beckford's *Vathek*, James Marier's *Hajji Baba*, and Thomas Hope's *Anastasius*. In the same vein and with a zealous determination to prove the moral and material inferiority of a civilization associated with Islam, the Right Reverend Cameron Mann formulated a system of comparison and contrast between the *Nights* and *Morte D'Arthur*.[3] Provoked, perhaps, by Burton's preferences for the religion of the *Nights*, Mann is driven to assert that the tales reveal nothing but cruelty, brutality, sensuality, and sordidness. Overlooking the typical Arabian tales of chivalry or religious piety in Scheherazade's and other collections, and focusing on secular and urban practices in individual stories, he quite boastfully declares the *Nights* inferior to *Arthur* in themes of friendliness and sacred love. To round off his thesis, he assumes that both works reveal aspects of medieval life and culture "in the light of the current religion with its blessings and its bans" (p. 151). He further expounds on this point, emphasizing that each work provides a "concrete illustration of what the Kuran did for the civilization of one world and the New Testament for that of another." In a word, Islamic theology is reduced to tales of petty aspirations and futile concerns, and the attractions of Scheherazade's art amount to no more than humorous anecdotes and childish escapades in an encompassing "panorama of hateful and contemptible human beings" (p. 154).

One can trace another variation upon the same theme in writings which betray obvious vacillation between attachment to the *Nights* on the one hand and resentment to Islam and to Orientals on the other. In his *Life of Mahomet* (1840; p. 298), the Reverend Samuel Green, for example, appreciates the "beauty and moral instruction of the *Arabian Nights*" despite his disparagement of Islamic theology. Both Hattersley and the *Eclectic* reviewer maintain a similar attitude. Leaving aside their avowed intention to exercise a catholic taste and "a resolute determination not to yield to the first shock of prejudice," they base their adverse criticism of Islam on Scheherazade's scattered references to the wiles of women;[4] for while glossing over the common themes which the eighteenth century had already recognized, nineteenth-century adverse criticism of Islam developed new criteria that were also at variance with conventional standards. As the available information on the strictness of Islamic public morality made traditional distortions no longer tenable, unfavorable criticism centered upon polygamy and the seclusion of women, treating both as manifestations of contempt for the fair sex. While catering to the *bourgeois* aspiration for liberty, this criticism partook, too, of the arrogant airs of superiority which partly stimulated colonial expansion abroad. No less complicated is William Ernest Henley's response in *Views and Reviews* (p. 256). Notwithstanding his infatuation with the tales, he separates their aesthetic charm from the socio-religious substratum, detecting beneath Scheherazade's tantalizing narrative only the "absolute failure of Islamism as an influence that makes for righteousness." Because of its talismanic power of enchantment and magic, the *Nights* does evoke favorable responses even from such a racist dilettante as Alexander William Kinglake. Unwilling to attribute Scheherazade's inventiveness and freshness to the Asiatics, Kinglake avails himself of the occasion by ascribing the work to Greek origin. He further maintains that while these stories "disclose a complete and habitual *knowledge* of things Asiatic, [they] have about them so much of freshness and life, so much of stirring and volatile European character, that they cannot have owed their conception to a mere Oriental, who, for creative purposes, is a thing dead and dry."[5] Like many who anticipated Ernest Renan or accepted his racist divide of languages, Kinglake was only one among many who prided themselves on belonging to the Empire.[6]

Even with these implications in mind, we cannot arrive at a fair estimate of the diverse efforts to reconstruct the socio-cultural structure of the tales unless we take into account the particular circumstances and historical factors which conditioned each translator's attitude to the social content of the *Nights*. Aside from its universal themes and exotic charm, the *Nights* must contain some other attractions to appeal so strongly to the English mind. It is worth noting, to be sure, that when the *Nights* and the *Persian Tales* were introduced to the French public, the latter tales enjoyed a better reception than Scheherazade's. Paradoxically, the English reader proved impervious to those Persian stories, demonstrating instead a life-long devotion to the "sole, unparalleled *Arabian Nights*." The implications of this situation are not without interest to the student of literary history, especially as both the *Nights* and the *Persian Tales* have many things in common and both cater to the taste for the exotic. But while the latter is "far more sentimental, more fantastic, more brilliant in colour," the *Nights* has the air of solid reality as Burton, Martha Conant, and Gibb rightly explain.[7] With this fact about the *Nights* in mind, Conant suggests probable interplay between Scheherazade's realistic temper and the typical English distrust of the wayward and the nonsensical. "May not this be one reason," she asks, "why the *Arabian Nights* has always been a greater favourite in England than the *Persian Tales;* and why, in France, the popularity of the *Persian Tales* has equaled, if not surpassed, that of the *Arabian Nights?*"[8]

No less significant is the fact that the *Nights* rather than the typical Arabian romance *Antar* has been accorded such a hearty reception. Although given considerable critical attention, and regarded as the most representative form of Arabic fictional literature,[9] this Bedouin romance has never proved popular with the English common reader. It is appropriate to mention in passing that the heroic and war-like tone of this romance sharply contrasts with the urban atmosphere of the *Nights,* a fact which the *Athenaeum* critic (no. 572, Oct. 13, 1838, 739) stressed. Dealing with Antar's heroic adventures in the desert with its scorching sun and tornados, this romance "breathes a spirit of freedom" which is manifested in its hero's horror of city life. But in the *Nights,* the same critic argued, despotism is rampant. More significant, however, is the urban setting of the tales; for "whether it be the Khalif surrounded by his courtiers, or the opulent citizen in the midst of his slaves, or the adventurous merchant travelling in distant and unknown regions for the sake of gain, the reader meets in every page with evident signs of a refined and superior civilization." As this is the marked difference between the two works, it is not too much to suggest that the *Nights* has also appealed to the *bourgeois* taste for refinement, order, and prosperity.

In line with this *bourgeois* interest which culminated in the publication of Edward William Lane's edition, nineteenth-century dramatic adaptations, abridgements, and selections from the *Nights* were mostly limited to tales of urban themes like "Aladdin," "Ali Baba," "Sindbad," and "The Sleeper Awakened." Aside from these, nineteenth-century critics have often dwelt on tales of middle-class ethics. Thus, Bagehot, for instance, contends that "those tales are infinitely the best and the most characteristic which deal with city life and city intrigues and adventures" (*NR,* p. 68). It is no mere coincidence, to be sure, that G.W. Peck writes for the *American Review* of December 1847 (p. 603), "as most of the inhabitants of the Arabian Nights are people of irreproachable morals ... we have a great variety among those whose society we can enjoy as that of agreeable and instructive acquaintances." For him, as for many other mid-century writers,

Sindbad is to be commended for his effort to regain his fortune, thereby maintaining a social order of rank and privilege. For his industry, perseverance, and resolution, Sindbad "well deserved the prosperity he finally acquired, and the especial favor of his sovereign. The very occasion of his narrating his adventures [hearing the porter's lament on social inequality]," affirms Peck, "shows him to be what gentlemen are, who are not laboring under an error of opinion—a true conservative in feeling, one who wishes to improve those about him, by enabling them to take rational views of the causes of social inequality."

Sindbad's voyages must have been more appealing because the narrator concludes by stressing some concepts that are in line with the middle class ethos of hard work, seriousness, and skill. The porter in the closing episode not only acknowledges Sindbad's right to prosperity after undergoing so many hardships and demonstrating shrewdness and tact but also endorses his view that social inequality is inevitable in a universe where only prudence and perseverance lead to affluence. This maxim is among many which testify to the urban outlook of the *Nights* and partly explain its popularity with the Victorian and American middle-class reading public. Inseparable from this aspect, however, is the fact that the *Nights* depicts a well-ordered and peaceful world where commerce and business flourish.[10] Hence, with the medieval Arab's high regard for trade in mind, Peck elaborates on the orderliness and security of a society in which all abide by rules of mercantile integrity and honest enterprise. "The sea captains with whom Sindbad sailed in the course of his adventures," remarks Peck (p. 605), "present examples of mercantile integrity worthy of the highest respect, and which, it is to be hoped, has had its proper effect on the minds of many boys who have afterwards engaged in the pursuits of business."

It is worth noting, moreover, that nineteenth-century critics seem to have accepted the story-teller's principles of poetic justice. Along with numerous elaborations on the moral frame of the tales, there also developed a deep interest in the narrator's method of retributions and rewards. For Peck (p. 603), the sultan in "Aladdin" proves to be a man of the world. Although aware of the magical sources of Aladdin's wealth, he accepts him as a son-in-law, siding thereby with a characteristic middle-class preference for commercial marriages. It is only when glossing over Aladdin's subsequent wealth and concentrating on his early life of dissipation and idleness that Victorian critics misunderstand the sultan's "careless disposal of his daughter in marriage . . . to Aladdin, an idle, incorrigible, disobedient and dissipated vagabond," as James Mew describes him (p. 731). The preceding remark, however, is hardly consistent with the vogue of the tale in Victorian England. What the critic obviously overlooked is the fact that Aladdin's early life is deliberately introduced to set off and consequently enhance the effectiveness of his evolution into an accomplished, prudent, and prosperous man.

While this urban atmosphere of the *Nights* partly accounts for its sustained popularity with the English reading public, we have to recognize as well each translator's susceptibility to the temper of the times. The major translations of the *Nights* were undertaken, after all, in periods of distinctive socio-cultural aspirations and, as such, were closely related to and dependent upon contemporary, intellectual, economic, and social conditions. When evaluating the outlook of each new translation of the *Nights,* nothing is more revealing than contemporary and immediately subsequent estimates of its moral and social content. These can unmistakably serve as an index of the public temper, setting, as it were, the preoccupations of their times against earlier aspirations and attainments. Victorian critical reactions to Galland's translation, for instance, largely partake of the growing middle class concern with correctness, reticence in sexual matters, and with scientific exactitude and concise detail. It should not be wondered at, therefore, that Bagehot related the "coarseness" of Galland's version to the prevalent taste "of the translator's time" (*NR*, p. 64), whereas Edward Stanley Poole went so far in his "Editor's Preface" for Lane's *Nights* (p. xviii) as to accuse the French translator of "indecency." On the other hand, James Mew, in his essay

Figure 5.1. Walter Crane: Aladdin in China

for *Cornhill* (p. 720), censured Galland for imposing his own taste upon the original text and casting "one mask of Gallic *délicatesse*" over the social, moral, and religious manners of the East, presenting, as a result, an "Oriental . . . in the fashionable French hat, gloves, and boots of the last century."

Such Victorian responses obviously build upon Lane's own criticism of the French translation and his subsequent endeavor to retain local color in an edition that was also meant to serve as a drawing-room book. In embarking on this project, Lane was only responding to a two-fold demand (that had already been voiced by early nineteenth-century writers) for a faithful but decorous version. Indeed, as early as 1825 Robert Ferguson recognized the prospects and limitations of such an undertaking. After voicing the need for a complete translation of the *Nights* that can shed a greater light on "Asiatic manners, and literary history in general," Ferguson hurriedly qualified his call by specifying the "translateable" tales, "for some of the *escapades* of the Asiatic writers are too free for our northern ears."[11]

Although conditioned by the prevailing taste of his reading public and by his attachment to Arabic classical concepts of composition, Lane's sense of propriety savors at times of prudery rather than mere delicacy, as the *Asiatic Journal* and, later, James Mew noticed.[12] Along with outspoken descriptions and indecent scenes, he suppressed a number of passing references to naked mermaids, and motivational details dealing with seduction and incest, thereby bringing upon himself Burton's condemnation and censure and provoking the latter to lay undue stress on these very deleted passages. As readers tend to confuse Lane's edition with Burton's and to form inadequate views of Burton's voluminous work, it is also to the purpose of the present chapter to separate the latter's own penchant for the grotesque and the curious from the original text. It is quite pertinent as well to contrast his method of translation and annotation with Lane's, evaluating both in the light of the growing late nineteenth-century conflict between Victorianism, with its emphasis on propriety and decorum, and the new realistic preoccupation with unadulterated truth regardless of strict moralism and ethical considerations. Although apparently confined to those who accepted or opposed Lane's scholarship,[13] the broader context of the controversy in the eighties over the real meaning of Scheherazade's tales was the clash between Victorian moralists on the one hand and the naturalists and neo-romanticists on the other. But lest we be distracted into irrelevant complications, it is proper to concentrate on the difference in perspective between Lane and Burton, a difference which seems to have decided not only the tone and prospects of each redaction but also subsequent critical patterns of reaction and response.

In line with his conformity to standards of proper composition, Lane attempted to separate suspected interpolations from the main body of the tales, explaining that many of these digressions and possible interpolations were meant to gratify the curiosity of the uncultured native auditor.[14] Conversely, however, Burton read the *Nights* as a panorama of life in the East and as a picture of popular practices and beliefs which no other document presents. Lane's redaction was largely appreciated as an instructive entertainment, focusing on basic precepts and customs and evoking responses to these very well-defined socio-religious aspects. Burton's professed purpose was to provide "a faithful copy of the great Eastern Saga-book, by preserving intact, not only the spirit, but even the *mecanique,* the manner and the matter."[15] Accordingly, he draws the reader's attention to both the beautiful and the sordid aspects of what he deems Eastern life. On one hand, he points out the high and pure tone of the tales, their sweet and genuine pathos, their strong and multitudinous life, their poetic justice and transcendental morality, and their fusion of the spiritual and the material (*TF*, p. xv). On the other hand, he looks upon the coarseness of some portions as "a coarseness of language, not of idea,"[16] indecent but not depraved, for they reveal no "subtle corruption and covert licentiousness" (*TF*, p. xiv). It is Burton's ardent contention, too, that the story-teller must be taken as he really is, a professional reciter who earns his living by reciting tales and anecdotes. Driven by drollery and humor and uninhibited by an exaggerated sense of decorum, the Eastern reciter relishes, among other things, erotic verbalism, titillating thereby the frustrated desires of his auditor by ushering him "with a flourish, into the bridal chamber" and then narrating to him "with infinite gusto, everything he sees and hears" (*TF*, p. xiv). Leaving aside for a moment Burton's own penchant for the erotic and the grotesque, it is worth stressing that as far as the general tone and content of the text is concerned, Burton can rightly boast not only of recreating the life of the middle and poor social orders better than any preceding redactor but also of liberating the story-teller from English conventional restrictions that were utterly alien to his temperament. In comparing Burton with Lane, the *Athenaeum* for May 12, 1888 (LXI, No. 3159, 594) concludes that "Burton represents the Arab in his own country; Lane the Egyptian in Cairo, and, in some sense, the Oriental of the European stage and story-book." But while the "first startles the untravelled, but attracts the travelled Englishman; the second puts before his countrymen a picture of Eastern life with richer colours, it may be, but not less conventional than that to which they have heretofore been accustomed."

This view is valid only in so far as the distinction between the two works is concerned, for the *Athenaeum* never overlooks Burton's tendency to call a "spade" a "shovel," neither does this moderate journal entirely accept his method of annotation. Indeed, when considering the social content of Burton's edition, we need to distinguish between the real text and the translator's style and annotation. Although striving to capture the spirit of the original, Burton was nevertheless inclined either to stress the coarseness of some portions or to find an excuse for a discourse on physiological or merely personal matters. A great deal of caution and tact is required, therefore, if we are to gauge the true nature and impact of this project. It is necessary to begin by investigating the reasons behind the controversy over his translation, attempting throughout not only to separate sober evaluations from prudish reaction but also to dissociate Burton's own solid contributions from his over-shadowing egotistical poses and vapid attempts to shock. As Stanley Lane-Poole's essay in the *Edinburgh Review* (July 1886) provoked further discussion, it is only fair to start with Poole's objections to Burton's method and achievement. With the latter's tremendous familiarity with the Orient in mind, Poole chastised him (p. 185) for dwelling on the seamy side of Oriental life to the exclusion of other aspects that must surely prove profitable to the interested reader. Lane, the writer maintained, deleted passages that seemed to "have been introduced merely to amuse the rabble that hang about a low coffee house, for they contain expressions and record practices to which people in the ranks and positions of the characters described in the tales could never have descended." But constituting himself the "chronicler" of such vices, "Captain Burton has seized principally upon these elements and has addressed himself to a similar audience."

As an objection to Burton's undue stress on probable interpolations and coarse details, Poole's remarks seem quite reasonable. They are not so, however, when seen in the context of the whole argument. Like Edward William Lane, Stanley Lane-Poole is obviously driven by compelling snobbery to associate loose morality with the lower classes, an association which hardly obtains in a Muslim society. Furthermore, his attitude savors of Victorian squeamishness which is not quite identical with the Arab intelligentsia's low esteem of popular fiction. Although excluding popular writings from their concept of *belles lettres,* Arabs are not quite squeamish regarding allusions to human sexuality. In fact, Poole makes no secret of his belief that Burton's translation is bound to demoralize and corrupt by its very flouting of the Victorian sense of decorum. "Our standard of delicacy," he contends (p. 179), "may be wholly conventional, but its infraction is no less dangerous and reprehensible."

No less infuriated was the *Saturday Review,* which made it its mission to uphold upper-class standards and to speak "for the university-bred class of scholarly gentlemen and gentlemanly scholars."[17] "Abroad we English have the character of being the most prudish of nations," the reviewer explained in the number for January 2, 1886 (p. 26) soon after the private circulation of Burton's edition through the Kamashastra Society; "we are celebrated as having Bowdlerized for our babes and sucklings even the immortal William Shakespeare; but we shall infallably lose this our character should the Kamashastra Society flourish." Compared to other weeklies, the *Saturday Review* nevertheless did acknowledge the merits of Burton's translation. Others, like the *Pall Mall*, developed an attitude of utter hostility, showering Burton with biting and vituperative comments and denouncing his work as mere trafficking in pornographic literature.

The nature as well as the outcome of this controversy are worth considering at some length. It was not a mere coincidence, to be sure, that both Burton and Payne embarked in the eighties on producing unexpurgated editions, neither was it accidental that Burton went so far as to buttress his edition with notes which the *Saturday Review* for January 2, 1886 (p. 26) described as "foul blotches on the pages, being needlessly and therefore offensively gross." When seen in the light of the growing concern for scientific exactitude and the inevitable corresponding reaction against conventional restrictions on plain references to pathological and physiological facts, Payne's and Burton's projects must be numbered among the salient signals of this revolt. That John Payne's and Burton's enterprises in the eighties were closely related to the growing dissatisfaction with traditional standards of propriety and reticence was not lost upon some nineteenth-century moralists. In fact, Stanley Lane-Poole (*Edinburgh Review*, pp. 175–76) read in the taste for an unexpurgated *Nights* a sign of the modern "mania" which he called "anthrophobia" or the "dread of selecting only what is best." Although the "coarseness" of the "unexpurgated" editions is not "so revolting as the morbid nastiness of modern French fiction," it is "still emphatically disgusting." According to Lane-Poole, those who criticized his uncle for his excisions were merely "pedants of these latter days who consider that whatever is natural is right and must forthwith be proclaimed upon the housetops" (p. 171). Regarding Burton's attitude as representative of a growing naturalist opposition to "prudish" delicacy, Lane-Poole concluded his discussion of this broader context of the controversy with the following sarcastic remark: "The 'modest Lane', as Captain Burton styles him, is a being of the past; now we have—well, we have Captain Burton" (p. 176).

These as well as the remarks of the *Pall Mall* and the *Saturday Review* obviously represent the conservative opposition to the growing taste for scientific objectivity and exactitude which Burton and a number of his admirers claim to cultivate. As far as the latter group is concerned, however, it is needful to specify each writer's point of view. While such writers as Alfred Austin, John Addington Symonds, Bernard Shaw, and Yeats had strenuously combatted hypocrisy and conventionalism in criticism, there were others, like Burton himself, who were interested also in shocking the watchful moralist and thereby gratifying their rebellious hunger for uncharted freedom. As appreciative responses to the Eastern story-teller's uninhibited treatment of sexual relationships, which Payne's and Burton's editions manifest, Yeats' and Shaw's comments are worth considering at this point. Both look upon Scheherazade's outspokenness in descriptions of love scenes as educative. Writing to Ethel Mannin, Yeats, in a phrase taken from Mardrus' edition of the tales, affirmed that "it is not shameful to talk of the things that lie beneath our belts"; and he suggested that this saying might serve as an adequate "motto to such a book on the education of children as . . . [she] may have written."[18] While impressed by this natural and uninhibited treatment of sex, Shaw was also aware of the wide horizons of artistic creation which lay open before the Eastern story-teller but seem irretrievably lost to the English conventional dramatist and novelist. In "Preface to three Plays for Puritans" (1900), Shaw contrasts Scheherazade's respect for natural instincts with the English "intolerable perversion of human conduct," concluding that the Eastern frank treatment of love is preferable to a false and commercial ethos that restricts artistic expression: "In the Arabian Nights we have a series of stories, some of them very good ones, in which no sort of decorum is observed. The result is that they are infinitely more instructive and enjoyable than our romances, because love is treated in them as naturally as any other passion." Criticizing the conventional preoccupation with sexual love, Shaw draws the attention to the Arabian story-teller's freedom from literary conventions and social inhibitions. "These tales expose . . . the delusion that the interest of this most capricious, most transient, mostly easily baffled of all instincts [love], is inexhaustible, and that the field of the English romancer has been cruelly narrowed by the restrictions under which he is permitted to deal with it." Comparing the Arabian story-teller to the English, Shaw concludes that as the former is "relieved of all such restrictions," he can heap "character on character, adventure on adventure, marvel on marvel." The English novelist, on the other hand, "like the starving tramp who can think of nothing but his hunger, seems to be unable to escape from the obsession of sex, and will rewrite the very gospels because the originals are not written in the strenuously ecstatic style."[19]

In line with this same tendency but more concerned with vindicating Burton's enterprise, both Alfred Austin and Symonds were bent on meeting vituperative criticism on its own grounds. They detect nothing intentionally demoralizing in stories told in a language that is no more reprehensible than certain passages in the Bible or Shakespeare. In Austin's words, "the language is ... more frequently coarse than loose, and smacks more of childish plainness ... than of prurience or suggestiveness. The Oriental cannot understand that it is improper to refer in straightforward terms to anything which Allah has created, or of which the Koran treats."[20] With his notable freedom from literary prejudice and conventionalism, Symonds wrote about the same point in the *Academy* of October 3, 1885, siding with Burton and demanding from hostile critics consistent and honest criteria to evaluate literary works: "When we invite our youth to read an unexpurgated Bible ... an unexpurgated Aristophanes, an unexpurgated Juvenal, an unexpurgated Boccaccio, an unexpurgated Rabelais, an unexpurgated collection of Elizabethan dramatists, including Shakespeare, and an unexpurgated Plato," he argues "it is surely inconsistent to exclude the unexpurgated *Arabian Nights*."[21] In the same place, Symonds further explains the merits of Burton's translation, attacking middle-class standards of morality and exposing the confusion which marks these standards: "In the lack of lucidity, which is supposed to distinguish English folk," he intimates, "our middle-class *censores morum* strain at the gnat of a privately circulated translation of an Arabic classic, while they daily swallow the camel of higher education based upon minute study of Greek and Latin literature."

While Symonds' reasoning may well apply to the moral confusion of late Victorian England and while it aptly sums up the weaknesses of the moralistic criticism of Richard Burton's project, it cannot adequately pertain to the latter's complete edition. Unacquainted with Burton's subsequent anthropological and personal discourses, Symonds was bound to overlook the translator's exaggerated impatience with Victorian prudery and sense of propriety. Looking upon the East as a land of robust living and freedom from prejudice and cant, Burton sets his romantic vision of the Orient in opposition to Victorian England, criticizing the latter for her social and moral biases without necessarily providing a truthful picture of the East. More than any of his works, the heavily annotated *Nights* may serve as an autobiographical sketch of a restless adventurer, who was bent on confronting "silly prejudice and miserable hypocrisy" and on defiling Victorian "ultra-delicacy, the squeamishness of an age which is by no means purer or more virtuous than its predecessors."[22] Fully anticipating hostile criticism, Burton called Victorian reticence "innocence of the word not of the thought; morality of the tongue not of the heart, and the sincere homage paid to virtue in guise of perfect hypocrisy" (*TF*, xv).

Although there is a great deal of truth in Burton's criticism of Victorian prudery, it is worth keeping in mind that even before issuing his translation for private subscribers in 1885–86, Burton had already set out to challenge the moralists. Referring to the prudish cry against John Payne's unexpurgated translation of the *Nights,* Burton wrote to the translator on June 3, 1882, "Please send me a lot of advertisements. I can place a number of copies. Mrs. Grundy is beginning to roar, already I hear the bore of her. And I know her to be an arrant whore and tell her so and don't care a damn for her."[23] This disposition to shock moralists and to flout conventions was apparently known to and appreciated by Burton's friend Swinburne. Looking forward to being "reinvigorated" by Burton's revels in Eastern Billingsgate, Swinburne wrote to him on November 27, 1884, "I am hungrily anticipating the *Arabian Nights.* Of course, it is understood that Watts and I subscribe for a copy apiece. My moral sense is in need of reinvigoration since the perusal of old Lytton's prenuptial correspondence."[24]

So much for the many aspects of this controversy. The outcome, however, is no less colorful and many-sided than the controversy itself. Along with Burton's bent for hatching new schemes to make a fortune,[25] vituperative criticism must be considered among the factors which drove Lady Burton to delete two hundred and fifteen pages of an objectionable nature in order to furnish a drawing-room book which "no mother shall regret her girl's reading." [26] According to the *Athenaeum* of May 12, 1888 (LXI, No. 3159, 594), "this promise has, to all intents and purposes, been fulfilled. An edition has been produced far more thorough than any which has preceded it in England for general use, and it is no disparagement to the great ability of an admirable and a justly popular book of recent years to assert that its Arabicism is more real than Lane's." Writing for the *Academy* of December 11, 1886 (XXX, No. 762, 387), Amelia B. Edwards explains that while Burton's edition is meant for the interested scholar, Lady Burton's is made "for all who run and read." She further remarks that the absence of offensive details and the literary wealth of this Household Edition make it popular with the common and the critical reader alike. With an eye on Galland's and Lane's translations, she notes that the present edition is "not merely ... a book to be read by the fireside on a winter's night, ... one of the few companions to be selected for a vacation tour or a spring voyage; [or] ... merely ... a suitable gift for young folk, free libraries, and mechanics' institutes." Neither is it merely "an inexhaustible storehouse of Oriental legends, superstitions, proverbs, poetry, manners, customs, and the like." To her, it is "a most remarkable *tours de force* in the way of literary workmanship."

Although adequate as an assessment of the critical reputation of Galland's and Lane's editions, Amelia Edwards' estimate of the literary value of Burton's edition is overstated. Readers interested in the *Nights* as a literary production will always use John Payne's translation, as Poole wisely admits for the *Edinburgh Review* (p. 177), whereas those who search for basic information on the social background of the tales will continue to read Lane's. Indeed, although Burton manifests keen awareness of Arabic stylistic manners and modes of life and thought, the chief attraction of his work rests upon the translator's own gaudy amoralism and the vigorous egotism with which the footnotes overflow. It is evidently this fact about Burton's edition which explains the failure of his wife's emasculated production. Proposed as a compromise between the vigilant Grundyites and the new realists and romanticists, Lady Burton's Household Edition sold in the course of two years only 457 copies, a fact which Burton sarcastically cited as evidence "of modern taste in highly respectable England." Comparing this failure to the tremendous success of his own privately circulated edition, Burton concludes that his readers "would not condescend to aught save the thing, the whole thing, and nothing but the thing, unexpurgated and uncastrated."[27]

Regardless of Burton's exaggerations, there did seem, however, to be some demand for his work. This demand impelled Leonard Smithers to restore to his Library Edition four-fifths of the deleted material, satisfying thereby the collector of "curious" literature as well as the student of anthropology. For such sober weeklies as the *Athenaeum,* Smithers' Library Edition of Sir Richard Burton's *Thousand Nights,* "should very well serve the purpose of scholars—almost, if not quite, as well as the original issue and better far than Lady Burton's abridgement. But as to the 'lock and key'," the *Athenaeum* in the issue for February 23, 1895 (no. 3513, 247) explains, "We fear that the cautious paterfamilias will still deem them necessary." Although removing "a few . . . extreme examples of unnatural grossness in the text and over minuteness in the 'anthropological' notes," Smithers' is "still gross in parts, and describes physical operations with unblushing precision. The spade is called 'a spade,' but Burton's tendency to exaggerate it into a still more offensive 'shovel' is wisely checked." After touching on the obvious drawbacks of Burton's undertaking, the *Athenaeum* aptly concludes, "In all this the editor has acted with considerable judgement, and if Burton had adopted the present redaction for his original issue, a great deal of hostile criticism would have been averted."

Not many reviewers accepted the *Athenaeum* critic's fair estimate. With his uncompromising rejection of Burton's taste for Billingsgate, the *Saturday* reviewer, for example, holds a different opinion. In its number for March 9, 1895 (LXXIX, 323), the *Saturday* professes that Smithers' stylistic revisions have only made the unmitigated nudity of the original more suggestive, for "the new edition, with its nominal purification, reminds us of those sweet little cherubs of art whose reality is veiled by a fleecy cloud." The *Saturday* critic further argues that Burton's personality is so embedded in the text that it is futile to revise and emasculate his edition. As it shows his scholarship and intimate familiarity with some aspects of Eastern literature, Burton's *Nights* exposes as much his penchant for the prurient and the coarse, as manifested in his lengthy discourses on the seamy side of things. As such "to Bowdlerize Burton was more than forcing the Ethiopian to change his skin; it was depriving the work of its unique value." This value "lies in its curiously minute commentary on the seamy side of Oriental society. Here Burton was an expert, and his notes and excursus are undoubtedly of genuine importance to those who wish to make themselves familiar with a peculiarly unpleasant subject."

Such a conclusion must not be surprising for readers well acquainted with the critical reception of Burton's *Thousand Nights*. In contrast with Lane, Burton reacted against Victorian prudery by stressing the prurient and the sordid, overwhelming the reader with a tremendous amount of Billingsgate which overshadows his other penetrating remarks on the socio-literary value of Scheherazade's tales. As such Burton's edition evokes no marked responses other than the ones dealing with moral questions. Conversely, Lane, by minimizing or eliminating the bizarre, draws the reader's attention to the socio-religious substratum of the *Nights,* especially to beliefs and ideas which have informed a large body of relevant social criticism. In *An Account of the Manners and Customs of the Modern Egyptians* (1836) he had already maintained that "there is one work ... which presents most admirable pictures of the manners and customs of the Arabs, and particularly those of the Egyptians; it is 'The Thousand and One Nights,' or 'Arabian Nights' Entertainments': if the English reader possessed a close translation of it with sufficient illustrative notes, I might almost have spared myself the labour of the present undertaking."[28] Although considering the tales' accurate representations of Eastern life, Lane substantiated them with sociological annotations that were so warmly received by Victorian critics that Stanley Lane-Poole published them separately in book form in 1883.[29] Aside from its adaptability in matters of thoroughness and decorum to the early Victorian milieu, Lane's edition soon began to exert a tremendous influence on cultivated circles, an influence which was clearly manifested not only in the appearance of a number of tolerant and appreciative studies of Islamic theology and literature but also in the development of scholarly research in Oriental mythology and folklore. It was Lane's edition, too, which furnished mid-Victorian critics with background material to substantiate their sociological insights into the social content of the *Nights.*

Meant to be a repertory of sociological information, Lane's notes cover a variety of topics, ranging from discourses on Muslim precepts and Arab domestic manners to discussions of Islamic political and social institutions. Much of this material was hardly new to the English reading public, but when appended to a popular text, such notes were bound to make a deep impression on the reader's mind. It is of some significance, to be sure, that Lane's edition led to the growth of a vigorous tendency to adopt the historical method in the study of the *Nights,* as a means of evaluating the tales in terms of the socio-religious context in which they were produced. Consequent upon the appearance of his work, the *Eclectic Review* (VIII, 643), for instance, published a lengthy study in which the reviewer stressed the need not only for sufficient acquaintance with foreign literature but also for new evaluative standards that take into account relevant circumstances and ideas: "It is our part to make the requisite allowance for the circumstances under which the author has written; and so far from charging him with a want of taste because he does not comply with the conditions of *our* national taste," postulates the critic, "we ought rather to charge it upon him, if we found him doing so."

Although the *Eclectic* reviewer did not strictly abide by the rules which he himself devised, in theory at least he demonstrated great readiness to build upon previous discussions of the historical method. As far as the *Nights* is concerned, he draws the reader's attention (pp. 644–45) to a number of climatic and social circumstances which entail different manners of expression and conduct from the ones to which the English reader is accustomed. More important are his allusions to Lane's well-informed analysis of the Islamic mythological superstructure of the tales to point out that what seems improbable and fictitious to the English public is a matter of faith for the Muslim mind. This willing belief in the marvelous, which Lane cites in his "Introduction" to the *Nights* (n. 15, p. 58) as a remarkable advantage enjoyed by Muslim writers of fiction over others, is fostered and sanctioned by Islam.

While accounting for the colorful romantic machinery of the *Nights,* the unlimited faith in God's omnipotence must not be seen apart from the Arab's susceptibility to the art of story-telling. In asserting this characteristic of the medieval Arab mind, Lane was not a pioneer; neither were his Victorian reviewers. James Capper, Russell, and, especially, Joseph Von Hammer had already explained how the Arab's compelling taste for story-telling goes hand in hand with his admiration for God's supreme power.[30] Lane's special contribution lies, however, in the emphasis he lays on the bearing of this temper on the structural design of the *Nights.* Unless the reader is aware of the impact of eloquence on the

Arab mind, he is bound to look upon Scheherazade's confidence in her power of story-telling as mere folly. In the framing tale, for instance, the witchery of words is brought into full operation against Shahriar's unjust decree. In describing the social basis of Scheherazade's device, Lane observes in the first volume of his translation (n. 18, p. 63) that the main incident upon which the framing tale is founded, "the triumph of the fascination of the tongue over a cruel and unjust determination which nothing could annul, might be regarded, by persons unacquainted with the character and literature of the Arabs, as a contrivance too improbable in its nature; but such is not the case." Referring to his own residence in Egypt and to his own familiarity with the socio-cultural context of Arabic literature, he assures his readers that "perhaps there are no other people in the world who are such enthusiastic admirers of literature, and so excited by romantic tales, as those above mentioned. Eloquence, with them, is lawful magic: it exercises over their minds an irresistible influence."

Carried to such lengths, the appeal to conditioning circumstances and national taste makes it difficult even for dissenting voices to dispute publicly the validity of Scheherazade's romantic machinery. Instead, we notice the emergence of highly specialized studies in the mythological content of the tales which aim at giving "a full account of. . . . [their] machinery . . ., as written by eastern hands and told to eastern ears," as Hattersley plans to undertake in his article for *Dublin Review* (p. 107). In this learned essay, the writer develops Lane's discussion of this topic in order to enable readers to evaluate and appreciate Eastern romantic fiction from a Muslim perspective: "The ideas of Eastern fiction entertained by those who have formed their judgement solely upon European materials, . . . are naturally enough limited, and as naturally often inaccurate." This fact is more shocking because these readers constitute "the larger portion of the reading and criticizing public, both in England and on the Continent." Ultimately, the critic concludes, "This charming section of the fairy land of fiction is as yet very imperfectly known."

Viewed as a whole, these and other reviews indicate that Lane's annotated *Nights* has opened new vistas of interest in Arabic culture and made it possible for critics and reviewers to see through the limitations of contemporary knowledge and current evaluative criteria of Islamic life and literature. It is certainly within this tendency to establish and develop better perspectives that Carlyle's view of Islam and Muhammad falls. In his lecture on the Prophet, Carlyle remonstrated against adverse criticism of Islam, asserting that the "lies, which well-meaning zeal has heaped round this man, are disgraceful to ourselves only."[31] Although it is unfair to assume that Carlyle's concept of the hero as prophet is based upon Lane's illustrative notes, one can suggest that Lane's *Nights* had intensified Carlyle's interest in Islam and the Arabs. According to Froude, Carlyle was reading about the Arabs when preparing for his lectures *On Heroes, Hero-Worship and the Heroic in History* (1840). His diary for October 1839 reads as follows: "Arabian Tales by Lane; very pious. No people so religious, except the English and Scotch Puritans for a season. Good man Mahomet, on the whole; sincere; a fighter, not indeed with perfect triumph, yet with honest battle ... wish I knew Arabic."[32] 'While not exactly proposing that Lane's *Nights* was the sole source for Carlyle's second lecture, Froude's reference to the former's reading in autumn and his foregoing citation imply as much. For readers familiar with Lane's edition, this conclusion is only partly true. As Lane provides no profound comments on the Prophet's personality, it is quite proper to argue that while Carlyle might have based his description of the Arabs and the socio-political structure of Islam on Lane's notes, there must have been other sources for his discourse on the Prophet's personal appearance and character.

Apart from such attempts to reassess the image of Islam and the Arabs, Lane's impact can be traced in discussions especially concerned with the socio-religious meaning of the *Nights*. It was mostly after the publication of Lane's edition that the moral and religious themes of some tales attracted a great deal of critical attention. While admitting the existence of different moral perspectives that separate Islam and the West, James Mew remarked in his often quoted contribution to *Cornhill* (p. 731) that the *Nights* offers many examples of common precepts and ideas, for "a sentence is like a cheveril glove to a good wit, and one may preach Protestant sermons from the texts of the Imam." He thereupon cites teachings which can be passed off as part of the Western moral tradition. In the light of other nineteenth-century appreciations of Scheherazade's moralism, one can plainly see that Mew is not exaggerating. In reviewing a reprint of Lane's *Nights,* the *Spectator* for November 25, 1882 (p. 1513) explains that "in glancing over it we were struck more than we have ever been struck before with the presence of something in the tales to which we think justice has never been quite done, the existence in some of them of an element of poetic religious feeling." As he considers this piety and wisdom more inclusive than the teachings of one specific faith, the critic contends, "There is a wind of wisdom—wisdom, not of Islam, but of all creeds—which intermittently blows through all the jungle of growths, fair and foul, grand trees and poisonous creepers" (p. 1513).

The reviewer is not so superficial as to base his estimate upon recurrent principles of poetic justice that form the story-teller's stock-in-trade. What appeals to him most is that profound religiosity which permeates such stories as "The City of Brass," religiosity which is the more impressive for being tinged with "the mysticism of the Desert, the mysticism which teaches that all is evanescent, goodness included, save God, the Ordainer, alone" (p. 1514). Such an insight into the religious fabric of the tales is worth considering, for the writer regards both their pervasive sordidness and brilliant sublimity as functional atmospheric devices deliberately and alternately introduced to project a realistic view of life and, ultimately, to enhance the efficacy of their pensive teachings. Through "all the stories, turning up in the strangest places, amid scenes which the narrator intended to be virtuous, and scenes which in the original he purposely made foul," says the critic, "runs a stream of philosophic or, rather, religious thought, always in essence the same, the burden of which is older than Mahommedanism, older than Christianity, older than Hellenism, the refrain of the Wise King,—'Vanity of Vanities, all is vanity!'" Although "often no better than the moralising of the old nurse," and sinking at times "into a bathos which, to us at least, suggests conscious hypocrisy," this strain occasionally "breaks forth overpoweringly, till the wild legend becomes a high moral apologue." On one occasion at least, remarks the *Spectator,* "it conquers, drowns narrative, effaces description, and transmutes a mere 'tale,' a bit of *The Arabian Nights,* into a lesson which would not be wholly unworthy in meaning of the Wise King himself" (p. 1513).

But Lane's edition deserves attention not so much for the teachings of universal application which it displays as for its specific references to Islamic moral and social life. It inspired a great deal of discussion especially regarding such themes as the absolute faith in Providential interposition, social mobility, Muslim domestic morality, and class structure in medieval Islam. Foremost among these are Moir Bussey's "Introduction" to the 1839 edition of Forster's *Nights* and Walter Bagehot's assessment of "The People of the Arabian Nights." The former endorses Lane's explanations regarding every detail of topical interest, whereas Bagehot—aside from his classical bias in literary criticism—develops a scientific view independent of contemporary taste for historical interpretation. Concerning the rights of women, the laws of marriage and divorce and the Islamic distinctive kindness to slaves, both critics reach similar conclusions that echo Lane's own insights. It is in matters of theological speculation that they differ, for each writer's bent of mind tells plainly upon his selection of examples and, consequently, upon his final estimates.

As an admirer of the cardinal articles of the Muslim faith, Bussey, for instance, never looks upon the belief of predestination as mere fatalism. As the drift of his argument indicates, his understanding is not at variance with Muslim views on this point. While believing in God's supreme omnipotence and his predestination of man's fortunes, a Muslim must also accept the Qur'anic emphasis on purposeful endeavor and on energetic exploration of God's creation. Rather than detecting unwholesome social attitudes attendant upon this belief, Bussey asserts in his "Introduction" (p. xxv) that this faith renders the Muslim "patient under suffering of any kind, and submissive to his fate," a conclusion which Burton also accepts. Conversely, Bagehot regards this unlimited faith and social conformity as largely responsible for the passive temperament of the people in the *Nights*. Instead of being drawn to manifestations of forebearance and patience, Bagehot is both shocked by the pervading obsession with Providence and luck, and appalled by the readiness to forgive which is incompatible with his practical view of justice *(NR, p. 57)*.

In comparison with both Lane and Bussey, Bagehot stands on better grounds when attempting to delve into the socio-political reasons for both the medieval excessive reliance on Providence and the obsession with wealth which the *Nights* demonstrates. Although at times confusing the social with the religious and the medieval Cairene tale with the Abbasid narratives, Bagehot is nevertheless aware of the impact of economic instability and vicissitudes of political fortune on the medieval Muslim mind. To social mobility and extreme changes in financial and political circumstances he attributes the obsession with wealth to which many a tale testifies *(NR, pp. 52–53, 61)*. Whether expressing the wishful thinking of the medieval Egyptian or picturing actual changes of fortune, these tales depict a society in which despotism and institutional corruption are rampant. To this, too, he ascribes a great deal of medieval generosity and prodigality, for the prosperous who provide for others today may themselves be provided for in adversity: "The combined importance of possession and the precariousness of acquisition and tenure go far to account for that mixture of covetousness and generosity which is so common a trait in these tales," argues Bagehot, remarking further that the "sultan who scatters his thousand pieces of gold recruits his finances at the expense of the nearest wealthy subject who has incurred his anger or given a pretext for the robbery." Very much concerned with the sociology of behavior, he holds social mobility and institutional corruption largely responsible for lavish expenditure and luxurious living, for "he who knows his turn to be stripped may at any moment arrive is willing to taste the pleasures and gain the benefits of a lavish expenditure" *(NR, pp. 52–53)*.

More interesting are Victorian critics' responses to the reputed voluptuousness of the *Nights*. Of some relevance here are the insights of Bagehot, Bussey, Hunt, and Poole, especially their comments on the theme of love, the idea of beauty, and the social position of women. As far as the theme of love is concerned, it was

Poole who, in his essay for the *Edinburgh* (p. 194), first recognized its supremacy in Scheherazade's tales, for supernatural agents as well as the caliph interfere only to bring the lovers together. Whether appearing as violent passion or unselfish devotion, the real charm of this topic, according to Poole, is its "absolute *abandon*": "The lovers love, and that is enough; no power on earth can keep them apart—or if it can, they die."

This theme cannot be considered, however, apart from the rich sensual atmosphere of the *Nights*. Although no one disputes the fact that the story-teller appeals in many stories to his auditor's taste for bodily pleasures, many critics maintain different views of the purpose of this voluptuous maze. With the carping criticism of Islam in mind, Bussey, for instance, tends to be apologetic in his discourse on this point, remarking that promises of glowing and sensual enjoyments are as abundant in the Qur'an and the *Nights* as they are in the Bible. They must be seen, therefore, in the same light as the offers of the early Christian writers "to their first proselytes" (xiv). With little regard for conventional attitudes towards other faiths, Bagehot, on the other hand, is not concerned with such justifications. For him these tales of sensual pleasures reveal the temper of the people concerned and their uninhibited appreciation of human beauty. Instead of looking down upon the Arab concept of erotic love, Bagehot commends it because it is associated with beauty, refinement, and grace: "But these enjoyments, sensual though they be, cover a wide range, and indicate no despicable degree of refinement and delicacy. The arts, indeed, are made ministers to the senses; but a love of beauty always accompanies and gives a grace to their indulgence." But rather than a mere attraction to physical beauty, the "Arabian idea of female loveliness is a high one," explains Bagehot. Aside from the emphasis on beauty, grace, and eloquence, "the narrator places his lovers among scenes which shall be in keeping with themselves, in noble gardens or adorned palaces, amid the play of fountains and the song of birds; wine must have music to attend it, and wit and eloquence give a charm to convivial intercourse" (*NR*, p. 67). Although partly valid as an interpretation, Bagehot's preceding understanding is mainly based on the narrator's description of love scenes in tales of city origin. As such, it takes no account of the Arab view of beauty as a sign of God's munificence, a view which had already been discussed at length by both Joseph Von Hammer and Leigh Hunt.[33] By overlooking this sanctified idea of human beauty, Bagehot provides no adequate explanation for the seeming obsession with female loveliness which pervades medieval Arabian fiction.

But with Lane's detailed discussion of the rights and privileges of Muslim women in mind, Bagehot develops a better perspective when dealing with the domestic morality of the Islamic world. Like Bussey (xvi–xvii), Bagehot knows that monogamy is the normal form of domestic life in the Muslim East, but he observes, "there seems to be a fixed persuasion among Englishmen, that any man who has liberty to take four wives will avail himself of the privilege" (*NR*, p. 64). In touching upon popular impressions concerning the "utter listlessness and slavish seclusion of the harem life" (*NR*, p. 63), Bagehot explains that these impressions are reinforced by the reading of the *Nights*. Depicting the exceptional in "the private lives of princes," the tales, he believes, are bound to cater to the reader's love for the unfamiliar and, ultimately, to make the deepest impressions on his memory (*NR*, p. 63). As for Scheherazade's anecdotes on the wickedness of women, Bagehot maintains that similar stories "have occupied a place in the literature of nearly all nations" (p. 65), and therefore cannot be cited as evidence of contempt for the other sex. These stories attract especial attention also because they present unique and rare cases. "Little weight," he concludes, ". . . is to be placed on the presence of this class of anecdotes in the *Arabian Nights,* and no sensible man would take them as an indication of female character in general" (p. 65). Such a dispassionate examination of Islamic sexual morality is not new to the English reading public as we have already seen. But, as Bagehot observes, "we do not bring it home to our minds for the correction of these undefined impressions which often remain, though we have learned them to be false, the active part of our knowledge" (p. 64). Bagehot's remarks are penetrative enough to explain the common tendency to confuse the entertaining story with actual life in the East. Even Bentham, despite his distrust of hearsay, seems to have fallen under the spell of Scheherazade's romanticized love accounts. Hence, when Muhammad Ali, the ruler of Egypt, arranged to send his son Abbas to study in Bentham's household, the latter advised the ruler that Abbas be provided with one female to accompany him only in the hours of repose, an advice which was obviously inspired by readings of the *Nights*.[34]

No less critical attention has been paid to the hierarchical quality of the medieval Muslim society. In the light of the Victorians' preoccupation with similar problems, this interest should not seem surprising. Partaking of the contemporary search for solutions to class antagonism and benefitting greatly from Lane's notes, this criticism is worth investigating not so much for its elucidation of the sociology of Islam as for its exposition of each writer's attitude to social problems in England. Thus, after explaining how social ranks are as well defined in the *Nights* as in "an oriental Court Calendar" (p. xv), Bussey contends that such classifications entail no class prejudice or restraint upon free communication between people of different stations. With an eye on class distinctions in

England, he further observes, "It is not in the East, as in Europe, that the pursuit of trade is held to be derogatory to a man's dignity; but, on the contrary, a merchant is one of the most honourable men." Expounding on this same point, Bussey mentions: "To know no trade or profession by which, in case of necessity, a man may procure his own subsistence, is considered a disgrace, however high may be a man's rank, or however great his wealth." While the "possession of civil or military power conferred by the sovereign or by the magistracy, is the only real distinction between plebeian and aristocrat," this pervasive feeling of social equality makes "the intercourse between rich and poor, without regard to the difference of rank or station . . . almost free from restraint" (p. xx).

Apart from this understandable middle-class susceptibility to shows of respect and admiration for business and trade, there is something especially appealing to writers like Walter Bagehot in a society that betrays no discrepancy between uninhibited intercourse and social distinctions. In line with his socio-political criterion of deference to rank and wealth, Bagehot was impressed by the modes of obeisance and strict observance of social stations which the tales display. While admiring this community, Bagehot lamented the absence in England of "brotherly intercommunication, the ready sympathy, the easy trust, the free compassion, the unquestioning hospitality" (*NR*, p. 57). After comparing such modes with the English "jealous distrust of every stranger," Bagehot draws a contrast between the Muslim and the English societies to the disadvantage of the latter. The people of the *Nights,* he remarks echoing Bussey, "mix together much more freely than with us, and the various classes have an unrestrained intercourse of which we have no idea. Distinctions of rank are accurately marked and universally respected. Partly from this very reason, they offer no barriers to free intercourse" (*NR*, 57, 58).

As Bussey's and Bagehot's readings indicate, Lane's impact on the sociological interest in the *Nights* is especially manifested in investigations of obvious religious or social issues; for, as D.B. Macdonald remarks in the *Nation* (Aug. 30, 1900, Pt. I, p. 167), "Lane's forte was description, what he saw he could describe so that anyone else would see it." As such, his version evoked no spirited search either for the narrator's point of view or for the involved psychological aspects of social behavior. Furthermore, Lane's reputation as a solid scholar and distinguished Arabist has made it difficult for the more critical reader to dissent from his theory concerning the Egyptian origin of the tales and their assumed illustration of contemporary and medieval Cairene life. It is true that many tales may serve as brilliant pictures of some extant medieval Egyptian modes and customs, but, as C.H. Toy adroitly argues in the *Atlantic Monthly* for June 1889 (p. 762), "Lane is not thereby justified in regarding the present form of the book as wholly or substantially Egyptian, for Eastern customs remain long unchanged, and what one now observes in a Cairo Khan may have occurred a thousand years ago in a Bagdad bazaar." In every culture, there are some constants, to be sure, but these should not be taken as signs of dormancy. Soon after the publication of Lane's work, there appeared a number of disagreements with his sweeping generalization concerning the social setting of the work. Leigh Hunt, for example, maintained that such a story as the "Porter and Three Ladies of Bagdad" could not be Egyptian ("NT," p. 128), whereas Hattersley, in his article for *Dublin* (p. 119), stressed the need for careful sifting and classification of manuscript material before deciding upon the local color and origin of each tale: "The Arabic student is well aware that the arrangement, the number, the nature and length of the stories, differ in different copies," for "those made at Cairo exhibit the manners of the Egyptians," whereas "those written at Baghdad picture the customs of Mesopotamia and Syria." But while the collections "always contain certain stories unaltered in their general form," there are obvious indications that "these tales have been considered a sort of public property, which might be altered, rearranged, or interpolated at will."[35]

But valid as such objections are, they build on no substantial foundations and are, therefore, too sporadic to challenge seriously Lane's influential theory. In fact, both Hunt and Hattersley seem unaware of Joseph Von Hammer's penetrating analysis of the story-teller's point of view in the "Preface" to his own translation (pp. xviii–xix). Although anticipating Lane in suggesting the medieval Cairene setting of the tales, Hammer at least draws the reader's attention to the story-teller's nostalgic tone. He explains that the Baghdadi tales were composed "long after the age of that caliph [al-Rashid], whose love of poetry and thirst of knowledge afforded great encouragement to poets and compilers of anecdotes." In other words, Hammer was aware of the romanticized nature of a work composed during a period of political upheaval such as the Mameluke reign in Egypt. Long before modern scholars began to study the social reasons for this nostalgic yearning for the times of the "good Haroun Alraschid," Hammer had already explained, in his study of Arabic poetry in the *New Monthly Magazine* for February 1, 1820, that the story-teller looked back with regret upon the passing of Haroun's era (786–809 A.D.) and the disintegration of the Abbasid civilization in Baghdad, an era which was associated in the popular mind with prosperity, security, and order. In contrast with the corruption and instability of the Mameluk rule in Egypt, the Abbasid period on which the reciter dwells with affection was a time of cultural and commercial expansion. The book, according to Hammer (p. 158), was "first written under the government of the last Mameluke sultans in Egypt, at a time when the era of Haroun was considered as the golden age of the caliphate, and his court as the ideal of all oriental courts."

Read with caution like other generalizations about the collection, Hammer's recognition of this nostalgic bent must be seen as a significant contribution to the social study of the *Nights*. By setting the idealized vision of the Baghdadi court in contrast with the medieval Mameluk reign in Egypt, the storyteller provides a panoramic view of the historical growth and decline of a whole civilization. Unfortunately, this insight passed unnoticed and was later overshadowed by Lane's illustrative discourses on extant Egyptian manners and customs. Even in the last part of the century when efforts were made to read the *Nights* anew and to evaluate its social background in terms of the available internal evidence, the story-teller's perspective was overlooked in deference to the apparent allusion to the Baghdadi court. Thus, without attempting to classify the tales in terms of their social, moral, and topographical detail, W.G. Palgrave hastily claims, in his introductory note to "Alkamah ..." in *Macmillan's* (XXXI, March 1875, 448), that Scheherazade's tales "belong ... to the town and court of Baghdad, at that time an Imperial Capital, and the centre of an organized civilization." It is worth remarking that while Lane's experience in Egypt predisposed him to assign Egyptian origin to the tales, Palgrave's acquaintance with the rigid and war-like life of Nejd made him associate the whole refined and urban atmosphere of the *Nights* with the Abbasid court.

Although no less impressed by the Baghdadi portion of the *Nights,* John Payne was nevertheless perceptive enough to recognize types of tales that were particularly Egyptian or otherwise in form and content. On the whole, however, he regarded the non-Iraqi-Syrian parts insignificant in volume and wanting in artistry. His views are worth studying not only because he primarily uses internal documentation and graphic detail as the mainstay for his thesis but also because his is the most controversial reading of the *Nights,* developing, as it were, a point of view which is completely at variance with Lane's. Rather than accepting Lane's solid, though somewhat deficient, assessment of the main socio-religious patterns of the *Nights,* Payne is bent upon studying the tales themselves, resorting to external evidence only to corroborate a notion which he has already formulated. It is only when succumbing to an overwhelming sympathy for Haroun's graceful minister Ja'far the Barmecide that he leaves the tales aside to impose his own derogatory view of the caliph upon an interpretation which might otherwise prove consistent. Thus, he is at great pains to reinterpret the role of Haroun al-Rashid, assigning different reasons for his popularity that square with the writer's psychological presentation of him as a morose and hysterical monarch driven by insomnia and by an overpowering sense of guilt to encourage and patronize whatever might help to relieve him of his spasmodic illness. To appeal to the caliph's artistic sensibility, contends Payne in the first part of his contribution on the *Nights* for the *New Quarterly Magazine* (p. 161), is sufficient to "save the greatest criminal or the most hated enemy from the consequences of the furious outbursts of passionate frenzy to which the monarch was subject."

While this sensitiveness partly explains Haroun's popularity with the artists whom he patronized, it sheds little light on public admiration and love for him as manifested in the *Nights*. Here Payne provides two justifications. On the one hand, he admits that the caliph's accessibility to his humbler subjects made him quite popular with the people. On the other hand, Payne suggests that we must not accept these tales as truthful records of the caliph's dealings, for they were mostly written and circulated at his own instigation: ". . . indeed, we may well suspect, from the prominence that is given to him and the frequency with which anecdotes of his reign recur, that a great portion of the collection was taken bodily from notes or compilations prepared at his especial instance by the celebrated poets and musicians . . . that illustrated his court" (I, p. 161).[36]

Aside from this shaky analysis of the caliph's character, Payne provides genuine insights into the Baghdadi content of some urban tales, working out a coherent view of the socio-political system during the Abbasid period that seems incompatible with his image of the caliph. On the basis of internal detail, Payne describes Baghdad during that period as "the metropolis of Muslim civilization" (I, p. 169). Its prodigal court and thriving business attracted people from all over the world, as the tales indicate. It might not have been so prosperous, however, had it not been governed by scrupulous and just rulers. As Scheherazade's tales of roguery and intrigue demonstrate, order and security were preserved by "employing certain selected rascals of high capacity, such as Ahmed ed Denef, Hassan Shouman and Ali Zeibec (all of whom are mentioned in 'The Thousand and One Nights') as subordinate prefects of the police to coerce and checkmate their former comrades" (I, p. 169). It was surely this method which, in Payne's opinion, helped preserve the untroubled and rarefied life of the "Abode of Peace" as Baghdad was deservedly called at that time (I, pp. 163, 169).

But Payne's study of the society of the *Nights* is worth more attention for the writer's ingenious views on the morality of the urban classes. Rather than confusing religious precepts with social behavior as Bagehot has done or generalizing about customs and moral practices in the manner of Lane, Payne strives to formulate new assessments based on the narrator's descriptions of certain social groups, focusing on modes and dealings that are incompatible with religious teachings.

With such stories as "The Porter and the Three Ladies of Baghdad" and "The Barber's Brother Bacbarah" in mind, Payne states that among the upper classes "drunkenness and debauchery of the most uncompromising kind prevailed," betraying a state of licentiousness comparable to the laxity and corruption of the Roman decadence (I, p. 163). Thus, instead of dismissing descriptions of sensual indulgence as mere interpolations meant to titillate the auditor's repressed desires, Payne seizes upon these as adequate pieces of evidence to substantiate his thesis.[37]

Payne has one good reason, however, to assume that the upper classes did indeed indulge in sensual affairs and licentious habits. In the *Nights* he detects a tendency on their part to disregard religious practices (I, p. 164). In fact, Payne observes in some Baghdadi tales a disposition to cultivate a refined atheism which stood in contrast to the attitude of "the lower and middle classes of the people [who] were still profoundly and fanatically attached to the 'Faith of the Unity of God'" (I, p. 164). Within the broader context of his interpretation of the growth and fall of the Abbasid caliphate, Payne maintains that this material prosperity and lack of religiosity, which distinguished the Abbasid court, carried within it the germs of decline and decadence. But as tales like the "Devout Prince" demonstrate, the same materialistic tendency provoked ascetic piety and deep religious devotion that represented the other extreme response in the life of the period (I, p. 165).

That Payne stands on firm grounds whenever he builds his estimates on internal evidence is also indicated in his analysis of the social relevance of the conversational style of the *Nights*. More than any other nineteenth-century writer, Payne studied the adaptability of this style to the unschooled urban audience, emphasizing in the second part of his essay (p. 380) its "extreme simplicity" and freedom from Arabic classical conventions which made it so appealing to the coffee-house auditor. At variance with the customary English reference to the metaphorical splendor of the *Nights*,[38] Payne remarks that "nothing can be more unlike the idea of barbaric splendour, of excessive and heterogeneous ornament, that we are accustomed to associate with the name, than the majority of the tales that compose the collection" (II, p. 381). There are but isolated metaphorical descriptions that mostly depend on stock phrases and conventional comparisons. "A beautiful youth," Payne explains in the same place, "is always a full moon, a slender and graceful girl a willow wand or a thirsty gazelle." But rather than producing any monotony that might irritate the coffee-house auditor, such comparisons disappear in a vast store of sentiment and circumstance on which the story-teller draws, inducing "in the rigid scale of their ornaments fresh permutations of shifting colour and new harmonies of fantasy and impression" (II, p. 382).

Payne's as well as other nineteenth-century critical estimates of the salient social and cultural aspects of the tales cannot be fairly assessed, however, without being seen in relation to larger Victorian efforts to classify these stories and to decide their probable origin and date of composition.[39] In fact, it is almost impossible to pass definite judgments on the story-teller's meaning and circumstance without a fair knowledge not only of the type of each tale but also of its genealogical roots and immediate context. It is only when we bear in mind the countless implications and difficulties surrounding studies of popular culture that we can appreciate nineteenth-century endeavors to reconstruct the society of the *Nights*.

After making allowances for all these complications, a modern reader may still, however, miss many things in the preceding evaluations, Nineteenth-century critics showed no adequate understanding of the subtle cynicism which informs the thematic patterns of many tales in the collection, neither did they discuss that compelling disgust with authority which permeates the Egyptian stories of roguery. Aside from these omissions, little was said about the psychological implications of the obsession with fate in tales set in medieval Cairo, where social oppression drove helpless individuals to nourish dreams and superstitions that would provide a temporary escape from uncongenial circumstances. In some of these tales, too, principles of poetic justice can hardly obtain, for the story-teller is too realistic to impose an idealistic conclusion on uncontrollable situations. It is in the Baghdadi tales, however, that such principles are usually stressed. Regarding Haroun's reign as an era of peace and justice, the story-teller depicts the caliph as an instrument of fate, a Providential means to redress wrongs and to bring about prosperity and happiness. But although these and many other points received little or no attention from Victorian critics, their endeavors and diverse responses reveal an awareness of the thematic complexity of the *Nights* and its presentation of a panoramic view of popular customs and beliefs that cannot easily be found in books meant for the erudite and the learned. Furthermore, while a twentieth-century perspective enables us to see through such omissions, it should not, however, blind us to the accomplishments of nineteenth-century periodical criticism of the tales. Aside from differences in manner of treatment, Victorian reviewers have displayed considerable diligence and concern to keep up with the growing interest in the *Nights,* a practice which we miss nowadays. In their estimates of the successive editions of the tales, they have all aimed at inclusiveness and thoroughness. It is a mark of their concern, to be sure, that each has striven to cover in a single review a variety of themes, ranging from the genesis of the tales to their intrinsic aesthetic merit. As they attest to the literary richness of the work itself, the diversity and freshness shown in such periodical evaluations testify to the vitality and exuberance of the critics and their own times. More preoccupied with instructiveness and practical values, but sensitive nonetheless to the story-teller's exquisite blend of form and content, they have introduced their readers to a wide range of issues that have become basic to further criticism of the *Nights*. Although at times conditioned and limited by their predilections, nineteenth-century critics have dwelt on the tales with a close intimacy and warm affection that can hardly be matched in current impersonal researches. In spite of disagreeing on specific topics, nineteenth-century critics were unanimous in appreciating the *Nights* as a rich record of Muslim popular culture. In this same vein the American Orientalist Crawford Howell Toy wrote on the subject for the *Atlantic Review* of June 1889 (p. 762), summing up the views of the period in an apt comment with which we may bring this discussion to a close: "The book is both the history of Moslem culture and the record of Moslem *esprit* in the palmy days of the Arabs in Asia; it gives a truer as well as a more vivid picture of their life than all the ordinary histories combined." In this book, he further stated, we have not only "the self-respecting courtesy of the Arab gentleman, the devotion of friendship" but also the "wiles and tricks, passion and treachery, soberness and silliness, nobility and meanness, the Arab individual independence standing beside the utterest political despotism, the high intellectual and social position assigned to women,—all the elements of life."

Notes

1 Bernard Cracroft, "The True Meaning of the 'Arabian Nights,'" in his *Essays, Political and Miscellaneous* (London: Trubner, 1868), II, 73—hereafter cited as *Essays* and incorporated with page number in the text at the end of each quotation. It is worth noting that Cracroft here only reasserts what Bagehot has already mentioned concerning Lane's annotations (*NR*, p. 71).

2 Apart from the tendency to exercise scientific objectivity and tolerance in the study of the socio-religious content of the tales, one can detect (especially in mid-Victorian travel accounts about the Near East) a cynical note and a disposition to deflate romantic expectations. In his *British Expedition to the Crimea* (London, 1858, p. 38), the *Times* correspondent W.H. Russell describes a Turkish Commission seated upon a divan as follows: "In the height of his delusions respecting Oriental magnificence and splendours, led away by reminiscences of *Tales of the Genii* and the *Arabian*

Nights the reader must not imagine that this divan was covered with cloth of gold, or glittering with precious stones. It was clad in a garment of honest Manchester print."

3 Further references to Mann's article in *North American Review* will be incorporated with page number within the text.

4 Citation from the *Eclectic Review*, n. ser. VIII (1840), 643. See also Hattersley's essay for *Dublin Review*, pp. 107, 122.

5 *Eothen, or Traces of Travel Brought from the East* (N. Ed.; New York: Putnam, 1950), chap. vi, p. 53—first published in 1844.

6 See Renan, *Histoire générale*, in *Said, Orientalism*, 143.

7 "Terminal Essay," p. 112; *Oriental Tale*, p. 25; and "Literature" in *Legacy of Islam*, eds. Sir Thomas Arnold and Alfred Guillaume (Oxford: Clarendon, 1931), pp. 202–03, respectively.

8 *Oriental Tale*, p. 25.

9 In England *Antar, A Bedoueen Romance* appeared in full in 1820 (3 vols.) translated by Terrick Hamilton, who also supplied a well-informed preface to the work. Among the best discussions of *Antar* are Joseph Von Hammer's study in the *New Monthly Magazine* of January and April 1820; a short essay in the *Penny Magazine*, VI (Feb. 1837), 55–56; and a lengthy one in *Blackwood's*, IV (Jan. 1819), pp. 385–94.

10 For some of the nineteenth-century comments on the *bourgeois* origin of the tales, see Stanley Lane-Poole, "The Arabian Nights," p. 195; and J.F. Hewitt, "History as Told in the Arabian Nights," pp. 255–56.

11 "Eastern Stories," *Blackwood's Edinburgh Magazine*, XVIII (July 1825), 63. Signed "R.F." and identified as Robert Ferguson by A.L. Strout, *A Bibliography of Articles in Blackwood's Magazine, 1817–1825* (Texas: Texas Tech. Coli. Library, 1959), p. 131.

12 For the *Asiatic Journal*, seen. ser. XXX, no. 117, 1839, 72 n. Mew's "Some Unedited Tales from the 'Arabian Nights'," appeared in *Tinsley's Magazine*, No. 176 (Mar. 1882), 229.

13 Thomas Wright provides some information on the conflict between Burton and the "Laneites" in *Life of John Payne* (London: Fisher Unwin, 1919), esp. pp. 72–76. See also Burton's "Biography of the Book and Its Reviewers Reviewed," *Supplemental Nights*, VI, 311–66—hereafter cited as "Biography of the Book."

14 See, for example, n. 87 to chap. 10 in the *Nights*, II, 213–14.

15 "Translator's Foreword," p. xii, hereafter cited as *TF* and incorporated with page number in the text at the end of each reference.

16 "Terminal Essay," p. 176, hereafter cited as *T* and incorporated with page number in the text at the end of each quotation.

17 John Gross, *Rise and Fall of the Man of Letters* (London: Weidenfeld, 1969), pp. 63, 64, 65.

18 *Letters*, ed. Allan Wade (London: Rupert Hart-Davis, 1954), 832. Although the above reference is to Mardrus' edition (which falls beyond the time scope of this

study), it is inserted here because of Yeats' intimate association with the literary circles which celebrated Burton's project. See B. Bjersby, *Interpretation of the Cuchulain Legend in the Works of W.B. Yeats* (Upsala, 1950), p. 127, n. 3.

19 *Prefaces by Bernard Shaw* (London: Constable, 1934), p. 710. In another place ("Parents and children" [1910], pp. 67–68), Shaw dwells on the same problem as manifested in the upbringing of children. Citing his own childhood experience as an example, he explains that English families tended to bring up their children to be physically strong and morally timid.

20 Reprinted from *Standard* (Sept. 12, 1885) in Burton's "Biography of the Book," p. 318.

21 "The Arabian Nights' Entertainments," XXVIII, No. 700, 233—reprinted in Burton's "Biography of the Book," p. 361. It is worth mentioning that Edward Peacock also expressed similar views in a note on "The Arabian Nights," *Academy*, XXVIII, No. 702 (Oct. 17, 1885), 258.

22 "Biography of the Book," p. 347.

23 Cited by Thomas Wright in the *Life of John Payne*, p. 73. Burton might have had in mind Reginald Stuart Poole's and William Wright's premature denunciations of Payne's "aesthetic 'culture'" as the former called the project. See *Academy* (Apr. 26, 1879), pp. 369–70; (Nov. 26, 1881), p. 421, and (Dec. 17, 1881).

24 *Swinburne Letters*, ed. Cecil Lang (New Haven, CT: Yale Univ. Press, 1962), V, 89.

25 It is needless to assert that Burton appropriated Payne's translation in order to provide copies for the rest of the subscribers to the latter's edition. For more on this point, see Mia Gerhardt, p. 81. Burton's contemporaries were aware of the partly commercial nature of such enterprises. The "remarkable success" of Payne's edition, according to Poole, "was chiefly due to the attractions offered to investors by a limited subscribed edition, sure to become rare" ("Arabian Nights," p. 177). The *Saturday Review* mentioned that "the competition of the collector, or the market-wisdom of the cornerer, has run up [Burton's edition] to an auction price of over £30 for the sixteen volumes" (Mar. 9, 1895, pp. 322–23).

26 From Isabel Burton's "Preface" to her Household Edition of the *Nights* (London: Waterlow, 1886), I, vi.

27 "Biography of the Book," p. 357.

28 "Author's Preface," Everyman Library edition (1963), pp. xxiv–xxv, n. 1.

29 *Arabian Society in the Middle Ages: Studies from the Thousand and One Nights* (London: Chatto & Windus, 1883).

30 For a review of these, see Scott's "Preface," pp. iv–viii; Forster's, pp. xli–xliii; Burton's "Terminal Essay," pp. 144–46; and Hammer in *New Monthly Magazine* (Jan. 1, 1820), pp. 16–17.

31 *Heroes, Hero-Worship, Works*, XII, 275.

32 James Anthony Froude, *Thomas Carlyle: A History of His Life in London, 1837–1881*, 2 vols. (London: Longmans, 1884), I, 176.

33 See *New Monthly Magazine* (Jan. 1, 1820), p. 17; and "NT," pp. 118–19, respectively.

34 Reference to Jeremy Bentham's letter, B.M. Add. MSS. 25663, f. 145, cited by Norman Daniel, pp. 46–47.

35 On the same point, see also the *Athenaeum*, No. 572 (Oct. 13, 1838), 737–38 (Review of Lane's *Nights*); and No. 622 (Sept. 28, 1839), 741 (Review of Henry Torrens' the *Book of the Thousand and One Nights*).

36 Although it is probable that many of these tales were based on anecdotes written or circulated during Haroun's reign, Payne's generalization is unconvincing because he has not taken into account later interpolations and redactions that indicate the temper of the medieval period. In the late eighties, De Goeje wrote more cautiously about this topic, suggesting that "most of the tales, in substance and form alike, are Arabian, and so many of them have the capital of the caliphs as the scene of action that it may be guessed that the author used as one of his sources a book of tales taken from the era of Baghdad's prosperity" ("Thousand and One Nights," *Encyclopaedia Britannica*, edit. 1888, XXIII, 317).

37 In view of Payne's analysis of the place and date of composition, such an assumption cannot be easily defended. It is safer to say that these scenes give evidence of a late temper (from the tenth century onwards), without necessarily pointing to a prevalent attitude among the upper classes in Haroun's times. The orgiastic detail in the story of the porter and the three ladies may be cited either as a possible interpolation of native reciters whose fancy loves to associate orgy with splendor and wealth, or as a sign of a slowly emerging decadent movement provoked by strict conventions and rigid rules of expression. The discrepancy between these scenes and Muslim morality has already been noticed by the *Athenaeum* critic (No. 572, Oct. 13, 1838, 739). To him such an incongruity indicates a non-Muslim source, for in Muslim literature proper "women appear but seldom, and when they do, it is not to expose their licentious habits like the three ladies of Baghdad."

38 In "Persian Passion Play" Arnold, for instance, maintains such a view of Scheherazade's narrative. Describing a scene in this play, he remarks that "the whole spectacle has just the effect of prodigality, colour, and sumptuousness which we are accustomed to associate with the splendours of the Arabian Nights." See the *Prose Works of Matthew Arnold*, ed. R.H. Super (Ann Arbor: Univ. of Michigan Press, 1960–1974), VII (1970), 22.

39 For information on this subject, see the present writer's the "Growing Scholarly Interest in the *Arabian Nights*," *Muslim World*, 1980.

6

The Growth of Scholarly Interest in the *Arabian Nights*

Even a casual survey of late nineteenth- and early twentieth-century criticism of Scheherazade's tales will indicate a heavy bias in favor of textual and literary-historical research. Numerous essays have appeared dealing with the literary genesis of the tales and their place in fictional literature. At the close of the century the investigations of August Muller, Noldeke, Oestrup, and others into the typological, generic, and genetic characteristics of the various layers of the work were widely known.[1] The immediate impact of these researches is manifested not so much in the subsequent critical concern with specific tales and motifs as in the relative disappearance of sweeping generalizations about the composition of the *Nights*, a point which will become obvious in due course. No less influential, but more comprehensive and thorough, is Victor Chauvin's *Bibliographie des ouvrages Arabes*, esp. vols. IV-VII.[2] Besides the excellent listing of numerous European editions and imitations, Chauvin supplies exhaustive bibliographic references to Western criticism of the major translations. Soon after its publication, interested scholars embarked on studying the early history of the *Nights* and assessing its impact on world fictional and legendary lore.[3] William E.A. Axon admits, in a review of Lane's version,[4] that "Prof. Victor Chauvin's 'Bibliographie Arabe' is a perfect storehouse of information about the literary history of the 'Thousand and One Nights', and of the analogues of the tales of which it is composed. It is in this direction we must look for the scientific value of the 'Arabian Nights'." No less indicative of Chauvin's influence was Macdonald's address of September 23, 1904, to the International Congress of Arts and Sciences at St. Louis. Obviously provoked by Chauvin's meticulous listing of analogous tales and conventions, Macdonald invoked researchers to inquire more thoroughly into the impact of Arabic fiction on such romances as "Aucassin et Nicolette."[5] Whether seen as part of the rise of academic scholarship or as a manifestation of the evolving taste for the freshness and vitality of folklore and romance, this rather specialized pursuit is a marked advance in the criticism of the *Nights*.

Unlike early nineteenth-century philologists, late century European scholars first embarked on examining and classifying individual stories before attempting to tackle the genealogical implications of the whole work. Their achievement in this respect is significant, for rather than adducing sporadic evidence from one exclusive portion, they wisely began establishing the different layers that form the collection, classifying each according to its prevailing topographical detail and generic characteristics. This endeavor quite legitimately entailed extensive search not only for internal circumstantial or stylistic peculiarities but also for external evidence. Besides Arabic literary histories, Indo-Persian, Babylonian, and Greek documents were investigated to decide the milieu, origin and possible transmission or migration of specific motifs and story elements. But before sketching the bearings of these efforts on subsequent undertakings, it is worth stressing that late nineteenth-century and modern Oriental scholarship owes more to early and mid-Victorian writings than is readily acknowledged in current bibliographic surveys. It is only proper, therefore, to assess in the following sections the real significance of some Victorian contributions that are developed but not invalidated by later researches.

Insofar as the textual and literary-historical study of the *Nights* is concerned, it is fair to say that landmarks had already been laid down in the first decades of the nineteenth century. Aside from his enduring contribution to the sociological interest in the tales, Edward William Lane's endeavor to establish a sound test still elicits admiration and respect.[6] No less pertinent is the periodical criticism of the years 1838–41, which was mainly provoked by the latter's significant achievement.[7] Within the limits of this overview, it is enough to refer to the *Athenaeum* effort to elucidate the involved history of the *Nights*. Although taking into account the then current views of De Sacy, von Hammer, Schlegel, and Lane, the *Athenaeum* critic was fully aware of the pitfalls of basing final judgments regarding the date of composition on scattered references to historical events.[8] No great value must be set on these allusions in a book that passed into many redactions and underwent a number of omissions, changes, and interpolations. A "careful and critical examination of the tales," he postulated, "would convince the reader that they were chiefly composed by illiterate persons, unacquainted with the history of their country; and it is unfair, therefore, to assume the accuracy of some particular date referred to, considering the numberless anachronisms contained in the work, and urge it as an argument either in favour or against opinions respecting the authorship, or age when written."[9] Disapproving of Lane's conclusion that the social and cultural setting points to an Egyptian origin, the reviewer observed that Islam regulates and models certain manners of communication and customs or every day practices in the whole Muslim East, establishing a seeming social conformity to which the *Nights* plainly attests. As for the very distinctive Egyptian traits, the reviewer urged that they ought to be seen in the light of the tendency of copyists and compilers to impose their regional predilections on the text.[10]

No less articulate is the critic's discussion of the genealogy of the work. Well acquainted with the Arab's taste for the marvelous and his appetite for story telling, the *Athenaeum* reviewer acknowledged the existence of some historical romances anterior to the ᶜAbbasid reign. He distinguished these from the *Nights,* not only because they depict a chivalrous and warlike atmosphere but also because they make hardly any reference to domestic practices.[11] He regarded these romances as true to the spirit of the pre-Islamic Arabian society. But following on the urban expansion in Iraq, Syria, and Egypt, such tales gave way to a new narrative art which drew quite heavily on bourgeois manners and aspirations. Rather than developing a sociological interpretation of the evolution of the *Nights,* the *Athenaeum* reviewer was, however, bent on proving that the increasing urban demand for entertainment drove story-tellers not only to invent or record accounts of adventure and roguery but also to ransack the light literature of neighboring nations. Like contemporary scientists and philologists, Arab story-tellers, he argued, must have appropriated a portion of this literature during a period of commercial and cultural expansion. Thus, although largely Arabian and Muslim in spirit and temper, the *Nights* contains some sporadic foreign elements. To round off his genetic criticism of the tales, the reviewer partly sided with von Hammer, concluding that the Indo-Persian *Hezār Afsāneh* (which the Arab historian al-Masᶜūdī had mentioned in *The Golden Meadows*) was "either in whole or in part translated into Arabic, and served as a ground work to the various collections of tales circulated in the East."[12]

Beyond these insights into the early history of the *Nights,* the *Athenaeum* critic came across some external evidence to corroborate the existence in the twelfth century of a work called the *Thousand and One Nights*. His citation from al-Maqqari "History of Spain Under the Moslems"[13] is still included, although without due acknowledgment, among the pertinent documentary findings of von Hammer, Torrey, Ritter and, lastly, Nabia Abbott.[14] Taken together this significant documentation as well as the reviewer's effort to reconstruct the historical growth of the *Nights* must be considered basic to the foundations upon which subsequent Orientalists have built. Aside from minor disagreements regarding the history and volume of some cycles, such twentieth-century scholars as Littmann, Macdonald, and Nabia Abbott have reached conclusions that are not basically different from those of the *Athenaeum* reviewer. From the Islamized *Hezār Afsāneh,* they conclude, was borrowed the framing tale, around which clustered a few Arabized and numerous genuine Arabian tales that continued to accumulate till the early sixteenth century. The reviewer's method is no less rewarding than the substance of his argument. Rather than confusing the general with the particular and treating the collection as homogeneous, he demonstrated some awareness of the component parts and genres that comprise the whole. By pointing to the need for separating possible interpolations from essential detail, he touched on a topic that has engaged the attention of a number of scholars, ranging from August Muller and Oestrup to Horovitz and Eli'sseeff.

Another Victorian contribution to modern academic scholarship of the *Nights* is John Payne's classification of the genres that make up its colorful and highly entertaining body. In his study of the history and character of the work, Payne divides the tales into four main categories: histories and romances partly founded on historical data, anecdotes, and short accounts concerned with historical figures and daily adventures, romances and romantic fictions of different proportions, and didactic stories. In the section dealing with romantic fiction, Payne distinguishes between three cycles. Apart from the romantic stories that make free use of the supernatural agency, there are narratives in which the fictional blend with the realistic. More entertaining, however, are the "nouvelles" and tales of roguery, to which Payne traced back many medieval European romances.[15] In these classifications, Payne has worked out a basic pattern which later scholars have continued to appropriate in their descriptive critiques of the generic richness of the *Nights*.[16]

A survey of Victorian contributions to modern Oriental scholarship would not be complete, however, without due mention of a number of nineteenth-century attempts to assess not only the impact of the *Nights* on medieval romance but also its probable, although meager, indebtedness to Greek, ancient Egyptian, and Babylonian sources. A few late eighteenth- and early nineteenth-century writers advanced some ideas regarding possible Greek elements in the *Nights.* A century and a half later, the late Gustave von Grunebaum attempted to track down classical conventions in Scheherazade's intricate web. Well acquainted with Arabic and Greek literatures, von Grunebaum has come to some interesting conclusions concerning the process of borrowing and adapting literary patterns.[17] Similarly, Biblical and Sanskrit scholars have continued to search for relevant echoes in the *Nights* to substantiate their respective views of the transmission and diffusion of folk literature.[18] But whether engendered by late eighteenth-century apologetic admirers of the *Nights,* the advocates of *new* philology, *or* by Biblical and Oriental scholars, this search for foreign elements represents a mere eddy when set beside the more solid tendency to trace Arabian motifs and details in European literature.[19]

Although mainly provoked by Huet's and, later, Warton's speculations on the origin of romance, late eighteenth- and early nineteenth century attempts to tackle the involved genesis, and growth of popular fiction evolved into two different schools. The first accepted the theory of Benfey, Gödeke, Köhler, Nödeke, and Liebrecht respecting the Oriental origin of a great body of European legendary and fictional lore, whereas the second followed Cox, Dasent, and Max Müller in stressing direct Aryan descent.[20]

This latter trend is the direct sibling of new philology, with its strong advocates like Ernest Renan and Joseph Arthur de Gobineau. As far as the present topic is concerned, it is worth mentioning that the most obvious medieval borrowings from Arabic romantic fiction were noticed by such scholars as Henry Weber, Dunlop, Charles Swan, Francis Douce, Keightley, B. E. Pote, and, later, John Payne.[21] But no matter how valuable these writings might be, they were done at a time when comprehensive surveys of the Arab impact on Sicilian and Spanish popular literatures were inaccessible and when the study of folklore was as yet undeveloped. In fact, as late as July 1876, T. F. Crane complained that it was too soon to decide upon matters of transmission and diffusion of popular tales, for the science of folklore had not yet advanced beyond the primary stage of collecting and arranging materials.[22]

In the closing decades of the nineteenth century and with the publication of sound surveys of South European and Asian popular fictions and the appearance of some detailed researches into the typology and semantics of the *Nights,* there has been established a solid foundation for thorough analysis of single themes and motifs. Clouston's investigations into the Arabian origin of several European folk tales must be cited among the prominent developments in the study of the *Nights.*[23] No less rewarding are the writings of Edward Yardley,

E. Rehatsek, Henry Charles Coote, W. F. Kirby, Sidney Hartland, and, later, John W. Mackail.[24] Whether tracing the Arabian origin of some motifs, modes and thematic conventions or examining the process of their migration and diffusion into European literatures, these and other writers have demonstrated keen awareness of the echoes of Arabic fiction in European literature. But although many penetrating remarks and sharp insights into the nature of this impact could be gathered from the foregoing surveys to be synthesized and developed into a brilliant chapter in comparative literature, modern scholarship has left this field virtually untouched. With this sad situation in mind, Joseph Campbell criticized those occidental literary historians who, while collaborating in "a curious fiction of the virtual nonexistence of our debt beyond the boundaries of Europe," have continued to "rehearse the outdated schoolbook story about the Greeks and the Renaissance."[25]

The foregoing contributions must be numbered among the factors that have exerted a marked influence on modern literary taste for the *Nights*. Whether substantiating critical inquiries into the amalgam of the tales, stimulating creative use of their thematic and structural properties, or provoking a reaction against the increasing preoccupation with factual detail, academic scholarship has left noticeable traces on some twentieth-century creative and critical writings. While recognizing this influence, we must, however, not assume that modern criticism of the *Nights* has not benefited greatly from relevant Victorian insights. In fact, the main body of twentieth-century criticism builds on and, at times, echoes the patterns of response which I have already discussed. Another point which needs elucidation before sketching some current appraisals of the *Nights* is the cosmopolitan nature of modern criticism. With the collapse of cultural frontiers, it is no longer tenable to speak of a particular English or American response. With such qualifications in mind, we can briefly assess the modern literary reputation of the *Nights*. But within the limitations of this chapter in relation to the foregoing ones, I shall dwell only on some salient features of this interest, focusing at first on literary studies that have drawn directly on academic research before considering the more theoretic appraisals of the work.

Since the publication of late nineteenth-century academic studies of the *Nights,* several literary critics have embarked on making good use of these achievements to develop psychoanalytic, sociological, or general literary critiques. Numerous articles and book-length essays have appeared dealing with individual themes in the *Nights* and pursuing a variety of topics, ranging from its "teachings" and pictures of social conditions to its subtle Freudian implications.[26] As it is beyond the scope of a concluding chapter to cover these twentieth-century studies, I shall consider only Moffitt Cecil's and Mia Gerhardt's critical estimates of the major generic and literary features of the *Nights*.[27]

In a brief but very penetrating survey of the generic characteristics which distinguish the *Nights* as a work of fiction, Moffitt Cecil has stressed the elemental aspects for which we must look when evaluating the impact of the tales on Western writers. In his analysis of this impact on Edgar Allan Poe, the critic has first established these features before embarking on tracing patterns of borrowing and assimilation in Poe's writings. As it is not part of my concern to appraise Cecil's estimate of Poe's indebtedness, I shall limit my review to his analysis of the inherent richness of the *Nights*. Echoing Leigh Hunt and, among twentieth century writers, Walter de la Mare, Cecil rightly explains that the narrated event is the center of attraction.[28] Whether exciting wonder and terror or titillating one's desire for wealth and adulation, the story is appealing enough to arouse the listener's curiosity and sustain his interest. A second aspect on which he has dwelt is the casually identified narrator. A fisherman, a trader, or a barber may step in at the most unexpected moments to narrate his own life story which must always prove more fascinating than the preceding. No less notable is the absolute faith in God. The medieval Arab story-teller draws no lines of demarcation between the natural and the supernatural in a universe which merely stands as one manifestation of God's sovereignty. Hence in Scheherazade's world, the "supernatural, ordinarily hidden from us, might at any moment crowd miraculously over into the sphere of the senses."[29] But although dominating the whole atmosphere, this faith in Providence is not incompatible with ingenuity, cunning, and perseverance. As the fisherman and the demon in the frame tale, Sindbad and Morgiana (Ali Baba's female slave) demonstrate, one should benefit to the utmost from these human attributes to avert impending disasters and to turn events to one's own gain.

As far as the main generic aspects of the *Nights* are concerned, it is fair to say that Moffitt Cecil shows some acute understanding. When set against the whole discussion of Poe's "Arabesque," his estimate, however, is not comprehensive enough. In justifying Poe's use of the term to describe his own tales, Cecil draws the reader's attention to Poe's acquaintance with medieval Arabic fiction and Islamic theology in general, as well as to his familiarity with the graphic implications of the term. But like all other critics of the *Nights*, Victorian or modern, Cecil fails to stress the applicability of the term "Arabesque" to medieval Arabic fiction. The ᶜAbbasid or medieval story-teller was no less susceptible to the prevailing religious teachings and traditions than his contemporary, the graphic designer. Although the term is still exclusively applied to Islamic geometric, vegetal, calligraphic, and (only occasionally) figural ornaments and designs, its early genesis coincided with the origin and growth of the *Nights*. Its very form (a denaturalized vegetal ornament with leaves spreading from a spiral, interlaced, or undulating main stalk) is also similar to the involuted structure of the *Nights*.[30] Finally, the principles of "Arabesque," such as reciprocal repetition and density, are identical with the stereotyped formulas that begin and end each tale as well as with the abundant detail with which each story abounds.

A more impressive testimony to the value of academic research for the literary critic is Mia Gerhardt's *Art of Storytelling,* mentioned above. Using Littmann's sound edition of the *Nights* and drawing profitably on the outstanding scholarship of Chauvin, Eli'sseeff, Horovitz, Macdonald, and Oestrup, she has produced the first thorough literary appraisal of the work. Aside from her fair evaluation of the major translations, she has demonstrated a sharp insight and a great deal of meticulousness when analyzing the form and content of the work. She divides the thematic contents into stories of love, crime and travel, fairy tales, and tales of piety and learning. In so doing, Gerhardt supplies a comprehensive survey of the thematic diversity of the *Nights*. As the Haroun's cycle forms a major portion in the collection, she has treated it in a separate section, where she dwells with particular care on the caliph's character as well as on the *bourgeois* substance and the narrative skill displayed in the whole cycle. No less rewarding is her description of the structure of the *Nights*. By pointing to the oblique and witnessing narrative systems employed in the work and classifying the thematic nature of the framing tales, she has brought to the reader's mind the artistic richness and literary wealth of Scheherazade's peerless *Nights*.

While Mia Gerhardt is primarily interested in describing the thematic and technical richness of the work, more theoretic critics have probed into the aesthetics of story-telling. Foremost among these is Tzvetan Todorov. Whether seen as a pure expression of structuralist poetics , the broadly   modernist concern with the intrinsic and total value of the work, or as an indirect flowering of late nineteenth-century researches into the generic and typological features of the tales, Tzvetan Todorov's formalist approach to their marvelous element represents a prominent current in modern literary criticism of the *Nights*.[31] His analysis is worth considering at some length because it deals with the aesthetic totality of the *Nights,* its musical blend of form and content.[32]

According to Todorov, the supernatural in the *Nights* is of the "marvelous" rather than the "uncanny" type, for it transcends the laws of reality and plunges into a world of totally different obligations. Todorov classifies the marvelous into three categories: the hyperbolic, the exotic, and the instrumental. Under the first heading, the hyperbolic, he places Sindbad's descriptions of enormous fish, huge birds, and serpents. In such accounts the sailor reports about beings that are "supernatural" only by virtue of their superiority to the commonplace and the familiar. Whether occurring as mere rhetoric or as an observation of strange lands, this element does no excessive violence to reason. From Sindbad's voyages, too, are cited examples to describe the "exotic marvelous." In this case, the listener is supposed to be ignorant of the remote regions which the sailor describes. He has no reason, therefore, to doubt things he is unfamiliar with. The "instrumental marvelous," however, denotes a different genre. As a term, it is applicable to such devices of magical nature as the enchanted carpet and the healing apple in Prince Ahmed's story or the evolving stone in "Ali Baba" (p. 54). In analyzing the literary function of the "supernatural," Todorov explains that this element involves the collapse of the limits between matter and mind, between the physical and the spiritual. It claims its own conditioning laws which transcend our commonplace explanations of coincidence and chance. He cites the story of the second calendar (mendicant) to elaborate on the semantic function of the supernatural. In this tale the realistic theme is sustained as long as the protagonist complies with certain taboos. Soon after violating these, the "supernatural" intervenes in the shape of a wicked genie who is bent on punishing the princess and her amorous companion. According to Todorov, the intrusion of the supernatural is a salient constant in the literature of the fantastic. Rather than merely symbolizing dreams of power, the existence of beings superior to ourselves compensate for "a deficient causality." While most *events* in our daily life are explained by logical reasoning, many are inexplicable and as such are usually passed off as mere coincidence. Coincidence or chance, however, have no place in the realm of the fantastic, for although we tend to consider the intrusion of the genie upon the amorous frolic a sign of the calendar's bad luck, we have to realize that the protagonist himself as well as his listeners consider this intrusion inevitable. To them a conditioning and determining cause is no less so for being of a supernatural order (pp. 107–10).

Todorov assigns another function to the supernatural in imaginative writings. Apart from its literary significance, the supernatural is introduced as a cover to transgress institutionalized censorship or to escape self-imposed taboos. But as the nature of taboos varies from one society to another, the "social" function of the supernatural must be viewed in relation to the moral and religious standards of a given milieu. Thus, when considering the function of the supernatural in the Gothic romance or in the *Nights,* we need to understand that the former was the product of a milieu that was puritanical in its attitude towards sexual love. It should not be surprising, therefore, that in the Gothic romance the supernatural is usually used to elude such inhibitions and taboos. On the other hand, medieval Arabic fiction depicts a society that cherishes rather than condemns sexual love. Hence, the supernatural assumes another function. It is mainly introduced to transgress class distinctions and, thereby, to fulfill the protagonist's wish to marry the princess. In "Aladdin and the Wonderful Lamp," for example, Aladdin's love for the Sultan's daughter "would have remained a dream forever without the intervention of the supernatural forces" (pp. 138, 158–59, 166).

No less engaging is Todorov's discussion of the syntactical function of the supernatural, in which he cites a number of stories where the supernatural intrudes to mobilize the action and to accelerate the narrative. In the story of Kamaralzaman, for instance, the imprisonment of the protagonist in the tower represents a static situation. But as soon as the "jinniya" Maymuna intervenes, "the median disequilibrium" gives way to rapid action (pp. 164–65). The same explanation applies to the second calendar's tale, for as long as the prince retains his sobriety and refrains from touching the talisman, he can live happily with the imprisoned princess. Such immobility means, however, the termination of the story, a thing which runs counter to the story-teller's design. To work out a good story, the reciter explains how a glass of wine provokes the prince to violate the ban and touch the genie's talisman, a move which brings about the intrusion of the genie to break the established equilibrium. In this, as in many other tales, the supernatural agency becomes identical with the artist's knack for story-telling. With this fact in mind, Todorov concludes that "every test in which the supernatural occurs is a narrative, for the supernatural event first of all modifies a previous equilibrium" (p. 166).

Different from Todorov's structural approach, but indicative nonetheless of the increasing interest in the elemental charm of Scheherazade's art, are the writings of such critics as Laura Spencer Portor, E. M. Forster, G. K. Chesterton, and P. H. Newby.[33] In his estimate of the irresistible appeal of this art, Newby elaborates on the most obvious thematic dimensions of the tales, stressing the obsession with luck, the belief in the supernatural, and the seeming indulgence in love and money fantasies. In these explications as in his preference for the more realistic tales, Newby repeats what nineteenth-century critics have already said. What is new in his appraisal, however, is the awareness of the story-teller's extreme cynicism and raillery. Rather than mere willful fantasies, Newby traces in the *Nights* thematic patterns that are heavily charged with irony. According to the writer, the story-teller figures throughout as the "keenest mocker" of self-deceptions despite his seeming indulgence in agreeable illusions.

Both Portor and Chesterton were more attracted to the meaning of Scheherazade's experience as a story-teller, a point which would receive great attention from novelists and critics throughout the early twentieth century. . Early in the century, Portor regarded Scheherazade's involuted story-telling as no mere narrative thread. It is synonymous with the very magic which permeates the whole work. As magic transforms the commonplace into lovely and majestic forms, so does Scheherazade's imagination recreate enchanting narratives from familiar themes, thereby engaging the Sultan's attention and simultaneously transforming him into a perceptive admirer of literature. Portor's conclusion is not very different from Chesterton's estimate of Scheherazade's aesthetics. In "The Everlasting Nights," Chesterton looks upon the scenes of splendor in the *Nights* as symbols of the richness of life itself: "The richness of gold, silver and jewels is a mere figure and representation of that which is the essential idea, the deep and enduring richness of life." Expounding on this point, he further explains that the "preciousness of emerald and amethyst and sandalwood is only the parable and expression of the preciousness of stones, dust, and dogs running in the streets." The length of the tales is, therefore, essential to the meaning of the collection, for it signifies the devouring desire for life. As long as Scheherazade can engage the tyrant's attention and arouse his curiosity, she will continue to live:

> The tyrant can sway kingdoms, and command multitudes, but he cannot discover exactly what happened to a fabulous prince or princess unless he asks for it. He has to wait, almost to fawn upon a wretched slave for the fag-end of an old-tale. Never in any other book, perhaps, has such a splendid tribute been offered to the pride and omnipotence of art.

Chesterton was not the only one who dwelt on the aesthetic dimension of Scheherazade's experience. E. M. Forster has already elaborated in his *Aspects of the Novel* on Scheherazade's capacity "to wield the weapon of suspense" in order to avoid her fate.[34] Although recognizing her other qualifications as an accomplished novelist (exquisite descriptions, tolerant judgments, ingenious incidents, advanced morality, vivid delineations of character, and expert knowledge of three Oriental capitals), Forster argues that Scheherazade "only survived because she managed to keep the king wondering what would happen next." Thus, in line with the general drift of his thesis, Forster cites her experience as conclusive testimony to the importance of a well-sustained narrative in novel writing.

No less varied than the preceding theoretic and critical approaches are twentieth-century literary efforts to assimilate and appropriate some Arabic themes and techniques. As it is not part of my intention to cover even the most significant of these, I shall devote the remaining concluding pages to a survey of a number of creative writings that reveal a pattern of relation and reaction to some academic and critical investigations that I have already studied. In such a consummate exercise in Oriental exoticism as Flecker's *Hassan,* for instance, the reader will notice that the author's picture of the caliph is inspired by a late nineteenth-century view of al-Rashid as less just and wise than Tennyson's idealized hero.[35] Impressed perhaps by Payne's analysis of al-Rashid's character, Flecker has willfully manipulated his source (the tale of Aladdin Abū al-Shamāt) to present the caliph in a very unfavorable light.[36] An entirely different literary recreation of the Orient is Chesterton's deliberate use in "Lepanto" of a medieval image of the Muslim faith. In reaction against the accumulation of factual and historical information about Islam and the Arabs, Chesterton in this poem seizes upon an obsolete convention to retain a clerical picture of the Muslim East.[37]

In line with these early literary recreations, but more closely related to their authors' everyday experiences, are the attempts on the part of some modern story-tellers to emulate Scheherazade's hypnotic art. Although no less dissatisfied with his reading public than was Poe,[38] William Sidney Porter (0. Henry) continued to derive inspiration from the *Nights*. Mainly fascinated by the caliph's role in this collection, Porter reads in the former's nocturnal adventures an expression of the Arabian story-teller's search for subject matter in the streets of Baghdad. These same adventures have suggested to Porter the idea of roaming his own "Bagdad-on-the-Subway" (as he used to call New York), looking for incidents and detail.

> You may be familiar with the history of that glorious and immortal ruler, the caliph Harun al-Rashid, whose wise and beneficent excursions among his people in the city of Bagdad secured him the privilege of relieving so much of their distress. In my humble way I walk in his footsteps. I seek for romance and adventure in city streets—not in ruined castles or in crumbling palaces.[39]

No less attached to Scheherazade's art is John Barth. In his "Dunyazadiad," the genie of story-telling poses throughout as the author's surrogate who draws on Scheherazade's mine of fictional devices.[40] To Barth, setting his surrogate in a remote and alien culture is inevitable, for to escape standardized and stereotyped modes and genres he has to go back to the vital sources of literary forms.[41] Barth admires the convoluted structure of the *Nights* as a symbol of the very richness of Arabian fiction and a testimony to the creator's fecund imaginativeness.[42] By hypnotizing the reader without letting him into the secret of this seductive art, the story-teller demonstrates a superb narrative skill which must be drawn upon to escape the dry conventions of modern writing.

Although it is too early to attempt an adequate assessment of the main currents in twentieth-century English criticism of the *Nights,* it is hardly too much to suggest that the preceding selections indicate a greater awareness of the aesthetic richness of the tales and the complexity of their socio-cultural milieu. Compared to Victorian literary journalism, a considerable portion of twentieth-century treatment of the tales recognizes their composite nature, a recognition which is manifested at its best in the more or less specialized analyses of specific modes, thematic cycles, and artistic patterns. Along with other reasons, this specialized pursuit informs current impersonal researches and indicates therefore a drastic break from the nineteenth-century reception of the *Arabian Nights.* Although its countless simplified versions still entertain children all over the world, its complete texts attract only the specialist. Thus, for the ethnologist, the sociologist, and the student of aesthetics, the *Nights* is a rich storehouse of information and modes that invites investigation and research.

In sum, the *Thousand and One Nights,* or the *Arabian Nights' Entertainments* as the Grub Street translator baptized them in 1705-1706, is no mere index of popular taste. Its popularity with the common reader has never detracted from its enormous presence in informed literary analysis, reading, assessment, and reflections. In theory, it is obvious that twentieth century histories of the novel as well as studies of narrative theory have been tethered to a Eurocentric position that could not accommodate to present an alien in their one-track reading of the novelistic tradition as a pure urban production centered in Paris, London, and little in New York or Boston. A counter direction is taking place, not only because an enormous body of novelistic engagements happen to proliferate all over the world that take at least the frame tale and a few significant ones like those of the mendicants as frames of reference, but also because academic scholarship has been showing great attention to a storehouse of fiction that should have been central to the theory of narrative. This departure is also a departure from the early excursions of Huet, Warton, and Dunlop and their effort to search for origins of a fictional tradition. It is an exploration of motifs, dynamics, characters, events, structures, and deviations that do not fit under Vladimir Propp's schema, or that of N. Elisseeff and Stith Thompson, Hasan El-Shamy, and a number of other folklorists. Upon looking back at the enormous amount of criticism in England, we have the right to argue the case of the *Arabian Nights* as a substantial presence in English literary theory.

Notes

1 For a brief bibliographic survey of these, see Enno Littmann, "Alf Layla wa-Layla," E.I., New Edn. I, 361; C. Brockelmann, *Geschichte der Arabischen Litteratur,* 2nd Edn. (Leiden: E. J. Brill, 1938), II, 72–74; *Suppl.*, II (Leiden: E. J. Brill, 1938), S9–63; and Mia Gerhardt, *The Art of Story Telling* (Leiden: E. J. Brill, 1963), pp. 475–87.

2 Liege: H. Vaillant-Carmanne; Leipzig: 0. Harrassowitz, 1900–1903.

3 As far as Anglo-American studies are concerned, Duncan Black Macdonald's writings stand among the best scholarly researches in the history of the collection, while the literary accounts of Martha Pike Conant, R. C. Whitford and William Axon represent early twentieth-century interest in the impact of the *Nights* on English (mainly eighteenth century) literature. A comparison between Macdonald's output with the latter's brief and hardly exhaustive surveys will tell much about the bias in favor of philological, editorial, and ethnographic research. For Macdonald's writings, see *The Macdonald Presentation Volume*, Essay Index Reprint Ser. (1933; rpt. New York: Books for Libraries Press, 1968), pp. 473–86; and John Jermain Bodine, "The Romanticism of Duncan Black Macdonald," (Ph.D. dissertation, Hartford Seminary Foundation, 1973), pp. 232–44.

4 Bookman, XXXI (Mar. 1907), 258.

5 Duncan Black Macdonald, "The Problems of Muhammadanism," *Hartford Seminary Record*, XV (Nov. 1904–Aug. 1905), 82.

6 See, for example, Gerhardt's comments, *Art of Story Telling*, pp. 62, 252–53.

7 The reviewer for the *Asiatic Journal*, n. ser. XXX, No. 117 (Sept.–Dec. 1839), 84, was impressed by the growing academic interest in the *Nights*, noticing that it "is becoming more than ever an object of grave attention and research." The reviewer might be C. Forbes Falconer as Burton guessed (see the "Terminal Essay" in the *Burton Club Edition* [no date], X, 87) for he, at times, could hardly be distinguished in style and substance from the *Athenaeum* reviewer of the *Nights* in the late thirties. The latter was identified as Falconer by Chauvin, *Bibliographie,* IV, I 16. Although Chauvin's reference was to the authorship of the Sept. 28, 1939, item, the reviewer himself made cross-references to his other writings: Nos. 572–74 (Oct. 13, 20, 27, 1838), pp. 737–39, 759–60, 773–75, and Nos. 622, 624 (Sept. 28, 1839, Oct. 12, 1839), pp. 741–42 and 773–75 respectively.

It is quite possible, however, that Chauvin was mistaken in this identification, for in the late thirties the outstanding Spanish Orientalist Don Pascual de Gayangos (later Minister of Public Education and Senator in Spain) worked as a reviewer of Oriental works for the *Athenaeum*. His citations from manuscript material accessible at the British Museum testify to his authorship of the aforesaid contribution, for during his residence in England the British Museum put him in charge of cataloguing its Spanish manuscripts.

8 The views of these philologists and literary historians were widely known at that time. Aside from their original appearance in French and in German, the writings of De Sacy and von Hammer were available in English. De Sacy's discussion of the Syrian origin of the *Nights* appeared in the *Asiatic Journal* XXVIII (July 1829), whereas von Hammer's documentary evidence respecting the genesis of the framing tale appeared in his article, "On Arabian Poetry," *New Monthly Magazine*, XIII (Jan. 1820), 15–16n, and in the introduction to his version of the *Nights*. Lane's survey of the question of origin and date of composition formed a large portion of the introduction and concluding "Review" to his translation. All these views were discussed by Leigh Hunt, "New Translations of the Arabian Nights," *Westm. Rev.*, XXXIII (Oct. 1839), 132–33; B. E. Pote in "Arabian Nights," *Foreign Quarterly Review*, XXIV (Oct. 1839), esp. 143–45; and by John Payne, "The Thousand and One Nights," pt. I, *The New Quarterly Magazine*, II (Jan. 1879), 154–61. For Schlegel's observations and Henry Torrens' rejoinder, see the latter's "Remarks on M. Schlegel's Objections to the restored editions of the Alif Leilah, or Arabian Nights Entertainments," *Journal of the Asiatic Society*, No. 63, March 1837, pp. 161–68.

9 *Athenaeum*, No. 572 (Oct. 13, 1838), p. 737.

10 *Ibid.*, No. 622 (Sept. 28, 1839), p. 742.

11 *Ibid.*, No. 572 (Oct. 13, 1838), pp. 738–39.

12 *Ibid.*, p. 738. The writer for the *Asiatic Journal*, n. ser. XXX No. 117 (Sept.–Dec. 1839), 83, fully developed this point. The *Nights,* he noticed, "is rather a vehicle for stories, partly fixed and partly arbitrary, than a collection fairly deserving, from its constant identity with itself, the name of a distinct work, and the reputation of having wholly emanated from the same inventive mind." As for the foreign elements, he qualified von Hammer's early sweeping conclusion, postulating that a "work there may have been similar to the *Arabian Nights,* whether in Persian, Pahlavi, or Arabic, we will not dispute; but we cannot imagine that this has furnished anything but the ground-work of what we now call the *Arabian Nights.*"

13 British Museum MS. No. 7, 334, fol. 136.

14 The citation was transcribed from Ibn Sa'id who in turn cited it from al-Qurtubi. See *Athenaeum*, No. 622 (Sept. 28, 1839), p. 742; and Littmann, "Alf Layla wa-Layla," E.I., New Edn., I, 361.

15 "The Thousand and One Nights," pt. 2, *New Quarterly Magazine,* n.s. 2 (Apr. 1879), 378–80.

16 See, for instance, Littmann, "Alf Layla wa-Layla," *I.*, New Edn., I, 363.

17 See, for example, his "Greek Elements in the Arabian Nights," *Journal of the American Oriental Society*, LXII (1942), 277–92.

18 It is another testimony to the strong hold of the *Nights* on the European mind that around the turn of the century Biblical scholars were exceedingly rapturous to discover that the Biblical story of Ahikar crept into the body of the *Nights*. See, for

instance, George A. Barton, "The Story of Ahikar and the Book of Daniel," *American Journal of Semitic Languages and Literatures,* XVI (July 1900), 242–47; and Eb. Nestle, "The Story of Ahikar," *Expository Times,* X (1898), 276–77. The latter concluded as follows: "Startling as it seemed at first, that a story from the *Thousand and One Nights* should have connexions with our Bible, not as the offspring of a Biblical book, but as an ancestor of it, it is no longer incredible, and this is reason enough for anyone who has his eyes wide open to join in Hutten's sentiment: 'Century, what a joy to live!'" Schlegel's unsatisfactory discourse on the Sanskrit origin of the *Nights* was echoed in part by Louis H. Gray in "The Sanskrit Novel and the Arabian Nights," *Wiener Zeitschriftfür die Kunde des Morgenlandes,* XVIII (1904), 39–48. In "History as Told in the Arabian Nights," *Westm. Rev.,* CXLIII (March 1895), 276, J. F. Hewitt attempted to prove that the "Arabian Nights is not only a living picture of eastern Mahommedan life, but a storehouse of the unwritten archives of primeval history derived from the tribal traditions and customs of northern and southern nations." More grounded in Hindu mythology, a writer for the *British and Foreign Review,* XI, No. 21 (1840), 224–74, studied the impact of Eastern fiction on European literature. But instead of stressing the influence of the *Nights,* he concluded that most medieval writings "were indebted to the East for many of their 'findings,' and that the Hindus occupy an early and a prominent place in the History of Fiction" (274).

19   In this brief survey, I am mainly concerned with inquiries into the Arabic element in medieval and Renaissance writings. References to probable influences on eighteenth century literature were too scanty to deserve special attention. Apart from Beattie's remark on Swift's indebtedness to the *Nights* and Goldsmith's allusion to the Arabian origin of Thomas Parnell's "Hermit," there appeared no other significant suggestions. In the nineteenth century and aside from the references to obvious dramatic adaptations, George Brandes devoted a chapter to "The Lake School's Oriental Romanticism," whereas W. A. Clouston and James Mew wrote on Parnell's probable indebtedness to the *Nights* and the Qur'an. See Brandes' *Main Currents in Nineteenth Century Literature,* IV (1875; rpt. London: Heinemann, 1905), 90–101; William A. Clouston's *Popular Tales and Fictions* (Edinburgh: Blackwood, 1887), I, 27–28; and Mew's "Some Unedited Tales from the 'Arabian Nights,'" *Tinsley's Magazine,* Mar. 1882, pp. 235–36.

20   On Warton and his indebtedness to Huet and Warburton, see Manzalaoui, "Pseudo Orientalism," in *William Beckford of Fonthill, 1760–1844, Bicentenary Essays,* ed. Fatma Moussa Mahmoud (1960; 2nd ed. Port Washington, New York: Kennikat Press, 1972), pp. 135–38. William Alexander Clouston supplies an excellent survey of these two schools in the "Introduction" to his *Popular Tales,* (1887). See also T. F. Crane, "Italian Popular Tales," *North American Review,* CXXIII (July 1876), esp. 26.

21   For an apt summary of Swan's and Douce's views, see Manzalaoui, "Pseudo Orientalism," in *Beckford,* pp. 138–39. For other explications, see Henry Weber

"Introduction" to *Tales of the East* (Edinburgh: Ballantyne, 1812); John C. Dunlop, *The History of Fiction* (1814; revised by Henry Wilson, London: G. Bell and Sons, 1888), II, 29–30, 39–42, 132, 21 I, 476–77; Thomas Keightley, *Tales and Popular Fictions* (London: Whittaker, 1834) (esp. on the Perso-Arabian origin of "Cleomades and Claremond," "Peter of Provence and the fair Maguelone," *Le Notti Piacevoli*, better known as the Pleasant Nights of Straparola}, pp. 40–127; Pote "Arabian Nights," *Foreign Quarterly Review*, XXIV (Oct. 1839), 144–46; and Payne, "The Thousand and One Nights," *New Quarterly Magazine*, n.s. 2 (Apr. 1879), pt. 2, 379–80.

22 "Italian Popular Tales," *North American Review*, CXXIII (July 1876), 26.

23 In *Popular Tales and Fictions*, Clouston has quite intelligently discussed the nature of this impact on European literature. While taking into account the theories advanced by other mythologists, he handled the question of influences with great tact. He began establishing the origin of some tales and examining probable ways of transmission. Throughout, he has made good use of preceding investigations into the subject.

24 See Edward Yardley, *The Supernatural in Romantic Fiction* (London: Longman & Green, 1880); E. Rehatsek, "A Few Analogies in 'The Thousand and One Nights' and in Latin Authors," *Journal of the Bombay Branch of the Royal Asiatic Society*, XIV (1880), 74–85; Henry Charles Coote, "Folk-lore the Source of Some of M. Galland's Tales," *The Folk-lore Record*, III, Pt. 2 (1881), 178–91; W. F. Kirby, "The Forbidden Doors of the Thousand and One Nights," *Folk-lore Journal*, V, Pt. 2 (1887), 112–24; E. Sidney Hartland, "The Forbidden Chamber," *Folk-lore Journal*, 111, Pt. 3 (1885), 193–242; and John W. Mackail, *Lectures on Poetry* (London: Longman & Green, 1911).

25 Joseph Campbell, ed., *The Portable Arabian Nights* (1952; rpt. New York: Viking Press, 1967), pp. 35, 33, respectively.

26 For a good listing of these, see bibliography in Gerhardt, *Art of Story Telling* and *Index Islamicus* and *Supplements*, Section XXXVII, "Arabic Literature," subsection "i. Legends and Stories."

27 Cecil's estimate forms part of his study of "Poe's 'Arabesque,'" *Comparative Literature*, XVIII (1966), esp. 63–65.

28 See Hunt's "New Translations," *Westm. Rev.*, XXXIII (Oct. 1839), 135–36; and for de la Mare, see "The Thousand and *One*," in his *Pleasures and Speculations* (1940; rpt. New York: Books for Libraries Press, 1960), pp. 71–76.

29 "Poe's 'Arabesque,'" *Comp. Lit.*, XVIII (1966), p. 65.

30 On "Arabesque," see E. Kuhnel in *E.l.*, New Edn. I, 559–61. In *Two Essays on Robert Browning* (Philadelphia: n.p., 1890), Felix E. Schelling devotes one essay to study the Arabesque in Browning's poetry. In this he explains that "Arabesque . . . was an elaborate style of ornamentation used among the earlier saracens or Arabs, in which the most indulgent play of the fancy was permitted, except that a literal interpretation of the second commandment forbade the representation of a living creature therein"

(p. 1). Richard A. Moulton beautifully describes this involution in the *Nights* where it "is perfectly carried through; all the dropped threads are regularly recovered, and the whole brought into symmetry": *World Literature* (New York: Macmillan, 1927), p. 307.

31 See *The Fantastic*, tr. Richard Howard, with a "Foreword" by Robert Scholes (1970; rpt. Ithaca, NY: Cornell University Press, 1975). Further citations will be incorporated in the text.

32 Although not a formalist, Andras Hamori deals with the story of "The Porter and the Three Ladies of Baghdad" from a similar perspective; see *On the Art of Medieval Arabic Literature* (Princeton, NJ: Princeton University Press, 1974), pp. 164–80.

33 For the essays of Portor, Chesterton, and Newby, see "The Greatest Books of the World: "The Arabian Nights, *Women's Home Companion*, XL (Feb. 1913), 16; "The Everlasting Nights," in *The Spice of Life and Other Essays*, ed. Dorothy Collins (Beaconsfield, England: Darwen Finlayson, 1964), pp. 58–60; "The 'Thousand and One Nights,'" *The Listener*, 39 (Jan. 29, 1948), pp. 178–79, respectively.

34 (1927; rpt. Penguin, 1968), p. 34. Further references are to this and the following page.

35 On Flecker's grounding in Oriental studies, see Geraldine Hodgson, *The Life of James Elroy Flecker* (Oxford: Basil Blackwell, 1925).

36 It is worth mentioning that Yeats strongly disapproved of Flecker's misrepresentation of the caliph's character, condemning *Hassan* as "nothing but the perversity and petulance of the disease from which its author was already fading." In Yeats' opinion, the *Nights* provides sufficient testimony to the amiability and justice of the caliph: "We know Harun ar-Rashid through the *Arabian Nights* alone, and there he is the greatest of all traditional images of generosity and magnanimity"; from "On the Boiler," *Explorations* (London: Macmillan, 1962), pp. 447, 448.

37 See *Collected Poems* (London: Cecil Palmer, 1927), pp. 100–03. Chesterton's image of the East is worth contrasting with that of Kipling. Especially in *Kim*, Kipling manifests some loving intimacy with the Orient which also contrasts quite sharply with the apathetic attitudes of Southey and Moore. In this story, the exotic is absorbed into the homely and the whole picture overflows with liveliness and breathes robust understanding of other manners. After reading the story, the reader may feel, however, that Kipling's view is fixed within the larger imperialist contention that the East is a component part of the British Empire, known and cherished as such. See *Kim* (1908; rpt. London: Macmillan, 1930).

38 Although Poe's "Thousand-and-Second Tale of Scheherazade" is often cited as a parody of Scheherazade's framing tale in the *Nights*, it was meant as "a parable which deplores the plight of the story-teller, Poe himself, in the modern world." After listening with due admiration to her early stories, the King was outraged when she reported modern discoveries and inventions. Consequently, Poe's story-teller was bowstrung. According to Levi Moffitt Cecil, "the bowstringing of the modernized

Scheherazade suggests ... Poe's own failure to gain admiration and support as an author in his day"; "Poe's 'Arabesque,' " *Comp. Lit.*, XVIII (1966), 62, 63.

39 In "A Madison Square Arabian Night," Porter is disillusioned with the public demand for mere amusement. Plumer the painter, who undertakes Scheherazade's role in the same story, explained how, after being a fashionable painter, he suddenly found himself out of business because he "had a knack of bringing out in the face of a portrait the hidden character of the original." People, he concluded, "don't want their secret meanness shown up in a picture"; *The Trimmed Lamp* (New York: Doubleday, 1919), pp. 28, 29.

"A Bird of Bagdad," *Strictly Business* (New York: Doubleday, 1919), p. 188.

40 See *Chimera* (New York: Random House, 1972), p. 20.

41 Richard Moulton has already advised students of literature to return to the *Nights*, for "it alone brings us in touch ... with the processes of evolution which built up romance ... [and as such] has ... great interest for the student of literary form"; *World Literature* (New York: Macmillan, 1927), p. 306.

42 Speaking of this very aspect in an essay of 1940 and citing the framing story of the three ladies of Baghdad as an example, Walter de la Mare makes this adroit remark ("The Thousand and One," *Pleasures and Speculations*, p. 70): "Two black dogs are barbarously beaten with rods, their tears and lamentations are kissed away, the porter, egged on by his betters, addressed but one intrusive little question to the fair ladies, and presto, all but a round dozen of narratives, opening out like incense-breathing water-lilies on some moon-haunted swamp, break one after another into full bloom under our noses."

A Selected Bibliography

Preliminary Remarks

The material listed below is largely limited to writings in English that have proved directly relevant to the present topic. It is divided into four main parts: reference works as defined below (pp. 325–28), editions of the *Nights*, primary, and secondary sources.

The part dealing with editions consists of eighteenth- and nineteenth century English translations of the tales and their significant abridgements, excluding reprints, reissues, adaptations, and imitations which the interested reader can easily find in the British Museum and the Library of Congress Catalogues of printed books as well as in the bibliographic aids cited in the first part.

Primary sources cover imitations, editorial comments, autobiographical recollections, and periodical criticism written in English between 1704 and 1910, covering thereby the responses to the basic editions of the *Arabian Nights* accessible to eighteenth- and nineteenth-century readers. This part is subdivided into two sections. The first includes book-length studies, reminiscences, and comments as well as notable adaptations and writings drawing directly on the *Nights*. In the second section of primary material are listed periodical articles, reviews, and notes arranged alphabetically by periodical title.

Secondary works consist mainly of critical studies published after 1910, and are entered under two sections, distinguishing between published and unpublished material.

I Bibliographic Aids and Reference Works

The following list is compiled for the convenience of readers interested in further bibliographic pursuit of this subject. Besides the British Museum and the Library of Congress Catalogues, Poole's *Index to Periodical Literature*, Helen G. Cushing's and Adah V. Morris' *Nineteenth Century Reader's Guide to Periodical Literature*, the *British Humanities Index, Essay and General Literature Index, 1900–1933* (and Supplements), the *Book Review Digest*, the *Bibliographic Index* and other primary indices, the following aids and specialized surveys are particularly valuable.

Altick, Richard D. and William R. Matthews. *Guide to Doctoral Dissertations in Victorian Literature, 1886–1958*. Urbana, IL, 1960; rpt. Westport, CT: Greenwood Press, 1973.

Baker, Ernest and James Packman. *A Guide to the Best Fiction, English and American, Including Translations from Foreign Languages*. New ed.; London: Routledge, 1967.

Baldensperger, F. and Werner P. Friederich. *Bibliography of Comparative Literature*. 1950; rpt. New York: Russell, 1960.

Bateson, F.W., ed. *The Cambridge Bibliography of English Literature*. 4 vols. Cambridge, England: Univ. Press, 1941.

Block, A. *The English Novel, 1740–1850: A Catalogue Including Prose Romances, Short Stories, and Translations of Foreign Fiction*. New ed.; London: Dawsons of Pall Mall, 1961.

Brockway, Duncan. "The Macdonald Collection of Arabian Nights: A Bibliography." *Muslim World*, LXI (1971), 256–66; LXIII (1973), 185–205; LXIV (1974), 16–32.

Burton, Richard F. "Terminal Essay." In *Book of the Thousand Nights and a Night*. Vol. 10. London: Burton Club for Private Subscribers only, n.d.

———. "Biography of the Book and Its Reviewers Reviewed." In *Supplemental Nights* Vol. 6. London: Burton Club for Private Subscribers only, n.d.

Catalogue of Additions to the MSS. Plays Submitted to the Lord Chamberlain, 1824–1851. B.M. Publications, 1964.

Chauvin, Victor. *Bibliographie des ouvrages arabes ou relatijs aux Arabes publies dans l'Europe Chretienne, 1810–1885*. Vols. IV–VII, *Les Mille et une nuits*. Liege: H. Vaillant-Carmanne, 1897–1904.

Conant, Martha Pike. *The Oriental Tale in England in the Eighteenth Century* (with appendices). New York: Columbia Univ. Press, 1908.

Dibdin, Charles (the elder). *Complete History of the English Stage*. 5 vols. London: The Author, 1797–1800.

Dyson, A.E., ed. *The English Novel: Select Bibliographical Guides*. London: Oxford Univ. Press, 1974.

Farrar, C.P. and A.P. Evans. *Bibliography of English Translations from Medieval Sources*. New York: Columbia Univ. Press, 1946.

Firkins, Ina T. Eyck. *Index to Plays, 1800–1926*. New York: H.W. Wilson, 1927. Supplement, 1935.

Friederich, Werner P. and David H. Malone. *Outline of Comparative Literature from Dante Alighieri to Eugene O'Neill*. Chapel Hill: Univ. of North Carolina, 1954.

Genest, J. *Some Accounts of the English Stage, from the Restoration in 1660, to 1830.* 10 vols. Bath: T. Rodd, 1832.

Hachicho, M. Ali. "English Travel Books about the Arab Near East in the Eighteenth Century," *Die Welt Des!slams*, IX (Leiden, 1964), 1–206.

Houghton, Walter E., ed. *The Wellesley Index to Victorian Periodicals, 1824–1900.* Toronto: Toronto Univ. Press, 1966.

Kirby, W.F. "Contributions to the Bibliography of the Thousand and One Nights and their Imitations," Appendix II to Burton's *Book of the Thousand Nights and a Night. Lowndes, William Thomas. The Bibliographer's Manual of English Literature.* 6 vols. 1834; rev. ed. by H. Bohn. London: Bell & Baldy, 1869.

Mcburney, W.H. *A Check List of English Prose Fiction, 1700–1739.* Cambridge, MA: Harvard Univ. Press, 1960.

———. *English Prose Fiction, 1700–1800, in the University of Illinois Library.* Urbana: Univ. of Illinois Press, 1965.

Macdonald, D.B. "A Bibliographical and Literary Study of the First Appearance of the 'Arabian Nights' in Europe," *Library Quarterly*, II, no. 4 (Oct. 1932), 387–420.

McNamee, Lawrence F. *Dissertations in English and American Literature Accepted by American, British and German Universities 1865–1964.* New York: R.R. Bowker, 1968 (with two supplements covering 1964–1968, 1969–1973).

Manzaloui, Mahmoud A. "Arabian Nights," *Cassell's Encyclopaedia of Literature.* Ed. S.H. Steinberg. 2 vols. London: Cassell & Co., 1953.

Mayo, Robert D. *The English Novel in the Magazines, 1740–1815: With a Catalogue of 1375 Magazine Novels and Novelettes.* Evanston: Northwestern; and London: Oxford Univ. Press, 1962.

Nicoll, Allardyce. *A History of English Drama, 1660–1900.* Rev. ed. 6 vols. Cambridge: Univ. Press, 1952–1959. Vol. 6 titled: *A Short-Title Alphabetical Catalogue of Plays Produced or Printed in England from 1660 to 1900.*

Pearson, J.D. *Index Islamicus. A Catalogue of Articles on Islamic Subjects Published in Periodicals, 1906–1955.* Cambridge: Univ. Press, 1960 (with four supplements jointly edited). "Register of Lord Chamberlain's Plays," Vols. I–VI, covering 1824–1897. B.M. Add. MSS. 53, 702–07.

Sadleir, M. ed. *Nineteenth-Century Fiction: A Bibliographical Record Based on His Own Collection.* 2 vols. Cambridge: Cambridge Univ. Press, 1951; rpt. New York, 1969.

Schweik, Robert C. and Dieter Riesner. *Reference Sources in English and American Literature; an Annotated Bibliography.* New York: Norton, 1977.

Selim, G., ed. *American Doctoral Dissertations on the Arab World.* Washington: Library of Congress, 1970.

Stucki, C.W., ed. *American Doctoral Dissertations on Asia, 1933–1958.* Ithaca, NY: Cornell Univ. Press, 1959.

Tobin, J.E. *Eighteenth Century English Literature and its Background: A Bibliography.* New York: Fordham Univ. Press, 1939.

Ward, Williams, ed. *Literary Reviews in British Periodicals, 1798–1820.* A Bibliography with a Supplementary List of General (Non-Review) Articles on Literary Subjects. 2 vols. New York: Garland, 1972. (Another vol. covering 1821–1826, 1977).

Wright, L.H. *American Fiction, 1774–1850: A Contribution Toward a Bibliography*. San Marino, CA: Huntington Library, 1969.

———. *American Fiction; 1851–1875: A Contribution Toward a Bibliography*. 1957; 2nd ed., San Marino, CA: Huntington Library, 1965.

———. *American Fiction, 1876–1900: a Contribution Toward a Bibliography*. San Marino, CA: Huntington Library, 1966.

Wright, R.G. and B.E. Rosenbaum (comps). *Chronological Bibliography of English Language ·Fiction in the Library of Congress Through 1950*. 8 vols. Boston, MA: Hall, O.K. & Co., 1974.

———. *Title Bibliography of English Language Fiction in the Library of Congress through 1950*. 9 vols. Boston, MA: Hall, O.K. & Co., 1976.

II Major Editions, Popular Abridgements and Famous Illustrated Copies

Here is not the place to dwell on the first appearance in English of Galland's *Nights* (see chap. I, n. 3; and W.H. Mcburney, *Check List*, pp. 10–11). One may notice in passing, however, that Bell's 1708 twelve-volume edition (*Term Catalogues*, III, 592) is probably a reissue of the 1704 copy. A copy of a 1706 edition is at Princeton University Library. An advertisement for a newly published three-volume copy appeared in the *Diverting Works of the Countess D'Anois* (1707). A third edition in seven volumes was on sale in 1711 *(Term Catalogues*, III, 677–78). The following editions, mentioned in the British Museum and the Bodleian Library Catalogues, will give a bibliographic indication of the vogue of the *Nights* in the eighteenth century: the fourth edition (in 12 vols., Andrew Bell, 1713–1715); the fifth (bound in 4 vols., Andrew Bell, 1717–1722); the sixth (12 vols., Osborne & Longman, 1725); the seventh (6 vols., bound in 4, Dublin: Powell & Risk, 1728); the eighth (8 vols., Longman, 1736); the tenth (4 vols., Dublin: Whitestone, 1776); the fourteenth (4 vols., London: Longman, 1778); the eighteenth (4 vols., Montrose: Buchanan & Mudie, 1793); the nineteenth (4 vols., Montrose: Buchanan, 1798); Harrison's (the *Novelist's Magazine)* with plates by E.F. Burney in 1785. For serialized issues, see Robert D. Mayo; and for cheap prints, see Chauvin, IV. Excepting some editions of individual tales, most of the items below are based on the major English translations which are marked with asterisks. Arrangement is mainly by author (redactor, translator, or editor) or by title in cases of anonymous editions and translations. Chronology is preserved whenever anonymous works bearing the same title are cited.

Adventure of the Hunch-back, and the Stories Connected with It. From the Arabian Nights Entertainments. With engravings by William Daniell from pictures by Robert Smirke. London: Daniell, 1814.

Aladdin; or, the Wonderful Lamp. A Delightful Story, Selected from the Arabian Nights' Entertainments, and on Which the Pantomime of That Name Is Founded; Which Is Now Performing, with Universal Applause, at the Theatre Royal. London: Hardy & Co., 1789.

———. London: Tabart, 1805.

———. A new and corrected edition. London: New Juvenile Library, 1816.

————. Corrected and adapted for juvenile readers . . . by a lady. London: Dean, 1840.

————. With an introductory sketch. New York: Maynard, Merrill, 1894.

————. Retold in rhyme by Arthur Ransome. London, n.d.

Arabian Nights Entertainments: Consisting of One Thousand and One Stories: Translated into *French* from the *Arabian* MSS. by M. Galland of the Royal Academy; and now done into *English* from the last Paris edition. 4 vols. London: Longman, 1783.

————. 3 vols. London: Suttaby, 1807 (with an interesting prefatory discourse).

————. *To Which Is Added a Continuation of the Arabian Nights' Entertainments.* 2 vols. Liverpool: Nuttall & Fisher, 1814.

————. Illustrated with engravings from designs by R. Westall. 4 vols. London: Brockers & Baldwin, 1819.

————. *Selected and Revised for General Use, to Which Are Added Other Specimens of Eastern Romance.* Select Library Edition. 2 vols. London: James Burns, 1847 (with a preface).

————. In 39 pts. London: Lloyd, 1847.

————. A new and complete edition with illustrations by S.J. Groves. 2 vols. Edinburgh: Nimmo, 1865.

————. In which *Vathek* is included. London: Griffin, 1866.

————. With numerous illustrations by Frederick Gilbert. London: Dicks, 1868.

————. With illustrations by Thomas B. Dalziel. London: Routledge, 1877.

————. With forty four illustrations by Dalziel Brothers. Sixpenny Series. London: Routledge, 1882.

————. Aldine edition. London: Pickering & Chatto, 1890.

————. Lubbock's Hundred Books, no. 57. Routledge, 1893.

————. With sixteen illustrations by F. Pegram. London: Service & Paton, 1898.

————. With illustrations by W.H. Robinson, Helen Stratton, A.D. McCormick, A.L. Davis, and A.E. Norbury. London: Newnes, 1899.

————. With hundred illustrations in photogravure by S. Wood. 6 vols. London: Dent, 1901.

"Arabian Story," *Classical Journal*, XXI, no. xli (Mar. 1820), 33–35. (An abridged translation of "Keid al nesa," also retold in Alaric A. Watts' *Literary Souvenir*, 1831, as "Woman's Wit," p. 217. See Chauvin, vi, 173).

Baskett, George C., ed. *Selections from the "Arabian Nights."* Rewritten from the original English version of Dr. Scott, for use in schools. Bell's Reading Books. London, 1885.

Beaumont, G.S., tr. *Arabian Nights' Entertainments: Or, the Thousand and one Nights, Accurately Describing the Manners, Customs, Laws, and Religion of the Eastern Nations.* 4 vols. London: Mathews & Leigh, 1811 (Kelly's edition, 4 vols. in one, appeared in 1817).

Beauties of the Arabian Nights Entertainments, Consisting of the Most Entertaining Stories. London, 1792 (Dick's edition appeared in 1808).

Beloe, William, tr. Arabian Tales; or, A Continuation of the Arabian Nights Entertainments. 3 vols. London: Faulder, Hookham and Carpenter, 1794 (with a preface). (For Beloe's contribution, see D.B. Macdonald's marginal note in his own copy, deposited at the Case Memorial Library; and Chauvin, IV, 82, 209).

————, tr. *Miscellanies, Consisting of Poems, Classical Extracts, and Oriental Apologues.* 3 vols. London, 1795.

Bleeck, A.H., tr. "Story of the Cadi and the Robber," Colburn's *New Monthly Magazine*, XCIX (Sept. 1853), 85–91.

Braddon, M.E., ed. *Aladdin; or, the Wonderful Lamp, Sindbad the Sailor; or, the Old Man of the Sea, Ali Baba; or, the Forty Thieves*. London: Maxwell, 1880.

Burnside, Helen M., ed. *Arabian Nights*. London: Tuck, 1893.

*Burton, Sir Richard F. *The Book of the Thousand Nights and a Night. A Plain and Literal Translation of the Arabian Nights Entertainments*. 10 vols. Kamashastra Society for private subscribers only, 1885–1886 (the Burton Club edition is used, n.d.).

———. *Supplemental Nights to the Book of the Thousand Nights and a Night with Notes Anthropological and Explanatory*. 6 vols. 1886–1888.

———. *Lady Burton's Edition of her Husband's Arabian Nights Entertainments Translated Literally from the Arabic*. Prepared for household reading by Justin H. McCarthy. 6 vols. London: Waterlaw, 1886–1887.

———. *The Library Edition of the Arabian Nights' Entertainments*. Reprinted from the original edition and edited by Leonard C. Smithers in 12 vols. London: Nichols, 1894 (illustrated by Albert Letchford).

Bussey, G. Moir, ed. *Arabian Nights' Entertainments*. Translated by the Reverend Edward Forster: Carefully revised and corrected, with an explanatory and historical introduction. Illustrated by twenty four engravings from designs by R. Smirke. London: J. Thomas, 1839 (the 1842 edition is used).

Clarke, Michael, ed. *Stories from the Arabian Nights*. Eclectic School Readings. New York: American Book Co., 1897.

Collection of Tales, Extracted from the Arabian Nights' Entertainments. Carlsruhe, Brawn, 1828.

Cooper, J. *The Oriental Moralist; or the Beauties of the Arabian Nights Entertainments*. Translated from the original and accompanied with suitable reflections adapted to each story. London: Newbery, 1790 (?). (American rpt. Dover, 1797).

Dalziels' Illustrated Arabian Nights' Entertainments. Revised and amendated throughout by H.W. Dulcken, with illustrations by eminent artists, engraved by the Brothers Dalziel. London: Ward & Lock, 1864 (in pts.)

Daniel, G., ed. *Aladdin; or the Wonderful Lamp: A Grand Romantic Spectacle in Two Acts*. Printed from the acting copy (Charles Farley's), with remarks, biographical and critical. London, n.d.

Davidson, Gladys, ed. *Arabian Nights' Entertainments*. Selected and retold for children, and illustrated by Helen Stratton. London: Blackie, 1906.

Dixson, C., ed. *Fairy Tales from the Arabian Nights*. London: Dent, 1893.

Dulcken, H.W., ed. *Dalziel's Illustrated Arabian Nights' Entertainments* (in full, 1878).

Ehot, Samuel, ed. *Arabian Nights' Entertainments*. Six Stories Authorized for Use in Boston Public Schools. Boston, MA: Lee & Shepard, 1880 (1879).

Enchanted Horse and Other Tales from the Arabian Nights' Entertainment. London: Blackwood, 1877.

Fairy Tales from the Arabian Nights. With twelve illustrations by T.H. Robinson. London: Dent, 1899 (same item reissued by Everyman's in 1907, illustrated jointly by Robinson and Dora Curtis).

Far-Famed Tales from the Arabian Nights' Entertainments. London: Addey, 1852 (under that same title appeared Hogg's edition in 1883).

Finter, Edward, tr. *Arabian Nights Entertainments*. Translated into English from the Arabic with a new collection of tales. 5 vols., 1810. (Scarce, see Macdonald's marginal notes and clippings in his own copy of Chauvin).

*Forster, Edward, tr. *The Arabian Nights*. 5 vols. London: Miller, 1802 (with a preface).

Forty Thieves; or, the Banditti of the Forest. New York: Turner & Fisher, 1841 (?)-with moral reflections interspersed.

*Gough, Richard, tr. and ed. *Arabian Nights Entertainments*. Translated into French from the Arabian MSS. by M. Galland ... and now rendered into English. 4 vols. London: Longman, 1798 (with a preface).

Green, Mrs. F.G., ed. *Arabian Nights*. London: Dean, 1904.

Griffis, W.E., ed. *Alij Laila wa Leila: The Arabian Nights Entertainments; adapted for American readers from the text of Jonathan Scott, with an introduction*. 4 vols. Boston, MA: Lothrop, 1891.

Hale, Edward E., ed. *A Selection of Stories from Alif Laila wa Laila, the Arabian Nights Entertainments*. Boston, MA: Ginn & Co., 1888.

*Hanley, Sylvanus, tr. and ed. *Caliphs and Sultans: Being Tales Omitted in the Usual Editions of the Arabian Nights Entertainments*. London: Reeve, 1868.

*Heron, Robert, tr. *Arabian Tales; or the Continuation of the Arabian Nights Entertainments* ... in four volumes, newly translated from the original Arabic into French by Dom Chavis a native Arab and M. Cazotte, and translated into English by Robert Heron. Edinburgh: Bell & Bradfute, 1792 (with a preface).

History of Ali Baba or the Forty Thieves Destroyed by a Slave. Newcastle: W. & E. Fordyce, 1890.

"History of Djouder," *Lady's Magazine* (Jan. 31, 1830), 11–15 (Hurried in style, annotated with remarks on Eastern manners and customs).

Holden, Edward Singelton, ed. *Stories from the Arabian Nights*. Appleton's Home Reading Books. New York: Appleton & Co., 1900.

Housman, L., ed. *Stories from the Arabian Nights*, with drawings by Edmund Dulac. New York: Scribner's, 1907.

Jacobs, J., ed. *The Thousand and One Nights; or the Arabian Nights Entertainments*. Translated by Edward W. Lane. 6 vols. London: Gibbings, 1896 (with introduction and appendices).

Johnson, Clifton, ed. *Arabian Nights' Entertainments*; with notes and an introduction. Macmillan's Pocket Classics. New York and London: Macmillan, 1904.

*Kirby, W.F., tr. *New Arabian Nights. Select tales not included in Galland or Lane*. London: Sonnenschein, 1882.

*Lamb, George, tr. *New Arabian Nights' Entertainments*, selected from the original MS. by Jos. von. Hammer; now first translated into English. 3 vols. London: Henry Colburn, 1826 (with a preface).

*Lane, Edward William, tr. and ed. *A New Translation of the Tales of a Thousand and One Nights; Known in England as the Arabian Nights' Entertainments*; with copious notes by Edward William Lane. Illustrated with many hundred woodcuts. London: Charles Knight & Co., 1838–1840 (in 32 pts.).

———. *The Thousand and One Nights, Commonly Called, in England, the Arabian Nights Entertainments*. A new translation from the Arabic, with copious notes. Illustrated by

William Harvey. 3 vols. London: Charles Knight, 1839–1841 (with a foreword and substantial review).

————. *Arabian Tales and Anecdotes: Being a Selection from the Notes to the New Translation of "The Thousand and One Nights."* London: Charles Knight, 1845 (pt. of Knight's weekly vols.).

Lane-Poole, Stanley, ed. and tr. *Stories from the Arabian Nights.* Selected from Lane's version, with additions newly translated from the Arabic. 3 vols. New York: Putnam, 1890 (1891) (with a preface and notes).

————. ed. *The Thousand and One Nights: The Arabian Nights' Entertainments* translated by Edward William Lane. 4 vols. London: George Bell, 1906.

Little Hunchback, from the Arabian Nights Entertainments. In 3 cantos with illustrations. London: Harris, 1817.

Martin, A.T., ed. *Stories from the Arabian Nights.* Edited for schools. London: Macmillan, 1908.

Mason, J., ed. *Arabian Nights' Entertainments.* Revised and Annotated. London: Cassell, 1875.

Mew, James. "Some Unedited Tales from the 'Arabian Nights'." *Tinsley's Magazine* (Mar. 1887) (later incorporated in Kirby's).

Miscellany of Eastern Learning. Translated into French by M. Cardonne. English translation in 2 vols. London: Wilkie, 1771 (containing some tales, and a useful preface).

Mohan, Hari, ed. *Beauties of the Arabian Nights.* Calcutta, 1839.

Oliver, Edwin, ed. *Arabian Nights.* Rewritten for Children, with illustrations by R. Coutts Armour. London: Treherne, 1909.

Oriental Anecdotes: Or, the History of Haroun Al Raschid. 2 vols (in one). Dublin, 1764.

Oriental Tales: Being Moral Reflections from the Arabian Nights' Entertainments calculated both to amuse and improve the minds of youth. 2 vols. London: Tegg, 1829.

*Payne, Jon, tr. *The Book of the Thousand Nights and One Night:* now first completely done in to English prose and verse, from the original Arabic. In nine vols. London: Printed by Villon Society for private subscription and private circulation, 1882–1884 (with well-informed booklength essay appended to vol. 9).

*————. *Tales from the Arabic of the Breslau and Calcutta (1814–1818) Editions of the Book of the Thousand Nights and One Night,* not occurring in the other printed texts of the work now first done into English. 3 vols. London: Villon Society, private subscription and circulation 1884.

*————. *Tales from the Arabic of the Breslau and Calcutta (1814–1818) Editions of the Book of the Thousand Nights and One Night,* not occurring in the other printed texts of the work now first done into English. 3 vols. London: Villon Society, private subscription and circulation 1884.

*————. *Alaeddin and the enchanted lamp; Zein ul asnam and the king of the Jinn:* Two stories done into English from the recently discovered Arabic text. London: private subscription, 1889.

*————. *Abou Mohammed the lazy, and Other Tales from the Arabian Nights.* Publications of John Payne Society. Olney: Thomas Wright, 1906.

People's Edition of the Arabian Nights' Entertainments, illustrated by J.E. Millais, J. Tenniel, J.D. Watson. London: Ward & Lock, 1882.

Pictorial Penny Arabian Nights' Entertainments. Pt. 1. London: Moore, 1845.

Piguenit, C.P., ed. *Arabian Nights Entertainments: Consisting of One Thousand and One Stories Freely Transcribed from the Original Translation.* 4 vols. London: C.D. Piguenit, 1792.

Poole, Edward Stanley, ed. *The Thousand and One Nights, Commonly Called in England the Arabian Nights Entertainments*. A new translation from the Arabic, with copious notes by Edward William Lane. Illustrated by William Harvey. A new edition, from a copy annotated by the translator. 3 vols. London: Murray, 1859 (reprinted many times; Bickers' 1977 threevolume copy used) (Lane's foreword incorporated in Poole's).

———. Same edition with a preface by Stanley Lane-Poole. 3 vols. London: Chatto & Windus, 1883.

Readings from the Arabian Nights' Entertainments. Murray's Railway Readings. Glasgow, 1867.

Robinson, W. Heath, ed. *Child's Arabian Nights*. London: Grant Richards, 1903.

Rouse, W.H.D., ed. *Arabian Nights*, with an introduction, illustrated by Walter Paget. London: Nister, 1907.

Savile, the Hon. C. Stuart, tr. and ed., "The Adventures of Khodadad," *Colburn's New Monthly Magazine*, LVIII (Feb.–Mar. 1840), 180–93; 373–84.

*Scott, Jonathan, tr. and ed. *Tales, Anecdotes, and Letters*, translated from the Arabic and the Persian. Shrewsbury: J. & W. Eddowes, 1800.

*———. To which is added, a selection of new tales, now first translated from the Arabic originals. Also an introduction and notes, with engravings from printings by Smirke. 6 vols. London: Longman & Hurst, 1811.

Sindbad the Sailor, Aladdin, and Other Stories from the Arabian Nights' Entertainments. London: Ward & Lock, 1886.

Sindbad the Sailor [Lane's trans.] and Ali Baba and the Forty Thieves [Scott's], illustrated by William Strang and J.B. Cark. London: Lawrence & Bullen, 1896.

Sindbad the Sailor (Lane's trans.), with illustrations by Helen Stratton. London: Blackie, 1908.

Stead, W.T., ed. *The Story of Aladdin and the Wonderful Lamp*. Philadelphia, 1908.

Steedman, Amy, ed. *Stories from the Arabian Nights*, told to children . . .; with pictures by F.M.B. Blaikie. London and New York: Jack, Dutton, 1907 (?).

Stories from the Arabian Nights, with an introductory note. Riverside Literature Series. 2 pts. Boston, MA: Houghton & Mifflin, 1897.

Stories from the Thousand and One Nights, . . . revised by Stanley Lane-Poole, with an introduction, notes, and illustrations. Harvard Classics. New York: Collier, 1909.

Story of Ali Baba and the Forty Thieves, an Extract from Dr. Weil's German Translation of the Arabian Nights. Boston, MA: L.H. Kilborn, 1888.

Sugden, the Hon. Mrs., ed. *Arabian Nights' Entertainments*; Arranged for the Perusal of Youthful Readers. London: Whittaker, 1863; and New York: Routledge, 1863.

Tales from the Arabian Nights' Entertainments, as related by a mother for the amusement of her children with . . . engravings by Butler, from designs by J. Gilbert. New edition. New York: Walker, 1848.

Tales from the Arabian Nights' Entertainments. Included in H.B. Stowe's *Library of Famous Fiction* . . .. New York: Ford, 1873.

———. *English School Texts*. London: Blackie, 1905 (reissued with illustrations by Helen Stratton, 1908).

———. *Aladdin and the Wonderful Lamp, Ali Baba and the Forty Thieves, Sindbad the Sailor*. Chamber's Supplementary Readers. London: Edinburgh, 1908.

Tales from the East: A Picture-Book for Children by Harlequin. Containing sixteen coloured plates and about fifty line illustrations, with tales adapted from the Arabian Nights' Entertainments, and written by W. Mord. London: Fisher & Unwin, 1908.

Thousand and One Nights, or the Arabian Nights' Entertainments. A new edition adapted to family readings. Boston, MA, 1869.

———. (Scott's version), with etchings by A. Lalauze. 4 vols. London: Nimmo, 1883.

———. (Lane's edition), with the addition of *Aladdin* and *Ali Baba.* London: Bliss, 1895.

*Torrens, Henry, tr. *Book of the Thousand Nights and One Night:* from the Arabic of AEgyptian ms. as edited by Wm. Hay Mcnaghten. London: Allen, 1838.

Townsend, the Rev. George Fyler, ed. *The Arabian Nights' Entertainments.* A new edition, revised, with notes. London: F. Warne & Co., 1866 (with a preface).

Tweed, Anna, ed. *Arabian Nights,* illustrated by Caspar Emerson and Leon D'Emo. New York: Baker & Taylor, 1910.

Valentine, Mrs., ed. *Eastern Tales by Many Story-Tellers.* London: Warne, n.d.

Warner, A.&A., ed. *Five Favourite Tales from the Arabian Nights in Words of One Syllable.* London: Lewis, 1871.

Weber, Henry, ed. *Tales of the East: Comprising the Most Popular Romances of Oriental Origin; and the Best Imitations by European Authors.* To which is prefixed an Introductory Dissertation. 3 vols. Edinburgh: James Ballantyne, 1812.

Wiggin, Kate Douglas and Nora Smith, eds. *The Arabian Nights: Their Best-Known Tales Retold.* With illustrations by Maxfield Parrish. New York: Scribner's, 1909.

Wilson, Epiphanius, ed. *Arabic Literature . . . with Critical and Biographical Sketches.* London and New York: Colonial Press, 1902 (containing selections from the *Nights*).

III Primary Sources

(A) Printed Books (1704–1910)

A'Beckett (G. Arthur). *The Modern Arabian Nights.* 4 vols. London: Bradbury, 1877.

Addison, Joseph. *The Spectator.* Ed. Donald F. Bond. 5 vols. Oxford: Clarendon, 1965 (For his relevant contributions to the *Spectator* and *Guardian,* see Conant, pp. 271–72).

Alger, W.R. *Poetry of the East.* Boston, MA: Whittemore, Niles & Hall, 1856.

Alkalomeric, the Son of Maugraby: An Arabian Tale. 1814.

Anstey, F. (Thomas Anstey Guthrie). *The Brass Bottle.* London: Smith, 1900.

Arnold, Sir Edwin. *Poetical Works.* 2 vols. Boston, MA: Roberts, 1889.

Arnold, Matthew. *Prose Works.* Ed. R.H. Super. Vol. VII. Ann Arbor: Univ. of Michigan, 1970.

Ashton, John. *Chapbooks of the Eighteenth Century.* London: Chatto & Windus, 1882.

Bage, R. *The Fair Syrian.* 2 vols. Dublin: J. Walter, 1787.

Beattie, J. *Dissertations Moral and Critical in Philosophical and Critical Works.* London: W. Strahan, 1783.

Beckford, William. *History of the Caliph Vathek.* London: J. Johnson, 1786.

———. *Episodes of Vathek.* Translated by Sir Frank T. Marzials, with an introduction by L. Melville. London: Swift, 1912.

———. *Story of Al Raoui—A Tale from the Arabick.* 2nd ed., London: C. Geisweiler, 1799.

Berquin, A. *The Blossoms of Morality.* London: Newbery, 1789.

Besant, Walter. *The Life and Achievements of Edward Henry Palmer.* 2nd ed., London: Murray, 1883.

Bignon, Jean Paul. *Adventures of Abdallah, Son of Hanif . . .*, done into English by William Hatchett. London: T. Worrall, 1729.

Blair, Hugh. *Lectures on Rhetoric and Belles Lettres.* 3 vols. 1783; 3rd ed., London: A Strahan & Cadell, 1787.

Bolingbroke, Lord Viscount (Henry St. John). *On the Study and Use of History.* 1738.

Brandes, George. *Main Currents in Nineteenth Century Literature: Naturalism in England.* Vol. IV. 1875; rpt. Heinemann, 1905.

Broadbent, R.J. *A History of Pantomime.* London, 1901.

Browning, Robert and Elizabeth Barrett. *The Letters . . . 1845–46.* Ed. E. Kitner. Cambridge, MA: Harvard Univ. Press, 1969.

Burne-Jones, Georgiana. *Memorials of Edward Burne-Iones.* 2 vols. New York: Macmillan, 1904.

Bussey, G. Moir, ed. *Fables, Original and Selected*, by most esteemed European and Oriental Authors, with an introductory dissertation on the history of fable. London: C. Tilt, 1839.

Button, Edward, tr. *A New Translation of the Persian Tales.* London, 1754.

Byron, H.J. *Aladdin, or the Wonderful Scamp.* London: Lacy's Acting Edition of Plays, 1861.

———. *Ali Baba.* London: Lacy's Acting Edition of Plays, 1864.

———. *Camaralzaman and the Fair Badoura.* London: Lacy's Acting Edition of Plays, 1872.

Callaway, John. *Oriental Observations.* Colombo: Printed for the author, 1823.

Campbell, J.F. *Popular Tales of the West Highlands.* 4 vols. Edinburgh: Edmonston, Douglas, 1860–1862.

Campbell, Killis. *A Study of the Romance of the Seven Sages with Special Reference to the Middle Ages Version.* Baltimore, MD: *PMLA*, 1898; rpt. XIV, 1899.

Capper, James. *Observations on the Passage to India.* London: W. Faden, 1783.

Carlyle, Joseph D. *Specimens of Arabian Poetry.* 2nd ed., London: Cadell & Davies, 1810.

Carlyle, Thomas. *Correspondence of Thomas Carlyle and Ralph Waldo Emerson, 1834–1872.* 2 vols. London: Chatto & Windus, 1883.

———. *Works.* 16 vols. New York: Collier, 1897.

Carne, J. *Letters from the East.* 2 vols. London: Henry Colburn, 1826.

Chandler, Izora and Mary W. Montgomery. *Gold in the Gardens of Araby.* New York: Eaton & Mams, 1905.

Clark, Charles H. *Transformations.* London: Ward & Lock, 1883.

Clerk, Mrs. G., tr. *I*c*lam-En-Nas.* London: H.S. King, 1873.

Clouston, W.A. *Arabian Poetry for English Readers.* Glasgow: privately printed, 1881.

———. *Book of Sindibad.* Privately printed, 1884.

———. *A Group of Eastern Romances and Stories.* Privately printed, 1889.

———. *Literary Coincidences . . . and Other Papers.* Glasgow, 1892.

———. *Popular Tales and Fictions, Their Migrations and Transformations.* 2 vols. New York: Scribner's, 1887.

————. *Variants and Analogues of Some of the Tales in Sir Richard F. Burton's Supplemental Nights.* 3 vols. London: privately printed, 1887.

Coleridge, Samuel T. *Coleridge's Miscellaneous Criticism.* Ed. T.M. Raysor. Cambridge, MA: Harvard Univ. Press, 1936.

————. *Coleridge's Shakespearean Criticism.* Ed. T.M. Raysor. 2 vols. Cambridge, MA: Harvard Univ. Press, 1930.

————. *Collected Letters of Samuel Taylor Coleridge.* Ed. Earl L. Griggs. 4 vols. Oxford: Clarendon, 1956–1959.

————. *Collected Works, The Friend.* 2 vols. Ed. Barbara E. Rooke. London: Routledge & Kegan, 1969.

————. *Letters of Samuel Taylor Coleridge.* Ed. Ernest H. Coleridge. London: Heinemann, 1895.

————. *The Notebooks of Samuel Taylor Coleridge.* Ed. Kathleen Coburn. 2 double vols. London: Routledge & Kegan Paul, 1957–1962.

Comparetti, Domenico. *Researches Respecting the Book of Sindibad.* London: Folklore Society Publications, 1882.

Conybeare, F.C., J.R. Harris and A.S. Lewis, trs. and eds. *The Story of Ahikar from the Syriac, Arabic, Armenian, Ethiopic, Greek and Slavonic Versions*, with an introduction and . . . texts. London: Clay, 1898.

Cooke, Mrs. Rose Terry. *Poems.* New York: W.S. Gottsberger, 1888.

Cooper, Thomas. *The Life of Thomas Cooper, Written by Himself.* London: Hodder & Stoughton, 1872.

Cornwall, B. *The Poetical Works.* 3 vols. London: Henry Colburn, 1822.

————. *A Sicilian Story . . . and Other Poems.* London: Oilier, 1820.

Crabbe, George. *Life and Poetical Works.* By his son. London; Murray, 1861.

————. *Poems.* Ed. Adolphus W. Ward. 3 vols. Cambridge: Univ. Press, 1907.

Cracroft, Bernard. *Essays Political and Miscellaneous.* 2 vols. London: Trubner, 1868.

Crawford, F.M. *Kaled. A Tale of Arabia.* London: Macmillan, 1891.

————. *Mr. Isaacs.* New York: Macmillan, 1882.

Crellin, H.N. *Romances of the Old Seraglio.* With illustrations by S.L. Wood. London: Chatto & Windus, 1894.

————. *Tales of the Caliph.* A new ed., London: Chatto & Windus, 1895.

Croly, George. *Angel of the World: An Arabian Tale . . . with Other Poems.* London: J. Warren, 1820.

Croxall, Samuel. *Select Collection of Novels and Histories.* 6 vols. 2nd ed., London: John Watts, 1729.

Dacre, Charlotte. *Zofloya; or the Moor.* 3 vols. London: Longman, 1806.

Dallaway, James. *Constantinople Ancient and Modern.* London: Cadell & Davies, 1797.

Daly, A., tr. *An Arabian Night in the Nineteenth Century.* A Comedy in Four Acts, from the German of von Moser. New York, 1844 (?)

Darley, G. *Labours of Idleness; or, the Seven Nights Entertainments.* London: John Taylor, 1826.

Dasent, Sir G.W. *Tales from the Norse.* London: Blackie, 1906.

Dawson, A.J. *African Nights' Entertainments.* New York: Dodd & Mead, 1900.

Denon, Vivant. *Travels in Upper and Lower Egypt.* 2 vols. London: James Ridgway, 1802.

De Quincey. *Collected Writings.* Ed. David Masson. London: Black, 1896.

————. *Selections from* . . .. Ed. with introduction and notes by Milton Haight Turk. Boston and London: Ginn & Co., 1902.

Dibdin, C. *The Mirror; or, Harlequin Everywhere.* 2nd ed. London: Kearsley, 1779.

Dibdin, T. *Il Bondocani; or the Caliph Robber.* London: Longman, 1801.

————. *Haroun Alraschid; or Wants and Superfluities.* Dicks' Standard Plays, no. 513. London: Dicks, 1884.

————. *Letters of Charles Dickens.* Edited by his Sister-in-Law and his Eldest Daughter. 3 vols. New York: Scribner's, 1879.

————. *The Ninth Statue; or, the Irishman in Bagdad.* London: John Miller, 1814. Dickens, Charles. *Thousand and One Humbugs.* (See Sec. B of this bibliography).

————. *Uncollected Writings from Household Words,* 1850–1859. Ed. with introduction and notes by Harry Stone. Bloomington: Indiana University, 1968.

————. *Writings, with Critical and Bibliographical Introductions* by Edwin P. Whipple and others. 32 vols. Boston and New York, 1894.

Disraeli, B. *Home Letters, Written . . . in 1830 and 1831.* 2nd ed., London: Murray, 1885.

Disraeli, Isa'ac. *Loves of Majnoun and Leila.* Rpt. Calcutta, 1800?

————. *Romances.* London: Cadell & Davies, 1799.

Dobson, Henry Austin. *Thomas Bewick and His Pupils.* London: Chatto & Windus, 1884.

Douce, F. *Illustrations of Shakespeare, and of Ancient Manners.* 2 vols. London, 1807.

Drake, Nathan. *Literary Hours; or Sketches Critical, Narrative, and Political.* 2 vols. 4th ed., London: Longman, 1820.

Driver, Henry Austen. *The Arabs; a Tale,* in four cantos. London, 1825.

Dunlop, J.C. *The History of Prose Fiction* (1814). Revised by Henry Wilson. 2 vols. London: Bohn's Standard Library, 1888.

Excursion of Osman, Son of Abdallah. A Political Romance. Liverpool: T. Schofield, 1792.

Fielding, Henry. *Joseph Andrews* (1742). (Edition used is the 1961 Houghton Mifflin *Joseph Andrews and Shamela*).

Fields, Mrs. Annie Adams. *A Shelf of Old Books.* London: Osgood & McIlvaine, 1894.

Fiske, J. *Myths and Myth-Makers.* Boston and New York: Houghton Mifflin, 1872.

Fitzball, E. *The Barber of Bagdad.* Dicks' Standard Plays, no. 975. London, 1888.

Flecker, J.E. *Hassan.* New York: A. Knopf, 1924.

Flloyd, Thomas, tr. *Tartarian Tales* (by Thomas S. Ouellette). London: J. & R. Tonson, 1759.

Forbes, Duncan. *The Adventures of Hatim Tai: A Romance.* London, 1830.

Forbes, J. *Oriental Memoirs,* 2 vols. 2nd ed., London, 1837.

Forster, J. *The Life of Charles Dickens.* 3 vols. 1872–1874; rpt. London: Chapman and Hall, 1904.

Froude, J.A. *Thomas Carlyle. A History of his Life in London, 1834–1881.* 2 vols. London: Longman, 1884.

Galt, John. "Haddad ben Ahab," in *The Romancist and Novelist's Library.* Ed. Wm Hazlitt. New series. Vol. II. (1841).

Garnett, R. *Essays of an Ex-Librarian.* London: Dodd & Mead, 1901.

Gibbon, Edward. *Memoirs of My Life.* Ed. from manuscripts by G.A. Bonnard. London: Nelson, 1966.

Gildon, Charles. *The Golden Spy; or, a Political Journal of the British Nights Entertainments of War and Peace, Love and Politics*. London: Woodward, 1709.

Gissing, George. *Charles Dickens: A Critical Study*. London, 1904.

Goeje, De. "Thousand and One Nights," *Encyclopaedia Britannica*, XXIII (1888), 316–18.

Goldsmith, Oliver. *Collected Works*. Ed. Arthur Friedman. 5 vols. Oxford: Clarendon, 1966.

Gomme, G.L. and H.B. Wheatley, eds. *Chap-Books and Folk-Lore Tracts*. Villon Society, 1885.

Gosse, Edmund. *Critical Kit-Kats*. New York: Dodd, 1897.

———. *Gossip in a Library* (1891). 3rd ed., London: Heinemann, 1893.

Gottheil, Richard. "The Arabian Nights." In *The Library of World's Best Literature*, edited by Charles Dudley Warner. 3 vols. New York: Peale & Hill, 1896. Vol. 2.

Gray, Louis H. "Literary Studies on the Sanskrit Novel: I. The Sanskrit Novel and the Arabian Nights," *Wiener Zeitschrift für die Kunde des Morgenlandes*, XVIII (1904), 39–45.

Green, Thomas. *Extracts from the Diary of a Lover of Literature*. Ipswich: John Raw, 1810.

Gregory, Benjamin, *Autobiographical Recollections*. Edited, with memorials of his later life, by his eldest son (J.R. Gregory). London: Hodder & Stoughton, 1903.

Grolier Society Prospectus of the Thousand Nights and a Night. The Library Edition prepared by Leonard C. Smithers. London, 1897.

Grundy, Sidney. *The Arabian Nights. A Farce Comedy*. Lacy's Acting Edition, 1893.

Hajira; a Turkish Love Story. London: E. Arnold, 1896.

Hamilton, Terrick, tr. *Antar, A Bedoueen Romance*. 4 vols. London: Murray, 1820.

Harrison, Frederick. *Among My Books*. London: Macmillan, 1912.

Hartland, Edwin Sidney. *The Science of Fairy Tales*. An Inquiry into Fairy Mythology. New York: Scribner's, 1891.

Hassan Abdallah; . . . and Other Tales: A Companion to the Arabian Nights. With an introduction by Miss Pardoe. Baltimore: Kelly, 1860.

Hauff, Wilhelm. *Arabian Days' Entertainments*. Translated from the German by Herbert P. Curtis. Boston, MA: Phillips, 1858.

Hawkesworth, John. *Adventurer*, nos. 4–5, 20–22, 32, 72, 91, 114, 132.

———. *Almoran and Hamel:* An Oriental Tale. 2 vols. London: Payne & Cropley, 1761.

Haywood, Mrs. Eliza. *The Unfortunate Princess*. London, 1741.

Hazlitt, W., ed. *History of English Poetry*. Percy Society Series. London: Reeves & Turner, 1871.

———. *Miscellaneous Works*. 5 vols. Philadelphia: Carey and Hart, 1848.

———. *The Plain Speaker: Opinions on Men, Books and Things*. 2 vols. London: Henry Colburn, 1826.

Henley, William Ernest. *Works*. 7 Vols. London: David Nutt, 1908.

History of the Fisherman and the Genius, taken from the real ms. of the Arabian Tales, recently discovered in Baghdad. London: Mclean, 1859 (A political skit).

History of the Forty Vezirs. TrJE.J.W. Gibb. London: George Redway, 1886.

Hockley, W.B. *Tales of the Zenana: Or a Nuwab's Leisure Hours*. 3 vols. London: Saunders & Otley, 1827.

Holcroft, Thomas. *Memoirs . . . Written by Himself*. 3 vols. London: Longman, 1816.

Hole, Richard. *Arthur or the Northern Enchantment*. London, 1789.

————. *Remarks on the Arabian Nights Entertainments, in Which the Origin of Sindbad's Voyages . . ., Is Particularly Considered*. London: Cadell & Davies, 1797.

Hood, Thomas. *Letters of . . .* Ed. Peter F. Morgan. Toronto: Univ. Of Toronto Press, 1973.

————. *Selected Poems*. Ed. John Clubbe. Cambridge, MA: Harvard Univ. Press, 1970.

Hoops, J. *Present Problems of English Literary History*, in *Congress of Arts and Science, Universal Exposition*, St. Louis, 1904. Ed. Howard J. Rogers. Boston and New York, 1906. Vol. III (esp. 415).

Hope, T. *Anastasius, or the Memoirs of a Greek*. 3 vols. London: Murray, 1819.

Hoppner, J. *Oriental Tales Translated into English Verse*. London: Hatchard, 1805.

Houghton, Richard Monckton Milnes, ed. *Life and Letters of John Keats*. London: Moxon, 1867.

————. *Palm Leaves*. London: Moxon, 1844.

Housman, Laurence. *Arthur Boyd Houghton*. London: Kegan & Paul, 1896.

Huet, P. *A Treatise of Romances and Their Original*. London, 1672.

Hughes, John. *The Siege of Damascus*. London, 1720. 3rd. ed., London: Watts, 1735.

Hume, James S., ed. *Selection from the Writings, Prose and Poetical, of the late Henry Torrens*, with a Biographical Memoir. 2 vols. Calcutta and London: R.C. Lepage, 1854.

Hunt, Leigh. *Autobiography*. 3 vols. London, 1850.

————. *A Book for a Corner; or Selections in Prose and Verse*. 2 vols. London: Chapman & Hall, 1849.

————. *A Jar of Honey from Mount Hybla*. 1848.

————. *Leigh Hunt's Literary Criticism*. Eds. L.H. and C.W. Houtchens. New York: Columbia, 1956.

————. *Lord Byron and Some of his Contemporaries*. 2nd ed., London, 1828.

————. *Poetical Works*. Ed. S.A. Lee. 2 vols. Boston, MA, 1866.

Ireland, Alexander, ed. *Book Lover's Enchiridion: Thoughts on the Solace and Companionship of Books*. London: Simpkin, 1883.

Irving, P.M., ed. *Life and Letters of Washington Irving*. New York: Putnam, 1864.

Irving, W. *Alhambra*. London. 1896.

————. *Journal of Washington Irving 1823–24*. Ed. Stanley T. Williams. Cambridge, MA: Harvard Univ. Press, 1931.

Irwin, Eyles. *Eastern Eclogues*. London, 1780.

James, G.P.R. *Camaralzaman: A Fairy Drama*. London, 1848.

John Bull and His Wonderful Lamp-A new reading of an old tale, by Homunculus (W.M. Thackeray?). London: Petheram, 1849.

Johnson, S. *Idler*, nos. 75, 99, 101. *Rambler*, nos. 17, 38, 65, 120, 190, 204, 205.

————. *The Prince of Abissinia. A Tale*. 2 vols. London: R. & L. Dodsley, 1759.

————. *The Yale Edition of the Works of Samuel Johnson*. 8 vols. New Haven, CT, 1958–1969.

Johnston, Grace L. Keith. *Alasnam's Lady; a modern Romance*. 3 vols. London: Bentley, 1882.

Johnstone, Charles. *The History of Arsaces, a Prince of Betlis*. 2 vols. London: T. Becket, 1774.

Jones, Sir William. *The Letters*. Ed. G. Cannon. Oxford: Clarendon, 1970.

————. *Works, with the Life of the Author* by Lord Teignmouth. 13 vols. London: Stockdale, 1807.

Kames, Henry Home. *Elements of Criticism*. Ed. Abraham Mills. New York: Huntington & Savage, 1846.

————. *Sketches of the History of Man*. 2nd ed., London: Strahan and Cadell, 1778.

Keats, John. *The Letters of John Keats, 1814–1821.* Ed. H.E. Rollins. 2 vols. Cambridge, MA: Harvard Univ. Press, 1958.

———. *The Poetical Works and Other Writings.* Ed. Harry H. Forman. 4 vols. London: Reeves & Turner, 1889.

Keeve, Henry George. *Persian Stories.* 7th ed., London: J.W. Parker, 1844.

Keightley, Thomas. *The Fairy Mythology; Illustrative of the Romance and Superstition of Various Countries.* 1828; rev. and enl., London: Bohn, l850.

———. *Tales and Popular Fictions, Their Resemblance and Transmission from Country to Country.* London: Whittaker, 1834.

Kinglake, Alexander William. *Eothen, or Traces of Travel Brought from the East.* 1844; new ed., New York: Putnam, 1850.

Kipling, Rudyard. *Something of Myself.* London: Macmillan, 1937.

———. *Writings in Prose and Verse.* 36 vols. New York: Scribner's, 1920–1937.

Kirby, W.F. *Ed-Dimiryaht. An Oriental Romance; and Other Poems.* London: Williams and Norgate, 1867.

Knight, Charles. *Once Upon a Time: Sketches.* New and enlarged edition. London: Routledge, 1865.

———. *Passages of a Working Life.* 3 vols. London: Bradbury, 1864.

Knight, Ellis Cornelia. *Dinarbas; a Tale: Being a Continuation of Rasselas, Prince of Abissinia.* London: Dilly, 1790.

Knight, Henry Gaily. *Eastern Sketches: In Verse.* 2nd ed., London: Murray, 1819.

Knight, William. *Memoir of John Nichol.* Glasgow: J. MacLehose, 1896.

Knox, Vicesimus. *Essays Moral and Literary.* New enl. ed., 2 vols. 1782.

Landor, Walter Savage. *Poems from the Arabic and the Persian; with Notes by the Author of Gebir.* London: Sharpe & Rivingtons, 1800.

———. *The Works, Poems.* Ed. Stephen Wheeler. 3 vols. London: Chapman & Hall, 1933.

Langhorne, J. *Solyman and Almena, an Oriental Tale.* London: H. Payne & W. Cropley, 1762.

Lane, Edward W. *An Account of the Manners and Customs of the Modern Egyptians.* 1836, reprinted in 1837 by the *Society for the Diffusion of Useful Knowledge.* (The 1963 Everyman's Library ed. is used).

Lane-Poole, Stanley, ed. *Arabian Society in the Middle Ages: Studies from the Thousand and One Nights.* London: Chatto & Windus, 1883.

———. *Life of Edward William Lane.* London, 1877.

Lee, A.C. *Decameron: Its Sources and Analogues.* London: Nutt, 1909.

Lefanu, A. *Memoirs of the Life and Writings of Mrs. F. Sheridan.* London, 1824.

Lewis, Matthew Gregory. *Romantic Tales.* 4 vols. London, 1808.

Light, H. *Travels in Egypt, Nubia, Holy Land, Mount Lebanon, and Cyprus, in the Year 1814.* London, 1818.

Lowell, James R. *Poems.* Boston and New York: Houghton Mifflin, 1897 (his "Aladdin" first appeared in Putnam's *Monthly Magazine,* 1853). Lytton, Edward B. *Leila; or the Siege of Granada,* 1838.

Maccabe, Belinda, ed. *The Wonderful Book; or, Tales for the Merry, Stories for the Studious, and Marvels for the Morose* (Tales of Sheikh al Mohdy). 2nd ed., Dublin: Duffy, 1849.

Macdonald, D.B. *Development of Muslim Theology, Jurisprudence and Constitutional Theory.* New York: Scribner's Sons, 1903.

———. *The Religious Attitude and Life in Islam:* Being the Haskell Lectures on Comparative Religions Delivered before the University of Chicago in 1906. Chicago: The Univ. of Chicago Press, 1909.

———. "Story of the Fisherman and the Jinni, transcribed from Galland's MS. of the 'Thousand and One Nights'," *Orientalische Studien, Theodor Noldeke zum siebzigsten Geburtstag,* I (1906), 357–83.

Macdonald, H.B. *Abdul Medjid and Other Poems.* Edinburgh, 1854.

Macmichael, William. *The Gold-Headed Cane.* 2nd ed., London: Murray, 1828.

Malcolm, Sir John. *Sketches of Persia, from the Journals of a Traveller in the East.* 1827.

Manley, Mrs. M. de la R. *Almyna or the Arabian Vow.* London, 1707.

Manning, Anne. *The Adventures of the Caliph Haroun Alraschid.* London: Richard Clay & A. Hall, 1855.

Marryat, Florence. *Open Sesame.* 3 vols. London, 1875.

Marryat, Frederick. *The Pacha of Many Tales.* 1835; London: Bentley, Standard Novels Ser., 1838.

Martin, Theodore, tr. *Aladdin, or the Wonderful Lamp* (by A. Oehlenschlager). London, 1857.

Masson, David. *Edinburgh Sketches and Memoirs.* London and Edinburgh: Adam and Charles Black, 1892.

Massouf, or, the Philosophy of the Day: An Eastern Tale. London: Minerva, 1802.

Maturin, Charles. *Melmoth the Wanderer.* 1820; Lincoln: Univ. of Nebraska Press, 1972.

Meredith, George. *The Critical Heritage.* Ed. Ioan Williams. London: Routledge & Kegan, 1971.

———. *Poems.* Surrey ed., London Times Club, 1912.

———. *Works.* Memorial ed., New York: Scribner's Sons, 1909–1912.

Mitford, A.B. Freeman (Lord Redesdale). *Memoirs.* 2 vols. London: Hutchinson, 1915.

Modern Arabia Displayed, in four Tales. London: Harris, 1811.

Mohan, Hari. *Beauties of the Arabian Nights.* Calcutta, 1839.

Montagu, Lady Mary Wortley. *The Complete Letters.* Ed. Robert Halsband. 3 vols. Oxford: Clarendon, 1965–1966.

Moore, Thomas, ed. *Letters and Journals of Lord Byron, with Notices of His Life.* London: Murray, 1830.

———. *Poetical Works, Collected by Himself.* 10 vols. London: Longman, 1840–1841.

Morier James. *Adventures of Hajji Baba of Ispahan.* 3 vols. London: Murray, 1824 (Bentley's 1851 edition is used in the text).

———. *Adventures of Hajji Baba of Ispahan in England.* 2 vols. London: Murray, 1828.

———. *Ayesha, the Maid of Kars.* Paris: Baudry, 1834.

———. *The Mirza.* 2 vols. London: Bentley, 1841.

———. *Misselmah, a Persian Tale.* Brighton, 1847.

———. *Zohrab, the Hostage.* 3 vols. London: Bentley, 1832.

Morris, William. *The Collected Works.* New York: Russell & Russell, 1966.

Moser, G. *Haroun Al-Raschid.* London, 1879.

Murray, Sir Charles. *Hassan; or the Child of the Pyramid.* 2 vols. London, 1857.

———. *Nour-ed-dyn; or the Light of the Faith.* London: Christian Knowledge Society, 1883.

Newman, John Henry. *Apologia Pro Vita Sua.* Ed. David J. De Laura. New York: Norton, 1968.

Nichols, John. *General Index of Gentleman's Magazine, 1787–1818*. London, 1821.

———. *Literacy Anecdotes of the Eighteenth Century*. 9 vols. London: Nichols Son and Bentley, 1812–1815 (esp. vol. 6, p. 318, on Gough's ed.).

Noble, James. *The Orientalist; or, Letters of a Rabbi*. Edinburgh, 1831.

Ockley, Simon. *History of the Saracens*. 2 vols. 2nd ed., London, 1718.

Oriental Tales, or the Ruby Heart . . . and the Enchanted Mirror. New ed. London, 1802.

The Orientalist, a Volume of Tales after Eastern Taste. Dublin, 1773 (by Tobias G. Smollett).

O'Keeffe, J. *Aladdin*. London, 1789.

———. *The Dead Alive*. Dublin, 1783.

———. *The Little Hunchback, or, a Frolic in Baghdad*. London, 1789.

Ottley, Thomas Henry. *Rustum Khan; or, Fourteen Nights' Entertainments*. 3 vols. London: Published for the Author, 1831.

Ouseley, William, ed. *Oriental Collections*. 2 vols. London, 1797–1798.

Pardoe, J. *City of the Sultan, and Domestic Manners of the Turks in 1836*. 2 vols. London, 1837.

———. *Romance of the Harem*. 3 vols. London, 1839.

———, ed. *Thousand and One Days; a Companion to the "Arabian Nights."* With an introduction by Miss Pardoe. London, 1857.

Parr, Bartholomew. *A Slight Sketch of the Life of the Reverend Richard Hole*. Exeter, 1803.

Payne, John. *Book of the Thousand Nights and One Night: Its History and Character*. Rpt. from the month volume of the complete work, London, 1884.

———. *Hamid the Luckless*. 1904.

Peacock, Miss Lucy. *The Adventures of the Six Princesses of Babylon*. London: Printed for the Author by T. Bensley, 1785.

The Persian and the Turkish Tales, Compleat. 2 vols. 3rd ed., London: Mears & Clay and Browne, 1729 (first ed. 1714).

Persian and Turkish Tales. With a Biographical Preface. 2 vols. London: J. Walker 1809?

Phelps, W.L. *The Beginnings of the English Romantic Movement: A Study in Eighteenth Century Literature*. Boston, MA: Ginn & Co., 1893.

Pickthall, M. William. *Children of the Nile*. London: Murray, 1908.

———. *The House of Islam*. London: Methuen, 1906.

———. *Sai'd the Fisherman*. London: Methuen, 1903.

Pilkington, Mrs. Mary. *The Asiatic Princess*. 2 vols. London: Vernor and Hood 1800

Piozzi, Hester Lynch Thrale. *Anecdotes of the Late Samuel Johnson*. London: T. Cadell, 1786.

Planche, J.R. *Recollections and Reflections*. 2 vols. London, 1872.

Pococke, Edward. *Specimen Historiae Arabum*. Ed. Joseph White. Oxford, 1806.

Pococke, Richard. *A Description of the East and Some Other Countries*. 2 vols. London: J. & R. Knapton, 1743–1745.

Poe, E.A. *The Thousand-and-Second Tale of Scheherazade*, in *The Complete Works*. Ed. James A. Harrison. 17 vols. New York: Thomas Y. Crowell & Co., 1902.

Poole, Stanley Lane. See Lane-Poole, S.

Poor, L.E. *Sanskrit and its Kindred Literatures*. Boston, MA: Roberts, 1880.

Pope, Alexander. *The Correspondence*. Ed. George Sherburn. 5 vols. Oxford: Clarendon, 1956.

————. *The Works.* Ed. Whitwell Elwin and William Courthope. 10 vols. London: Murray 1871–1889.

Pratt, S.J. *The Fair Circassian.* London: R. Baldwin, 1781.

Prior, M. *Poems on Several Occasions* (1718). Ed. A.R. Waller. Cambridge: Univ. Press, 1904.

Procter, Bryan Waller. See Cornwall, B.

Pye, Henry James. *A Commentary Illustrating the Poetic of Aristotle.* London: Stockdale, 1792.

Raleigh, W. *The English Novel.* 5th ed., London: Murray, 1903.

Redding, C. *Memoirs of William Beckford of Fonthill.* 2 vols. London: Charles Skeet, 1859.

Reeve, Clara. *The Progress of Romance.* Colchester, 1785.

Reynolds, John Hamilton. *Safie, an Eastern Tale.* London, 1814.

Richardson, John. *Dissertation on the Language, Literature, and Manners of the Eastern Nations.* Oxford: Clarendon, 1778.

————. *A Grammar of the Arabic Language.* London: Murray, 1776.

Ridley, James. *Tales of the Genii; or, the Delightful Lessons of Horam the Son of Asmar.* Translated by Charles Morell. London: Wilkie, 1764.

Roberts, Emma. *Notes of an Overland Journey . . . To Bombay.* London: W.H. Allen, 1841.

————. *Oriental Scenes, Dramatic Sketches and Tales, with Other Poems.* London, 1832.

Rossetti, Christina Georgina. *Family Letters.* Ed. William Michael Rossetti. London: Brown, 1908.

————. *Poetical Works, with Memoir and Notes . . .,* by William Michael Rossetti. London: Ellis & Elvey, 1895.

Rossetti, Michael, comp. *Rossetti Papers, 1862 to 1870.* London: Sands & Co., 1903.

Ruskin, John. *The Works.* Library Edition, Eds. E.T. Cook and A.D.O. Wedderburn. 39 vols. New York: Longmans & Green, 1908.

Russell, Alexander, *Natural History of Aleppo.* 2 vols. London; 1756. 2nd ed. enl., rev., and annot. by Patrick Russell. London: G.G. & J. Robinson, 1794.

Russell, Thomas. *Sonnets and Miscellaneous Poems.* Oxford, 1789 (esp. sonnet no. v).

Russell, W.H. *British Expedition to the Crimea.* Rev. ed., London, 1858.

St. John, James Augustus. *Tales of the Ramad'han.* 3 vols. London: Bentley, 1835.

Saintsbury, George. *A History of Nineteenth Century Literature, 1780–1895.* London: Macmillan, 1896.

Sale, George, tr. *The Koran.* London, 1734 (with a preliminary discourse).

Salt, H.S. *The Life of James Thomson.* London: Reeves & Turner, 1889.

Schelling, F.E. *Two Essays on Robert Browning* (1890).

Schlegel, Frederich. *Lectures on the History of Literature, Ancient and Modern,* from the German. 2 vols. Edinburgh: Blackwood, 1818.

School for Majesty . . . An Oriental History. London: W. Lane, 1783.

Scott, John. *Oriental Eclogues* in *The Poetical Works.* London: J. Buckland, 1782.

Scott: The Critical Heritage. Ed. John O. Hayden. London: Routledge, 1970.

Scott, Sir Walter. *Ivanhoe.* Ed. W.M. Parker. Everyman's edition, 1965.

————. *Miscellaneous Prose Works.* 6 vols. Edinburgh: Cadell, 1827.

————. *Sir Walter Scott: On Novelists and Fiction.* Ed. Ioan Williams. London: Routledge &Paul, 1968.

Seally, John. *Moral Tales After the Eastern Manner.* 2 vols. London, 1814.

Shaftesbury, Anthony. *Characteristics.* Ed. John M. Robertson. 2 vols. 1900; rpt. Gloucester, Mass.: P. Smith, 1963.

Shaw, Bernard. *Prefaces.* London: Constable, 1934.

Sherer, J.M. *Scenes and Impressions in Egypt and Italy.* London, 1824.

Sheridan, Mrs. F. *History of Nourjahad.* London: Dodsley, 1767.

Simonde de Sismondi, J.C.L. *Historical View of the Literature of the South of Europe.* Translated T. Roscoe, with notes and a Life of the Author. 2 vols. 3rd ed., London: H. Bohn, 1850.

Southey, Robert. *The Complete Poetical Works, Collected by Himself.* New ed., New York: Appleton & Co., 1856.

Spence, Joseph. *Observations, Anecdotes* (1820). Ed. James M. Osborn. Oxford: Clarendon, 1966.

Steele, Sir Richard. *Selections from the Tatter, Spectator, and Guardian.* Ed. Austin Dobson. Oxford: Clarendon, 1885.

Stevenson, Robert Louis. *Essays on Travel and in the Art of Writing.* New York: Scribner's, 1923.

———. *Island Nights Entertainments.* 1891; new ed., London: Macmillan, 1928.

———. *Letters.* 4 vols. Ed. Sidney Colvin. New York: Scribner's, 1911.

———. *Letters and Miscellanies.* New York: Scribner's, 1893.

———. *Memories and Portraits.* New York: Scribner's, 1887.

———. *New Arabian Nights.* London: Chatto, 1882.

———. with Fanny v. de G. Stevenson. *More New Arabian Nights: The Dynamiter.* London, 1885.

Stoker, B. *Personal Reminiscences of Henry Irving.* 2 vols. London: Macmillan, 1906.

Stowe, Harriet Beecher, ed. *A Library of Famous Fiction, Embracing the Nine Standard Masterpieces.* New York: Ford, 1873.

Swynnerton, Charles. *Indian Nights' Entertainments.* London: Stock, 1892.

Tale of the Four Durwesh. Translated by Lewes F. Smith. Calcutta: Greenway, 1813.

Tales from the Eastern Land. London, 1845.

Tales of the Caliph, by Al Arawiyah. London: Fisher & Unwin, 1887.

Taylor, Bayard. *Poems from the Orient.* Boston, MA: Ticknor & Fields, 1855.

Temple, R.C. *The Legends of the Panjab.* London: Triibner, 1884.

Tennyson, Alfred Lord. *The Poetic and Dramatic Works.* Student's Cambridge edition. New York: Houghton Mifflin, 1898.

Tennyson, Hallam. *Alfred Lord Tennyson. A Memoir.* 2 vols. New York: Macmillan, 1897.

Thackeray, W.M. *Letters and Private Papers of W.M. Thackeray.* Ed. Gordon N. Ray. 4 vols. Cambridge, MA: Harvard Univ. Press, 1946.

———. *Notes of a Journey from Cornhill to Grand Cairo.* London, 1848.

———. *Works.* 30 vols. Kensington Edition. New York: Scribner's, 1904.

Thomson, J. *The Poetical Works.* Ed. B. Dobell, with a memoir of the author. 2 vols. London, Reeves & Turner, 1895.

Thousand and One Days: Persian Tales. Translated from the French by Mr. Philips. 5th ed., 3 vols. London, 1738.

Trench, Richard. *Poems from Eastern Sources.* 1842; 2nd ed., London: Parker, 1851.

Tucker, T.G. *The Foreign Debt of English Literature.* 1907; rpt., New York: Haskell House, 1966.

Turkish Evening Entertainments. Translated by John P. Brown. New York: Putnam, 1850.

Upham, Edward. *Karmath; an Arabian Tale.* London: Cook, 1827.

Urquhart, D. *The Spirit of the East.* 2 vols. London, 1838.

Victorian Scrutinies: Reviews of Poetry 1830–1870. Ed. Isobel Armstrong. Athlone Press, Univ. of London, 1972.

Volney, C. *Travels Through Syria and Egypt, in the Years 1783, 1784 and 1785.* 2 vols. London, 1787.

Wainewright, Thomas Griffiths. *Essays and Criticism.* Ed. William C. Hazlitt. London: Reeves & Turner, 1880.

Walpole, Horace. *The Correspondence.* Ed. W.S. Lewis. Vol. XI. New York: Yale Univ. Press, 1954.

————. *The Works.* Ed. R. Berry, with the assistance of his daughter Mary. 5 vols. London 1798.

Warburton, W. *Dissertation on the Origin of Books of Chivalry,* prefixed to Charles Jarvis' translation of Don Quixote, *The Life and Exploits of the Ingenious Gentleman Don Quixote.* 2 vols. London, 1738–1742.

Warner, Charles Dudley. *Being a Boy.* Boston, MA: James R. Osgood, 1878.

Warton, Thomas. *History of English Poetry.* 4 vols, 1774–1781. New ed. by Richard Price. London, 1824.

Wells, Charles. *Mehmet, the Kurd, and Other Tales from Eastern Sources.* London: Bell & Daldy, 1865.

White, Gleeson. *English Illustration: "The Sixties," 1855–1870.* 1897; Kingsmead Rpts., 1970.

Whittaker, G.B. *Karmath: An Arabian Tale.* London: Charles F. Cock, 1827.

Wood, Robert. *Essay on the Original Genius and Writings of Homer.* 1769; enl. ed. London: T. Payne and P. Elmsly, 1775.

Wordsworth, Christopher. *Memoirs of William Wordsworth.* Ed. H. Reed. Boston, MA: Ticknor & Reed, 1851.

Wordsworth, William. *The Poetical Works.* Ed. E. Dowden. 7 vols. London: Aldine Edition, 1892.

Wordsworth, William and Dorothy. *The Letters* (covering 1787–1850, early, middle and later years). 6 vols. Ed. E. De Selincourt. Oxford: Clarendon, 1935–1939.

Yardley, E. *The Supernatural in the Romantic Fiction.* London: Longmans, 1880.

Primary Sources

(B) Periodical Criticism (1704–1910)

A word must be said about this material. To identify authorship of some contributions, I have consulted Poole's, the *Wellesley* and other accessible indices listed among secondary works. For convenience, Anglo and/or American periodicals of identical titles are listed under one heading. Articles dealing with Arabic culture in general or with specific mythological and comparative aspects of the tales are selectively cited. Insofar as the controversy over Burton's "unexpurgated" edition is concerned, only a few comments are included, for Burton himself gave a good account of this in his "Biography of the Book, and its Reviewers Reviewed" appended to the sixth volume of his *Supplemental Nights.* Under each heading items are arranged chronologically in order to follow up the growing interest in the tales as well as the changing literary taste.

Academic
Review of Thomas Hope's *Anastasius*, XVIII (Oct. I, 1821), 345–50.

Academy
"*A Low-German Aesop,*" II (Mar. 1, 1871), 151 (Felix Liebrecht).
"*Captain Marryat a Plagiarist,*" VII (Feb. 27, 1875), 218–19 (H.G. Coote-on the indebtedness of the *Pasha of Many Tales* to Beloe's *Miscellanies*).
"Specimens of a New Translation of the 'Thousand and One Nights'," XV (Apr. 26, 1879), 369–70 (Reginald Stuart Poole).
"Arabic Poetry for English Readers," XIX, no. 472 (May 21, 1881), 375–77 (George Percy Badger).
"The Book of the Thousand and One Nights," XX, no. 499 (Nov. 26, 1881), 403 (George Percy Badger).
"The Book of the Thousand Nights and One Night," XX, no. 500 (Dec. 3, 1881), 421 (A. Granger Hutt).
"The Thousand and One Nights," XX, no. 500 (Dec. 3, 1881), 421 (Reginald Stuart Poole). "The Thousand Nights and One Night," XX, no. 501 (Dec. 10, 1881), 437–38 (George Percy Badger).
"The Book of the Thousand Nights and One Night," XX, no. 502 (Dec. 17, 1881), 457 (A. Granger Hutt).
On James Thomson's "Doom of a City" in *A Voice from the Nile and Other Poems*, XXIV, no. 604 (Dec. 1, 1883), 364.
"The Book of Sindibad," XXVI, no. 646 (Sept. 20, 1884), 175–76 (Richard Burton).
"The Thousand Nights and a Night," XXVIII, no. 693 (Aug. 15, 1885) (Richard Burton). Correspondence – "The Arabian Nights' Entertainments," XXVIII, no. 700 (Oct. 3, 1885), 223 (John Addington Symonds).
"The Arabian Nights," XXVIII, no. 702 (Oct. 17, 1885), 258 (Edward Peacock).
"Notes and News," XXIX, no. 738 (June 26, 1886), 450.
"Notes and News," XXX, no. 747 (Aug. 28, 1886), 135.
"Notes and News," XXX, no. 749 (Sept. 2, 1886), 167.
"Notes and News," XXX, no. 755 (Oct. 23, 1886), 277.
"History of the Forty Vezirs," XXX, no 759, n. ser. (Nov. 20, 1886), 337–38 (Richard Burton).
"The Orientalism of Galland's 'Arabian Nights'," XXX, no. 755 (Oct. 23, 1886), 277.
"The Final Aspirate in Arabic," XXX, no. 760 (Nov. 27, 1886), 760 (J.W. Redhouse).
"Lady Burton's Edition of her Husband's 'Arabian Nights'," XXX, no. 762 (Dec. 11, 1886), 387–88 (Amelia B. Edwards).
"Tales of the Caliph," XXX, no. 764 (Dec. 25, 1886), 425.
"Thousand and One Nights," XXXI, no. 767 (Jan. 15, 1887), 43.
"Notes and News," XXXI, no. 768 (Jan. 22, 1887), 58.
"The Thousand and One Nights," XXXI, no. 768 (Jan 22, 1887), 58.
"Notes and News," XXXII, no. 794 (July 23, 1887), 53.
"The Kama Shastra Society," XXXII, no. 814 (Dec. 10, 1887), 389–90.

"Lady Burton's Edition of her Husband's 'Arabian Nights'," XXXII, no. 817 (Dec. 31, 1887), 438–39.
"The Supplemental 'Nights'," XXXIV, no. 848 (Aug. 4, 1888), 72 (Richard Burton).
"Reprints of the 'Arabian Nights'," XXXIV, no. 850 (Aug. 18, 1888), 103–04.
"The Treasury of King Rilampsinitus," XXXVIII (Nov. 29, 1890), 509–10.
"The Ancient East," LVI (Feb. 18, 1899), 213–14.

Ainsworth's Magazine
"Sultan Stork: Being the One Thousand and Second Night," 2 pts. (Feb. and May 1842), 33–38, 233–37 (W.M. Thackeray).

American Journal of Philology
"Ali Baba and the Forty Thieves," XLVII, 307–09.

American Journal of Semitic Languages
"Story of Ahikar and the Book of Daniel," XVI (July 1900), 242–47 (George A. Barton).

American Review
"The Thousand and One Nights," VI (Dec. 1, 1847), 601–18 (G.W. Peck).

Antijacobin Review
Review of *Massouf; or, the Philosophy of the Day*, XII (July 1802), 300.
Review of Landor's *Gebir*, XVII (Feb. 1804), 182–84.
Review of Hope's *Anastasius*, LVII (Jan. 1820), 442–50.

Antiquary
"A Variant of the Legend of Mab's Cross in the 'Thousand and One Nights'," XXXVIII (1902), 24–25 (William E.A. Axon).

Asiatic Journal and Monthly Register
Review of Moore's *Lalla Rookh*, IV (Nov. 1817), 457–67.
"On the Origin of the 'Arabian Nights'," XXVIII (July 1829), 560–66 (rpt. in *Selections from the Asiatic Journal*, covering Jan. 1816 to Dec. 1829 [Madras, 1875], 996–1001, by Baron De Sacy).
"Literary Intelligence," n. ser. XXII (1837), 84.
"Sir Richard Ryan's Proposition to the Asiatic Society of Bengal," n. ser. XXII (1837), 249–52.
"The Alif Leila, or Arabian Nights' Entertainments," n. ser. XXIII (1837), 64–69 (on Brownlow's Ms.)
"Remarks on M. Schlegel's Objections to the Restored Editions of the Alif Leilah, or Arabian Nights' Entertainments," n. ser. XXV (1838), 72–77 (Henry Torrens).
"The Romance of Antar," n. ser. XXVII (1838), 57–61. On Torrens' Translation, n. ser. XXVIII (1839), 121. "The Arabian Nights," n. ser. XXX (1839), 69–84.

"History of the Barmekides," n. ser. XXX (1839), 127–37.
"Alf-Lailah wa Lailat, or Thousand and One Nights," n. ser. XXX (1839), 177–84, 275–80.
"Persian Origin of the 'Arabian Nights'," n. ser. XXXI (1840), 237.
"Supplement to the 'Arabian Nights'," n. ser. XXXIII (1840), 56–62, 130–38.
"The Alif Laila," n. ser. XXXIII (1840), 203.

Athenaeum

"Contes Arabes du Cheykh ei Mohdy," no. 355 (1834), 605–06.
On Baron De Sacy's *Memoire* respecting the origin of the *Nights*, no. 355 (1834), 797.
"Memoires des L'Institut Royal de France," no. 367 (Nov. 8, 1834), 817.
"Tales and Popular Fictions," rev. of Keightley's work, no. 326 (Jan. 25, 1835), 67–68.
"The Arabian Nights' Entertainments: with copious Notes," no. 572 (Oct. 13, 1838), 737–39; Pt. 2, no. 573 (Oct. 20, 1838), 759–60; Pt. 3, no. 574 (Oct. 27, 1838), 773–75.
"The Book of the Thousand and One Nights," no. 622 (Sept. 1839), 741–42; no. 624 (Oct. 1839), 773–75.
"The Shaving of Shagpat; an Arabian Night Entertainment, by George Meredith," no. 1471 (Jan. 5, 1856), 6.
"Dalziels' Illustrated Arabian Nights' Entertainments" and Townsend's "Arabian Nights Entertainments." No. 1983(Oct 28, 1865), 572–73.
"The Arabian Nights," LIV, no. 2822 (Nov. 26, 1881), 703 (Richard Burton).
"Al Arawiyah," no. 3092 (Jan. 29, 1887), 159.
"Lady Burton's Edition of her Husband's Arabian Nights," no. 3159 (May 12, 1888), 594–95.
"A Source of the Book of Tobit," LXIII, no. 3292 (Nov. 29, 1890), 738–39 (W.F. Kirby).
"The Book of Sindibad," no. 3333 (Sept. 12, 1891), 355–56; no. 3336 (Oct. 3, 1891), 451–52 (W.A. Clouston).
"Aladdin and the Enchanted Lamp," no. 3378 (July 23, 1892), 130 (W.F. Kirby).
"Oriental Literature," no. 3406 (Feb. 4, 1893), 101.
"The Library Edition of Sir Richard Burton's Translation of the *Arabian Nights*," no. 3513 (Feb. 23, 1895), 247–48.
Review of *Sind bad the Sailor & Ali Baba and the Forty Thieves* (illustrated by W. Strang and J.B. Clark), no. 3553 (Nov. 30, 1895), 759.
"The Thousand and One Nights . . . with an introduction by Joseph Jacobs," no. 3596 (Sept. 26, 1896), 412–13.
"The Thousand and One Nights," Jacobs' remonstrance and a rejoinder, no. 3598 (Oct. 10, 1896)' 484–85.
"The Arabian Nights in French," no. 3752 (Sept. 23, 1899), 413–14.
Review of Stanley Lane-Poole's Bohn edition of his uncle's (Lane's) translation, no. 4130 (Dec. 22, 1906), 801.

Atlantic Monthly

"George Meredith," LXIII (Feb. 1888), 178–93.
"The Thousand and One Nights," LXIII (June 1889), 756–63 (C.H. Toy).

Augustan Review
Review of *Osman. A Turkish Tale*, I (Oct. 1815), 577–80. Review of *Vathek*, I (Dec. 1815), 843–48.

Blackwood's Edinburgh Magazine
Review of *Lalla Rookh*, I (June 1817), 279–85; concluded (August, 1817), 503–10 (John Wilson).
"Remarks on the Romance of Antar," IV (Jan. 1819), 385–94 (J.C. Lockhart).
"Hajji Baba of Ispahan," XV (Jan. 1824), 51–57 (Henry Thomson).
"Eastern Stories," XVIII (July 1825), 61–64 (Robert Ferguson).
"Gillies's German Stories," XX (Dec. 1826), 844–58–on the *Nights*, p. 845 (Thomas De Quincey).
"Tennyson's Poems," XXXI (May 1832), 721–41-on "Recollections . . .," pp. 738–40 (John Wilson).
"*Aladdin*, a dramatic poem, in two parts, by Adam Oschlenschlaeger," XXXVI (Nov. 1834), 620–41 (George Moir).
"Story of Bab-ey-buk," XLII (Nov. 1837), 648–60 (James White).
"A few Words about Novels-a Dialogue in a Letter to Eusebius," LXIV (Oct. 1848), 459–74-about the *Nights*, 472–73 (John Eagles).

Bookman
"Origin of the Arabian Nights Entertainments," XIV (Dec. 1901), 341.
"Thomas De Quincey," XXXI (Feb. 7, 1907), 207–12-on Quincey's "detailed reference" to the *Nights*, p. 208 (William E.A. Axon).
"The Thousand and One Nights," XXXI (Mar. 1907), 258 (William E. A. Axon).
Review of K.D. Wiggin's and N. Smith's edition of the *Nights* (Dec. 1909), 344 (Algernon Tassin).

Bookmart
Note on the editions of Burton and Payne (Oct. 1886), 180, 185.

British Critic
"Literary Intelligence,"-on Scott's projected translation, XII (1798), 692. Review of Landor's *Gebir*, XV (Feb. 1800), 190.
Review of William Gardiner's *The Sultana, or the Jealous Queen: A Tragedy*, XXVIII (Oct. 1806), 445.
Review of Moore's *Lalla Rookh*, n. ser. VII (June 1817), 604–16.

British and Foreign Review [or European Quarterly Journal]
"Eastern Storytellers and History of Fiction," VII (1840), 224-274.

British Lady's Magazine
Review of Moore's *Lalla Rookh*, n. ser. I (Sept. 1817), 180–81.

British Review
Review of Moore's *Lalla Rookh*, X (1817), 30–54.

Brighton Magazine
Review of George Croly's *The Angel of the World, an Arabian Tale*, I (1822), 79–84.

Century Magazine
"New Arabian Nights," XXV (1882), 628.

Contemporary Review
"On the Pleasure of Reading," XLIX (Feb. 1886), 240–51 (Sir John Lubbock). "About Fiction," LI (1887), 172–80 (R. Haggard).

Cornhill Magazine
"The Arabian Nights," XXXII (Dec. 1875), 711–32 (James Mew).

Cosmopolitan
"The Real 'Arabian Nights'," XXVI (Mar. 1899), 483–94.

Critic
"Mr. Comstock and the Arabian Nights," n. ser. III (April4, 1885), 161–62. "Notes," n. ser. VI (Dec. 4, 1886), 23.
On the *Nights*, XXIX, n. ser. XXVI (Nov. 12, 1896), 318.

Critical Review
Review of the *Tales of the Genii*, XVIII (1764), 40–41 (Owen Ruffhead).
"D'Alenzon's Bonze," XXVII (1769), 178–81.
"History of the Caliph Vathek," 1st ser. LXII (1786), 37–42.
Review of Landor's *Gebir*, n. ser. XXVII (Sept. 1799), 29–39.
Review of the 1798 ed. of the *Nights*, n. ser. XXVII (Nov. 1799), 356.
Review of *Massouf*, n. ser. XXXVI (Sept. 1802), 117.
Review of William Gardiner's *The Sultana*, 3rd ser. IX (Oct. 1806), 212.
Review of *Osman, a Turkish Tale*, 5th ser. II (Aug. 1815), 210–13.
Review of Moore's *Lalla Rookh*, 5th ser. V (June 1817), 560–81.

Dublin Examiner
Review of *Vathek*, I (Sept. 1816), 338–50.

Dublin Magazine
Review of *The Maid of Araby*, I (Apr. 1820), 314–15.

Dublin Review
"Arabian Nights' Entertainments," VIII (Feb. 1840), 105–33 (Mr. Hattersley).

Eclectic Review
Review of *Lalla Rookh*, IV (1817), 340–53.
Review of George Croly's *Angel of the World*, n. ser. XV (1821), 30–34.
Review of the *Adventures of Hajji Baba*, n. ser. XXI (Apr. 1824), 341–55.
"Lane's Arabian Nights," n. ser. VIII (1840), 641–60.

Edinburgh Review
Review of Moore's *Lalla Rookh*, XXIX (Nov. 1817), 1–35.
Review of *Anastasius*, XXXV (Mar. 1821), 92–102 (Sidney Smith).
"The Arabian Nights," CLXIV (July 1886), 166–99 (Stanley Lane-Poole).

European Magazine
Review of *Vathek*, X (Aug. 1786), 102–04.
Review of Moore's *Lalla Rookh*, LXXII (July 1817), 55–58.

Expository Times
"The Story of Ahikar," X (1898), 276–77.

Folk-Lore Journal
"Folklore the Source of some of M. Galland's Tales," III, Pt. 2 (1881), 178–91 (Henry Charles Coote).
"Forbidden Chambers," III, Pt. 3 (1885), 193–242 (S. Hartland).
"The Forbidden Door of the 1001 Nights," V (Mar. 1887), 112–24 (W.F. Kirby). Review of J. Jacobs' *Book of Wonder Voyages*, VIII (1897), 266–67.
"The Binding of a God: A Study of the Basis of Idolatry," VIII (1897), 325–55 (W. Crooke).
"Cairene Folklore," XI (1900), 354–95 (A.H. Sayee).
On other details related to the *Nights* in "Cairene Folklore,"-Pt. 3, XVI (1906), 191–200 (A.H. Sayee).

Foreign Quarterly Review
"Arabic Literature," III (Sept. 1828), 1–28 (W.D. Cooley).
"Professor Schlegel and the Oriental Translation Fund," XI (Apr. 1833, 315–33), (W.C. Taylor).
"New Arabian Tales," XIV (Dec. 1834), 350–69 (W.C. Taylor).
"Miscellaneous Literary Notices" (on De Sacy), XIV (Dec. 1834), 470–77-esp. 472 (John Macray).
"Arabian Nights," XXIV (Oct. 1839), 139–68 (B.E. Pote).

Fortnightly Review
"Burton as I Knew Him," LIV, n. ser. 48 (Dec. 1890), 878–84 (V.L. Cameron).
"Elegy," on the death of R.F. Burton, LVIII (July 1, 1892), 1–5 (A.C. Swinburne). "Richard Burton," LXXXV (June 1906), 1039–45 (Ouida).
"William Beckford of Fonthill," n. ser. LXXXVI (1909), 1011–23 (L. Melville).

Forum (N.Y.)
"New Story-Tellers and the Doom of Realism," XVIII (1894–1895), 471–80 (W.R. Thayer).

Fraser's Magazine
"Barmecide Banquets," XXXII (Nov. 1845), 584–93 (W.M. Thackeray).
"The Tale of an Arab Story-Teller," XXXIX (Jan. 1849), 112–17.
"Abdallah and Saida; a Tale of Mesopotamia," LV (June 1857), 718–22.

Freethinker
On the *Pall Mall Gazette's* Criticism of Burton (Oct. 25, 1885), 339–40.

Gentleman's Magazine
"Story from an Arabian Ms.," VII (Apr. 1737), 195–96. "An Arabian Story," VII (July 1737), 435–36.
"Story of Parizade in the Arabian Tales," XXIV (May 1754), 222–23.
"History of the Caliph *Vathek*," LVI, Pt. 2 (July 1786), 593–94.
Another note on *Vathek*, LVII (Jan. 1787), 55–56 (Stephen Weston).
"Conjectures Concerning the History of *Vathek* Obviated," LVII (Feb. 1787), 120 (Samuel Henley).
"Palace of Istaker," LX (Jan. 1790), 69–70, 163–65, 258-59-a poetic version of the concluding scene to *Vathek* ("A.V.").
On Voltaire's reference to Galland's edition, LXIV (1794), 527 ("Sciolus").
"Arabian Tales," LXIV (Sept. 1794), 783–84 ("M-S").
Another reference to Voltaire's statement and a rejoinder, LXVI (1796), 396 ("Sciolus").
On Galland's and Gazotte's editions, LXVI (1796), 488 ("P.Q.").
"Hole's Remarks on the Arabian Nights' Entertainments," LXVII (July 1797), 540–41 (Stephen Weston).
"Arabian Nights," LXVII (1797), 1019–20 ("M.N.").
"Remarks on the Arabian Nights' Entertainments," LXVII (Dec. 1797), 1047–49.
On the authenticity of Gazotte's *Tales*, LXVII (Sept. 1797), 1081 ("E.O.E.").
On dating the first English translation of the *Nights*, LXVIII (Jan. 1798), 19.
"Arabian Nights," LXVIII (Apr. 1798), 304–05 ("M.N.").
"Arabian Nights Entertainments," LXVIII (Sept. 1798), 757–58 ("W.W.").
"Arabian Nights Entertainments," (on Beloe's trans. of the *Continuation*), LXIX (Jan. 1799), 55.
"On the Authenticity of the Arabian Tales," LXIX, Pt. I (Feb. 1799), 91–92 (Patrick Russell).
Review of Landor's *Gebir*, LXIX (Suppl., 1799), 1144. "Tales, Anecdotes, and Letters," LXX (Dec. 1800), 1180–82.
On borrowings from a *Miscellany of Eastern Learning*, LXXII (Aug. 1802), 701–02 ("Altharicus").
"Oriental Collections," LXXIV (Nov. 1804), 1033–37.
"On Scott's use of Gough's revised edition of the *Nights*, LXXX (Jan. 1810), 39.
Review of *Osman, a Turkish Tale*, LXXXV and LXXXVII (Suppl., Jan.–June 1815 and July 1817), 611, 55–57, respectively.

Review of Moore's *Lalla Rookh*, LXXXVII (June 1817), 535–37.

Review of Mrs. Leman Grimstone's *Zayda; a Spanish Tale; and Other Poems*, XC (Aug. 1820), 150.

Hartford Seminary Record

"Problems of Muhammadanism," XV, 2 (1905), 77–97 (D.B. Macdonald).

Household Words

"A Christmas Tree" (Dec. 21, 1850), 289–95.

"The Child's Story," extra no. (1852), 5 (Dickens).

"Discovery of a Treasure Near Cheapside" (Nov. 13, 1852) – rpt. in Harry Stone's edition of *Uncollected Writings from Household Words*, II, 443–53 (Dickens).

"One Thousand and One Humbugs" (Apr. 21, 1855), 265–67; (Apr. 28, 1855), 289–92; (May 5, 1855), 313–16 (Dickens).

"The School of Fairies" (June 30, 1855), 509–13 (Henry Morley).

Illustrated London News

Review of Nelson Lee's pantomime, the *Forty Thieves* (Jan. 9, 1847), 26.

Independent

Review of George Croly's *Angel of the Hlorld*, no. VIII (Feb. 24, 1821), 120–22 (Eng. Per.).

"A Lesson from the 'Arabian Nights'," LIII (Jan. 3, 1901), 23–25 (M. Maeterlinck), New York.

Review of Stanley Lane-Poole's Bohn edition of his uncle's (E.W. Lane) translation, LXII (Jan. 17, 1907), 159, New York.

International Quarterly (N.Y.)

"Story of Ahikar," IV (July 1901), 122–26 (G.A. Barton).

Journal of American Folklore

"Filipino . . . version of Aladdin," XX (Apr. 1907), 117–18 (F. Gardener).

Journal of the Bombay Branch of the Royal Asiatic Society

"A Few Analogies in the 'Thousand and One Nights' and in Latin Authors," XIV, no. XX–XV (1879), 74–85 (E. Rehatsek).

Journal of the Royal Asiatic Society

"Jatakas in the Arabian Nights," n. ser. XXII (1890), 504.

"Maximilian Habicht and His Recension of the Thousand and One Nights" (1909), 685–704 (D.B. Macdonald).

"Ali Baba and the Forty Thieves, in Arabic, from a Bodleian Ms.," (1910), 327–86 (D.B. Macdonald).

Leigh Hunt's London Journal
"Genii and Fairies of the East, the Arabian Nights," I, no. 30 (Oct. 22, 1834), 233–37.

Leisure Hour
"Arab Story Tellers," XXIII (1874), 486–87, 748–50 (H. Hopley).
"Story-Telling in all Ages," XXXIV (1885), 199–202, 273–77, 351–54 (R. Heath).
"Gleanings from Story Tellers," XXXV (1886), 543–47 (G.L. Browne).

Literary Digest
Review of K.D. Wiggin's and N. Smith's edition of the *Nights*, LXXXIX (Dec. 1909), 1025.

Literary Journal
Review of Hoppner's *Oriental Tales*, V (Feb. 1805), 138–42.

Literary World
"The Origin of the Arabian Nights," III (Feb. 12 and 26, Mar. 18 and 25, May 13, 1848), 26–28,
    63–65, 123–25, 144–46, 284–86, respectively (E.G. Langdon).
"The Arabian Nights' Entertainments," III, no. 89 (Oct. 14, 1848), 724–25.
"The New Arabian Nights," rev. of Kirby's translation, XIV (1883), 5–6.

Longman's Magazine
"A Gossip on Romance," I (1882–1883), 69–79 (R.L. Stevenson).

London Magazine
Review of Hope's *Anastasius*, I (Jan. 1820), 76–79 (Baldwin's); and in (Gold's) I (1820), 57–67,
    294–302, 410–14.
"Eastern Story-Tellers," XX (May 1828), 183–86.

London and Westminster Review:
"New Translations of the Arabian Nights," XXXIII (Oct.1839), 101–37 (Leigh Hunt).

Macmillan's Magazine
"Alkamah's Cave: Story of Nejd," Pt. I, XXXI (Mar. 1875), 448–62; Pt. 2 (Apr. 1875), 535–49;
    and Pt. 3, XXXII (May 1875), 73–88 (W.O. Palgrave).

Monthly Magazine
Review of Landor's *Gebir*, Suppl. VIII (Jan. 20, 1800), 1051–52.
Review of *Massouj*, Suppl. XIV (Jan. 25, 1803), 599.
Review of William Gardiner's *The Sultana*, Suppl. XXII (Jan. 25, 1807), 642.
Review of Moore's *Lalla Rookh*, XLIII (June 1817), 450–51.
Review of Charles Phillips' *The Arab*, XLVIII (Aug. 1819), 49 (rpt. in *Fireside Magazine*,
    I [Sept. 1819], 355).
Review of Mrs. L. Grimstone's *Zayda*, XLIX (July 1820), 556.

Monthly Mirror

Review of *Massouj*, XIV (Aug. 1802), 108.

Review of William Gardiner's *The Sultana*, XXII (Dec. 1806) 408.

Monthly Review

"Review of Some Oriental Tales," XX (1759), 380.

Review of *Almoran and Hamel*, XXIV (May 1761) (Owen Ruffhead).

"On the Oriental Vogue," XXVI (1762), 263–64 (Owen Ruffhead).

"An Arabian Tale *[Vathek]*, from an Unpublished Manuscript." LXXVI (May 1787), 450.

"Arabian Tales," 1st ser. XI (June 1793), 153–59 (Thomas Holcroft).

"Hole's Remarks on the Arabian Nights' Entertainments," 1st ser. XXIV (Sept. 1797), 44–46.

"Arabian Nights' Entertainments" (rev. of the 1798 ed.), 1st ser. XXIX (1799), 474–76.

Review of Landor's *Gebir*, 1st ser. XXXI (Feb. 1800), 206–08.

"The Story of AI Raoui, a Tale from the Arabic," 1st ser. XXXII (1800), 429.

"Oriental Tales-tr. into English verse by J. Hoppner," 1st ser. XLVI (1805), 404–09 (L.E. Christopher).

Review of William Gardiner's *Sultana*, n. ser. LIX (Aug. 1809), 436–38.

Review of the *Parliament of Ispahan; an Oriental Eclogue*, LXII (May 1810), 104–05.

Review of *Osman, a Turkish Tale*, LXXVIII (Oct. 1815), 215–16.

Review of *Lalla Rookh*, LXXXIII (1817), 177–201, 285–99.

Review of Mrs. L. Grimstone's *Zayda*, XCIII (Oct. 1820), 215–16.

Review of *Antar*, XCIV (Mar. 1820), 277–92.

"New Arabian Nights' Entertainments," n. ser. I (1826), 362–70.

"The Arabian Nights' Entertainments: with copious Notes," n. ser. III (Dec. 1838), 583–94.

Nation

"On Translating the Arabian Nights," in 2 pts. LXXI, nos. 1835–36 (Aug. 30, Sept. 6, 1900), 185–86, respectively (D.B. Macdonald).

Review of a new edition of Lane's translation, LXXIII (Dec. 12, 1901), 460.

Review of Stanley Lane-Poole's Bohn edition of his uncle's translation, LXXXIII (Dec. 21, 1906), 555.

Review of vol. 4 of the same art., LXXXIV (Jan. 31, 1907), 106.

"Arabic Ms. of Ali Baba and the Forty Thieves," LXXXVII (Oct. 8, 1908), 335 (D.B. Macdonald).

Review of the Kate Wiggin, Nora Smith volume, LXXXIX (Dec. 2, 1909), 538.

National Review

"The People of the Arabian Nights," IX (July 1859), 44–71 (Walter Bagehot; rpt. in Littell's *Living Age*, LXII [1859], 327–42).

"Story-Telling in the East," (Sept. 1888), 79–86 (A.H. Sayee).

New Annual Register

Review of *Massouj*, XXIII (1802), 322.

Review of Hoppner's *Oriental Tales*, XXVI (1805), 355.

New London Review
Review of the *Enchanted Mirror*, I (June 1799), 616.

New Monthly Magazine
Review of Moore's *Lalla Rookh*, VIII (Aug. 1817), 52.
"On Arabic Poetry, Especially the Romance of Antar," XIII (Jan., Feb. 1820), 12–18, 151–61 (J. von. Hammer).
Review of Hope's *Anastasius*, XIII (1820), 56–62, 192–98.
Review of Grimstone's *Zayda*, XIV (July 1820), 92.
"New Series of Arabian Nights' Entertainments," 2nd ser. XVI (1826), 336–42 (Leigh Hunt).
"The Adventures of Khodadad," LVIII (Feb. and Mar. 1840), 180–93, 373–84 (Charles Stuart Savile).
"Recollections of the Author of 'Vathek'," LXXI (June 1844), 143–58, 302–19 (Cyrus Redding).
"Story of the Cadi and the Robber," XCIX (Sept. 1853), 85–91 (Tr. A.H. Bleeck).
"Gleanings from Anglo-Oriental Literature," IX (June 1877), 674–87 (P.Q. Keegan).

New Review
Review of *Vathek*, IX (1786), 410–12; X (1787), 33–39.
"Sir Richard Burton. An Explanation and a Defence," VII (Nov. 1892), '562–78 (Isabel Burton).

New Quarterly Magazine
"The Thousand and One Nights," in 2 pts., II (Jan.–Apr. 1879), 150–74, 377–401 (John Payne).

North American Review
"Italian Popular Tales," CXXIII (July 1876), 25–60 (T.F. Crane).
"The 'Thousand and One Nights' and the 'Morte d'Arthur'," CLXXXIV (Jan. 18, 1907), 150–56 (Cameron Mann).
Review of the Kate Wiggin & Nora Smith volume, CXC (Dec. 1909), 843.

Oriental Herald
Review of *Hajji Baba*, I (1824), 451–66.

Outlook
"Arabian Nights Stories," LIII (Feb. 15, 1896), 289 (Helen M. North).
Review of Stanley Lane-Poole's edition of his uncle's trans., LXXXV (Jan. 12, 1907), 94.
Review of the Kate Wiggin and Nora Smith volume, XCIII (Dec. 4, 1909), 787.

Pall Mall Gazette
"The Best Hundred Books," extra no. 24 (1886), 2–27.

Penny Magazine
"Antar, an Arabian Romance," VI (Feb. 1837), 55–56.

Quarterly Review

"Dunlop's *History of Fiction*," XIII (July 1815), 384–408 (Francis Palgrave).

Review of Henry G. Knight's *Eastern Sketches*, XXII (July 1819), 149–58 (Stratford Canning).

Review of Hope's *Anastasius*, XXIV (1821), 511–29 (William Gifford).

Review of *Hajji Baba of Ispahan in England*, XXXIX (Jan. 1829), 73–99 (Walter Scott).

"Hatim Tai, a Romance," XLIX (July 1833), 506–17 (M.J. Quin).

"Lane's *Manners and Customs of the Modern Egyptians*," LIX (July 1837), 165–203 (John Barrow).

"Foster on Arabia," LXXIV (Oct. 1844), 325–58.

"The Author of *Vathek*," CCXIII, no. 425 (Oct. 1910), 377–401 (Stanley Lane-Poole).

St. James Magazine

"A London Arabian Nights Entertainment," IX (Dec. and Mar. 1864), 364–72.

Saturday Review

"Shaving of Shagpat," (Jan. 19, 1856), 216 (G.H. Lewes).

"New Arabian Nights," LIV (Aug. 19, 1882), 250–51.

"The Arabian Nights," a review of both Stanley Lane-Poole's new edition of his uncle's and a reprint of Scott's (Nov. 4, 1882), 609.

"Arabian Society in the Middle Ages," LV (Mar. 3, 1883), 284–85.

"Burton's Arabian Nights," LXI (Jan. 2, 1886), 26–27.

"Burton's Arabian Nights" (Mar. 27, 1886), 448–49.

"The Thousand Nights and a Night," LXIII (Apr. 1887), 632–33.

"Lady Burton's Edition of the Arabian Nights" (Sept. 10, 1887), 367–68.

"Supplemental Nights" (July 21, 1888), 86–87.

"Arabian Nights Illustrated" (Aidine edition), LXX (Dec. 13, 1890), 688.

"The Thousand and One Days," LXXIV (Nov. 12, 1892), 569.

"Burton's 'Arabian Nights' Re-edited," LXXIX (Mar. 9, 1895), 322–23.

Scots Magazine

Review of Moore's *Lalla Rookh*, LXXIX (July 1817), 528–31.

Scribner's Magazine (N.Y.)

"Arabian Nights' Entertainments" (a poem), XIV (July 1893), 56–62 (W.E. Henley).

Spectator

"Mr. Stevenson's Stories," LV (Nov. 11, 1882), 1450–52.

"The Religion of the Arabian Nights," LV (Nov. 25, 1882), 1513–14.

Tinsley's Magazine

"Some Unedited Tales from the 'Arabian Nights'," (Mar. 1882), 229–37.

Westminster Review (**Also under** *London and Westminster Review*)
"New Translations of the Arabian Nights," XXXIII (Oct. 1839), 101–37 (Leigh Hunt).
"The Shaving of Shagpat," LXV, n. ser. IX (Apr. 1856), 638–39 (George Eliot).
Review of Murray's *Hassan*, LXIX, n. ser. XIII (Jan. 1858), 164.
"*Belles Lettres* and Art," LXIX, n. ser. XIII (1858), 291–93. (George Meredith reviewing Ochlenschlliger's *Aladdin*).
Review of Stevenson's *New Arabian Nights*, CXIX (Jan. 1883), 137–38.
"*Belles Lett res,*" review of Stanley Lane-Poole's *Stories from the Arabian Nights*, CXXXVII (1892), 347.
"History as Told in the Arabian Nights," CXLIII (Mar. 1895), 253–77 (J.F. Hewitt).

IV Secondary Works

(A) Published Material

Abbott, Nabia. "A Ninth-Century Fragment of the 'Thousand Nights': New Light on the Early History of the Arabian Nights," *Journal of the Near Eastern Studies*, VIII, no. 3 (July 1949), 129–64.

Abdel-Hamid, Samir. "Oriental Background of the *Monk* . . . and Its Impact on Horror Romantic Fiction in England during the late Eighteenth Century," *Bulletin of the Faculty of Arts*, University of Cairo, XXV, pt. I (May 1963), 13–27.

Abrams, M.H. *The Mirror and the Lamp: Romantic Theory and the Critical Tradition*. New York: Oxford Univ. Press, 1953.

Aldridge, A.O. "Addison's 'Vision of Mirza'," *Explicator*, VI, no. 6 (Apr. 1948), item 37.

Alexander, Boyd. *England's Wealthiest Son*. London: Centaur Press, 1962.

———. *Life at Fonthill, 1807–1822*. London: Rupert Hart-Davis, 1957.

Allen, B. Sprague. *Tides in English Taste, 1619–1800*. 2 vols. Cambridge, MA: Harvard Univ. Press, 1937.

Altick, Richard D. *The English Common Reader: A Social History of the Mass Reading Public, 1800–1900*. 1957; rpt. Chicago, IL: Chicago Univ. Press, 1963.

America. "Arabian Nights: Musical Comedy," XCI (July 10, 1954), 386; XCIII (Aug. 6, 1955), 458–59; and CXVII (Aug. 5, 1967), 139.

Anis, Mohammad. "British Travellers' Impressions of Egypt in the Late Eighteenth Century," *Bulletin of the Faculty of Arts*, Fouad I University-Cairo, XIII, pt. II (Dec. 1951), 9–37.

Arberry, A.J. *British Orientalists*. London: Collins, 1943.

———. *Oriental Essays: Portraits of Seven Scholars*. New York: Macmillan, 1960.

———, tr. *Scheherazade: Tales from the Thousand and One Nights*. London: Allen & Unwin, 1954.

Archer, J.C. "Our Debt to the Moslem Arab," *Muslim World*, XXIX (July 1939), 248–64.

Arnold, Sir Thomas and Alfred Guillaume, eds. *Legacy of Islam*. Oxford: Clarendon Press, 1931.

Asin, P.M. *Islam and the Divine Comedy*. London: Murray, 1926.

Athenaeum. Review of the Dodd's edition of the *Nights*, no. 4438 (Nov. 16, 1912), 584.

Babbitt, Irving. "Romanticism and the Orient," *Bookman*, LXXIV, no. 4 (Dec. 1931), 349–57.

Baird, James. "Critical Problems in the Orientalism of Western Poetry," *Asia and the Humanities*, II (1959), 38–57.

Bajraktarevic, F.D. "The Citizens of Dubrovnik and Zadar in the 'Thousand and One Nights'," *Istoriski Chasopis*, V (1954–1955), 155–65-with a summary in English, p. 165.

Baker, Ernest. *The History of the Novel*. 5 vols. London: Witherby, 1934.

Baker, F.G. "Sir Richard Burton as I Knew Him," *Cornhill Magazine*, no. 304 (Oct. 1921), 411–23.

Barchilon, Jacques. "Uses of the Fairy Tale in the Eighteenth Century," *Studies on Voltaire and the Eighteenth Century*, XXIV (1963), 111–38.

Barth, John. *Chimera*. New York: Random House, 1972.

Bator, Robert, J. "Eighteenth-Century England versus the Fairy Tale," *Research Studies*, XXXIX, no. 1 (Mar. 1971), 1–10.

Baumer, Franklin, L. "Romanticism." In *History of Ideas*, edited by Philip P. Wiener. New York: Scribner's, 1955 (IV, 198–204).

Becker, M.L. Review of a new edition of the *Nights* based on Lang's adaptation, *Weekly Book Review* (May 5, 1946), p. 8.

Beer, John. *Coleridge the Visionary*. New York: Macmillan, 1959.

Bennett, J.O. "Book of the Thousand and One Nights." In *Much Loved Books: Best Sellers of the Ages*. New York: Boni and Liveright, 1927.

Bernbaum, E. *Guide Through the Romantic Movement*. 1930; rpt. New York: Ronald Press, 1949.

Beveridge, H. "A Supposed Missing MS. of the Arabian Nights," *Journal of the Royal Asiatic Society*, I (1913), 170–71.

Beyer, Werner W. *Keats and the Daemon King*. New York: Oxford Univ. Press, 1947.

Bjersby, B.M.H. *The Interpretation of the Cuchulain Legend in the Works of W.B. Yeats*. Upsala: Upsala Irish Studies, no. 1, 1950.

Bleiler, E.F., ed. *Three Gothic Novels*. New York: Dover, 1966.

Booklist. Review of a new edition based on Lang's adaptation, XLII (June 15, 1946), 334.

———. Review of Joseph Campbell's *Portable Arabian Nights*, XLVIII (Apr. 15, 1952), 266.

———. Review of Marcia Brown's abridgement of the *Nights* (Scribner's, 1956), LIII (Dec. 15, 1956), 204.

———. Review of A. Williams-Ellis' edition of the *Nights*, LV (Oct. 15, 1958), 104.

Bookman. Review of Dodd's edition of the *Nights*, XXXVI (Jan. 1913), 523.

Bookmark. Review of Marcia Brown's edition of the *Nights*, XVI (Oct. 1956), 11.

Booth, Michael R. *English Melodrama*. London: Jenkins, 1965.

———. *English Plays of the Nineteenth Century*. 5 vols. Oxford: Clarendon, 1969–1976.

Boston Transcript. Review of Dodd's edition (Dec. 7, 1912), 5.

Botsford, J.B. *English Society in the Eighteenth Century as Influenced from Oversea*. 1924; rpt. New York: Octagon, 1965.

Braddy, H. "The Oriental Origin of Chaucer's Canacee-Falcon Episode," *Modern Language Review*, XXXI (1936), 11–19.

Brett, R.L., ed. *Writers and Their Backgrounds: S.T. Coleridge*. London: Bell, 1971.

Brocklemann, C. *Der Arabischen Literatur*. Leiden: Brill, 1938. 2 vols. and supplements.

Brockman, C.J. "Chemistry and Alchemistry in the Arabian Nights," *Science*, n. ser. LXII (July 3, 1925), 16.

Brown, Wallace Cable. "Byron and the English Interest in the Near East," *Studies in Philology*, XXXIV (1937), 55–64.

———. "English Travel Books and Minor Poetry about the Near East, 1775–1825," *Philological Quarterly*, XVI (1937), 249–71.

———. "The Near East in English Drama, 1775–1825," *The Journal of English and German Philology*, XLVI (1947), 63–69.

———. "The Popularity of English Travel Books about the Near East, 1775–1825," *Philological Quarterly*, XV (1936), 70–80.

———. "Prose Fiction and English Interest in the Near East, 1775–1825," *PMLA*, LIII (1938), 827–37.

———. "Robert Southey and English Interest in the Near East," *English Literary History*, V (1938), 218–24.

———. "Thomas Moore and the English Interest in the Near East," *Studies in Philology*, XX–XIV (1937), 575–88.

Buckley, Jerome Hamilton. *The Victorian Temper: A Study in Literary Culture*. 1951; rpt. Vintage edition, Toronto: Random House, 1964.

———. *William Ernest Henley: A Study in the "Counter Decadence" of the Nineties*. Princeton, NJ: Princeton Univ. Press, 1945.

Campbell, Joseph. *The Hero with a Thousand Faces*. Bollingen ser. XVII, 1949; 3rd ed. Princeton, NJ: Princeton Univ. Press, 1973.

———. *The Masks of God: Primitive Mythology*. New York: Viking Press, 1959.

———. *The Portable Arabian Nights*. 1952; rpt. New York: Viking Press, 1967.

Cannon, Garland H. *The Letters of Sir William Jones*. 2 vols. Oxford: Clarendon, 1970.

———. *Oriental Jones: A Biography of Sir William Jones (1746–1794)*. London: Asia Publishing House, 1964.

———. *Sir William Jones, Orientalist: An Annotated Bibliography of His Works*. Honolulu: Univ. of Hawaii Press, 1952.

Catholic World. Review of Rosa Van Rosen's edition of the *Nights* (Hyperion Book), CLX (Dec. 1944), 280.

———. "Arabian Nights," CLXXIX (Aug. 1954), 391.

Cecil, Moffitt L. "Poe's 'Arabesque'," *Comparative Literature*, XVIII (1966), 55–70.

Chapman, Guy. *Beckford: Life and Letters*. 1940; new ed. London: Rupert Hart-Davis, 1952.

———, with John Hodgkin. *A Bibliography of William Beckford of Fonthill*. London: Constable, 1930.

Chatterji, Suniti Kumar. "A World Classic: The Arabian Nights," *Indo-Asian Culture* (1960), 141–59. Same art. IX (1961), 264–82.

Chesterton, O.K. *The Collected Poems*. London: Cecil Palmer, 1927.

———. "The Everlasting Nights." In *The Spice of Life and Other Essays*, edited by Dorothy Collins. 1964; rpt. Beaconsfield: Darwen Finlayson, 1967.

Chew, Samuel. *The Crescent and the Rose; Islam and England During the Renaissance*. 1937; rpt. New York: Octagon, 1965.

Chicago Sunday Tribune. Review of Marcia Brown's edition of the *Nights* (Scribner's, 1956) (Nov. 2, 1956), 18.

———. Review of A. Williams Ellis' edition of the *Nights* (Nov. 2, 1958), 14.

———. Review of *Sindbad* (Atheneum Publishers, 1962) (May 13, 1962), 2.

Christian Century. Review of Joseph Campbell's *Portable Arabian Nights*, LXIX (Apr. 23, 1952), 498.

Christian Science Monitor. Review of Jean Stafford's abridgement (Macmillan, 1963) (Nov. 15, 1962), 8.

Christides, V. "An Arabo Byzantine Novel 'Umar b-ai-Nu'man' compared with Digene's Akritas," *Byzantion*, XXXII (1962), 549–604.

Christy, A. *The Orient in American Transcendentalism: A Study of Emerson, Thoreau and Alcott.* 1932; rpt. New York: Octagon Books, 1969.

Cimino, Maria. Review of Marcia Brown's abridgement, *Saturday Review*, XXXIX (Nov. 17, 1956), 48.

Clark, T. Blake. *Oriental England: A Study of Oriental Influences in Eighteenth-Century England as Reflected in Drama.* Shanghai, 1939.

Clay, B., and C. Spurling. *Plays from the Arabian Nights.* London: Wells Gardner, 1913.

Clement, N.H. *Romanticism in France.* New York: MLA, 1936.

Colby, Elbridge. *A Bibliography of Thomas Holcroft.* New York: The New York Public Library, 1922.

Colvin, Sidney. *John Keats: His Life and Poetry, His Friends and Critics, and After-fame.* 1917; rpt. New York: Octagon, 1970.

Conkling, G.H. "To Elsa: With a Volume of the Arabian Nights; a Poem," *The Century Illustrated Magazine*, LXXXVII (Nov. 1913), 36–38 (also in *Current Opinion*, LV [Dec. 1913], 439).

Cook, E.T. *Life of John Ruskin.* 2 vols. London: George Allen, 1912.

Cooper, E. Taber. *Some English Story-Tellers.* London: Henry Holt, 1912.

Cox, R.G. "The Reviews and Magazines." In *Pelican Guide to English Literature: From Dickens to Hardy*, edited by Boris Ford. 1958; rpt. Penguin, 1966.

Craig, Alec. *The Banned Books of England.* London: George Allen & Unwin, 1937.

Cruse, Amy. *The Victorians and their Books.* 1935; 3rd ed., London: George Allen & Unwin, 1962.

Dance Magazine. "Arabian Nights: Musical Comedy," XXIX (Aug. 1955), 30–35; XLI (Aug. 1967), 24–25.

Daniel, Norman. *Islam, Europe and Empire.* Edinburgh: Edinburgh Univ. Press, 1966.

Darling, F.C. Review of a New Edition Based on Andrew Lang's Abridgement, *Christian Science Monitor* (Sept. 24, 1946), 10.

Darton, F.J.H. *Children's Books in England: Five Centuries of Social Life.* Cambridge: Univ. Press, 1932.

Dearden, Seton. *The Arabian Knight: A Study of Sir Richard Burton.* 1936; rpt. London: Baker, 1953.

Decker, Clarence Raymond. *The Victorian Conscience.* New York: Twayne Publishers, 1952.

De La Mare, Walter. "The Thousand and One." In *Pleasures and Speculations.* Essay Index Series. 1940; rpt. New York: Books for Libraries Press, 1960.

Dodds, John W. *The Age of Paradox; a Biography of England, 1841–51.* New York: Rinehart, 1952.

Downs, Robert B. "World of Wonders: The Book of a Thousand Nights and a Night." In *Famous Books Ancient and Modem.* 1964; 3rd printing, New York: Barnes & Nobel, 1968.

Draper, J. "Shelley and Arabic Persian Lyric Style," *Revisti Campara*, XIII (1960), 92–95.

Duffy, Maureen. *The Erotic World of Faery*. London: Hodder & Stoughton, 1972.

Dufrenoy, Marie-Louise. *L'Orient romanesque en France: 1704–1789*. 2 vols. Montreal, 1946.

Dutt, S. *The Supernatural in English Romantic Poetry, 1780–1830*. Calcutta: Univ. of Calcutta Press, 1938.

Eaton, Horace Ainsworth. *Thomas De Quincey: A Biography*. New York: Oxford Univ. Press, 1936.

Eddy, William A. *Gulliver's Travels: A Critical Study*. Princeton, NJ: Princeton Univ. Press, 1923.

Elisseeff, Nikita. *Themes et motifs des Mille et une nuits: Essai de classification*. Beirut, 1949.

Ellmann, Richard, ed. *Edwardians and Late Victorians*. New York: Columbia Univ. Press, 1960.

Elwin, Malcolm. *Victorian Wallflowers*. London: Jonathan Cape, 1934.

Esdaile, Arundel!. *A List of English Tales and Prose Romances Printed Before 1740*. London: Bibliographical Society, 1912.

Ettinghausen, Richard. "The Man-made Setting: Islamic Art and Architecture." In *Islam and the Arab World*, edited by Bernard Lewis. New York: Alfred A. Knopf, 1976.

Farmer, Henry George. *The Minstrelsy of "The Arabian Nights": A Study of Music and Musicians in the Arabic "Alif Laila wa Laila."* Bearsden (Scotland): The Author, 1945.

———. "The Music of the *Arabian Nights*," *Journal of the Royal Asiatic Society*, 2 pts (Oct. 1944, and 1945), 172–85, 39–60.

Farwell, B. *Burton: A Biography of Sir Richard Francis Burton*. New York: Holt, 1963.

Fedden, Robin. *English Travellers in the Near East*. London: Longmans & Green, 1958.

Finkelstein, Dorothee Metlitsky. *Melville's Orienda*. 1961; rpt. New York: Octagon, 1971.

Fitch, G. Hamlin. "Arabian Nights and Other Classics." In *Comfort Found in Good Old Books*. Grosset, 1911.

Ford, George H. *Dickens and His Readers*. Princeton, NJ: Princeton Univ. Press, 1955.

Forster, E.M. *Aspects of the Novel*. 1927; rpt. Penguin, 1968.

Gaal, E. "Aladdin and the Wonderful Lamp," *Acta Orientalia* (Academia Scientiarum Hungaria), XXVII (1973), 291–300.

Gail, Marziah. *Persia and the Victorians*. London: Allen & Unwin, 1951.

Gallaway, W.F., Jr. "The Conservative Attitude Toward Fiction, 1770–1830," *PMLA*, LV (1940), 1041–59.

Gerhardt, Mia A. *The Art of Story-Telling: A Literary Study of the Thousand and One Nights*. Leiden: Brill, 1963.

Gerin, Winifred. *Charlotte Bronte: The Evolution of a Genius*. Oxford: Clarendon, 1967.

———. *Emily Bronte: A Biography*. 1971; rpt. Oxford: Clarendon, 1972.

Germanus, Abdul Karim. "Sources of the Arabian Nights," *Islamic Review* (Sept. 1951), 16–19.

Gibb, H.A.R. "Literature." In *Legacy of Islam*, edited by Sir Thomas Arnold and Alfred Guillaume. Oxford: Clarendon, 1931.

Gibson, Byron Hall. *The History, from 1800 to 1832, of English Criticism of Prose Fiction*. Urbana, IL, 1931.

Goitein, S.D. "The Oldest Documentary Evidence for the Title *Alf Laila wa-Laila*," *Journal of the American Oriental Society*, LXXVIII (1958), 301–02.

Golden Book Magazine (N.Y.), "Hunchback Who Died Four Times," XVII (May 1933), 454–58.

———. "Tale of the Kadi," XXI (May 1935), 430–35.

Goldknopf, David. *The Life of the Novel*. Chicago, IL: Univ. of Chicago Press, 1972.

Gose, Elliott, B., Jr. *Imagination Indulged: The Irrational in the Nineteenth-Century Novel*. Montreal: McGill & Queen's Univ. Press, 1972.

Gottheil, R.J.H. "Arabian Nights with Selections." In *Columbia University Course*. Warner Library, vol. I.

Gowen, Herbert H. "Dante and the Orient," *Sewanee Review*, XXXII (1924), 434–45.

Graham, Kenneth. *English Criticism of the Novel 1865–1900*. Oxford: Clarendon, 1965.

Graham, Walter. *English Literary Periodicals*. New York: T. Nelson, 1930.

———. *Tory Criticism in the "Quarterly Review," 1809–1853*. New York: Columbia Univ. Press 1921.

Grob, Shirley. "Dickens and Some Motifs of the Fairy Tale," *Texas Studies in Literature and Language*, V, no. 1 (Spring 1963), 567–79.

Gross, John. *The Rise and Fall of the Man of Letters: Aspects of English Literary Life since 1800*. London: Weidenfeld, 1969.

Grunebaum, G.E. von. "Creative Borrowing; Greece in the Arabian Nights." In *Medieval Islam*. Chicago, IL: Chicago Univ. Press, 1946.

———. "Greek Form Elements in the Arabian Nights," *Journal of the American Oriental Society*, LXII (1942), 277–92.

Gupta, J. "The East in English Literature," *Calcutta Review*, XXX (Jan. 1929), 45–66.

Hachicho, Mohamad Ali. "English Travel Books about the Arab Near East in the Eighteenth Century," *Die Welt Des Islams*, IX (Leiden, 1964), 1–206.

Haight, G.S. "George Meredith and the 'Westminster Review'," *Modern Language Review*, LIII (Jan. 1958), 1–16.

Haller, William. *Early Life of Robert Southey: 1774–1803*. New York: Columbia Univ. Press, 1917.

Halliday, W.R. "The Story of Ali Baba and the Forty Thieves," *Folklore*, XXXI (1920), 321–23.

Hamori, Andras. "An Allegory from the Arabian Nights: The City of Brass," *Bulletin of School of Oriental and African Studies* (London Univ.), XXXIV (1971), 9–19.

———. *On the Art of Medieval Arabic Literature*. Princeton Essays in Literature, Princeton, NJ: Princeton Univ. Press, 1974.

Hardy, Barbara. "Dickens' Story-Tellers," *Dickensian*, LXIX (Spring, 1973), 71–78.

Haupt, P. "Ali Baba and the Forty Thieves: Note on 'Open Sesame'," *American Journal of Philology* (Oct. 1926), 307–09.

Havens, Raymond D. *The Mind of a Poet*. 1941; 4th printing, Baltimore, MD: John Hopkins Press, 1967.

Hawari, Rida. "Poetical Orientalization in 18th and 19th Century England," *Bulletin of the Faculty of Arts*, Riyadh Univ., I (1970), 7–19.

———. "On Some Oriental Sources of English Literature in Eighteenth and Nineteenth Century England," *Bulletin of the Faculty of Arts*, Riyadh Univ., II (1971–1972), 31–59.

———. "A Study of Thackeray's 'Sultan Stork' as an Orientalization with Special Reference to the Thackerary-Hauff Relationship," *Bulletin of the Faculty of Arts*, Riyadh Univ., III (1973–1974), 7–22.

Hearn, Lafcadio. *Interpretations of Literature*, ed. John Erskine. 2 vols. New York: Dodd & Mead, 1915.

Heidler, Joseph Bunn. *The History, from 1700 to 1800, of English Criticism of Prose Fiction.* Urbana: Univ. of Illinois, 1928.

Hewitt, R.M. "Harmonious Jones," *Essays and Studies by Members of the English Association*, XVIII (1942), 42–59.

Hibbard, L.A. *Medieval Romance in England.* New York: Oxford Univ. Press, 1924.

Highet, Gilbert. "On First Looking into the Arabian Nights." In *Explorations.* New York: Oxford Univ. Press, 1971.

Hill, T.W. "Books That Dickens Read," *Dickensian*, XLV (1949), 81–90, 201–07.

Hilles, F.W. *The Literary Career of Sir Joshua Reynolds.* New York: Macmillan, 1936.

Hinckley, H.B. "The Framing Tale," *Modern Language Notes*, XLIX (1934), 64–80.

Hodgson, G. *The Life of James Elroy Flecker.* Oxford: Blackwell, 1925.

Hollenback. J.W. "The Image of the Arab in Nineteenth Century English and American Literature," *Muslim World*, LXII (1972), 195–208.

Holloway, J. *Widening Horizons in English Verse.* Evanston: Northwestern Univ. Press, 1967.

Holt, P.M. "The Treatment of Arab History by Prideaux, Ockley and Sale." In *Historians of the Middle East.* London: Oxford Univ. Press, 1962.

Hormel, O.D. Review of Marcia Brown's abridgement of the *Nights. Christian Science Monitor* (Nov. 15, 1956), 20.

Horn Book Magazine. Review of Marcia Brown's abridgement (Scribner's, 1956), XXXII (Dec. 1956), 441.

———. Review of A. Williams-Ellis' edition of the *Nights*, XXXIV (Dec. 1958), 474.

———. Review of Charles Mozley's edition of the *First Book of Ancient Araby* (Watts, 1960), XXXVI (Dec. 1960), 511.

———. Review of *Sindbad* (Atheneum Publishers, 1962), XXXVIII (Aug. 1962), 371.

———. Review of William Wiesner's *Joco and the Fishbone* (Viking, 1966), XLII (Oct. 1966), 567.

Horovitz, J. "The Origins of the 'Arabian Nights'," *Islamic Culture*, I (1927), 36–57.

Houghton, Walter E. *The Victorian Frame of Mind, 1830–1870.* 1957: 10th printing, New Haven, CT: Yale Univ. Press, 1971.

Hussain, I. "Oriental Elements in English Poetry," *Venture*, I (June 1960), 156–65.

———. "Beckford, Wainewright, De Quincey and Oriental Exoticism," *Venture*, I, no. 3 (Sept. 1960), 234–48.

———. "Orientalism and Coleridge," *Venture*, I, no. 4 (Dec. 1960), 336–46.

Hussain, S.M. "Traces of Sufism in Tennyson's Poetry," *Tennyson Research Bulletin*, II, no. I (1972), 6–14.

Jack, Ian. *English Literature, 1815–1832.* Oxford: Clarendon, 1963.

Jackson, Charlotte. Review of William Wiesner's *Jaco and the Fishbone, Atlantic Monthly*, CCXVIII (Dec. 1966), 150.

James, Louis. *Fiction for the Working Man, 1830–1850.* London: Oxford Univ. Press, 1963.

Jeffares, A. Norman and K.G.W. Cross, eds. *In Excited Reverie: A Centenary Tribute to William Butler Yeats, 1865–1939.* Toronto: Macmillan, 1965.

John Rylands Library Bulletin. "Collection Comprising Upwards of 1000 Vols. in the Various Editions and Languages Given to the Case Memorial Library at Hartford by Dr. Duncan B. Macdonald," XXVI (May 1942), 244–45.

Keller, J.E., tr. *The Book of the Wiles of Women.* Chapel Hill: Univ. of North Carolina, 1956.

Khulusi, S. "The Probable Author of the Early Stories of the Arabian Nights," Trud. XX Mezhdunarodnogo Kongressa Vosloko (Moskua), 1960, tom II 1963, 110–13.

Kiely, Robert. *Robert Louis Stevenson and the Fiction of Adventure.* Cambridge, MA: Harvard Univ. Press, 1964.

Killham, J. *Tennyson and the Princess: Reflections of an Age.* Athlone Press, Univ. of London, 1958.

King, M.B. Review of Charles Mozley's *First Book . . ., Chicago Sunday Tribune* (Nov. 6, 1960), p. 18.

Kinkead, K.T. Review of Marcia Brown's abridgement, *New Yorker,* XXXII (Nov. 24, 1956), 230.

Kirkus' (Bulletin of Virginia Kirkus' Bookshop Service), XII (Oct. 1, 1944), 450 (review of Rosa van Rosen's abridgement).

———. XIV (Feb. 1, 1946), 67 (review of a new edition based on Lang's).

———. XX (Jan. 15, 1952), 43 (review of Joseph Campbell's *Portable Arabian Nights*).

———. XXVI (July 15, 1958), 504 (review of William-Ellis' edition).

———. XXVIII (July 1, 1960), 498 (review of Nathaniel Benchley's translation of *Sindbad the Sailor*, Random House, 1961).

———. XXVIII (Sept. 1, 1960), 755 (review of Mozley's edition of the *First Book . . .*).

———. XXX (Feb. 1, 1962), 109 (review of *Sindbad*).

Knipp, Christopher. "The Arabian Nights in England: Galland's Translation and Its Successors," *Journal of Arabic Literature,* V (1974), 44–54.

Lach, Donald F. *Asia in the Making of Europe.* Chicago, IL: Univ. Press, 1965.

Lanes, S.G. Review of William Wiesner's edition of *loco and the Fishbone* (Viking, 1966) (Oct. 30, 1966), 24.

Landre, Louis. *Leigh Hunt.* 2 vols. Paris, 1935.

Lask, Thomas. Review of *Sindbad, New York Times Book Review* (May 13, 1962), 37.

———. Review of J. Stafford's abridgement (Macmillan, 1963), *New York Times Book Review* (Nov. 2, 1962), pt. 2, p. 62.

Leaf, M. "Arabian Nights, by the Princess Scheherazade," *American Magazine,* CXXIX (June 1940), 62.

Leavis, Q.D., ed. *Jane Eyre.* 1966; rpt. Penguin, 1972.

Lecky, W.E.H. *History of England in the Eighteenth Century.* New York: Appleton, 1878–1890.

Lefebure, Molly. *Samuel Taylor Coleridge: A Bondage of Opium.* London: Victor Gollancz, 1974.

Leidecker, K.F. "Edgar Allan Poe's Orientalism," *Modern Review* (Calcutta), LIX (Jan.–June 1936), 277–82.

Leturmy, M. "Thousand and One Nights or the Secret of Scheherazade," *UNESCO Courier,* XXIV (Oct. 1971), 40–43.

Levi Della Vida, G. "A Christian Legend in a Moslem Garb," *Byzantion,* XV (1940–1941), 144–57.

Libby, M.S. Review of Marcia Brown's abridgement, in *New York Herald Tribune Book Review* (Nov. 18, 1956), pt. 2, p. 4.

———. Review of A. Williams-Ellis' edition, *New York Herald Tribune Book Review* (Nov. 2, 1958), pt. 2, p. 12.

———. Review of Benchley's translation of *Sindbad* (Legacy Books, 1961), in the *New York Herald Tribune, Lively Arts* (Jan. 29, 1961), p. 39.

———. Review of *Sindbad* (Atheneum Publishers, 1962), *New York Herald Tribune Books* (May 13, 1962), sect. 12, p. 28.

Library Journal. Review of Mozley's *First Book* . . ., LXXXV (Nov. 15, 1960), 4227.

Littmann, E. "Alf Layla Wa-Layla," *Encyclopaedia of Islam* (Brill, 1960), I, 358–64.

Long, C.R. "Aladdin and the Wonderful Lamp," *Archaeology*, IX (1956), 210–14.

Lovecraft, Howard Phillips. *Supernatural Horror in Literature.* 1927; rpt. New York: Ben Abramson, 1945.

Lowes, John Livingston. *The Road to Xanadu.* Boston and New York: Houghton & Mifflin, 1927.

Maar, Harko, G. De. *A History of Modern Romanticism.* 1924; rpt. New York: Haskell House, 1964.

McAiarney, K.H. Review of a new edition based on Lang's abridgement, *Literary Journal*, LXXI (June 15, 1946), 920.

McBurney, W.H. "The Authorship of the Turkish Spy," *PMLA*, LXXII (1957), 915–35.

MacCunn, Florence. *Sir Walter Scott's Friends.* Edinburgh: Blackwood, 1909.

Macdonald, Duncan Black. "A Missing Manuscript of the Arabian Nights," *Journal of the Royal Asiatic Society* (1913), 432.

———. "Further Notes on 'Ali Baba and the Forty Thieves'," *Journal of the Royal Asiatic Society* (1913), 41–53.

———. "From Arabian Nights to Spirit," *Muslim World* (Oct. 1919), 336–48.

———. "A Preliminary Classification of some MSS. of the Arabian Nights." In *A Volume of Oriental Studies Presented to Professor E.G. Brown,* edited by T.W. Arnold and R.A. Nicholson. Cambridge: Univ. Press, 1922.

———. "Earlier History of the Arabian Nights," *Journal of the Royal Asiatic Society* (1924), 353–97.

———. "Oriental Tales," *Times Literary Supplement* (May 15, 1930), 414.

———. "Aif Laila wa-Laila," *Encyclopaedia of Islam*, Supple., no. 1 (Leiden, 1934), 17–21.

McIntosh, Carey. *The Choice of Life: Samuel Johnson and the World of Fiction.* New Haven, CT: Yale Univ. Press, 1973.

Mackail, J.W. *Lectures on Poetry.* London: Longman & Green, 1911.

Mahmoud, Fatma, Moussa. "The Oriental Fashion in the Work of the Romantics," *Annual Bulletin of English Studies* (Cairo, 1955), 137–48.

———. "Rasselas and Vathek," *Supplement to Cairo Studies in English* (1959), 50–57.

———, ed. *William Beckford of Fonthill, 1760–1844: Bicentenary Essays. Supplement to Cairo Studies in English.* 1960; 2nd ed. Kennikat Press, 1972.

———. "Orientals in Picaresque: A Chapter in the History of the Oriental Tale in England," *Cairo Studies in English* (1961–1962), 145–88.

Manzaloui, Mahmoud. "Pseudo-Orientalism in Transition: The Age of Vathek," in *William Beckford of Fonthill, 1760–1844: Bicentenary Essays.*

Marchand, Leslie A. *The Athenaeum: A Mirror of Victorian Culture.* Chapel Hill: Univ. of North Carolina Press, 1941.

Marriott, J.A.R. *The Eastern Question.* Oxford: Clarendon, 1917.

Maxwell, Emily. Review of *Sindbad* (Atheneum, 1962), *New Yorker*, XXXVIII (Nov. 24, 1962), 225.

Melville, Lewis. *Life and Letters of William Beckford of Fonthill.* London: Heinemann, 1910.

Mentor. "Story of the Arabian Nights," X (Mar. 1922), 13–28.

Miner, Earl Roy. *Japanese Tradition in British and American Literature.* Princeton, NJ: Princeton Univ. Press, 1958.

Mommsen, K. *Goethe und 1001 Nacht.* Berlin: Inst. fur deutsche Sprache und Literature, 1960.

Monod, S. *Dickens the Novelist.* Norman: Univ. of Oklahoma Press, 1968.

More, Paul Elmer. *The Drift of Romanticism.* Shelburne Essays, 8th ser. Boston and New York: Houghton & Mifflin, 1913.

Morley, Edith J. *The Life and Times of Henry Crabb Robinson.* London: Dent, 1935.

Moslem World. "Collections of Arabian Nights," XXXII (Apr. 1942), 178.

Moulton, R.G. *World Literature.* New York: Macmillan, 1927.

Muir, P.H. *English Children's Books.* 1600–1900. London: B.T. Batsford, 1954.

Muller, B.E. "Arabian Nights in America; Fascinating Architectural Fantasy," *Country Life,* LV (Nov. 1928), 67–69.

Myer, H. Review of Mommsen's *Goethe und 1001 Nacht, Germ. Review,* XXV (Dec. 1960), 315–18.

Nangle, B.C. and W.H. McBurney. *The Monthly Review, First Series, 1749–1789. Indexes of Contributors and Articles.* 2 vols. Oxford: Clarendon, 1934.

Nasr, Seyyed Hossein. *Ideals and Realities of Islam.* 1966; rpt. London: Allen & Unwin, 1971.

Nation, XCV (Dec. 12, 1912), 561 (Review of Dodd's edition).

Nesbitt, George L. *Benthamite Reviewing: The First 12 Years of the "Westminster Review," 1824– 1836.* New York: Columbia Univ. Press, 1934.

Newby, P.H. "The Thousand and One Nights," *Listener,* XXXIX (Jan. 29, 1948), 178–79.

Nolen, Barbara. Review of Benchley's *Sindbad, New York Times Book Review* (Nov. 13, 1960), pt. 2, p. 39.

Oaten, E.F. *A Sketch of Anglo-Indian Literature.* London: Kegan Paul, 1908.

Oliver, D.J.W. *Life of William Beckford.* London: Oxford Univ. Press, 1932.

Osborne, Edna. "Oriental Diction and Theme in English Verse, 1740–1840," *Bulletin of the University of Kansas Humanistic Studies,* II, no. 1 (May 1916), 8–141 (with a bibliography).

Paden, W.D. *Tennyson in Egypt: A Study of the Imagery in His Earlier Work.* Univ. of Kansas Publications, Humanistic Studies, no. 27 (1942).

Park, William. "Change in the Criticism of the Novel after 1760," *Philological Quarterly,* XL VI (1967), 34–41.

Paston, George. "The Monthly Review in the Eighteenth Century," *Monthly Review,* VIII (Aug. 1902), 123–37.

Penzer, Norman M. *An Annotated Bibliography of Sir Richard Burton.* 1923; London: Dawsons of Pall Mall, 1967.

Perry, B.E. "The Origin of the Book of Sindbad," *Fabula,* III (1959), 1–94.

Phelps, Robert. Review of Jose Campbell's edition of the *Nights, Nation,* CLXXIV (Mar. 15, 1952), 256.

Pinto, V. de Sola. "Sir William Jones and English Literature," *Bulletin of the School of Oriental and African Studies,* XI, no. 4 (1946), 686–94.

Pippitt, Aileen. Review of W. Wiesner's *Joco and the Fishbone, New York Times Book Review* (Nov. 6, 1966), pt. 2, p. 60.

Ponsonby, F. *Sidelights on Queen Victoria*. New York: Sears Pub. Co., 1930.

Popper, W. "Data for Dating a Tale of the Nights," *Journal of the Royal Asiatic Society* (Jan. 1926), 1–14.

Porter, William Sidney (O. Henry). *The Trimmed Lamp*. New York: Doubleday, 1919.

————. *Strictly Business*. New York: Doubleday, 1919.

Portor, L.S. "Greatest Books in the World: The Arabian Nights," *Woman's Home Companion*, XL (Feb. 1913), 16.

Praz, Mario. *The Romantic Agony*. Translated by Angus Davidson. 1933; 2nd ed. London: Oxford Univ. Press, 1970.

Proceedings of the Sir William Jones Bicentenary Conference (held at Univ. College, Oxford, Sept. 2–6, 1946). London: Royal India Society, n.d.

Puccetti, R. "Lorca and Arab Andalusia," *Mid-East Forum*, XXXV (July 1956), 22–25.

Qalmawi, S. *Alf Laila wa Laila* (in Arabic). Cairo, 1943.

Quinlan, M.J. *Victorian Prelude, a History of English Manners, 1700–1830*. New York: Columbia Univ. Press, 1941.

Reynolds, E. *Early Victorian Drama, 1830–1870*. Cambridge: Heffer & Sons, 1936.

Rice, Warner G. "Early English Travellers to Greece and the Levant," *Univ. of Michigan Publications* (Language and Literature), X (1933), 205–60.

Richardson, A.E. *Georgian England*. 1931; rpt. New York: Books for Libraries Press, 1967.

Ridley, M.R. *Keats' Craftsmanship: A Study in Poetic Development*. Oxford: Clarendon, 1933.

Rihani, Ameen. "The Coming of the Arabian Nights," *Bookman* (N.Y.), XXXV (1912), pt. I, 366–70; pt. II, 503–08.

Roe, Frederick. *Thomas Carlyle as a Critic of Literature*. New York: Columbia Univ. Press, 1910.

Ronkel, P.S. Van. "A Malay Version of an Arabic Popular Romance," *Acta Orientalia*, V (1927), 68–73.

Rosenthal, F. "The Tale of Anthony," *Oriens*, XV (1962), 35–60.

Roth, G. "The City of Iron in Ancient Indian Literature and in the Arabian Nights," *Journal of Bihar Research Society*, XLV (1959), 53–76.

Rushdy, Rashad. "English Travellers in Egypt During the Reign of Mohammed Ali," *Bulletin of the Faculty of Arts*, Fouad I Univ., Cairo, XIV (Dec. 1952), 1–51.

————. "The English Travel-Book (1780–1850), A Popular Literary Form," *Bulletin of the Faculty of Arts*, Cairo Univ., XV (Dec. 1953), 159–79.

————. "English Writings on Egypt, 1780–1850: A Bibliography of Primary and Secondary Sources," *Cairo Studies in English* (1963–1966), 77–96.

Saintsbury, George. *The English Novel*. London: Dent, 1913.

San Francisco Chronicle. Review of A. Williams-Ellis' edition (Nov. 9, 1958), p. 13.

————. Review of *Sindbad* (May 13, 1962), p. 29.

Sanders, M.E. *The Life of Christina Rossetti*. London: Hutchinson, n.d.

Saturday Review. Review of Andrew Lang's edition, XXIX (June 15, 1946), 45.

Saunders, J.J. "Harun al-Rashid and His Times," *History Today*, XIII (Jan. 1963), 52–62.

Scaglione, Aldo D. "Shahryar, Giocondo, Kote. Three Versions of the Faithless Woman," *Oriens*, XI (1958), 151–61.

Scarborough, D. *The Supernatural in Modern English Fiction*. New York: Putnam, 1917.

Schach, Joseph and C.E. Bosworth, eds. *Legacy of Islam*. 2nd. ed., Oxford: Clarendon, 1974.

School and Society. Review of Andrew Lang's edition, LXIII (May 11, 1946), 351.

Scott, V.W. Review of R.V. Rosen's edition of the *Nights, Library Journal*, LXIX (Dec. 15, 1944), 1105.

Segalowitsch, B. *Benjamin Disraeli's Orientalismus*. Berlin, 1930.

Selincourt, Ernest De. *The Prelude, or Growth of a Poet's Mind*. Oxford: Clarendon, 1926.

Sencourt, R. *India in English Literature*. London: Simpkin & Marshall, 1924.

Shaffer, E.S. *"Kubla Khan" and the Fall of Jerusalem: The Mythological School in Biblical Criticism and Secular Literature, 1770–1880*. Cambridge: Univ. Press, 1975.

Shaw, Bernard. "Books of My Childhood," *Literary Digest* (Oct. 1946), p. I.

Shaw, Sheila, G. "Early English Editions of the Arabian Nights: Their Value to Eighteenth Century Literary Scholarship," *Muslim World*, XLIX (1959), 232–38.

———. Review of N. Benchley's *Sindbad, Library Journal*, LXXXV (Oct. 15, 1960), 3856.

———. Review of the Atheneum edition of *Sindbad, Library Journal*, LXXXVII (Mar. 15, 1962), 1322.

———. "The Rape of Gulliver: Case Study of a Source," *PMLA*, XC (Jan. 1975), 62–68.

Shine, Hill and Helen Chadwick. *The Quarterly Review under Gifford: Identifications of Contributors, 1809–1824*. Chapel Hill: Univ. of North Carolina Press, 1949.

Singh, B. *A Survey of Anglo-Indian Fiction*. London: Oxford Univ. Press, 1934.

Slythe, R.M. *The Art of Illustration, 1750–1900*. London: Library Association, 1970.

Smith, Byron Porter. *Islam In English Literature*. Beirut: American Press, 1939.

Social Studies. Review of Andrew Lang's edition, XXXVII (Nov. 1946), 336.

Spectator. Review of Dodd's edition, CIX (Nov. 2, 1912), 681.

Staffa, Susan Jane. "The Culture of Medieval Cairo as Reflected in Folk Literature," *Middle Eastern Studies*, X (1974), 333–47.

Stallworthy, Jon. *Between the Lines: Yeats's Poetry in the Making*. Oxford: Clarendon, 1963.

Stang, Richard. *The Theory of the Novel in England, 1850–1870*. London: Routledge & Kegan, 1959.

Stedman, Jane W. "Good Spirits: Dickens's Childhood Reading," *Dickensian*, LXI (Sept. 1965), 150–54.

———. "The Genesis of the Genii," *The Bronte Society Transactions*, XIV (1965), 16–19.

Steegman, J. *The Rule of Taste from George I to George IV*. London: Macmillan, 1936.

Stephens, G.A. "Arabian Nights and Arthurian Romance," *Comparative Literature Studies*, XX (1946), 11–15.

Stevenson, Lionel. *The Ordeal of Richard Meredith: A Biography*. London: Scribner's, 1953.

Stone, Donald David. *Novelists in a Changing World*. Cambridge, MA: Harvard Univ. Press, 1972.

Stone, Harry. "Dark Corners of the Mind: Dickens' Childhood Reading," *Hornbook Magazine*, XXXIX (June 1963), 306–21.

Strout, A.L. *A Bibliography of Articles in Blackwood's Magazine, 1817–1825*. Lubbock: Texas Tech. College Library, 1959.

Stuart, Dorothy M. *Christina Rossetti*. London: Macmillan, 1930.

Symons, Arthur. "A Neglected Genius: Sir Richard Burton." In *Dramatis Personae*. Indianapolis, IN: Bobbs-Merrill, 1923.

Taylor, John T. *Early Opposition to the English Novel: The Popular Reaction from 1760 to 1830*. New York: King's Crown Press, 1943.

Thomas, Della. Review of W. Wiesner's edition of *Joco and the Fishbone, Library Journal,* XCI (Oct. 15, 1966), 5242.

Tillotson, G. '"Rasselas' and the 'Persian Tales'." In *Essays in Criticism and Research.* 1942; with a new preface, Hamden, CT: Archon Books, 1967.

Times Literary Supplement. "Biographical Notes" (Mar. 16 and 30, 1922), pp. 176, 212.

———. "Notes on Sales" (Apr. 10, 1930), p. 324.

———. A note on *Aladdin and Other Tales* (Penguin, 1957) (July 5, 1957), p. 418.

———. A note on J. Stafford's abridgment (Nov. 23, 1962), p. 905.

Todorov, T. *The Fantastic.* Translated by Richard Howard. 1970; rpt. Ithaca, NY: Cornell Univ. Press, 1975.

Tompkins, J.M.S. *The Popular Novel in England, 1770–1800.* 1932; rpt. London: Methuen, 1969.

Thompson, S., ed. *A Motif-Index of Folk Literature.* 6 vols. Bloomington: Indiana Univ. Press, 1932–1936.

Turberville, A.S. *English Men and Manners in the Eighteenth Century.* Oxford: Clarendon, 1926.

Varma, D.P. *The Gothic Flame.* New York: Russell & Russell, 1957.

Wahba, M. ed. *Bicentenary Essays on Rasselas,* Suppl. to *Cairo Studies in English,* 1959.

Walker, Kenneth, ed. *Love, War and Fancy: The Customs and Manners of the East from Writings on the Arabian Nights by Sir Richard Burton.* London: W. Kimber, 1964.

Wann, Louis. "The Oriental in Elizabethan Drama," *Modern Philology,* XII (1914), 423–47.

Wasserman, E.R. *Elizabethan Poetry in the Eighteenth Century.* Urbana: Univ. of Illinois, 1947.

Watt, Ian. *The Rise of the Novel; Studies in Defoe, Richardson and Fielding.* London: Chato & Windus, 1957.

Weisinger, Herbert. "The Middle Ages and the Late Eighteenth-Century Historians," *Philological Quarterly,* XXVII (Jan. 1948), 63–79.

Weitzman, A.J. "The Oriental Tale in the Eighteenth Century: A Reconsideration," *Studies on Voltaire and the Eighteenth Century,* LVIII (1967), 1839–55.

Wellek, Rene. *A History of Modern Criticism, 1750–1950.* Vol. 3. New Haven, CT: Yale Univ. Press, 1965.

Whicher, G.F. *The Life and Romances of Mrs. Eliza Haywood.* New York: Columbia Univ. Press, 1915.

Whitford, R.C. "'The Arabian Nights' and the English Novel," *Dial,* LX (Mar. 16, 1916), 270.

Whitney, P.A. Review of an edition based on Lang's abridgement, *Bookman* (June 2, 1946), p. 11.

Wickens, G.M. "Lalla Rookh and the Romantic Tradition of Islamic Literature in English," *Yearbook of Comparative and General Literature,* XX (1971), 61–66.

Wiener, H.S.L. "Byron and the East: The Literary Sources of the 'Turkish Tales'." In *Nineteenth Century Studies,* edited by Herbert Davis. 1940; rpt. New York: Greenwood, 1968.

Wiener, L. *Contributions towards a History of Arabico-Gothic Culture.* New York: Neale Pub!. Co., 1917.

Wiles, R.M. *Serial Publication in England Before 1745.* Cambridge: Cambridge Univ. Press, 1957.

Williams, Ioan, ed. *Novel and Romance, 1700–1800: A Documentary Record.* London: Routledge & Kegan, 1970.

Williams, R.D. "The Thousand and One Nights," *Central Literary Magazine* (Jan. 1939), 16–22.

Williams, Stanley T. "The Source of Landor's *Gebir*," *Modern Language Notes,* XXXVI (1921), 315.

————. "The Story of *Gebir*," *PMLA*, XXXVI (1921), 615–31.

Williamson, Kennedy. *W.F. Henley: A Memoir*. London: H. Shaylor, 1930.

Wright, Thomas. *The Life of John Payne*. London: Fisher & Unwin, 1919.

Yeats, W.B. *Explorations*. Selected by Mrs. W.B. Yeats. London: Macmillan, 1962.

————. *The Letters of* . . ., ed. Allan Wade. London: Rupert Hart-Davis, 1954.

Secondary Works

(B) Unpublished Materials (Dissertations)

Abdel-Hamid, M.S. "Oriental Satanism in English Literature with Special Reference to the Romantic Movement." Ph.D., London, 1958.

Abdullah, A.M. "The Arabian Nights in English Literature to 1900." Ph.D., Cambridge, 1962.

Ahmed Laila Nadine Abdel Aziz. "The Works of Edward William Lane and Ideas of the Near East in England, 1800–1850: The Transformation of an Image." Ph.D. Cambridge, 1971.

Ahmed, M. "Oriental Influences in English Poetry of the Romantic Period." Ph.D., Birmingham, 1959–1960.

Aljuboure, D.A.H. "The Medieval Idea of the Saracen." Ph.D., Leeds, 1972.

Ambastha, K.P. "Traces of Oriental Mysticism in the Poetry of the English Romantic Revival. Ph.D., Edinburgh, 1955–1956.

Annan, M.C. "The Arabian Nights in Victorian Literature," Ph.D., Northwestern Univ., 1945.

Asfour, M.H. "The Crescent and the Cross: Islam and the Moslems in English Literature from Samuel Johnson to Thomas Moore." Ph.D., Indiana, 1973.

Bodine, J.J. "The Romanticism of Duncan Black Macdonald." Ph.D., Hartford Seminary Foundation, 1973.

Broughton, E.S. "Orientalism in English Poetry." M.A., London, 1919.

Brown, Wallace Cable. "The Near East as Theme and Background m English Literature, 1775–1825." Ph.D., Michigan, 1934.

Dawson, E. "Byron and Moore." Leipzig, 1902.

Duffy, John Dennis. "Arabian Literaria: Four Versions of the East, 1855–1926." Ph.D., Toronto, 1964.

Dunn, T.D. "Eastern Rogues in English Fiction," D. Litt., Glasgow, 1921.

Farag, F.F. "Oriental Mysticism in W.B. Yeats," Ph.D., London, 1942.

Haddawy, Hussain F. Ali. "English Arabesque: The Oriental Mode in Eighteenth Century English Literature." Ph.D., Cornell, 1962.

Hall, D.R. "Lamartine's Mirage of the East: The *Voyage en Onent*." Ph.D., Yale, 1966.

Hawari, R. "The Arabian Background of Tennyson. Thomson, and Meredith." B. Lit Oxford, 1962–1963

————. "A Study of the 'Exotic' East in the Works of Thackeray, with Reference to the Cult of the Oriental in Eighteenth and Nineteenth Century England." Ph.D., London, 1967.

Hellal, Farida. "Emerson's Knowledge and Use of Islamic Literature." Ph.D., Houston, 1971.

Holt, P.M. "Arabic Studies in Seventeenth Century England with Special Reference to the Life and Works of Edward Pococke (1604–1691)." B. Litt., Oxford, 1951–1952.

Hussein, H.S. "The Koran and Courtly Love: A Study of the Koran and Its Influence on the Development of Divine and Courtly Love." Ph.D., Southern California, 971.

Isan, Mukhtar Ali. "The Oriental Tale in America through 1865." Ph.D., Princeton, 1962.

Ishak, F.M. "The Philosophical Bearing of Eastern and Western Mysticism on the Poetry of Eliot." Ph.D., Liverpool, 1961–62.

Kararah, A.M.A. "Simon Ockley: His Contribution to Arabic Studies and Influences on Western Thought." Ph.D., Cambridge, 1955.

Khair-Ullah, F.S. "Orientalism in the Romantics." Ph.D., Edinburgh, 1952–1953.

Khatib, Issam al. "The Orientalism of Alfred, Lord Tennyson." Ph.D., Case Western Reserve, 1967.

Knipp, Christopher. "Oriental Types in the Eighteenth-Century." Ph.D., California, Berkley, 1974.

Lewis, A.D. "Oriental Influences in English Literature from 1800 to 1850." M.A., Wales 1953–1954.

Mahmoud, F.M. "The Oriental Tale in England in the Early Nineteenth Century, 1780–1824." Ph.D., London, 1957.

Manzaloui, M.A. "Some English Translations of Arabic Imaginative Literature (1704–1838): A Study of Their Portrayal of the Arab World, with an Estimate of Their Influence on Nineteenth Century Literature." B.Litt., Oxford, 1954.

Maynard, T.G.J. "The Literary Relevance of the Enclosed Garden as an Image in the Oriental Tale, 1704–1820." Ph.D., London, 1970.

Metlitzky, D. "Prolegomena for a Study of Arabic Influences on the Middle Ages." M.A., London, 1938.

Mowafy, M.I. El. "Arabia in English Literature, 1650–1750." Ph.D., Wales-Swansea, 1962.

Mukhlis, Naziha. "Studies in the Social Background of the *Arabian Nights*." Ph.D., School of Oriental & African Studies-Univ. of London, 1968.

Nanavutty, P. "Some Eastern Influences on William Blake's Prophetic Books." M.Litt., Cambridge, 1938.

Rushdy, Rashad. "English Travellers in Egypt during the Reign of Mohammed Ali, 1805–1847." Ph.D., Leeds, 1950.

Saigh, E.J.S. "Eastern Influences on Chaucer with Special Reference to the Arabs." Ph.D., London, 1946.

Sha'ban, Fuad. "The Mohammedan World in English Literature, 1580–1672." Ph.D., Duke, 1965.

Shaw, Sheila G. "The Influence of the *Arabian Nights* on Early Eighteenth-Century English Literature, with Special Reference to *Robinson Crusoe* and *Gulliver's Travels*." Ph.D., Bryn Mawr, 1959.

Shiber, Cornelia E. Sheider. "Echoes of 'Aiif-Layla wa-Layla' in E.T.A. Hoffman's Marchen." M.A., Tulane, 1967.

Stone, Harry. "Dickens's Reading." Ph.D., Univ. of California, Los Angeles, 1955.

Taylor, W. "A List of Arabic Words in the English Vocabulary." M.A., Leeds, 1932.

Tayseer, M.D. "India and the Near East in English Literature from the Earliest Times to 1924." Ph.D., Cambridge, 1936.

Weitzman, Arthur J. "The Influence of the Middle East on English Prose Fiction, 1600–1725." Ph.D., New York Univ., 1963.

Index